Look again™ 52

Look Again 52

Published by Monty Williams

Produced by Kaye Burson of Mastercraft Printed Products
2150 Century Circle, Irving, Texas 75062

Project Managed by
Ministry Solutions: Gene Amason II

Editor
Lea Collins

Cover Design by
Ministry Soutions: Bobby Moore

Interior Design by
The Typecrafter: Wayne Muirheid

ISBN
Hardback: 978–0–9767161–4–3
Paperback: 978–0–9767161–8–6

Printed in the United States of America

Acknowledgements

I wanted to take time out and give our Heavenly Father what is due to Him, if that is possible. This project has been a huge leap of faith for me and it could not have finished without His guidance. There were days when I wanted to quit and say "forget it," but God showed up in ways that only He and I know about. Even though this book has taken so much time to write, design, publish, print, advertise, and distribute, God made most of the process seem like a blessing because of the time spent in His Word and the people that we have built relationships with over the past few years. Thank you, Father.

I also want to thank my wife, Ingrid, for her strength, encouragement, and willingness to tell me the truth no matter what my reaction might be. She is my best friend; there is no one more important in my life.

My children, Lael, Faith, Janna, and Elijah deserve many thanks for giving up time spent with mommy and daddy. They lost their whole summer of 2008 while we got this project off and running. The same goes for Tessa and Jackson, as Dave and Kaci also spent months researching and writing.

Dave and Kaci, WOW! Your input, friendship, and willingness to collaborate with us made this project complete. You two will never know how it made me feel when you said "yes" to write this book with us. I know that God appointed you two for the task and, like I have said before, many people are going to be blessed by the gifts that have been trapped in you for so long. Thank you both so much.

Kaye Burson—the guiding light, mountain of wisdom, and mother of this project—you have been a blessing to me over these past few years. I know this for sure: if you were not in my life, this project would have fallen into the wrong hands and that would have been tragic. Thanks a million, as you would often tell me. To Gene Amason II and his team, thank you so much for your creative spirit and willingness to go out of the box with ideas that are going to make the world look again.

Rick Godwin and Sandy Ross, thanks for affirming me. When I came to San Antonio that summer of 2008, it was to see what the Godwin's and Ross' thought of me writing a book. When you two said go for it, I felt like I did years ago when the grown men would pick me to play on their teams when I was 12 years old back on the court in Oxon Hill Village. The guidance and support from your families has changed my life. Pat and BJ Magley, thanks for your support and mentorship over the past 20 years.

To my mother, Joyce Williams, thank you for the tough love and countless sacrifice. To my father, Tavares Williams, thank you for being a great friend even when I was not friendly.

For the people I may have forgotten, please forgive my oversight, but know that you have not been forgotten by God.

Table of Contents

FOREWORD

Everyone needs a coach. Coaches have the gift to lift your play to a higher level of performance and maximize your potential. Even coaches are mentored by great coaches.

So, who's coaching *you*?

Monty Williams is an assistant coach for the Portland Trailblazers and a former NBA player. God has gifted Monty to help people maximize their understanding of God's Word, just like a coach can diagram a play. Out of his own frustration with reading a different devotion every day and trying to remember what he read, he realized there was a problem for him with the modern devotional structure. He also realized that he probably wasn't the only one with that difficulty.

His solution? Focusing on one Scripture for an entire week with a different aspect emphasized on each of these seven days. Repeating the same verse each day for a week helps to stick it in your memory bank, which means it's unlikely that you'll forget it.

Like all good coaches, Monty knows that it doesn't just take a team of players to get the job done; it also takes a team of coaches to take care of winning players. Dave & Kaci Bullis as well as Monty's wife Ingrid Williams caught the vision for this project and partnered with him to make it happen. Their four unique perspectives give you the benefit of a wider range of insight into the Word of God, just like the team benefits from the additional experience and expertise of each coach.

Remember: Practice doesn't make perfect. It makes permanent. And God's Word, hidden in your heart and mind, will be a lamp to your feet and a light to your path. God's Spirit can flash that

Word into your mind and give you warning or wisdom for the moment, but it has to be there for you to remember it when you really need it.

Buckle up and get ready for an exciting adventure through God's Word.

— Rick Godwin
Founder and Senior Pastor
Summit Christian Center
San Antonio, Texas

Introduction

Before talking about how this devotional works, I must begin withow and where the idea originated.

On May 24, 2008, I was on my way to Battleground, Washington to see a friend of mine named Joeri Goedertier. Joeri is a Rottweiler breeder, and I am a dog lover. I live in Oregon, about 45 minutes away from Joeri. On my days off, if I have some free time, I take a ride to Joeri's house to sit and talk about the dogs, family, basketball, and other guy stuff.

During my drive up to Washington that May, I turned off my radio and tried to think about what I had studied that morning in my devotional. Driving alone is usually a nice time for me to do so without any distractions. Well, for the life of me, I could not remember one thing I had studied that morning. It was so frustrating! Different verses were running through my head from the previous week, and pieces of lessons clouded my thoughts. This was not the first time that this had happened to me. But this time I was more affected than ever before. I could not blow it off and turn on my favorite song from my i-Pod®.

As my frustration built, I began to feel condemnation, as if I had done something wrong. The truth was that I was doing all that I could to understand God's Scriptures and their lessons. With about 10 minutes left before arriving at Joeri's house, an overwhelming peace come over me and I knew that the Holy Spirit was telling me something. This had happened to me before; it led to me feeling pressed to *do* something, pushed in a certain direction, felt a warning or conviction about some sin in my life.

The peace that I felt at this time was amazing and somewhat surreal—kind of like when you make a great play on the court, everything seems to slow down while life's pace is still going on.

As I drove, the idea came to me that I was not the only person who had gone through this ordeal, when remembering the passages and lessons learned in church or seminar were hard to recall. I know without a doubt that God was pushing me to do something about this dilemma. I would love to tell you that the sky parted, a rainbow covered my car, a tingling sensation took over my body, and a beautiful white dove brought me a scroll with the answer on it. But that was not the case.

However, the next thing that *did* happen was amazing. The very next thought that I had was to come up with a devotional that would allow people like me to understand God's Word in a way that would be simple but without compromise. The problem was, I am not a writer or a Bible scholar. So, I called my wife Ingrid and told her what had just happened to me. We talked for a minute about coming up with a devotional that would allow people to understand the Word who would never pick up a Bible, something that would encourage those who have a hard time understanding the good news that God has given us. The amazing part is (I told you there was one) that she immediately got excited, which is not like her. We decided to pray about it and see where the Holy Spirit directed us, if anywhere. The more we prayed and talked, the more we felt driven to do something about this concept. But, with excitement comes the reality of all the work and research that it would take to finish a project like this one.

We decided to call our friends Dave and Kaci Bullis. Dave and Kaci are pastors and people that have put God at the head of their lives. They've been a great encouragement to me and my family. Being people that we really respect and spend a lot of time with, they were the first ones we thought of collaborating with to do this project. So we invited Dave, Kaci, and their two children, Tessa and Jackson, over for dinner one Sunday evening. We told them what happened to me on the drive to Washington and the idea we felt God was giving us. More importantly, we told them that we wanted them to be a part of this project. And just like I thought, Dave said that he would have to pray about it and they would get back to us. You have to know Dave to really know what this meant. It meant that he was not sure, but it was also "typical Dave." He would never make a move like this without seeking God in prayer and having a peace about it. This characteristic is one of the things that has drawn me to Dave over the past two years of our friendship.

While they were deciding, I took the time to pray and talk about the project with some people whom I trusted to be straight up with me (Rick Godwin, Sandy Ross, and Pat Magley, to name a few) about whether or not I was way out of my sphere of ability. Although to be honest, I know that I would have gone forward with this book anyway, because I knew that the idea came from the Holy Spirit. It is the only time that I would have considered going against wise counsel. Well, a week went by, and the Bullis' wanted to sit down and talk about the project. Dave and Kaci, after a week of prayer and talking, decided that they wanted to be a part of this endeavor.

You might wonder why we would need other people to join us in the writing of this devotional. The answer is that I wanted to do something different, something out-of-the-box that would give different perspectives on the Word of God without compromising Scripture. So we decided that each person, myself (an assistant basketball coach), Ingrid (homemaker and mother of 4 beautiful children), Dave (pastor and basketball coach), and Kaci (homemaker and pastor), would pray over 13 Scriptures that we felt would work in this project. Once we finalized our Scriptures, we would take time to research each one and write a seven-day devotional for each passage, allowing the reader to spend a full week on each verse for an entire year. We would call the book *LOOK AGAIN 52*, describing exactly what the book does: it gives people a chance to look again, to look deeper, at the Word of God by devoting an entire year—365 days—to 52 Scriptures.

Our hope and prayer is that at the end of a calendar year, readers will be able to say that they knew more about God's Word because they actually studied (not just read) the verses, even though it's a smaller number of verses than many devotionals cover. Our hope is that in this way, we can help people get more out of their devotional times, to help people really hide the Word in their hearts. We're not saying that everyone will be able to recall all 52 verses at the end of this devotional book, but we think you will be more familiar with the Truth of the Scripture because you took time to really digest the lessons, breakdowns, stories, and examples that we used in this project. Even if you still have a tough time with the verses, we believe you will still benefit from seeing the same one every day for seven consecutive days. We also believe that this method will create a habit of spending greater amounts of time on bits and pieces of God's Word, with the hope that the Holy Spirit will give you more and more revelation.

I must say that this is not an attempt to compete with or discredit anyone else who creates devotionals. We are simply trying to advance the Kingdom, encourage more people to read God's Word, and make the Word less intimidating to those who might not pick up the Bible or Matthew Henry's Commentary to study the Scriptures.

I know that there are people just like me who need the Word of God broken down so that they can understand it better. There are also many who only know something about the Bible because of tradition, folklore, media, or word of mouth. I was surprised when I learned that a number of Christians don't believe that the Bible is totally accurate; in 2006, The Barna Group did a study which showed 12% of born again Christians disagree that the Bible is totally true. That is alarming.

My mentor, Rick Godwin, taught me that most people don't go to church because they have already been. He means that they have not had a good experience or have been turned off by something or someone within the body. (That's not saying these are good reasons, but it is what it is.) As a result, those who don't attend church are missing out. Also, a great many who do attend don't enjoy what God has for them, because they don't understand or they just play the "church game." We are trying to meet their needs, too, because if we don't, Satan will fulfill their worldly desires and take them further away from God.

The Bible is the most believable, inspiring, credible book you will ever read. There is a reason that over 150,000 copies are sold, given away, or distributed every day in the United States. It has 1,260 promises, 6,464 commands, and over 6,000 prophecies. There is a reason there are 540+ million believers worldwide. There is a reason why men like Martin Luther, Hudson Taylor, William Tyndale and others risked their lives to make sure everyone had an opportunity to read God's Word. There is a reason why the apostle Paul wrote in 2 Timothy 3:16-17 NIV: "*All scripture is God-breathed and is useful for teaching, rebuking, correcting and training in righteousness so that the man of God may be thoroughly equipped for every good work.*" There is a reason why Billy Graham and Luis Palau, by sharing the Bible all over the world, have won more than 3.5 million souls for the Kingdom of God.

The Bible is our blueprint for life and has been given to us so that we can know our heavenly Father better. We live in a day when there is little excuse for not understanding God's Word and being able to apply it to our lives, regardless of our culture, race, gender, or past or present indiscretions. We hope that this resource will bring you closer to Him. In the New International Version NIV of the Bible, Proverbs 9:6 says, "*Leave your simple ways and you will live; walk in the way of understanding.*"

Our main goal in this project is to encourage everyone to keep God and His Word first in their lives while living in a society that regularly pushes Him to the backseat. Our jobs, goals, current events, fashion, place in society, financial portfolios, past sins, pursuit of power, along with the American Dream, can tempt us to take God out of the equation. But look at what God did when a human being tried to usurp the position in which only God can reign. Matthew 17 records what happened when Jesus took Peter, James, and John up into a mountain to witness what is called the "transfiguration" or metamorphosis of Christ. At this event, Elijah and Moses appeared and were talking to Jesus. Peter, with good intentions, got excited and wanted to do something to memorialize these three men. He said (verse 4): *"Lord, it is good for us to be here. If you wish, I will put up three shelters—one for you, one for Moses and Elijah..."* The word "shelter" was another way of saying "booth," or a place where people could gather and worship. But before Peter could finish his eloquent proposal, God interrupted him by saying (verse 5): *"This is my Son, whom I love; with him I am well pleased. Listen to him!"*

One point that we can take from this story is that nothing can take the place of Jesus, the Living Word of God, in our lives—not even the things and people that seem (and probably are) really important. Even though Moses led 2.5 million people out of Egyptian slavery and Elijah called fire down from the sky, God made the point that even they were not to replace God the Father, God the Son, Jesus Christ, and God the Holy Spirit.

It is our prayer that you will be blessed by this project and that you will keep God and His Word the number one priority in your life. We also pray that this book will help you to understand the Scriptures so that you can know God more intimately, live out the plan and purpose that God has for your life, and learn to rely on Him as your source of strength.

Remember, the best commentary on the Bible is the Bible.

— *Monty Williams*

WHY LOOK AGAIN?

Your journey to study—to hide God's Word in your heart and to dig deeper into the truth of Scripture—is just beginning.

If I had to pinpoint a foundational verse from the Bible that inspired the writing of this book, it would be Psalm 19:7-8 NIV. In these verses, King David says, "*The law of the Lord is perfect, reviving the soul. The statutes of the Lord are trustworthy, making wise the simple. The precepts of the Lord are right, giving joy to the heart. The commands of the Lord are radiant, giving light to the eyes.*"

Unfortunately, too many Christians are living off of their grandparent's faith, what the national media wants to propagate, or the newest and hottest trend that make us feel more comfortable. The apostle Paul talked about this in 2 Timothy 4:3 NIV: "*For the time will come when men will not put up with sound doctrine. Instead, to suit their own desires, they will gather around them a great number of teachers to say what their itching ears want to hear.*" My friend, we are right in the middle of 2 Timothy 4:3! This is not God's plan.

Many churches, self help books, and other religious outlets are preaching what they think will make the listening audience feel good. They use catchy slogans to attract more people into the building. I'm sure you've heard at least a few: "Jesus built us a bridge to God by using 2 boards and 3 nails;" "Give God what is right, not what is left;" "Give Satan an inch and he will be a ruler;" and my favorite (because it's true) "God is good, all the time, and all the time, God is good." These slogans might not be what bring people in, but the life-coach style of church services is very popular —as evidenced by the continually growing number of mega churches that utilize this type of service approach. Consequently, the numbers of attendees are growing in our churches, but the body of believers has become shallow in our understanding of God's Word. The Christian ability to witness to nonbelievers (the way we read about in Acts) has not been as effective as it should be, either; just read *"Christianity is No Longer Americans' Default Faith"* on barna.org (January 12, 2009). Why? Because the Bible is seldom properly and fully taught. When we stop studying and preaching the Word of God, we lose our ability to bear fruit that will last. When anecdotes, funny stories, 12 steps to this, 40 days to that, and hanging on to "the way it used to be" for no other reason than familiarity replace Scripture, we no doubt grieve our Father in Heaven.

In Jeremiah 23:32 NIV, God says *"Indeed I am against those who prophesy false dreams….they tell them and lead my people astray with their reckless lies, yet I did not send or appoint them. They do not benefit these people in the least."* God told us to take the *"helmet of salvation and sword of the spirit, which is the word of God"* in Ephesians 6:17 NIV. He did not say take the funny story, the "touchy feely thingy," or any other churchy exercises and sayings. None of those sermon devices are in themselves bad, but without the Word of God, these are used so we—the church—can remain on good terms with the listening audience and not offend anyone. That leads to soaring popularity and excitement, but it lacks eternal impact. Mark 7:13 NIV says that we make *"the word of God of no effect"* because of our *"traditions"* that have been *"handed down."*

So why look again? Because John 10:35 says that *"Scripture cannot be broken."* God's Word must be taken for what it is and not diluted in any way. Matthew 24:35 NIV says *"Heaven and Earth will pass away, but My words will not pass away."* Although it was written thousands of years ago in Greek, Hebrew, and Aramaic, the Bible still has so much to say to us today.

Why look again? Because *"the word of God is living and active. Sharper than any double-edged sword, it penetrates even to dividing soul and spirit, joints and marrow…"* (Hebrews 4:12, NIV) Why look again? Because *"in the beginning was the Word, and the Word was with God, and the Word was God."* (John 1:1, NIV)

Why look again? Because Proverbs 12:8 NIV says "A man is praised according to his wisdom, but men [and women] with warped minds are despised."

Why look again? Because millions of people will believe a talk show host's view on faith before they believe the One who created them.

Why look again? Because what you think or may have heard about God does not validate or invalidate who He is; only His Word can do that.

Why look again? Not because we have to study the Bible; because we *get* to study the Bible.

I encourage you to continue meditating on the Word, not just reading something every day. Give it the time to lodge itself in your mind and your heart. If you make this a habit, you will never be the same.

Blessings.

— *Monty Williams*

"...so that Christ may dwell in your hearts through faith. And I pray that you, being rooted and established in love, may have power, together with all the saints, to grasp how wide and long and high and deep is the love of Christ, and to know this love that surpasses knowledge—that you may be filled to the measure of all the fullness of God. Now to him who is able to do immeasurably more than all we ask or imagine, according to his power that is at work within us, to him be glory in the church and in Christ Jesus throughout all generations, forever and ever! Amen." Ephesians 3:17-21, NIV

Week 1

"Study to show yourself approved to God, a workman
that needs not to be ashamed,
rightly dividing the word of truth."

2 Timothy 2:15, AKJV

DAY 1

"Study to show yourself approved to God, a workman
that needs not to be ashamed,
rightly dividing the word of truth."

2 TIMOTHY 2:15, AKJV

What does the Word of God mean to you? Is it just a book of heroic stories that would make a good SportsCenter highlight reel? Is it a decoration perfectly placed on your coffee table to be easily seen by guests? Is it a book of tales and prophecies that were only meant to inspire, but not to be taken literally as God's inspired Word? Or, is it the most important book ever written, with true stories, principles, prophecies, and promises that were inspired by the God of the universe, and written down by people that He chose? You must decide.

In a survey of 1,027 people, "Open Air" magazine (fall 2008 issue) asked participants what they would most want to have with them if they were snowed in at a cabin for a month. Thirty-two percent (the greatest number for one object in this survey) said that they would rather have the Bible over anything else. You might focus on the fact that almost seventy percent chose something else to take. But I found the 32 percent statistic encouraging, because the question was not "What book would you want to take with you?" The survey question asked, "*What* would you most want to take?" These people could have chosen anything, but they chose the Bible. More and more people from all walks of life are reading the Bible. And it is up to us to "rightly divide" the Word so that we can understand it better.

> IT IS UP TO US TO "RIGHTLY DIVIDE" THE WORD.

Here are some important characteristics that I know about the Bible:

- It is alive. Studying the Word can lead us to better understand God and help us build a relationship with Him. Check out Hebrews 4:12 NIV: *"For the word of God is living and active…it judges the thoughts and attitudes of the heart."*
- Jeremiah 23:29 says, *"Does not my word burn like a fire? Is it not like a mighty hammer that smashes rock to pieces?"* God's Word purifies in the same way fire purifies. God's fire can also burn down the traditional and cultural beliefs that build up when we look for truth outside of the Bible.
- Ephesians 5:26 shows the Word of God as a cleanser, *"washing of the water with the word of God"* NAS.
- Hebrews 6:4-5 speaks of the Word of God as food that provides nourishment (the kind that deep-dish pizza could never provide). The New American Standard NAS translation says, *"For in the case of those who have tasted of the heavenly gift and have been made partakers of the Holy Spirit, and have tasted the good word of God…"*

One of the most important descriptions of God's Word is revealed in John 12:48 NIV, where the Word is described as something that should not be discarded: *"There is a judge for the one who rejects me and does not accept my words; that very word which I spoke will condemn him at the last day."* Regarding this verse, the Wiersbe Bible Commentary remarks: "His words are the very words of God; faith in Him brings salvation; to reject Him is to face eternal judgment. In fact, the very Word that he rejects becomes his judge! Why? Because the written Word points to the Living Word, Jesus Christ."

God's Word leads us to Jesus Christ. If you want to be more like Christ, study His Word.

DAY 2

"Study to show yourself approved to God, a workman
that needs not to be ashamed,
rightly dividing the word of truth."
2 TIMOTHY 2:15, AKJV

What does the phrase "rightly dividing (also known as hermeneutics) the word of truth" actually mean?

According to the *New Strong's Exhaustive Concordance* of the Bible, the Greek word "divide" (*orthotomeo*) used in 2 Timothy 2:15 means "to make a straight cut" or "to dissect (expound) correctly." Paul commands Timothy to study the Word of God—by dissecting and cutting—to find out what God really means when He speaks through His chosen ones.

For example, when you rightly divide the Word, you find out that the meaning of the word "world" in John 3:16 and in 1 Corinthians 3:19 is totally different. One refers to the people whom God loves; the other refers to the fallen system of doing things that contradicts God's Word.

Another word worthy of study is love. The Hebrew language offers several variations of the word "love," such as the word *ahab* (ah-hab) or *ahabah*, which is an affection. *Chashaq* (khaw-shak) means "to join" or "delight in." The word *racham* in Hebrew (raw-kham) is used to express compassion. The Hebrew word *rayah* (rah-yaw) is a feminine form of love often used in the Old Testament.

In the Greek language, two of the words for "love" are *agape* (uh-gah-pay) and *phileo* (fil-eh-o). Agape is used to describe an “affection” or “benevolence,” and is the same word used when the Bible describes God’s love toward us (seen in John 3:16). *Phileo* is a term used to describe “friendly” love in the Greek, from which we get the word “Philadelphia”—the city of brotherly love. Other Greek words used for “love” are *eros* and *stergo*. *Eros* is used to describe a sensual, sexually gratifying type of love, and *stergos* is used to describe the kind of love between parents and children. In 2 Timothy 3:3, *stergos* is used in a negative sense to describe the breaking down of family ties or the loss of “natural affection.”

As you can see, the Bible uses the word “love” in many ways. It is up to us to know which variation is being used, and why it is being used in that context.

I really like the way *Jon Courson’s Application Commentary* explains why we should “rightly divide” the Word of God: “We are to understand how the Word is divided and then allow the Word to divide us” (p. 1404).

Without knowing it, you may be guilty of eisegesis, which is interpreting and reading information into the Scriptures that is not there. The Mormons have done this with 1 Corinthians 8:5 KJV, “*For though there be many that are called gods, whether in heaven or in earth*....” They use this text to promote the idea of many gods, but the text plainly says that there are many that are “called” gods, not many gods. Study the Word so you don’t make this kind of mistake.

Day 3

"Study to show yourself approved to God, a workman
that needs not to be ashamed,
rightly dividing the word of truth."
2 Timothy 2:15, AKJV

I would like to share with you a story about a man that I met who desired to study and comprehend the Word of God enough to overcome a major obstacle.

I met this man when I accompanied my mentor Rick Godwin, his assistant, and some others on a trip to a church located in a very remote part of Mississippi. Rick shared the gospel one night at a men's meeting and I stayed in the lobby to help set up the tape and book stand. When the meeting was over, all the men came out of the sanctuary and into the lobby to buy books and CDs by Rick. I did my best to keep up with Rick's assistant, but I was not as adept at running the table as she was.

> Some of us can live inside our little cocoons and forget about the world around us.

After about 15 or 20 minutes of selling merchandise, up walked the man I mentioned. Instead of looking over the items on the table, he looked right at the assistant and me and said, "Do you all have stuff that I can listen to?" Before we could tell him about the CDs and other articles we had, he added, "Cuz I can't read, and I need something that I can listen to." Rick's assistant was used to this kind of customer, but I was not. Some of us can live inside our little cocoons and forget about the world around us—like I did with illiteracy in America. In February of 2008, ABC News did a story called *Living in the*

Shadows: Illiteracy in America, which showed that seven million Americans are illiterate, 27 million cannot read well enough to fill out a job application, and 30 million cannot read a simple sentence. Yes… in America.

That man had an impact on me because he would not let his inability to read stop him from knowing more about God's Word. In Psalm 143:10 NAS, David said "*Teach me to do your will, for You are my God…*" Some people, like our friend in Mississippi, may need to be taught a different way. Technological advances have greatly benefitted those who may have a weakness or handicap, such as being illiterate or suffering from blindness. But the truth is, we all should have the attitude of our friend from the good ole' South.

Let's allow nothing—not illiteracy, blindness, deafness, being too busy or lazy or anything else—keep us from comprehending the Word and learning more about our God and King.

What hinders you from studying God's Word?

Do you feel ashamed because you don't understand the Bible?

Does the Bible confuse you to the point that you stop reading it?

If so, I encourage you to pray that the Holy Spirit would direct you to a church that teaches the Word

Day 4

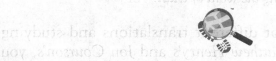

"Study to show yourself approved to God, a workman
that needs not to be ashamed,
rightly dividing the word of truth."
2 Timothy 2:15, AKJV

After looking at a few different translations of this week's verse, I thought it would be a good idea to look at some other renditions of 2 Timothy 2:15. Check out the different Bible versions and the different words used in the verses.

> *Do your best to present yourself to God as an* ***approved worker*** *who has nothing to be ashamed of, handling the word of truth with precision.* ISV
>
> *Be diligent to present yourself approved to God as a workman who does not need to be ashamed,* ***accurately handling*** *the word of truth.* NAS
>
> *Do your best to present yourself to God as a* ***tried-and-true worker*** *who isn't ashamed to teach the word of truth correctly.* GW
>
> ***Let it be your care*** *to get the approval of God, as a workman who has no cause for shame, giving the true word in the right way.* BBE
>
> *Strive diligently to present thyself approved to God, a workman that has not to be ashamed,* ***cutting in a straight line the word of truth****.* DAR
>
> ***Give diligence*** *to present yourself approved by God, a workman who doesn't need to be ashamed,* ***properly handling*** *the Word of Truth. [Earnestly seek to commend yourself to God as a servant who, because of his straightforward dealing with the word of truth, has no reason to feel any shame].* WEB

*Be diligent to present thyself approved to God—**a workman irreproachable**, rightly dividing the word of truth.* YLT

I hope that by looking at different translations and studying such commentaries as *Matthew Henry's* and *Jon Courson's*, you will be able to rightly divide, cut in a straight line, and accurately and properly handle God's Word.

DAY 5

"Study to show yourself approved to God, a workman
that needs not to be ashamed,
rightly dividing the word of truth."

2 TIMOTHY 2:15, AKJV

"Dispensationalist," "Hypostatic Union," "Harmitiology," and "Amillenialism" are all terms heard in theological debating circles. If you are looking for thought-provoking discussions on these topics, you should know that this is not that type of devotional. Instead, I want to encourage people to study the Word of God so that He can lead them to more peace, a better lifestyle, and more importantly, a better relationship with God.

The Church (including me) can spend a lot of time answering questions that no one is asking. Some of us may even stand in the middle of a big city holding a sign and shouting that people who are not like us are "going to hell." Neither of these activities heeds Matthew 4:19 and Mark 1:17 on how to become "fishers of men."

I do believe it's important for believers to be well-versed in such Bible prophecy as the book of Daniel (especially chapter 9). At some point in their walk, I believe every believer needs to give some thought to the lessons in Matthew 24 and 1 Thessalonians 4:13-18 on the rapture, tribulation, and the second coming of our Lord and Savior. I also believe that we believers need to understand the book of Romans, because it is our version of Christianity 101. Romans sheds light on the continuation of Adam's sin (chapter 5) and the sovereignty of God (chapter 9). Some of my "theologically-heavy" friends are very knowledgeable on the terms that I mentioned in the first paragraph. But

I believe that the terms used in Galatians 5:22-23—love, joy, peace, patience, kindness, goodness, faithfulness, gentleness, and self-control—should be equally studied and imprinted on our hearts and minds.

As I have matured in my walk with God, I've learned that we each grow at a different pace. Some learn in a seminary and some in a coffee shop. The things that interest me may not intrigue someone else. Some of us want to study the Apocalypse of Peter and some just want to go to church and get involved in local home groups. I think both activities please our Father in heaven, because both show an interest in knowing Him more intimately.

I'VE LEARNED THAT WE EACH GROW AT A DIFFERENT PACE.

I love to listen to Hank Hanegraaff, The Bible Answer Man. On both his show and website he often uses the term "equip." His goal is to help us study the Word so that we can be equipped for the journey ahead. As Psalm 119:105 NLT says: "*Your word is a lamp to my feet and a light for my path.*"

Take a look at the verses right before verse 105, which explain why we need to study God's Word, including "*How sweet are your words to my taste, they are sweeter than honey. Your commandments give me understanding...*"

Day 6

"Study to show yourself approved to God, a workman
that needs not to be ashamed,
rightly dividing the word of truth."

2 Timothy 2:15, AKJV

One of the coolest things about God's Word is that it supernaturally displays more and more revelation as you mature. The reverse can be said about the things of this world. When I look in the mirror, I don't see the spry 25-year-old who used to jump 38 inches off the ground and run for days. I have to speak Deuteronomy 34:7 over myself daily. The truth is that the things of this world are decaying every second because of sin and death. If not for regular maintenance, your house would fall apart and be taken over by weeds, bugs, and mold. Our national landmarks, like the Washington Monument and Mount Rushmore, seem permanent but are frequently in a rehab state because they suffer the wear of old age. Remember the movie "Star Wars" which debuted in 1977? It was a cinematic marvel when it came out. Chewbacca, C3PO, and the light saber were all wonders back then. But when we watch that movie today, Chewy looks like an oversized Yorkshire Terrier and the storm troopers look like bike reflectors.

God's Word gets better with time and diligent study.

Amazingly, God's Word does the exact opposite. It gets better with time and diligent study. Growing up, I saw the story of David and Goliath as a miraculous tale of a young man who, by chance and some help from God, pounded a giant who bullied everyone around.

As I have matured in my faith and study, I have since learned a few more important facts about David the king:

- 1 Kings 9:4 says David was a man who walked with a heart filled with *"integrity and uprightness."*

- 1 Samuel 16:18 NIV describes David as a skillful musician, *"a brave man and warrior,"* fine looking and most importantly, *"the Lord is with him."*

- 1 Samuel 17:36 speaks of David killing both a lion and a bear. Now wrap your mind around that for a second. The hunters on ESPN and Fox Sports use high caliber rifles to kill big game in the wild, and they are usually accompanied by other hunters. At best, David—while living alone on the side of a remote mountain—carried a sling and a staff, which he used in close proximity as he protected his father's sheep.

- To me as an adult, the most important fact I've learned about our brother David is found in 2 Samuel 7:8-9 NIV when God says: *"...I took you from the pasture and from following the flock to be ruler over my people Israel. I have been with you wherever you have gone, and I have cut off all your enemies from before you. Now I will make your name great, like the names of the greatest men of the earth."* David's skill, power, musical talent, mental toughness, and favor all came from God.

It's amazing what you find out when you study the Word.

In Matthew 24:35 Jesus teaches that *"Heaven and earth will pass, but my words will never pass away."* What story in the Bible has taken on new meaning for you as you have matured in your walk?

Day 7

"Study to show yourself approved to God, a workman
that needs not to be ashamed,
rightly dividing the word of truth."

2 Timothy 2:15, AKJV

In 2 Timothy 2:15, the apostle Paul is admonishing Timothy to correctly handle the "word of truth," instead of being like Hymenaeus, Philetus (2 Timothy 2:17), and Alexander (1 Timothy 1:20), who were labeled as false teachers. Paul says that people like them, who do not "rightly divide" the Word, will become more ungodly and will be "*handed over to Satan to be taught not to blaspheme*" (1 Timothy 1:20). This meant that these men and those like them would be thrown out of the church, losing the covering that God's children enjoy when they live under His grace. *The Wiersbe Bible Commentary* states: "The fellowship of the local church, in obedience to the will of God, gives a believer spiritual protection." This is the reason that Satan had to ask for permission to attack Job (check Job 1 and 2), as Job was under God's protection.

> NOT EVERY BELIEVER IS IN A POSITION TO TEACH OR PASTOR A CONGREGATION, BUT THAT DOES NOT ABSOLVE US FROM DOING WHAT GOD IS COMMANDING: STUDY THE WORD.

What is my point? Not every believer is in a position to teach or pastor a congregation, but that does not absolve us from doing what God is commanding in 2 Timothy: study the Word. Sometimes some of our brothers and sisters—whom I believe have good intentions— preach and teach doctrines that are not Biblical. The problem is that their listeners do not know if they are hearing Biblical teaching because they don't diligently study the Word.

The Bible warns us about Satan in John 8:44 (NIV), "*When he lies, he speaks his native language, for he is a liar and the father of lies.*" We have seen many fall prey to Satan's lies in the past, like the death of more than 900 people in 1978 because of the false teachings of Jim Jones. The death of 54 adults and 21 children rocked our nation in 1993 when many were led to believe that the Branch Davidian religious sect, headed up by David Karesh, was a true religion founded in the Bible. These false sects are nothing new, as 1 Timothy 4:1 NIV explains: "*The Spirit clearly says that in later times some will abandon the faith and follow deceiving spirits and things taught by demons.*"

How can we, as believers in Christ, avoid these tricks of the enemy? These three steps will help us greatly.

1. First, we must believe that God's Word is the truth, as John 17:17 declares.
2. We must also know that the words in the Bible are straight from God, as Jesus teaches in John 14:24 NIV: "*These words you hear are not my own; they belong to the Father who sent me.*"
3. Additionally, we must allow the Word of God to reign in us, as Colossians 3:16 NLT tells us: "*Let the words of Christ, in all their richness, live in your hearts and make you wise.*" Psalm 119:11 NAS adds: "*Your word I have treasured in my heart, that I may not sin against You.*"

"Touch, tilt, look at, look through" is what government agents are taught to detect counterfeit money. Interestingly enough, these experts become great at detecting illegally-produced currency by becoming familiar with the real thing. This should be our approach as believers in Jehovah. We should know the Bible so well that as soon as we hear or see something that contradicts the Word of God, we are able to detect it and count it as false.

This can only happen if we study the Word and handle it correctly.

Week 2

"...anyone who comes to him must believe
that he exists and that he rewards
those who earnestly seek him."

Hebrews 11:6, NIV

DAY 1

"...anyone who comes to him must believe
that he exists and that he rewards
those who earnestly seek him."

HEBREWS 11:6, NIV

One reward for diligently seeking our Father is the way that it builds our faith. I read a quote from Kenneth Copeland that said "Faith is developed by meditating on God's Word. Fear is developed by meditating on Satan's lies." Romans 10:17 NIV says "*consequently, faith comes from hearing the message, and the message is heard through the word of Christ.*"

You don't have to go far to hear a surplus of Satan's lies, whether on television, at work, or at school. As God's children, we are to be the "salt" and the "light" that Jesus spoke of in Matthew 5:13-14. Salt brings flavor to every situation (it was also the primary means of food preservation in Jesus' time) and light illuminates dark situations so true reality can be seen. We cannot be either if we are not pursuing God the way we pursue pensions, more square footage on our homes, club memberships, or tighter abs.

As believers, we are to first seek the Father in every situation. Matthew 6:33 NKJ says we are to "*...seek ye first the kingdom of God and his righteousness, and all these things will be given unto you as well.*" This text is talking about God's Kingdom and the only way to enter that Kingdom is through a relationship with, and submission to, Jesus Christ. Without that relationship, the other things are never in their proper place.

Without Christ, our destinations are the equivalent of a mirage in the desert. They give us something to chase after, but once we arrive we discover that they're not there. Like the mirage, the things we were chasing after appear to have moved to another place, leaving us more frustrated and confused than we were when we started.

We are always so sure that if we attain a certain desire or achieve a certain goal we will finally be happy, that we will finally find our fulfillment. But we never find it where we thought we would, so we are off to the next thing—again and again. So many people spend their entire lives chasing mirage after mirage, never finding the fulfillment they're seeking. And they won't, because there is nothing in this world that can satisfy what we really desire.

Why? Because we were created with pieces of eternity in us that pull us toward God with an almost magnetic force (Ecclesiastes 3:11). The eternity we carry in us has given us a deep thirst for the eternal that nothing on earth can fulfill. Only God, the source of eternity, can fulfill what we really crave—and He will if we seek Him. Look at Isaiah 64:4 NLT where it says *"For since the world began, no ear has heard, and no eye has seen a God like you, who works for those who wait for him!"*

Stay in the Word of God daily; meditate on it. It's something you can never overdose on. We have the Holy Spirit living on the inside of us, teaching, leading, and helping us apply what needs to be in our lives so we can be used for God's Glory.

Are you really seeking God? Or are you playing church?

Have you grown spiritually? Or are you so used to the church ritual that you have not even noticed?

DAY 2

"…anyone who comes to him must believe
that he exists and that he rewards
those who earnestly seek him."

HEBREWS 11:6, NIV

There are so many resources that can help you earnestly seek God by studying Scripture. There are scores of Bible translations that can help you understand the text and thousands of study tools to help you dig into it as deeply as you want to go. Articles, devotionals, and short studies are available online from very well-known biblical teachers—and even more *un*known ones. Radio broadcasts share the truth of God's love in most of the 2700 spoken languages all around the world. You can listen to podcasts of sermons, hear Christian radio stations online, and download teachings from i-Tunes.

My favorite study resource is teaching tapes, and my favorite teacher is Rick Godwin. Rick is funny and relevant, but without compromise. I have been on the other end of one of his uncompromising "sit-down, let me tell you something" talks and it was not fun at all—but it helped me to mature.

There are so many powerful teachers of the Word: Creflo Dollar, John McArthur, Hank Hanegraaff, Charles Stanley, Beth Moore, Joyce Meyer, Chuck Swindoll, John Piper, Derek Prince, Dr. Leroy Thompson, William Branch, Eric Mason, Brett Meador, Luis Palau, and many others who have blessed millions of people with a deeper understanding of God's Word.

You may not think you have enough time in your day to add one more person telling you what to do and how to live your life. I never used to listen to Christian radio broadcasts or look online for ministries, either. But then I found out how easy it was to make room for it in my life. And *then* I discovered the benefits of knowing God in a deeper way. Now it's all I listen to in my car when I'm on the road. At least once a day I pull out a devotional from one my favorite teachers. It takes about 15 minutes and changes my day.

If you live in America, there is no excuse for not knowing more about God. We are blessed with a multitude of resources that have made it so easy to study.

The pressure is on you to find out more about Him.

How much time do you waste on stuff that adds no value to your life?

Begin with just 10 minutes a day to get started in your diligent search for God.

Spend some time online and choose a Biblical teacher to "sit under" for awhile.

DAY 3

"...anyone who comes to him must believe
that he exists and that he rewards
those who earnestly seek him."
HEBREWS 11:6, NIV

Would you like to be a producer of good things? I know that even on your worst day, you have a desire to finish stronger than you started. I know that on days when I snap at my wife and kids, dishonor my boss (inwardly or outwardly), or just have a bad day all by myself, I can still bring the Father glory because I can go to the Word (at home or at church) and fill up on God. I usually end up reminding myself that He still loves me and my stuff is not impossible for Him to fix.

God loves us just the way we are, no matter what your condition, but He refuses to leave us where we are. Luke 6:45 NIV says *"The good man brings good things out of the good stored up in his heart, and the evil man brings evil things out of the evil stored up in his heart. For out of the overflow of his heart his mouth speaks."*

The pathway to your heart is your eyes, ears, and the atmosphere that you allow yourself to be in. If we fill up on Satan or the trends of our culture, we will produce things that might feel good at the time, but in the end will lead to our demise. Proverbs 14:12 NAS says, "There is a way that seems right to a man, but its end is the way of death." Proverbs 8:34-35 NIV says *"Blessed is the man who listens to me, watching daily at my doorway. For whoever finds me finds life and receives favor from the LORD."* So who are you listening to? Better yet, who are you diligently seeking?

Listen to this quote from Luis Palau in a book written by his wife Pat and Peggy Sue Wells called *When You Don't Want to go to Church:*

> *"My advice to every Christian is the same: Attend church regularly. Follow the prescribed procedures to become a member of your local church. Inform the church leaders that your desire is to become an active member and work positively and productively under their leadership."*

This is from a man who has been influential in 1.5 million recorded conversions to Christianity, as he has traveled all over the world and preached the gospel in 70 different countries. I think it is amazing that this man and his wife still find time to be part of their local church in Portland, Oregon because they understand the importance of fellowshipping with other believers. Being under Christ-centered leadership will help you to produce fruit for the Kingdom.

BE CAREFUL OF THE ATMOSPHERE THAT YOU ALLOW YOURSELF TO FREQUENT BECAUSE IF YOU ARE NOT IMPACTING IT, IT WILL SURELY HAVE AN IMPACT ON YOU.

Be careful of the atmosphere that you allow yourself to frequent because if you are not impacting it, it will surely have an impact on you. I encourage you to be more active in your local church gathering, it will be a blessing to you, and your gifts, talents, and wisdom will help someone else to be a producer of good things.

Remember that Psalm 119:2 NIV says "***Blessed*** *are they who keep his statutes and* ***seek*** *him with all their heart.*" And lastly, look at Philippians 1:11 NLT where it says *"May you always be filled with the fruit of your salvation—* ***those good things that are produced*** *in your life by Jesus Christ —for this will bring much glory and praise to God."*

Peace and Blessings.

Day 4

"…anyone who comes to him must believe
that he exists and that he rewards
those who earnestly seek him."

Hebrews 11:6, NIV

I like the simplicity of this verse. It gets right to the point and includes several items of clarification that can go unnoticed if you skim through it like you would a newspaper or a magazine.

It starts by saying "*…anyone who comes to him.*" This means no matter what color, culture, or class, you can come to Him. It means even if you just committed what you may deem as the most despicable sin in the world, you can come to Him. It means if you have worshiped other gods and practiced other religions, you can come to Him. There is nothing that can stand between us and the love of God. You can't do anything to stop that principle from working for you.

> There is nothing that can stand between us and the love of God.

But once you come, you must believe that He exists. You cannot accept Jesus as your Lord and Master and think of Him as a mythological being. You must know that He sits at the right hand of God as Mark 14:62 says. You must know that when God said, "*Let us make man in our image*" in Genesis 1:26, that He is making reference to the Trinity: Father, Son, and Holy Spirit. You must have a firm grip on this fact—HE EXISTS; He always has and always will. What society or a scientist of eloquent speech says about Him does not validate or invalidate who He is; He is because He is.

Lastly, you can't just *think* to yourself that God rewards those who earnestly seek Him; you must also *believe* it. Look at the verse again. It says that you must believe that he exists *"and."* That "and" is a bridge between two action phases: we believe and He rewards. You have to know that God wants what is best for you. That does not mean that He has predestined you to be like your daddy if that is not what He has called you to be. It does not mean He has ordained you to work in the field that your degree is listed under. What it means is that if we believe that He rewards those who earnestly seek Him, we also believe that He knows what is best for us. Look at Isaiah 64:4 in the NAS: *"No eye has seen a God besides You that acts in behalf of the one who waits for Him."* Mark 9:23 in the NIV says that *"Everything is possible for him who believes."*

But we can't forget the clincher: we must seek Him! *Webster's New World Dictionary* defines "seek" with terms like "to try to find," "search for," and "to try to get." Look at Acts 17:26-27: *"From one man he made every nation of men, that they should inhabit the whole earth; and he determined the times set for them and the exact places where they should live. God did this so that men would seek him and perhaps reach out for him and find him, though he is not far from each one of us."* NIV

God has made it easier for us to find Him. Once we diligently seek Him, all things are possible.

Day 5

"…anyone who comes to him must believe
that he exists and that he rewards
those who earnestly seek him."

Hebrews 11:6, NIV

Today I want to talk about a consequence for *not* seeking God. That consequence is living your life without knowing your purpose and God's plan for you.

You may say, "I attend church and am a member of a small group that meets once a week." You may say, "I keep a Bible open on my coffee table and wear a cross around my neck." All those things are fine, even good, but they do not automatically mean that we are seeking God.

One of the main reasons why seeking God is so important is that church activities can become just that: nothing more than church activities. Church goers often forget most of what they heard in the service by the end of the day they went. I know this firsthand; it's part of the reason why this devotional came into existence.

As we began to write this book, we all agreed that even if this effort came to nothing and we flopped as authors, we would know our Heavenly Father better because of the time studying for it—and *that* would be well worth the months invested in writing it. The more I wrote and studied, the more I began to see what God was doing in my life. As I studied these Scriptures, the Holy Spirit reminded me of things I needed to do and things that needed to be corrected.

That's what happens when we get into the Word: our spirits line up with God and it becomes easier to know His heart—not just for our future but for each part of our lives. For example, there is nothing like reading Proverbs 31:10-31 to remind me that my wife is the MVP of our household as I see her in the light of Proverbs' virtuous woman. But it does more than just make me proud of her; it makes me want to do all I can so she can be at her best, to keep an atmosphere in our home that makes it easier for her to reach her full potential in Christ. To be honest, I thought that once you were married you were automatically entitled to happiness; eventually you threw in a few kids and just continued to do whatever you did before you got married and it resulted in eternal bliss. I had no idea that God had so much purpose in the union of Ingrid, myself, and Him. I had no idea that I needed to seek Him to discover my purpose as a husband. I don't know if I would have been able to understand her value and purpose if God had not made it plain for me through His Word.

A similar thing is seen in the way many people approach church. We go to a service and treat it like it is only a schedule obligation or a social activity, forgetting the purposes behind the praise, the worship, the message, and the fellowship with other believers. Some days we go to church and we are uplifted; other times we uplift the church leadership with prayers, encouragement, or just our presence. But most importantly, we please God in that we make Him the most important part of our lives. Now *that* is purpose.

The point is this: the closer we are to God, the easier it is to know our purpose in all facets of our lives. In order to get close to God, we must seek Him. Rick Warren, in *The Purpose Driven Life*, says "Nothing matters more than knowing God's purposes for your life, and nothing can compensate for not knowing them."

Do you read the Word for guidance and wisdom or because it is a habit?

Do you mark up your Bible because you are studying or so others will think, "Wow they really know the Word?"

Day 6

"...anyone who comes to him must believe
that he exists and that he rewards
those who earnestly seek him."

Hebrews 11:6, NIV

How would you like to be like God?

Now, don't get offended. I am not about to give you the blueprints to create your own universe and reign as the "King of Kings." Just think about it for a moment.

Proverbs 1:7 NAS tells us that *"The fear of the Lord is the beginning of knowledge; fools despise wisdom and instruction."* As you are already investing yourself in study of the Word, I know that you are not a fool; our goal in biblical study is to seek God's wisdom and instruction so we can better serve Him.

Listen to this commentary from the *MacArthur Study Bible* on Proverbs 1:7: "The fear of Lord is a state of mind in which one's own attitudes, will, feelings, deeds, and goals are exchanged for God's." How would you like, by faith and in the natural world, to exchange your *bag of bones*, with its habits, mood swings, and selfish desires, for a personality like that of Jesus (Immanuel, God with us)? In essence, we become like God. It will never happen if we don't diligently seek after the One who first programmed us to be like Him.

A quick look at Psalms 42:1 NAS gives us an idea of what kind of determination it takes to seek the Father: *"As the deer pants for the water brooks, so my soul pants for You,* O GOD*."* In that psalm, we see a deer that is desperate for a drink. Notice it did not say a pond or lake, where there is no flow and the water is stagnate. David used "brook" as a reference intentionally, not a river which can flow out of control but a brook which moves but slowly enough to drink from without choking or being pulled in by the current.

The key in this verse, though, is the desperation of the deer. We must desire to know God like we desire the things that our culture tricks us into going after (only to find out later that it was not as good as advertised). God should be our greatest desire, as we were His. Take a look at how much detail God took in the planning of our existence: *"You saw me before I was born. Every day of my life was recorded in your book. Every moment was laid out before a single day had passed. And when I wake up in the morning, you are still with me!"* (Psalm 139:16, NLT)

God made you.
He knows you.
He wants what is best for you.
He is waiting on you.

It is up to us to believe in and seek Him. The closer we are to Him, the more we become like Him. In Ephesians 4:13 AMP, Paul says *"Until we attain oneness in the faith and in the comprehension of the [full and accurate] knowledge of the Son of God, that [we might arrive] at really mature manhood (the completeness of personality which is nothing less than the standard height of Christ's own perfection) the measure of the stature of the fullness of the Christ, and the completeness found in Him."*

Remember that God made humanity in His image, as Genesis 1:26 NIV says *"Then God said 'Let us make man in our image, in our likeness, and let them rule…."* That plan was not aborted because of the fall of man; it was just delayed.

Now is the time to get back what is ours: our rightful place of dominion that comes from being made in the image of God (see, it wasn't a heretical question after all).

Seek Him.

DAY 7

"…anyone who comes to him must believe
that he exists and that he rewards
those who earnestly seek him."

HEBREWS 11:6, NIV

As we close this week, I want to talk about some of the rewards for diligently seeking the Father. But first, let's take a look at another key word in this verse: earnestly.

Earnestly means diligently. *The Random House College Dictionary* says that "diligent" means to be in "constant effort to accomplish something or pursue with persevering attention." We know that "seek" means to "search for." So in other words, we are in a constant search or quest to know our Heavenly Father.

When we are seeking God and beginning to submit to His will, we find ourselves overcome by His blessings. Blessings of healing are one example, as Exodus 15:26 NIV explains: "*…If you listen carefully to the voice of the LORD your God and do what is right in his eyes, if you pay attention to his commands and keep all his decrees, I will not bring on you any diseases I brought on the Egyptians, for I am the LORD, who heals you.*" If you have time, look at Deuteronomy 7:12-15 and Deuteronomy 28 where God gives a blueprint for how our life will go if we will seek Him and do what His Word says to do. Interestingly enough, Deuteronomy 28 begins with "*Now it shall be, if you will diligently obey the Lord your God….*" which takes our devotional a step further this week. We are not only to seek the Father, but we are to diligently *obey* Him as well.

A little Old Testament wisdom will give us some food for thought as well as inspiration to do what Hebrews 11:6 commands. When these decrees were given to God's chosen people, it meant their obedience (you can't be obedient if you don't know Him) would put them in a lofty place (a place of promotion and protection) above all other nations. Study the book of Joshua to get a picture of all the nations that were destroyed as God gave favor to His people because of the obedience of people like Moses, Joshua, and Caleb.

As a child of God, you are an heir to all God has.

As covenant children who have been grafted into His family through faith in Jesus Christ (read Romans 11:24), we are also exalted to the same high place and receive the same protection from Jehovah Jireh (God who Provides) that the Israelites from the Old Testament received. Plus, we have the Holy Spirit inside of us. These and many other blessing are for God's children. Proverbs 10:6 NIV says, *"Blessings crown the head of the righteous, but violence overwhelms the mouth of the wicked."* As a child of God, you are an heir to all God has.

God must become our number one priority. He must be diligently sought after.

When we do, the rewards will blow us away.

Week 3

"But where sin increased, grace increased all the more."

Romans 5:20, NIV

DAY 1

"But where sin increased, grace increased all the more."
ROMANS 5:20, NIV

The grace that is available to us because of Jesus' atoning blood has tremendous power. It has the power to do something amazing, something that goes beyond our comprehension, but is available nonetheless to those who accept it: it has the power to reconnect humanity.

"Reconnect humanity to *what*?" you might ask. The short answer: reconnect us to God. As red-blooded men and women, we have all committed sin (Romans 3:23; Ephesians 2:1-3). The fact that all of us have made bad decisions, dishonored someone, gossiped, cheated in some form, displayed arrogance and pride, succumbed to any of our fleshly desires, along with a long list of other things, is only part of the problem. We were also born into an inherited, condemned nature (1 Corinthians 15:22)—a huge and debilitating debt—whether or not we wanted it or chose it.

EVERYONE INHERITED A BROKEN RELATIONSHIP WITH JEHOVAH. IT'S KIND OF LIKE BEING DIVORCED BEFORE YOU EVEN GET MARRIED, WITH NO CHANCE TO MAKE THE RELATIONSHIP WORK.

Our debt began to pile up a long time ago when Adam sinned against God. Because of Adam's transgression recorded in Genesis 3 (check Romans 5:12), everyone after him inherited a broken relationship with Jehovah. It's kind of like being divorced before you even get married, with no chance to make the relationship work. Starting with Adam and culminating with our personal choices, we have individually and collectively created and built upon an eternal debt that can only be paid for (redeemed) by the blood of a perfect sacrifice. This perfect sacrifice was Jesus Christ. His willingness to die on the cross, be raised from the dead, and ascend to heaven reconnects us to the Father so that we can personally have the relationship that He originally designed for humanity. This reconnecting is the epitome of grace.

The Bible says that when we have broken relationship with God, we are friends with the world (the system of doing things that contradicts the way God intended life to function). This is called "*enmity*" (James 4:4) and makes us "*objects of wrath*" (Ephesians 2:3). Without the grace that we receive through faith in Christ (Ephesians 2:4, 5), either we are or were at odds with God—depending on our relationship to Jesus.

Let's make something clear: you can stop gossiping, take a vow of celibacy, treat others with impeccable respect, and so on, but you will never be able to erase the consequences of your past sin on your own. No matter how hard you try or how good you are, you have inherited a sinful nature that disqualifies you from ever being able to pay back the debt to God, no matter how good a life you live. In the New American Standard NAS version of the Bible, Isaiah 64:6 says, "*...and all our righteous deeds are like a filthy garment...*" Paul considered all his good deeds "rubbish" (for more read Philippians 3:5-9).

So many people think they are okay because they are a "good person," but that doesn't take the entire situation into account. They don't understand the grace that is required to overcome the penalty for sin through our actions and our spiritual/genetic makeup. If you compare yourself to the world, you can conceivably reason that you are okay, based on that paradigm. But when comparing yourself to the standard set by Jesus (whose name Immanuel means "God with us") and acknowledging the debt caused by sin, you find the need for grace. My favorite music artist,

The Ambassador, says it this way in his song Psalm 23: "*Life's no joke...so even when you fight hard...you'll drown in your sin...if you don't meet Christ the Lifeguard.*"

The remedy to this situation is found in John 3:16. Christ's nature, shed blood, and perfection are superior to our lifestyles, ways of thinking, and the original fall of man in Adam. "*For it is by grace you have been saved, through faith—and this is not from yourselves, it is the gift of God—not by works, so that no one can boast*" (Ephesians 2:8-9).

If you are a believer, choose again today to walk in His grace.

If you are not a follower of Christ, make the decision now to receive His grace and reconnect yourself to God. Remember, where there is a drop of sin, there is an ocean of grace.

Don't focus on the drop; swim in and enjoy His grace.

DAY 2

"But where sin increased, grace increased all the more."

ROMANS 5:20, NIV

Let's do a simple exercise. Read through the list of words in the left column. In the right column, fill in the blank with the word that is its opposite, like the four examples already shown:

cold	**hot**
wet	____________
light	____________
confusion	**understanding**
moral	____________
above	**below**
exciting	____________
GOD	____________
foreign	**native**
faith	____________

Each of these words has been used by us at some point in our lives, so we pretty much understand the opposite of each. But if you wrote "Satan" as the opposite of God, there are two problems: one, that's the wrong answer; two, it's probably going to be hard for you to understand God's grace if you think Satan has that much power.

John 10:10 describes Satan as a thief who comes to steal, kill, and destroy. This illustrates a personality that almost sounds like a spoiled, selfish, miserable child. Revelation 20:1-3 describes how Satan is defeated, and thrown into the lake of fire (also Revelation 9:1). There are many more illustrations in the Bible that show that Satan is no contest for God and doesn't stand a chance of winning in any sort of cosmic struggle. He was actually created by God and his name was originally Lucifer, which means Angel of Light. Technically, this makes him the antagonist (or opposite) of Michael, another angel God created.

Sin started with Satan and his rebellion against God; grace began with God as His initiative to reconnect us to our intended relationship with Him. The Scripture reinforces what this means for us: that where there is sin, grace is also available, and that grace is so much more powerful than any sin. Look at the second part of Romans 5:21 NIV: *"So that, just as sin reigned in death, so also grace might reign through righteousness to bring eternal life through Jesus Christ our Lord."*

Choose life, so that the power of grace can work for you.

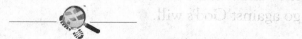

Two of Satan's greatest tricks are to make us think that he does not exist and to get us to think that he is equal to God. Why should we not see Satan as an equal to our Lord Jesus Christ?

Day 3

"But where sin increased, grace increased all the more."

Romans 5:20, NIV

Let's take a look at two verses which precede our meat for the week. "*So then as through one transgression there resulted condemnation to all men, even so through one act of righteousness there resulted justification of life to all men. For as through the one man's disobedience the many were made sinners, even so through the obedience of the* ***One*** *the many will be made righteous*" (Romans 5:18-19, NAS).

Some theologians call Adam's time with God before the fall the "covenant of works." God created, Adam enjoyed. God gave, Adam received. God commanded, Adam obeyed. All of this produced a perfect "way" if you will, until the "fall" (Adam's sin), which caused a powerful force to come into existence. This force—sin—is the same force that causes all believers and unbelievers to go against God's will.

Sin is the force that causes people to gossip. It is the force that causes men and women to commit adultery, even when they are in healthy marriages. It is the force that causes us to covet what others have or fall prey to what the culture says we should have so we end up living beyond our means or neglecting our children for a couple more square feet on our home. Sin is the force that causes addictions to drugs, power, sex, status, and even people. It causes natural and environmental catastrophes on Earth. It causes parents to get into physical fights at Little League games. It causes "*immorality, greed, obscenity, foolish talk, and coarse joking*," which are listed in Ephesians 5:3-4. And it is the same force that causes you to _______________ (fill in the blank).

We often feel alone in our struggle with sin, but this is not true. Listen to the apostle Paul in Romans 7:22-24 NIV: "*...but I see another law at work in the members of my body, waging war against the law of my mind and making me a prisoner of the law of sin at work within my members. What a wretched man I am!*" Earlier in that chapter we can see an even clearer picture of Paul's dilemma: "*...for I am not practicing what I would like to do, but I am doing the very thing I hate*" (Romans 7:15; NAS). Sound familiar?

We often feel alone in our struggle with sin, but this is not true.

Thank God for His grace! Because of that, we have the ultimate weapon that dominates this evil force and leaves it powerless—the Spirit of God. In Ezekiel 36:27 NAS God promises, "*I will put my spirit within you and cause you to walk in My statutes, and you will be careful to observe My ordinances.*" The spirit referred to here is the Holy Spirit, who lives in those who call Jesus their Lord and Savior This Spirit causes us to *"love God and love our neighbor"* (Luke 10:27). When we practice living a life of love by the power of God's Spirit, our world becomes a better place in which to live.

How has God's grace helped you stay in His will?

Do you remember a time when wanted to do the right thing, and felt overwhelmed by the "want" to commit sin?

Day 4

"But where sin increased, grace increased all the more."

Romans 5:20, NIV

Let's take a look at the word "grace" from a Greek point of view.

"Grace" comes from the Greek word *charis*. *Charis* embodies the idea of favor. *Charis* is also where the Greeks get the word *chara*, which in English means "joy." So we can conclude that joy comes from grace.

If we determine that God gives us the grace to do the things that are pleasing to Him, as 1 Corinthians 15:10 NIV says, "*But by the* ***grace*** *of God I am what I am, and his* ***grace*** *to me was not without effect. No, I worked harder than all of them—yet not I, but the* ***grace*** *of God that was with me*," then it makes sense that when we do the will of God, we feel good. I am talking about the good/joy that makes you walk with confidence because you have been obedient; the kind of joy that lets you sleep deeply at night, instead of tossing and turning because you went against the will of God.

I like 1 Corinthians 15:10 because Paul makes reference to himself as a hard worker. But he is also quick to mention that though hard work is important, it must remain in the passenger seat; the grace of God has to be the driver. No wonder so many people work all their lives for what they thought would satisfy them, only to find that they were missing something: GRACE. No wonder couples spend 30 and 40 years in marriage and suddenly fall out of love: NO GRACE. No wonder one out of three state lottery winners goes broke and ends up filing for bankruptcy: NO GRACE.

The only way you can have joy in this life is by having grace. Look at 1 Peter 5:10 in the NIV: "*And the God of all* ***grace****, who called* *you to his eternal glory in Christ, after you have suffered a little while, will himself restore you and make you strong, firm and steadfast.*" The importance of this statement is huge, because it promises that God is the source of all grace, and that even when we suffer, we have this grace. That means we can also have joy—which comes from grace—even when things don't go our way.

Some have taught that you can only enjoy God's grace by or through the Jewish nation, based on Galatians 3:16 NIV: "*Now to Abraham and his Seed were these promises made.*" Everyone has been blessed through Abraham's seed, with whom God's covenant and the Old Testament promises of the Messiah were made; Jesus was a descendent of Abraham (check Matthew 1:1-16). But look at a note from *Jon Courson's Application Commentary NT*: "*The promises of God to bless the world come not through the Jewish nation, but through Jesus; not through a national entity, but through Jesus Christ exclusively to all people, in all places.*"

God's grace is based on Him—not men, not nations, and certainly not anyone's deeds. Thank God for that!

Day 5

"But where sin increased, grace increased all the more."

Romans 5:20, NIV

I think it is essential that we understand that the sin of Romans 5:20 is increased because we are finally aware of it. How did we become aware of our sin? The Law made us aware of it, with all the "dos" and "do nots" from the Old Testament that we were unable to obey completely. Paul says in Romans 7:7 NIV, "*For I would not have known what sin was except through the law.*" This awareness of sin drives us to Jesus Christ: "*so the law was put in charge to lead us to Christ that we might be justified by faith*" (Galatians 3:24, NIV).

Matthew Henry's Commentary on the Whole Bible has an interesting take on this verse in Scripture. It says, "When the commandment came into the world sin revived, as the letting of clearer light into a room discovers the dust and filth which were there before, but were not seen."

Now, we must not forget that even though sin increased, "*grace increased all the more.*" Because of that grace, we win. It is interesting that some interpretations use "increased all the more," and some use the phrase "abounded all the more." *The MacArthur Study Bible* defines "abound" with terms like "excel" and "be plentiful." It seems we can conclude from the Word that grace excels and destroys the power of sin.

My friend and pastor Sam Hinn from The Gathering Place in Sanford, Florida has a profound way of teaching this principle that helps when we are feeling condemned by our mistakes or when the evil pull of sin tries to wear us down. He says that we have to see sin increasing in terms of addition, like 2 + 2 + 2 + 2 +2. But we must see and know that grace increases or abounds in terms of multiplication, like 10 x 10 x 10 x 10 x 10. Think of God's grace as something that is greater in value than a googolplex, which is the highest named number humans know. Sam also teaches that "God's way of overcoming the power of sin wasn't by giving laws to regulate sin, but by drowning sin with an abundance of grace."

GOD'S WAY OF OVERCOMING THE POWER OF SIN WASN'T BY GIVING LAWS TO REGULATE SIN, BUT BY DROWNING SIN WITH AN ABUNDANCE OF GRACE.

Look at Titus 2:11-12 in the NKJV: "*For the grace of God that brings salvation has appeared to all men, teaching us that, denying ungodliness and worldly lusts, we should live soberly, righteously, and godly in the present age.*" How has this grace appeared? Through Jesus Christ! "*For the law was given by Moses; grace and truth were realized through Jesus Christ*" (John 1:17 NAS).

You've probably never heard of A. A. Allen, but he had one of the largest healing ministries in the 1950's and 60's. A quick study of his ministry will reveal things that we (the Church) would call sinful. Nevertheless, many were impacted by his ministry. You may say, "How can that be?" I believe what God did through his ministry was based on God's faithfulness to Allen, not the other way around. That is the power of grace in the work of flawed human beings: God sharing His perfect power and love with less than perfect people. Remember, we are not perfect, but we are perfectly forgiven.

Day 6

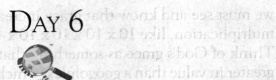

"But where sin increased, grace increased all the more."

Romans 5:20, NIV

When looking at Romans 5:20, we find ourselves most attracted to the word "grace" because we know we need it for living a life that is pleasing to the Father. But let's not ignore another important aspect of this verse: sin.

Webster's New World Dictionary and Thesaurus defines sin like this: "the willful breaking of religious and moral law" and "any offense or fault." The thesaurus from the same book uses terms like "error," "wrongdoing," wickedness," "evildoing," and "iniquity," to name a few.

It would be easy to say that sin started in Genesis 3 where the serpent, Satan, deceived Eve and caused Adam to sin. But sin started some time before Genesis 3 took place. It started before Scripture was Scripture. It started before…well, I will stop there. The truth is, nobody knows the exact date when sin started, but Isaiah 14:12-15 NIV gives us a recap of what happened: "*How you have fallen from heaven, O morning star, son of the dawn! You have been cast down to earth, you who once laid low the nations! You said in your heart, 'I will ascend to heaven; I will raise my throne above the stars of God; I will sit enthroned on the mount of assembly, on the utmost heights of the sacred mountain. I will ascend above tops of the clouds; I will make myself like the Most High.' But you are brought down to the grave, to the depths of the pit.*"

These verses are addressed to the king of Babylon, but the description is also a lowlight reel of what happened to Satan when he rebelled against God, fell from heaven, and began the cycle of sin. The Bible uses this same method when addressing the king of Tyre in Ezekiel 28:12-17. We know these two verses are more about Satan than the two kings because of the verbiage used, like *"fallen from heaven," "heights of clouds," and "anointed cherub."*

Some Hebrew words that are used for sin are *chattaah* or *chata*, meaning "offense." Two more are *avown*, which is used for "perversity," and *asham*, which is another way of saying "a fault."

The Greek word for sin is *anomia*. Listen to an excerpt from *Sparkling Gems from the Greek* by Rick Renner: "Translating the word *anomia* as "sin" is unfortunate, for the word *anomia* actually means without law and carries the idea of lawless attitude...this is a reference to the man of lawlessness or the antichrist." In Hank Hanegraaff's book *The Bible Answer Book*, sin is described as "...the deprivation of good. As such, sin is characterized by a lack of something rather than being something in itself."

> WE CANNOT BEGIN TO UNDERSTAND GRACE UNTIL WE UNDERSTAND WHY WE NEED IT. WE NEED GRACE BECAUSE IT IS THE ONLY WAY OUR SIN CAN BE ERASED.

There is no way around it: sin is not from God and it is the foundation of evil in our world. From the Old Testament we learn that sin brought a barrier between us and God. From the New Testament we learn that it causes us to grieve the Holy Spirit (Ephesians 4:30), among many other things. We cannot begin to understand grace until we understand why we need it. We need grace because it is the only way our in can be erased.

Grace is not just a catchy word. It is not just a valiant action. It is not just a benevolent institution. Grace is our Lord and Master,

Jesus Christ. Sin started with Satan and ended with Immanuel, our source of grace.

Before we close, check out 2 Corinthians 4:15 NLT where it says, "*All these things are for your benefit. And as God's grace brings more and more people to Christ, there will be great thanksgiving, and God will receive more and more glory.*"

Repeat Romans 5:20 over and over (sing it if you have to) until it gets down in your spirit like a song or commercial that you cannot get out of your mind.

DAY 7

"But where sin increased, grace increased all the more."

ROMANS 5:20, NIV

I want to end this week by looking at Abraham as a symbol of the church (followers of Jesus Christ) to see how God's grace shows up when we least deserve it.

Genesis 12:10-20 shows Abraham headed toward Egypt. Before he enters Egypt, he asks his wife Sarai (her name at the time) to lie and say that she is his sister. His reasoning was that Sarai was so beautiful that the men from Egypt would kill him and keep her for themselves. Verse 13 in the NIV says, "*Say that you are my sister, so that I will be treated well for your sake and my life will be spared because of you.*"

Just as he hoped, Abraham was treated well, even acquiring "*sheep, cattle, donkeys, menservants, and maidservants, and camels*" (verse 16). Before long, Pharaoh and his house were afflicted by God with disease for Sarai's sake, and Abraham's plan was brought to light by the Egyptian ruler.

Where is God's grace in all this? The answer is in verse 20: "*Then Pharaoh gave orders about Abram to his men, and they sent him on his way, with his wife and everything he had.*" That is amazing. Here we have Abraham, who is afraid for his life, puts his wife in harm's way, lies about who he and his wife are, and in the end, he is still blessed with a material blessing. He walks away with more than he had before he cooked up this crazy scheme.

I am not condoning lying or throwing our family members to the wolves to save our own necks. But I am making the point that even when we are at our worst, God's grace works on our behalf. Notice that the blessing of the Lord manifests itself right in the middle of this Biblical soap opera, right when Abraham is at his most undeserving point. Where sin increased, grace increased all the more.

We also should not forget that Abraham's butt was spared because he had an awesome wife. Ephesians 5:22 says that wives should submit to their husbands. I believe because Sarah submitted to his leadership and protection—not domination or devaluing—she was not only unharmed, but Abraham was abundantly blessed. That is God's grace at work.

When you hit rock bottom and all you can see is the belly of the whale, look for the grace of El Roi, the God who Sees you. When you are down to your last dollar and are tempted not to tithe, look for the grace of Jehovah-Jireh, the Lord who Provides. When you are weak physically, spiritually, and emotionally, look for the grace of Elohim, the God Most High. When you are sick and it seems like there is no hope in sight, look for the grace of Jehovah-Rapha, the Lord who Heals. When everything around you is out of sorts, look for Jehovah-Shalom, the Lord of Peace.

For a New Testament application, look at Luke 7:36-50. There we find a woman who had lived a sinful life. She heard that Jesus was having dinner with one of the Pharisees. She approached Jesus and washed His feet with her tears, wiped them with her hair, and poured perfume on them. This sinful woman did all this in front of the Pharisees, who believed they should not be in the company of a woman who was likely a prostitute.

Where's the grace? We see it in verses 48 and 50, when Jesus says to the woman, "*Your sins are forgiven,*" and "*Your faith has saved you; go in peace*." Now that is grace!

When we least expect it and we do not deserve it, God gives us what we do not deserve and shows mercy by not giving us what we do.

King David said in Psalm 4:1 NAS: *"You have relieved me in my distress…"*

When David was at his lowest, God showed His Grace to him.

Will God do any less for you?

Did you know abraham and Sarah were brother and sister. Check Genesis 20:12 where it says *"And yet indeed she (Sarah) is my sister; she is the daughter of my father, but not the daughter of my mother, and she became my wife."* KJV

WEEK 4

"But put ye on the Lord Jesus Christ,
and make not provision for the flesh,
to fulfill the lusts thereof."

ROMANS 13:14, KJV

DAY 1

"But put ye on the Lord Jesus Christ,
and make not provision for the flesh,
to fulfill the lusts thereof."

ROMANS 13:14, KJV

I first heard this verse from one of the best teachers of the Word that I know. Her name is Sandy Ross. Sandy and her husband Randy are the leaders of a young married couples' class at Eagles Nest Christian Fellowship, our old church in San Antonio, Texas (now known as Summit Christian Center). When I heard this verse, all I could think about were the times that I put myself in harm's way—the times when I knew exactly what I was doing and the consequences that would follow but made the choice anyway. Intentionally committing sin has severe penalties; trust me, I know. Proverbs 14:12 NIV says, *"There is a way that seems right to man but in the end it leads to death."*

I would like to take a quick look at the episode in 2 Samuel 11 involving King David and Bathsheba. In this story, David commits the sins of adultery, deceitful cover-up, and murder—all the while involving others in his lustful plot. A closer look at the beginning of this story reveals something that you'll miss if you only pay attention to the plot of the story or forget to study lessons preached in church.

Kings almost always led their troops out to battle, and as Israel's King David always went to battle with his troops, but 2 Samuel 11:1 mentions that David stayed home this time. It was evening, 2 Samuel 11:2 notes, and David may have just awakened. Now, whether he awoke from a nap or from the night before is not clear. What is clear is that David was not his normal, vigorous, ready-to-lead self. Furthermore, not only does David strategically put Bathsheba's husband Uriah in a location where he knew he would have a great chance of dying (2 Samuel 11:15), but he also destroys a marriage and causes a number of people to sin in the process (a servant and Joab, who was more than willing to do so).

We all succumb to lethargy at one time or another in our lives. Considering what David went through before this period of his life, most people would say that he deserved a break or sabbatical. But it's interesting to note that this was the first time we read of King David not going to war when there was a fight, from his first battle with Goliath and probably as far back as his battles with fierce animals. Ponder for a minute on the times you have put yourself in the devil's playing field because you were not where you were supposed to be. How quickly we forget the consequences of sin when the desires of our flesh are used as our compass.

This is not a finger-pointing session aimed at the man after God's own heart who was also one of the finest kings in the history of the world. Instead, this is a clear warning to all of us who believe in Christ, and even those who don't, that we should never redirect our calling or assignment until we get confirmation from GOD (which could also come through our boss, teacher, parents, etc.).

We know the flesh we live in has a plan of its own; deviating from God's plan to follow it has definite consequences. I pray that God shows you how to control that which He has given you authority over.

Have you ever put yourself in a situation where you knew you compromised your integrity?

What were the consequences? What does "put ye on the Lord Jesus Christ" mean to you?

Day 2

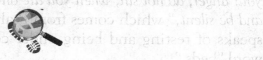

"But put ye on the Lord Jesus Christ,
and make not provision for the flesh,
to fulfill the lusts thereof."

Romans 13:14, KJV

The summer of 1999 was supposed to be a relaxing time for me and my family. I was looking forward to being rewarded with a brand new contract from the San Antonio Spurs. It was not going to be a mega-million dollar deal, but it was going to be more money than I had at the time—or at any point in my life.

As it turned out, we had a lockout (a work stoppage) that year and did not resume the season until February, which in a normal year would have been close to All Star break. That left about eight months to prepare, which involved lifting weights, track work, and a lot of pickup ball. In January I was playing with teammates and other guys from around the NBA and I severely sprained my ankle. At that time of the injury (though I did not know yet) I tore two ligaments in my ankle, which meant that I was literally playing on one leg for about a year and a half afterwards.

A few weeks later, the work stoppage ended and my contract talks with the Spurs went south...South Pole south. The Spurs graciously offered me a sign and trade deal to the Chicago Bulls for a clutch shooting guard, Steve Kerr. Because of pride, arrogance, and just being plain stubborn, I turned the deal down and signed a one year contract with the Denver Nuggets. Two weeks into the season I got "released"—cut, let go, fired.

I was devastated. I could have blamed it on my ankle, but that was just an excuse. The truth is that I went out of God's will because I acted out of premeditated anger. The Bible says, "*In your anger, do not sin; when you are on your beds, search your hearts and be silent,*" which comes from Psalms 4:4 NIV. That verse also speaks of resting and being under control, in reference to the word "beds."

As I look back on that situation, I have learned two things that I try to remember, though it is very hard in the heat of the moment.

1. I must keep my emotions out of any decision-making. I have made too many mistakes when I let my emotions and ego guide me. The Spurs motto, in reference to this, is "*GET* **OVER** *YOURSELF.*"
2. I should always seek wise counsel when making life changing decisions. Look at Proverbs 11:14 in the NIV, where it says, "*For lack of guidance a nation falls, but many advisers make victory sure.*"

Pray that GOD would show you your weaknesses in the flesh and how to keep them under control.

Has your anger and ego lead you into trouble?

Do you have a person you can rely on to tell you the truth no matter what you may think of them afterwards? Thank God for that person if you have one.

DAY 3

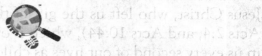

"But put ye on the Lord Jesus Christ,
and make not provision for the flesh,
to fulfill the lusts thereof."
ROMANS 13:14, KJV

I thought we'd take a minute and do a breakdown of the key words in Romans 13:14. Let's look at the word "provision." The American Dictionary of the English Language by Noah Webster defines provision with terms like "making previous preparation," "measures taken beforehand," and "the act of providing."

A "Christian's attitude toward" is how Strong's Exhaustive Concordance of the Bible describes the word "flesh" in reference to Romans 13:14. It is important to signify this reference because the same resource has two other meanings from other verses in the Bible that were translated using this same word "flesh." Webster's describes the word "lust" in this way: "to have a carnal desire, to have irregular or inordinate desire, an evil propensity," and carries on from there. Strong's cuts right to the chase, defining lust as an "evil desire."

LET'S MAKE IT PLAIN: ROMANS 13:14 IS COMMANDING US TO NEVER, NEVER, NEVER MAKE PREVIOUS PREPARATION FOR OUR NATURAL TENDENCY TO FOLLOW THE EVIL DESIRE OF THE FLESH.

Let's make it plain: Romans 13:14 is commanding us to never, never, never make previous preparation for our natural tendency to follow the evil desire of the flesh. We must be prayerful and cognizant of the fact that we are wrapped in a package that wants to lean on and reside in the state that was conceived in the fall of man in Genesis 3. Thank God for our Lord and Redeemer Jesus Christ, who left us the gift of the Holy Spirit (John 14-16, Acts 2:4, and Acts 10:44), which is our God who lives and reigns in us every second of our lives as children of Yahweh.

1 John 4:4 NIV says, "*You, dear children, are from God and have overcome them, because the one who is in you is greater than the one who is in the world.*" That "One" is the Almighty God. He is Jehovah (the Great I AM). He is EI-Shaddai (the God who is more than enough). He is the Alpha and Omega (the beginning and the end). He is the Creator, and nothing is impossible for Him—except your choices. He cannot choose for you, but what He can do and has done is leave us a blueprint for success.

Pray for the strength and will to follow it.

Day 4

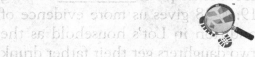

"But put ye on the Lord Jesus Christ,
and make not provision for the flesh,
to fulfill the lusts thereof."
Romans 13:14, KJV

There is a decision that Lot made thousands of years ago which can be a great lesson for us today in light of what Romans 13:14 is teaching us. Most people know Lot as Abraham's nephew or the husband of the lady who was turned into a salt pillar (Genesis 19:26). Genesis 13 shows Lot and Abram's herdsmen in a dispute that causes them to split into two caravans. This split puts a choice right in front of Lot as to where he will live with his family. Lot chooses to pitch his tent near the city of Sodom —apparently a good choice at the time as it was "*pleasing to the eye*" (Genesis 13:12).

As we move farther along in the story's timeline, Genesis 19 reveals not only what happened to Lot but what can happen to us when we choose to spend time in the wrong environments. Genesis 19:4 shows Lot's house under attack by the men of Sodom. These men wanted to have sex with the angels who had been sent by God to warn Lot of the destruction that was coming upon Sodom. Lot, who grew up with Abram and no doubt understood the covenant that God had established with his family, offered his two daughters to pay off the angry mob so they would leave the angels alone.

This was a decision that certainly would not have been made had Lot sought the counsel and protection of his uncle Abram (later to be called Abraham). You cannot overlook the fact that living near or in a city like Sodom had a corrupting effect on Lot and his decisions with regard to the well-being of his family. This is no different than when we choose to frequent __________ or hang with ___________. Genesis 19:30-38 gives us more evidence of the condition in Lot's household as the same two daughters get their father drunk and have sex with him so they could have children. The offspring of this union of father and daughter were the Moabites, who were an idolatrous nation that sacrificed their children to their false gods (1 Kings 11:7), and the Amorites who were worshipers of idols (Judges 6:10).

THIS FLESH WE LIVE IN IS TOUGH ENOUGH TO DEAL WITH. WE DON'T NEED TO HELP IT FULFILL THE CARNAL TENDENCIES THAT ARE WAITING TO REVEAL THEMSELVES EVERY DAY.

This flesh we live in is tough enough to deal with. We don't need to help it fulfill the carnal tendencies that are waiting to reveal themselves every day. The places where we choose to spend time have a direct effect on those tendencies being controlled or enabled. Pray that God would help you spend time in places and with people who can strengthen you. Then you will be able to stand strong and bring the light of Christ and share His grace, mercy, and love with those who don't know Him.

What places do you frequent that cause you to forget your assignment from God?

Is there anyone that you spend time with who causes you to not be the person you are called to be in Christ?

Day 5

"But put ye on the Lord Jesus Christ,
and make not provision for the flesh,
to fulfill the lusts thereof."

Romans 13:14, KJV

Today is going to be short, but profound. I wanted to share with you a principle that walks step by step with Romans 13:14. I got it from a good friend of mine, Randy Ross. Randy is a CPA with a thriving business in San Antonio, Texas. His lovely wife Sandy is an amazing Bible teacher. They are the parents of three godly daughters, five grandchildren, and have been married for more than 30 years.

Over a decade ago, Randy told me that he never has a woman in his office with the door closed. Back then, I thought that was pretty extreme. Now, after being married for 13 years and understanding how to protect myself from situations that have potential to happen behind closed doors (just flip through any Hollywood tabloid), I totally concur with Randy's methodology. I have definitely allowed myself to be in some suspect situations that could have cost me my marriage and my family. Thank God for His grace and the many people who have prayed over my future!

Let's be honest: a lot of passages in the Bible seem extreme—until we find ourselves dealing with the consequences of not following them.

Let's be honest: a lot of passages in the Bible seem extreme—until we find ourselves dealing with the consequences of not following them. There are choices to be made. Deuteronomy 30:19-20 in the NIV says *"Now choose life, so that you and your children may live, and that you may love the Lord your God, listen to his voice, and hold fast to him."*

I would also add that we should hold fast to the wisdom of those that God has put in our lives to warn us of the dangers that lay waiting, dangers that are able to steal our future if we don't avoid compromising situations. The Old Testament shows that King David had Nathan; in the New Testament, Timothy leaned on the wisdom of the apostle Paul. Who do you have? Hopefully there is someone in your life who is older than you and not exactly like you. Humble yourself and glean from their wealth of knowledge.

Have you ever received a pearl of wisdom that seemed extreme at the time, only to find out later that it was just what you needed to hear?

Thank God for the "Generals of the Way" that He has put in your life.

Day 6

"But put ye on the Lord Jesus Christ,
and make not provision for the flesh,
to fulfill the lusts thereof."
Romans 13:14, KJV

The first part of Romans 13:14 tends to be overlooked next to the emphasis on the lusts of the flesh, but it is probably the most important part of this verse.

The KJV says, "*...put ye on the Lord Jesus Christ...*" The NIV says, "*clothe yourselves with the Lord Jesus Christ...*" The Living Bible says, "*... ask the Lord Jesus Christ to help you live as you should...*"

This part of the verse speaks not only of what we shouldn't do but the course of action we should take, the action that takes place every day in the lives of believers as we strive to be more like Christ in each area of our lives.

The NIV says that we are to clothe ourselves with Christ. This speaks of taking off our old ways, our sinful nature, the stuff that kept us out of God's care. Listen to David in Psalms 51:10 NIV: "*Create in me a pure heart, 0 God, and renew a steadfast spirit within me.*" 2 Corinthians 5:17 NIV says, "*Therefore, if anyone is in Christ, he is a new creation; the old has gone, the new has come!*"

Before we can control the flesh, we must submit to, believe in, and imitate our Lord and Savior Jesus Christ. Contrary to popular belief, He is not after your money, career, or lifestyle. He is after your heart. If you give Him that, everything else will be more favorable, more exciting. Your desires will change as you allow the Holy Spirit to be your guide through life. Pray that you have an ear to hear the leadings of the Spirit of God.

If you don't know Christ as your Lord and Redeemer, I hope that you ask Him into to your life right now!

If you do know him as your Loving Father and Master, I want you to think about where you used to be and where you are now. It is amazing what Christ can do with those who are available.

DAY 7

"But put ye on the Lord Jesus Christ,
and make not provision for the flesh,
to fulfill the lusts thereof."
ROMANS 13:14, KJV

One of my best friends in the world is Charlie Ward. We were both drafted by the New York Knicks in the 1994 NBA draft. Upon getting drafted, we both realized that we were brothers in Christ. We also knew there were a lot of opportunities to get out of God's will with all the free time, money—and let's face it: being constantly approached by women was difficult to deal with healthily.

Charlie and I decided to do something unheard of in the NBA: we chose to be roommates on road trips during the season. It was a decision that would bring us closer as brothers and certainly kept me from yielding to my flesh, which is exactly what I wanted to do at the time.

> LOOKING BACK I CAN SEE GOD'S SOVEREIGN HAND KEEPING ME OUT OF SITUATIONS AND AWAY FROM CERTAIN PEOPLE THAT COULD HAVE DESTROYED MY FUTURE.

We spent a lot of nights talking, reading, and planning our futures. I was going through a rough time with my girlfriend, Ingrid (who is now my wife and mother of my four children). Back then, I was trying to push her away so I could enjoy myself (thank God for His Grace and her patience!), but Charlie's example and company was a blessing and an answer to prayer. Ecclesiastes 4:9-10 NIV says, "*Two are better than one, because they have a good return for their work; if one falls down, his friend can help him up…"*

To say that I did not fall spiritually and morally that year would be a lie. But I did not stay down because of people like Charlie and others during that very important year of my life. Looking back I can see God's sovereign hand keeping me out of situations and away from certain people that could have destroyed my future.

Today, Charlie and I are still best friends. We were both married that very next summer, almost exactly a month apart. We have done camps, Bible studies, youth rallies, men's retreats, and mission trips together. That year I was supposed to be a high draft pick in the NBA draft and Charlie was supposed to be one of the top quarterbacks in the NFL draft. Neither happened. Fortunately, the New York Knicks had two draft picks that year: 24 and 26.

Me and Charlie.

God knew exactly what I needed. I needed an example, a friend, a brother, a prayer partner, someone to laugh with and vent to. Charlie was and still is that person for me. Just when I was prepared to violate my conscience and God's Word, He sent just what I needed. By His grace, I chose to follow His lead. I just needed a little help. And He even provided that.

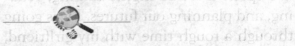

Have you ever been at a profound place in your life and thought that it was just a coincidence only to find out days, weeks, years later that it was the hand of God ordering your steps the whole time? Thank Him for caring so much for you. Remember that there are over 6 billion people on this planet and He cares about you.

Week 5

"…Forgetting what is behind and straining toward
what is ahead, I press on toward the goal
to win the prize for which God has called me
heavenward in Christ Jesus."

Philippians 3:13-14, NIV

Day 1

"…Forgetting what is behind and straining toward
what is ahead, I press on toward the goal
to win the prize for which God has called me
heavenward in Christ Jesus."
Philippians 3:13-14, NIV

Today I want to share a bit of what happened in my childhood and how reliving those episodes could have destroyed my future and my relationship with Jehovah. The first eight years of my life were filled with awesome memories with my mother and father. We traveled to many different states to live because my father served in the Air Force. Unfortunately, after eight years of marriage, my parents separated and finally divorced. As a result, my mother and I left my father to live with my grandparents in Fredericksburg, Virginia.

The next two years were filled with wonderful memories of spending my days with my two childhood heroes: my grandfather Philip and my cousin John. But these two years were also filled with images I wish I could forget, because a few of my family members did things to me that no child should ever have to experience.

As time went on, I began to struggle with issues that I could not explain, like anger and insecurity. They would reveal themselves in impulsive behaviors, physical fights with people who were older than me, or ducking my responsibilities as a young man. The sad part was that I was so popular from playing basketball that these issues were never addressed, because no one wanted to tell me the truth—except my mother. Because I was somewhat of a "golden egg" to a lot of people, no one was willing to confront me on these issues in my life. At the end of the day, all I wanted to do was blame my father for everything that happened to me—past, present, and future. I had a built-in excuse. It went like this: If my father would have done so and so, he and my mother would have remained married and I would not have been in situation X, Y, or Z. But the truth is those were just excuses to justify the choices and mistakes I was making in my own life.

After a lot of prayer by my wife, and by being around other godly men, I started to get an image of a Christ-centered man. I realized that my father was not my problem, and blaming him was not the answer. In fact, he has been one of my best friends over the years. He was just a convenient excuse. I am deeply sorry for the times I blamed him and spoke harshly about him. Did he do some things wrong? Yes. But what parent doesn't?

Deuteronomy 5:16 says to *honor* your parents, and it ends with a period, meaning we are to do this regardless of the situation. This does not mean we are to put up with abuse and neglect, but it does mean that we are not to defile our parents in any way, especially with our words. In fact, Ephesians 6:2-3 NIV promises, "*Honor your father and mother…that it may go well with you and that you may enjoy long life on the earth.*"

Things really hit home for me when I had an encounter with Mrs. Sandy Ross. She sat me down one day and told me that I was going to have to "suffer the wrong" and move on with my life and stop blaming my father, negative childhood memories, and other excuses. She said God had a plan for my life, but I was never going to enjoy it if I kept carrying all this baggage around. She spoke to me in a real, matter-of-fact way, without any regard for how I might respond. It was just what I needed: someone who loved me so much that they would risk our relationship to tell me the truth.

At the end of the day, it is true that some horrible things happened to me in my past, but I learned that God promised me a "future and a hope" (Jeremiah 29:11). Believing these promises and other principles from the Bible gives us the ability to have what Pastor

Kevin L. Adams Sr. calls "back-up praise" or faith. He means that no matter what you have been through, you know that God loves you and has a plan for your life that is *"immeasurably more than all we ask or imagine, according to his power that is at work within us"* (Ephesians 3:20, NIV). I love that verse because when we trust Him with our lives, it puts the ball in God's court.

We believers need to press on like Shadrach, Meshach, and Abednego from Daniel 3. When they were pressured to turn their back on God and worship false gods, they said: *"If we are thrown into the blazing furnace, the God we serve is able to save us from it, and he will rescue us from your hand, O king.* ***But even if he does not****, we want you to know, O king, that we will not serve your gods, or worship the image of gold you have set up"* (Daniel 3:17-18, NIV).

Friend, no matter what you have been through or are facing right now, you must do what the apostle Paul is commanding us to do: forget what is behind and *"press on toward the prize."* This is not a disregard for the things that happened in your past, but it is an attitude that truly believes that God is in control. He can change our nightmares into a life well lived for Him, a life filled with joy and peace that we never knew was possible.

DAY 2

"…Forgetting what is behind and straining toward
what is ahead, I press on toward the goal
to win the prize for which God has called me
heavenward in Christ Jesus."
PHILIPPIANS 3:13-14, NIV

When writing a book like this, scores of questions go through your mind: Did I really hear from God? Can I even write a book? Will anyone read this book? How much will it cost? How much work will it take? Will this project hurt the other things that are important in my life? But the most pressing question that I dealt with over the months of researching, studying, and writing this work was one that has come up several times in my life: What will people, who know my history, think of me writing a book like this?

I wish I could tell you that I have been a model Christian my entire "born again" journey. But the truth is that even after I gave my life to Christ, I did things that were despicable in the sight of man and God. As I struggled with this predicament, I thought of ways to make myself and my past look better than they really were, but that would have been a lie. More importantly, God could not get any glory out of tall tales and fabrications about my past.

This struggle came to an end one day when I was walking and felt the Holy Spirit tugging on my heart. I did not hear an audible sound or see anything visible to the human eye, but I knew God was telling me that I was exactly the man for this assignment—*because* of my past, not just in spite of it. In several ways, God told me that I was exhibit "A" for Romans 5:20 NLT: "*…but as people sinned more and more, God's wonderful kindness became* *more abundant*." That "kindness" is called *grace*. Grace is God's way of giving us what we do not deserve: relationship with Him, a pardon from eternal death, and an inheritance to all He has.

Unfortunately, we live in a society that believes God rules with an iron fist (although wrath and justice are part of His nature), which has even been taught by some in the church. But the Bible says that God is "*...slow to anger, abounding in love*" (Psalm 103:8, NIV). This means He did not cause the Yellow River Flood of 1332 where more than seven million people died, or Hurricane Katrina, or the tsunami started by an earthquake in the Indian Ocean resulting in more than 225,000 deaths. These disasters happened because we live in a fallen world; according to Paul, "*The whole creation has been groaning as in the pains of childbirth right up to the present time*" (Romans 8:22, NIV). Is God happy when we sin? Absolutely not! God is displeased with some of our actions, but He never hates the actors.

> I REALIZED THAT I REJECTED GOD'S GIFT OF WHAT JESUS DID ON THE CROSS FOR ME AND THE REST OF THE WORLD WHEN I BELIEVED THAT HE COULD NOT OVERCOME MY PAST.

I realized that I rejected God's gift of what Jesus did on the cross for me and the rest of the world when I believed that He could not overcome my past. This misbelief could keep me from pressing on into my destiny and completing the assignments that He had for me.

This viewpoint is also expressed in New Age parenting methods that say, "I used to abuse alcohol, drugs, and have had illicit sexual encounters in the past, so I can't blame my kids if they do the same." Instead, we need to tell our kids and the youth around us what we did, on a level that they can understand, and how it impacted our lives. Too many times we wait until our youth venture into territories that we have already paid taxes on to tell them, "Oh yeah, been there, done that." We think they cannot handle our advice or memories. We assume they are strong enough to venture into parts unknown without a road map. Our nation's thirty-fifth president, John F. Kennedy, said, "A child miseducated is a child lost."

Understand this: our former sins, covered in God's grace, can become a springboard for the generations to follow, instead of a comparison in hindsight, after the fact. But we must first see God as Jehovah-Tsidkenu, The Lord Our Righteousness, whose perfect past takes the sting out of our past sin.

I encourage you not to let your past rob you of your future and the destinies of those you love. Don't allow your past to keep you from writing a book, inventing a tool that can change humanity for good, saying sorry to a loved one or a stranger, or forgiving someone who has wronged you. Cemeteries are filled with those whose ideas, books, inventions, songs, "I love you's," "will you marry me's," and other rich possibilities never materialized because someone thought that they did not measure up to a false standard. You and I have to press on and know that *the* standard, Jehovah, has a purpose for our lives. We cannot let our past sin rob us of what He has for us.

Think about this today: "The surest way of severely upsetting yourself for hours is by continuing to consider what concerns you most for a single moment too long." (Christopher Spranger)

DAY 3

"...Forgetting what is behind and straining toward
what is ahead, I press on toward the goal
to win the prize for which God has called me
heavenward in Christ Jesus."
PHILIPPIANS 3:13-14, NIV

My mentor, Rick Godwin, taught me that most people fit into one of three categories: Quitters, Campers, or Climbers. These categories are not personality traits; they are choices. These choices can be shaped by our childhood experiences, circumstances, the people we spend time with, and by understanding our God-given purpose through a relationship with Jesus Christ.

The first place of residency, "Quittersville," is self-explanatory. It is usually occupied by those who are spurred on by excitement, the desire to be like someone else, or even an honest motivation to achieve a certain goal. Unfortunately, these same people neglect to "*count the cost*," a principle that Jesus talked about in Luke 14:28. They have a tendency to grow bitter and envy anyone who stays the course en route to fulfilling their destiny. I can remember the old folks from my childhood calling people like this "crabs in a bucket." As soon as one is just about to climb out of the pit, another crab will say, "Nope, you stay right here with me in misery," and snatches him back down to ground zero.

"Campers" happen to be in the majority. These residents are pursuing the American Dream. They are goal-oriented, disciplined, and dedicated to their particular objective. I know this person well; I used to be one. All I ever wanted was to make a lot of money, save some so I could live comfortably, buy a second home on a beach or a lake, and ride off into the sunset. The problem with this idea is that the Bible never mentions the word "retirement" or anything that resembles it. When we look at the life of Abraham, we see he lived vibrantly and fruitfully well passed 100. The Bible says that his wife Sarah died when she was 127 years old, which means Abraham was 137 at the time. Genesis 25 shows Abraham taking another wife, Keturah, and having six more children. Way to go, Abe! Many times we see "campers" having less or no children at all, so they can live their life. But this kind of life often involves a routine, boring, impotent existence, hoarding all they have accumulated over the years, only to find out that they won't get to take it with them when they die. Campers are people with so much to offer society, but the comforts of this world (though intoxicating) have led to a life of complacency. Some even fear losing their "spot" in a world in which we were never meant to be permanent residents. Jesus said that we are "*not of the world*" and neither was He (John 17:16).

"Climbers" are those who want it all. They want a life full in years; prosperity in every area of their lives; to be servants to others; and most importantly, they want to fulfill the call that God has placed on their lives. They press on. Climbers have a pit bull attitude that will not allow them to be abated, like former 49ers safety Ronnie Lott. He once had his finger cut off during a game so that he could continue to play. Climbers are like Joshua and Caleb from Numbers 13. These men were sent on assignment to explore the land of Canaan, along with 10 others. The 10 came back with reports of how Israel could not challenge the people, like the Nephilim who occupied the Israelites' Promised Land. But Joshua and Caleb had a different story to tell the entire gathered assembly: "*…do not rebel against the Lord. And do not be afraid of the people of the land, because we will swallow them up. Their protection is gone,* ***but the Lord is with us***." (Numbers 14:9, NIV)

The climber attitude of the apostle Paul is shown in this week's verse. He is saying that no matter what my past looks like, what others are doing, what the present situation is, whether I have failed before, whether my friends don't return my phone calls, whether co-workers stop hanging with me and call me a "Jesus Freak," whether the stock market crashes, etc, I…WILL… PRESS…ON.

Mark Twain put it this way: "Twenty years from now you will be more disappointed by the things you didn't do than by the ones you did do. So throw off the bowlines. Sail away from the safe harbor. Catch the trade winds in your sails. Explore. Dream. Discover."

> Ask yourself a tough question: Which category do I fit in—Quitter, Camper, or Climber?

DAY 4

"…Forgetting what is behind and straining toward
what is ahead, I press on toward the goal
to win the prize for which God has called me
heavenward in Christ Jesus."
PHILIPPIANS 3:13-14, NIV

I want to share an example of "pressing on" that you may not hear about in your average church circle: Bill & Melinda Gates and what they are doing through their Gates Foundation to help people live a better quality of life.

One of the many ways that their foundation has enabled people to have a measure of normalcy in an otherwise chaotic world is through "smart cards." You see, in Malawi, where life expectancy is less than 40 years, widowed women usually lose all of the possessions that were accumulated during their marriage to their former husband's family. This leaves these women and their children right smack in the eye of the poverty tornado, where the only options for supporting themselves are often begging or prostitution. Smart cards were created to allow these women to keep all their money in a secure bank account that will only recognize their thumbprint.

Most likely, this technology would never have reached this part of the world had the Gates chosen to keep all of their 50+ billion dollars to themselves. Because of this act, we are going to see more Nelson Mandelas, Hakeem Olajuwons, Dikembe Mutombos, and Ellen Johnson-Sirleafs (the President of Liberia) in our lifetime.

What does this have to do with "*straining toward*" and "*pressing on*"? It's pretty simple, actually, but it's very hard. The Gates' could have easily taken all of their money and lived a life that all of us can only dream about with a house in every country of the world. I can imagine MTV devoting a whole year of *Cribs* just to the Gates' houses. I'm sure their annual family budget is still well beyond what most of us will imagine, but they have decided to "*press on*" in a different way by serving others, which is what Jesus called us to do if we wanted to have significance. Jesus said, "*...the greatest among you should be like the youngest, and the one who rules like the one who serves....I am among you as one who serves.*" (Luke 22:26, NIV)

It is no surprise that one of the Gates' foundational premises on their website is "*to whom much is given, much is expected*" (Luke 12:48). As we "*press on*" to heaven, let us not forget that there is much work that needs to be done here on the earth. May we all be vessels used by God to encourage others to forget their past and move into what God has for their lives.

Nelson Mandela said, "After climbing a great hill, one only finds there are many more hills to climb."

DAY 5

"...Forgetting what is behind and straining toward
what is ahead, I press on toward the goal
to win the prize for which God has called me
heavenward in Christ Jesus."
PHILIPPIANS 3:13-14, NIV

In some translations of Philippians 3:13-14, we see the word "mark" used to refer to the thing that we should be pressing toward. The *Matthew Henry's Commentary on the Whole Bible* states, "Heaven is called here the mark...It is of great use in the Christian course to keep our eye upon heaven...There is no getting to heaven as our home but by Christ as our way."

As we ponder the thought of heaven and how being raptured will solve every problem that we have ever had, we cannot help but consider the first part of this week's verse: forgetting. What was the apostle Paul erasing from his memory? Today, let's take a brief look at the history of Paul and see what he was leaving behind in order to enjoy the wonderful gift of eternal relationship with God.

Paul was born in Tarsus, a city in modern day Turkey. This is also where Mark Antony and Cleopatra lived in first century B.C. Paul was a Roman and Pharisee by birth, as his father before him. He was well versed in Jewish history and Scripture, having finished training of the law under the brilliant Jewish scholar Gamaliel (Acts 22:3). Paul was also a tentmaker by trade (Acts 18:3).

It is possible that the apostle Paul was once married, but to assume this from Scripture would be jumping the gun. History says that members of the Sanhedrin were to be married, but Paul never states that he was a member. Galatians 1:14 records that he was "*advancing in Judaism beyond many Jews of my own age*," but this does not mean that Paul reached the level of the Sanhedrin. 1 Corinthians 9:5 makes you think that he was married, but 1 Corinthians 7:8-9 reveals that if he had been married in the past, he was not at the time of this address to the unmarried and widows.

PAUL IS A GREAT EXAMPLE OF A MAN WHO KNEW HIS PURPOSE AND REFUSED TO LET THE GOOD OR THE BAD OF HIS PAST SIDETRACK HIM.

Paul was a persecutor of those who believed in Christ: "*But Saul began to destroy the church. Going from house to house, he dragged off men and women and put them in prison.*" (Acts 8:3) Conversely, we see the grace of God in Acts 9:3-9, which shows the conversion of Saul (Paul) into a believer in Jesus Christ. God is so good to those of us who were at odds with Him.

Paul underwent training in Arabia, Damascus, Jerusalem, Syria, and Cilicia to prepare for the remarkable work that God was going to do through him as a missionary and church builder. He was a preacher to both the Jews (Acts 13:16-41) and to the Gentiles (Acts 17:22-31). Paul was also a writer, as the evidence of 14 out of 27 New Testament books proves.

Paul's attitude and approach to spreading the gospel of Jesus Christ is summed up in Acts 21:13 NIV: "*I am ready not only to be bound, but also to die in Jerusalem for the name of the Lord Jesus Christ.*"

This is just a portion of what Paul was leaving behind as he strained ahead to "*win the prize*" that we are all expecting from our Father in heaven. Paul is a great example of a man who knew his purpose and refused to let the good or the bad of his past sidetrack him. He was also a man who refused to let any physical shortcomings stop him from finishing his assignment, as most historical recounts talk of Paul as a short, bald, funny-looking guy with crooked legs.

I pray that Paul's life would encourage us believers to not get hamstrung by our past, so that we can keep our eyes on the prize. I believe life here on earth is never totally perfect, because we are not meant to stay here permanently. Paul's command and example can fuel our own efforts, as we are straining, forgetting, winning, and receiving that which God has for us.

Abraham Lincoln said, "I don't know who my grandfather was; I am much more concerned to know what his grandson will be."

DAY 6

"...Forgetting what is behind and straining toward
what is ahead, I press on toward the goal
to win the prize for which God has called me
heavenward in Christ Jesus."
PHILIPPIANS 3:13-14, NIV

In June of 2005, I was blessed to be part of a coaching staff that helped the San Antonio Spurs win their third world championship. It was the first time that I had won an NBA title as pro, and to me, it came about in a most unconventional way. You see, I played for the Spurs in the 1990s, then played for some really good teams and one really bad one (we were 20 and 62). But the year I left the Spurs is when they started their dynasty.

I was on the court after the buzzer sounded as we defeated the Detroit Pistons in game seven. The court was filled with family, friends, media, and officials from the team as well as the NBA. We took pictures on the court, in the locker room—even in a room that I had never known existed. Champagne, tears, smiles, hugs, and other giddy gestures filled every part of that arena. Many members from my former church, Eagles Nest Christian Fellowship, were there to share in this awesome moment.

After leaving the arena, many of us continued the celebration at a local restaurant. We ate, laughed, told stories, and realized how fortunate we were to accomplish this amazing feat. Before I knew it, it was 4 o'clock in the morning and a sudden shock came over me. Why? My position on the staff was assistant to Brett Brown, head of the player development program. It was my job to be at the gym by 8 a.m. the next morning to run the workout with the year's upcoming draftees preparing for the

2005 NBA draft. I did not want to let Brett or Pop (Gregg Popovich) down.

So I left the restaurant, got home as fast as I could, and got a couple of hours of sleep. The next morning, around 6:45, I woke with that numb feeling—the one you have when you've had about seven hours less sleep than normal. I got to the gym, put the guys through some drills, and did a good job, but something was pulling on my heart that whole morning. I could not help but ponder on the experience the Lord had blessed me with. In a matter of twelve hours, I was part of a championship and all that goes with that experience, and hours later, I was helping the team work on the next one, before the confetti could be cleaned up in the SBC Center. It was like God was saying, "Enjoy, but don't stay; there is more work to be done."

It was like God was saying, "Enjoy, but don't stay; there is more work to be done."

Did I enjoy my experience? Absolutely! But the next day and in the days to come, the whole staff diligently worked to make the Spurs even better than they were before. This is a good lesson for all of us, because we have a tendency to savor and relish our triumphs and tragedies longer than necessary. When you look at the Scriptures, God put a time limit on many things. Many Biblical celebrations still celebrated today—the Sabbath, Passover, Unleavened Bread, First Fruits, Weeks, Trumpets, Day of Atonement, Tabernacles, and others—had a limit on their length. God even puts time limits on the amount of time to mourn a person's death. In Genesis 50:10 Joseph set the time for mourning for his father Israel (Jacob) to be seven days. The Israelites mourned the deaths of Aaron and Moses for 30 days (Numbers 20:29, Deuteronomy 34:8). Maybe the mourning time was longer for these two men because of their importance to God's chosen nation.

The point of this day's devotional is to encourage you to "*press on*" and not wallow in or become complacent in the things, bad or good, that happen to us. We all have assignments. Society might teach that fulfilling one or a few is the end of the journey, and you are finally "there." But as we mature, we realize that there is no "there;" that life is an adventure; that goals achieved are not destinations. I think this is what the apostle Paul is calling us to do as we press toward heaven. Achieving goals along our journey must not keep us from focusing on God and His plan and mission for us.

Day 7

"...Forgetting what is behind and straining toward
what is ahead, I press on toward the goal
to win the prize for which God has called me
heavenward in Christ Jesus."
Philippians 3:13-14, NIV

Have you ever heard of the word *adiaphora*? No, it is not the name of a trendy cologne you can purchase on Rodeo Drive in LA. *Adiaphora* refers to "teachings and practices that are neither commanded nor forbidden in Scripture" (spiritrestoration.org). You will find examples of this in church when believers argue over the style of music being used, or when Christians have a difference of opinion on where or when we should worship. Storefront church, cathedral, basketball arena, Wednesday, Saturday, or Sunday—none of them are the right or wrong place.

Today I would like to give you a Biblical example of *adiaphora* from the Old Testament. I hope it will encourage you to "*press on*" and seek the power of God, not the vehicles that He has chosen in which to display His power.

Our example begins in Numbers 21, where we find the Israelites in the wilderness speaking against God and Moses, His chosen leader: *"There is no bread! There is no water! And we detest this miserable food!"* (Numbers 21:5 NIV) This food, manna, was a gift from God that would sustain them while on their journey. Their impatience caused them to forget the promise that God gave them in Numbers 13:1 about the Promised Land.

For their protests, God sent venomous snakes that bit the people and many died. The people who were left repented and asked

Moses to pray for them. Moses did so, and God told him to make a snake-like object and place it on a pole. The people were told that if they looked at the pole when they were bitten, they would live. God displayed His power through the use of this article and the faith of the people in Him and His command.

Let's flash forward about 750 years. A king of Jerusalem named Hezekiah began to remove all the places and things that were being worshiped in place of Elohim (The God Most High). In 2 Kings 18:3, 4 NIV the Scripture says that Hezekiah *"did what was right in the eyes of the Lord...he broke into pieces the bronze snake Moses had made, for up to that time the Israelites had been burning incense to it."* This is the same pole that Moses made earlier (Numbers 21), which, unfortunately, became a god to the Israelites. Thankfully, Hezekiah broke it into pieces, as he did with the other idols, so that the praise and honor would return to Jehovah.

Today, many well-intentioned saints put more stock into things like prayer cloths, vials of oil, palm leaves, dirt from the holy sites in Israel, buildings, songs, and seasons than into the power of God. Deuteronomy 5:8,9 NIV says, *"You shall not make for yourself an idol in the form of anything in heaven above or on the earth beneath or in the waters below... I, the Lord your God, am a jealous God..."*

The Bible uses the word "new" more than 150 times. I believe that we are to continue to "*press on*" and see the new ways and methods that God is going to choose to reveal His power, mercy, and grace in our lives. The means that He is using to heal us, get our attention, or cause a person to give their life to Christ may never be used again. It is up to us to sit at His feet and know what new thing He is doing.

We must remember that God's Truth is eternal and everything else has a shelf life. Paul's commands to "*forget*" and "*press on*" are critical if we are going to be led by the Spirit of God instead of by a trendy, expired method from our past.

Week 6

"Death and life are in the power of the tongue,
and they who indulge in it shall eat the
fruit of it [for death or life]."

Proverbs 18:21, AMP

DAY 1

"Death and life are in the power of the tongue,
and they who indulge in it shall eat the
fruit of it [for death or life]."
PROVERBS 18:21, AMP

To start this week off I want to take an excerpt from the *Wiersbe Bible Commentary* that should help Proverbs 18:21 become a part of your life.

Page 1086 reads this way:

> "A judge speaks some words and a guilty prisoner is taken to a cell on death row. A gossip makes a phone call and a reputation is blemished or perhaps ruined. A cynical professor makes a snide remark in a lecture and a student's faith is destroyed… Never underestimate the power of words. For every word in Hitler's book *Mein Kampf*, 125 people died in World War II."

That excerpt started some thoughts of my own. A parent gives a child confidence by encouraging her strengths; the child goes on to do things in life that she did not believe she was capable of before the parental charge. A friend cuts off a conversation because it is degrading someone else; a habit of gossip begins to break. A coach tells a struggling player, "You can do it—I believe in you;" the player performs in a way that he never performed before. A parishioner walks up to the pastor after church and says "thank you for your faithfulness, your words were just what I needed… please don't ever think that we don't appreciate you;" the pastor changes his mind about leaving the ministry.

The Wiersbe commentary breaks up speech into 4 propositions:

(1) speech is an awesome gift of from God;

(2) speech can be used to do good;

(3) speech can be used to do evil;

(4) only God can help us use speech to do good (GRACE).

Proverbs 18:21 in the New Century Version says, *"What you say can mean life or death. Those who speak with care will be rewarded."* WOW!

My hope is that the Holy Spirit will do a work in you this week, as has happened with me.

I would like to tell you that I have always obeyed this verse of Scripture, but I have not come close. Studying this verse has convicted me more than any other devotional I have written during this project.

My hope is that the Holy Spirit will do a work in you this week, as has happened with me, so the reward of *"those who speak with care"* can be yours.

DAY 2

"Death and life are in the power of the tongue,
and they who indulge in it shall eat the
fruit of it [for death or life]."

PROVERBS 18:21, AMP

God's Words have the ultimate power. *"By faith we understand that the universe was formed at **God's command**, so that what is seen was not made out of what was visible."* (Hebrews 11:3) This verse says that God created the universe with His Words. Genesis 1:3,6,9,11,14,20,24, and 26 all start with *"And God said"* NIV. From this, the whole world we know was created.

Our faith in Jesus Christ, which is also from God, is a spoken faith. *"If you **confess** with your mouth, 'Jesus is Lord,' and believe in your heart that God raised him from the dead, you will be saved."* (Romans 10:9, NIV) *"Whoever **confesses** that Jesus is the Son of God, God abides in him, and he in God."* (1 John 4:15) Notice that neither of those verses says anything about performing certain acts or thinking this or that. It says you must confess, speak, talk, verbalize, announce, decree… **SAY IT!!!** Psalm 107:2 AMP says, *"Let the redeemed of the Lord **say so**…"* We must "say so" to become saved; we must also "say so" when are presently atoned for, as a witness to the world that "this is who I am."

The world around you is a direct result of the words spoken by someone else. Instead of asking why your situation is the way it is, speak the Word of God over your present condition and watch your life change in an awesome way. Look at what God said to Jeremiah in Jeremiah

THE WORLD AROUND YOU IS A DIRECT RESULT OF THE WORDS SPOKEN BY SOMEONE ELSE.

1:12 HCSB, *"The Lord said to me, 'You have seen correctly, for I watch over my word to accomplish it'."* This was in reference to the word that was given to the Lord's prophet Jeremiah. You and I have the entire Bible (Jeremiah did not), full of God's promises that can change our situation for the better—and most importantly, give God the glory so that the world will know Him better—but we must **confess** God's Word.

God is waiting for His people to **declare** something, instead of letting the media, culture, and the president declare it for us. Job 22:28 NIV says, *"What you* ***decide*** *on will be done, and light will shine on your ways."* The Amplified says it this way: *"You shall* ***decide*** *and* ***decree*** *a thing, and it shall be established for you; and the light [of God's favor] shall shine upon your ways."* God is waiting on you to make a decision and declare it with your words. That does not mean you are going to be millionaire or a star or an idol, but it does mean you will be positioning yourself to live in the Lord's will for you. Neither money nor popularity can buy that.

The purpose of this devotional is to encourage people to study the Word of God, know it, and be able to confess it at the appropriate time. I do not want to condemn anybody. I want to give you hope and encourage you to fulfill your destiny. God's Word coming out of your mouth can help you do just that. Jesus said in Matthew 12:34 NIV, *"For out of the overflow of the heart the mouth* ***speaks****."* Remember: His Word created the world; it surely has the power to make your life better.

Gatorade will ask if their sports drink is in you. I am asking if God's Word is in you. If so, it will come out of your mouth, and change your life.

Day 3

"Death and life are in the power of the tongue,
and they who indulge in it shall eat the
fruit of it [for death or life]."

Proverbs 18:21, AMP

Our words have the power to propel people into their destiny. Proverbs 15:23 NIV says "*A man finds joy in giving an apt reply—and how good is a timely word.*" Proverbs 25:11 TLB says "*Timely advice is as lovely as golden apples in a silver basket.*"

Like most of you, I'd guess, I have experienced the truth of both of those verses. Two people had a particularly profound effect on the direction of my life because of the words they spoke to me at the right time: when I needed to hear the truth and was desperate for some encouragement. The first was my mother.

In 1986, we were like most homes with a single parent: barely making it but happy nonetheless. My mom, who worked eight to ten hours a day and went to school for two hours a night twice a week, was faced with a dilemma. She knew that she could not financially send me to college and it was bothering her deeply. So, when I was 14 years old, she sat me down one day and told me, "Baby, Momma cannot afford to send you to college, so you better get out there and run… I know you can do it."

At that point in my life I was an average basketball player who loved to play and had an okay work ethic. But my mother's words were like gas on a fire. I wanted to take the pressure off of her so she would not have to worry about me. That has been the greatest gift I have ever given my mother, and her statement is one of the greatest things she has done for me. My mom could have easily said, "Son, you are old enough to take care of yourself… you are becoming a burden and I need money to pay these bills off, so do whatever you have to do so you can earn your keep." But instead, she lovingly told me the truth. What I saw that day in her eyes pushed me to try to make her proud of me.

The second person was Todd Bozeman, the assistant coach from my high school basketball team. Somehow, he always knew what to say to give me confidence to play my best. When we had a game against guys who were older or ranked ahead of me, Todd would always say "Chise, I am telling you, you are better than those guys… you watch, you are going to destroy them tonight." Chise was my nickname; it was short for "franchise player." The fact that Todd called me "franchise" was enough to make me run through a wall to prove that he was right about me.

His confidence had even more effect on me because he was one of very few who felt that way about me at the time. Every publication and even kids at school thought that I was a "scrub" or just plain average. Todd and I were riding to a Five Star Basketball Camp in Radford, Virginia when Todd spoke some of the most encouraging words of my life to me. He said things like, "Chise, trust me: by the end of this camp, they are going to know who you are" and "I guarantee you that by the end of your senior year you will be ranked ahead of all these cats." He was right on both accounts; I played really well at my first camp appearance. By the end of my time in high school, I was one of the top players in the country, which helped me to earn a scholarship to the University of Notre Dame (Momma was happy about that). But it's unlikely that any of that would have happened without Mom and Todd speaking life into that part of me.

Maybe you didn't have anyone like my mom or Todd and you are bitter about it. If that's the case, pray that God would send you someone to speak life into you. If you did have someone who blessed you with inspiring words at the right time, I encourage you to continue the chain of blessing that timely advice can bring. There is life and death in our mouths. Speak life so you will be rewarded and others can benefit.

Day 4

"Death and life are in the power of the tongue,
and they who indulge in it shall eat the
fruit of it [for death or life]."
Proverbs 18:21, AMP

Our words have the ability to keep us in a state of perpetual victimization. Elizabeth Smart is the epitome of this statement; she is an amazing example of strength and courage in the midst of one of the most tragic things that could ever happen to a child. You may remember the summer of 2002 when Elizabeth was abducted by a man who was doing some handiwork around their house in Salt Lake City, Utah. This 14 year old was held hostage by the man and his wife for 9 months, and most of this time was spent at remote campsites in the Utah wilderness.

Elizabeth could have become bitter and used this episode in her life as an excuse to rebel and live contrary to the hopes and dreams she had before the night in June 2002. But look at what she said in a *People* magazine interview (June 23, 2008) when asked whether she was angry at the people who abducted her. She said, "It's just not worth holding on to that kind of hate. It can ruin your life. Nine months of my life had been taken from me, and I wasn't going to give them any more of my time."

WOW! You're talking about a 20 year old who spent 9 months kidnapped. Every second of those months was probably spent wondering if she would ever see the people she loved again. Elizabeth has an unbelievable future ahead of her because she has applied the principle of Job 22:28: she has decided/decreed what she is going to do with her life.

I know that you have something from your past that you have not settled in your heart. Your daddy may have mistreated you, your teacher may have broken your confidence, someone older than you may have abused you as a child, your former pastor may have done something that made you upset. All these things may be true, but the reality is this: living in "Victimville" will not change your situation and life is going to pass you by if you continue to take up residence there by saying, "I would take a risk but________"; "I am not that good at it"; "No one in my family ever graduated so I can't"; "This is how everyone from my neighborhood does things, so I am going to do the same"; "No biggie, divorce is normal for my family"; "I am always sick this time of year"—the list goes on and on. My mentor taught me that the most powerful opinion in your life is the one you have of yourself. What you think and say about yourself matters.

> The most powerful opinion in your life is the one you have of yourself. What you think and say about yourself matters.

The truth is we do live in a fallen world; just look around you. But you have to get past that and proclaim what the Bible says about you.

- "I am the righteousness of God."
- "No weapon formed against me will prosper."
- "In Christ I am new creation."
- "By Christ's stripes I am healed."
- "Greater is He that is in me than he that is in the world."
- "I am not a slave to sin and death."
- "If God feeds the birds of the air and clothes the lilies of the fields, he is certainly going to be sure I'm taken care of."
- "I am forgiven."

- "I am called, chosen, and cared for."
- "He is risen."
- "I am redeemed."

Start by declaring what you know and make sure it lines up with God's Word. At the same time, do not continue to speak death over yourself and your family. An easy way to check-in with this is to make sure you don't spend most of your time going through your list of everything that's wrong (money you don't have for your bills, crises you're in at school or work, relationships that are in trouble) that you don't know how to fix. You already know all of those things. Thinking about them and restating them over and over will not get you any closer to a change in that situation. Instead, begin spending more time declaring and thinking about the Bible's promise of God's provision in whatever that situation is.

There is life and death in the power of the tongue. Choices you make and things you say today really can change your future.

Take a minute and think of the words that you have said this week. Are they life giving or curse bringing? Does your past affect the way you speak?

Spend the day meditating on the promise of God for your situation rather than the thing you need. Pray that God would renew your heart so that from the overflow of it, your mouth would speak good things.

For *"out of the overflow of the heart the mouth speaks"* (Luke 6:45).

Day 5

"Death and life are in the power of the tongue,
and they who indulge in it shall eat the
fruit of it [for death or life]."

Proverbs 18:21, AMP

As I studied, contemplated, and finished the rough draft for this day, I felt more than convicted with today's topic than any other. Today's topic deals with the negative words we speak and their consequences. Galatians 5:22,23 NIV says, *"But the fruit of the Spirit is love, joy, peace, patience, kindness, goodness, faithfulness, gentleness, and self-control."* Negative criticism, back-biting, and gossip are not listed as fruits of the Spirit in any interpretation of the Bible. These are things I have struggled with, but I am determined to overcome these destructive practices. Colossians 3:8 lists slander as one of the things that plagued us before Christ, along with anger, rage, malice, and filthy language… but in Christ we are a new creation; the old has gone, the new has come! If we have been walking with Jesus for any amount of time, we should not have to battle with our tongues as much as we do.

Today, I want to take a look at a story in Numbers 12 where we see Moses (the leader and lawgiver of Israel), Aaron (the high priest), and Miriam (the prophetess) in conflict. There is one other character in this story that may have brought out the worst in Miriam and Aaron: Moses' wife.

Miriam felt a close kinship to her brother Moses; she had been there for him since he was a baby. Exodus 2:7 shows Miriam stepping in to make sure Moses was nursed by a Hebrew (his mother) when he was found by Pharaoh's daughter floating in a basket in the Nile River. For forty years, Moses and Miriam were confidants and friends. How quickly the tongue can shake the most time tested relationships.

Numbers 12:2 displays Miriam and Aaron degrading the importance of their brother and leader by saying, *"Has the LORD indeed spoken only through Moses? Has He not spoken through us as well?"* Did Moses' marriage to a non-Hebrew woman (the NIV describes her as a Cushite or an Ethiopian) bring this verbal lashing out of Miriam? Did she feel like she was being replaced as the only female leader of Israel? Did Miriam contrive this plan and also instigate her brother Aaron to join her in this act?

The answers to the first two questions are just my opinion; I believe they would be a resounding "YES." But the answer to the last question is found in Numbers 12:8-10. The Lord's anger burned against Miriam and Aaron because they spoke harshly against His servant Moses; Miriam (not Aaron) was inflicted with leprosy. She suffered from this skin condition for 7 days and had to leave the camp until she was well again.

I think it is interesting to note that the act of back-biting by this brother and sister duo caused the journey of Israelites to come to a halt; Numbers 12:15 says NAS, *"The people did not move on until Miriam was received again."* The negative words that come out our mouths have a direct affect on the people around us.

This should be a firm warning to us that our words should not be used to slander anyone—friend or stranger. Ephesians 4:29 NIV says, *"Do not let any unwholesome talk come out of your mouths, but only what is helpful for building others up according to their needs, that it may benefit those who listen."* Colossians 4:6 NIV says *"Let your conversations be always full of grace, seasoned with salt, so that you may know how to answer everyone."*

Join me in this pledge:

I will not speak a negative word about myself or anyone else today.

When I struggle with my tongue, I will yield it to the Holy Spirit.

I will use my mouth to help others and not destroy them.

Day 6

"Death and life are in the power of the tongue,
and they who indulge in it shall eat the
fruit of it [for death or life]."

Proverbs 18:21, AMP

Words are perpetual; they never die. This rings true for me on so many levels. I can still hear my grandfather saying (when I did something I was not supposed to), "Boy, you go to school 9 days and come home 10 days dumber." Then he would fix the situation, give me a chore to do, and pay me 50 cents to go get a bag of chips and a drink.

Think about some of the great, powerful speeches in American history. There is Patrick Henry with "Give me liberty or give me death;" the Gettysburg Address of President Abraham Lincoln; Dr. Martin Luther King Jr.'s incredibly famous "I Have a Dream" speech. As a sports fan, I love Tony Dungy's "No excuses, no explanations," Gregg Popovich's "You must be a part of your own rehab," and Nat McMillan's chant "If you mess with the game, the game will mess with you."

And have you ever heard of "Ubuntu"? It was the 2007-2008 Boston Celtics rallying cry for their season. My friend, Doc Rivers, adopted the term because he wanted to unite his team, which was comprised of a multitude of talented players, not to mention Kevin Garnett, Paul Pierce, and Ray Allen—future hall of famers. The term "Ubuntu" means "I am because of you." It is a term that comes from the Bantu languages of South Africa. The Celtics went on to win the NBA championship by beating their 80's rival, the Los Angeles Lakers.

Another group of words spoken by a man in the 19th century not only changed a nation, but also started a grassroots movement that empowered an entire race of God's people. William Wilberforce gave a speech to the House of Commons on May 12, 1789 to stop the European slave trade. The bill was denied but he kept fighting for it, fighting with powerful and well-chosen words. In 1807, the slave trade was abolished. Here is a segment from Wilberforce's speech to the House of Commons:

> "… I take courage—I determine to forget all my other fears, and march forward with a firmer step in full assurance that my cause will bear me out, and that I shall be able to justify upon the clearest principles, every resolution in my hand, the avowed end of which is, the total abolition of the slave trade."

Words are perpetual.

Words are perpetual. They never die. They can hurt for a long time or they can heal a wound in an instant. They can bring life to a nation. Proverbs 15:4 NIV says, *"The tongue that brings healing is a tree of life."*

Make your words count.

Day 7

"Death and life are in the power of the tongue,
and they who indulge in it shall eat the
fruit of it [for death or life]."

Proverbs 18:21, AMP

This verse talks about the power of the things that we verbalize—to ourselves, to others, and even to God. The tongue can be life giving or it can be as destructive as a bulldozer, and it's our choice.

But today I want to take at a look a different power that we possess through communication or lack thereof: the power of silence. Knowing when and when not to speak has great benefits; it has also been known to destroy many relationships. I heard once that the difference between a healthy marriage and an ugly divorce is 3 or 4 words, said or unspoken.

The tongue can be life giving or it can be as destructive as a bulldozer, and it's our choice.

The power of unspoken words ranges from a mother at the end of her patience, choosing to clean up the fourth glass of juice spilled that day in silence instead of screaming at the top of her lungs about that mess, to a dad refusing to talk to a desperate daughter looking for affirmation because the Golf Channel® is the focus of his attention.

The power of unspoken words can be seen when a husband rolls his eyes at a wife who changes her hairstyle to please him, to a proud fist pump from someone in the audience as his friend performs on stage in The Nutcracker.

The power of unspoken words can be seen as a wife waves good-bye to a husband boarding a naval ship headed to a base where he will be stationed for the next 2 years, or as a predator violates his secretary… needing her job, she keeps quiet and never reports the incident.

The power of unspoken words can be seen when we return phone calls with text messages because we are too busy to talk.

The power of unspoken words can be seen when all across our nation schools no longer recite "The Pledge of Allegiance" or sing "My Country 'Tis of Thee."

The power of unspoken words can be seen in Genesis 3 when Eve is deceived by the serpent into eating fruit from the forbidden tree, as her husband Adam, witnessing the whole episode, says nothing. Verse 6 in the NIV says, *"She also gave some to her husband, **who was with her**, and he ate it."*

It can also be seen in Luke 10, when Mary of Bethany sits at Jesus' feet giving Him her full attention while her sister Martha is distracted with "preparations." Luke 10:39 says, *"She had a sister called Mary, who sat at the Lord's feet **listening to what he said**."*

Psalms 32:3-4 reveals the power of an unspoken word that can hinder our relationship with the Father: sin that has not been confessed. This Psalm displays King David pouring his heart out to Jehovah after he had committed the sin of conspiracy with his servant, adultery with Bathsheba, and the murder of Uriah, in 2 Samuel 11. A big part of the problem was that David did not admit to these sins for almost a year. Listen to Psalm 32:3-4 NIV as David talks about the burden of his silence: *"When I kept silent, my bones wasted away through my groaning all day long. For day and night your hand was heavy upon me; my strength was sapped as in the heat of summer."* What a price to pay for trying to keep something away from God that He is already aware of! But, as He has been since before eternity, God is gracious and reveals it in verse 5 of the same chapter. David says *"Then I acknowledged my sin to you and did not cover up my iniquity... and you forgave the guilt of my sin."*

As we close this week, I want to leave you with some powerful wisdom from Ecclesiastes 5:2-3 NIV: *"Do not be quick with your mouth, do not be hasty in your heart to utter anything before God. God is in heaven and you are on earth, so let your words be few. As a dream comes when there are many cares, so the speech of a fool when there are many words."*

Our God is an awesome God.

Week 7

"Lord," Martha said to Jesus, "if you had been here,
my brother would not have died."

John 11:21, NIV

DAY 1

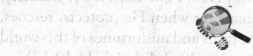

"Lord," Martha said to Jesus, "if you had been here,
my brother would not have died."
JOHN 11:21, NIV

In this verse, Martha seems to join in with those who end up blaming God for everything that goes wrong. The most profound statement I've ever heard in defense of our Father was spoken by Anne Graham (Billy Graham's daughter) and repeated by Ben Stein on the CBS Morning Commentary. According to Mr. Stein, interviewer Jane Clayson asked Ms. Graham regarding the Hurricane Katrina disaster: "How could God let something like this happen?" Ms. Graham answered: "I believe God is deeply saddened by this, just as we are, but for years we've been telling God to get out of our schools, to get out of our government and to get out of our lives. And being the gentlemen He is, I believe He has calmly backed out. How can we expect God to give us His blessing and His protection if we demand He leave us alone?"

We see this same attitude in the book of Nehemiah. In his prayer recorded in chapter 9, Nehemiah talks of how Jehovah (The Self-Existent One) rescues His people from captivity. But look at Nehemiah 9:28 NIV where he says, *"But as soon as they were at rest, they again did what was evil in your sight."*

These statements make two things clear.

1. We, like those from the Bible era, have created the calamities around us, not God.

2. We do serve a gracious God who rescues us from trouble time after time. He is Jehovah-Nissi (The Lord is My Banner), and He displays this character when He protects, rescues, and redeems us from the trials and misfortunes of this world (Exodus 17:15, Deuteronomy 20: 3-4, Isaiah 11:10-12).

Whatever the situation, seeking God, not blaming Him, is the key.

DAY 2

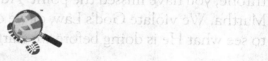

"Lord," Martha said to Jesus, "if you had been here, my brother would not have died."

JOHN 11:21, NIV

I am going to pick on Martha for a bit, just to make a point. In verse 21, Martha seems to show a lack of faith, though in the very next verse she redeems herself (or at least tries to) by acknowledging to Jesus that God will do whatever *"you ask."* But a second look at John 11:21, where Martha says *"if you had been here"* shows that she knew for sure that all they needed was the presence of Jesus and the outcome would have been different.

Martha is a type of our society. We blame God for everything that goes against our plans or what we think should happen. We ask, "How could God allow this to happen to sister so and so?" Or we are disobedient, things go south, and the first thing out of our mouths resembles what Martha said in John 11:21. For example, we blame God when certain music genres are having more of an impact than we want, instead of praying for both the entertainers and the listeners to have a relationship with God and that He can change their hearts. We blame God for the problems that exist in our government, but we don't even vote.

It's not just us who have accused God for the consequences of certain actions or lack thereof. Look at what Adam did in Genesis 3:12 NAS. Adam said to God, *"The woman you gave me, she gave me from the tree, and I ate"*—all but forgetting what God had told him (Genesis 2:16-17) about eating from a certain tree. It makes you wonder what would have happened if Adam had stood up for his wife and said, "It was me…I am the man who fell short." If you have read this story in Genesis and found yourself looking down at Adam from your seat on the high moral throne, you have missed the point. Adam is a type of you, me, and Martha. We violate God's Law, or we don't have enough patience to see what He is doing before we start spouting off at the mouth.

Take, for instance, our fuel situation in America. At one point, prices were well over $4.00 a gallon. And all we did was complain, complain, complain, instead of looking at what is happening because of these high fuel prices. In the magazine *Business Weekly*, John Carey, in his article "The Real Question: Should Oil Be Cheap," goes under the surface and looks at all the positive things that are happening in our country because we began making necessary adjustments in our lifestyles to combat the volatility of the economy. He talks about how we are much healthier because people are losing weight from walking or riding their bikes to work. He writes, "A study from Washington University in St. Louis suggests that 8% of the rise in obesity since the 1980s was due to low gas prices." Families spend more time together because they are not wasting fuel on random trips to the mall (and other places), staying home instead. Technological advances such as making jet fuel from plants and plug-in cars are on the horizon.

Adam is a type of you, me, and Martha. We violate God's Law, or we don't have enough patience to see what He is doing before we start spouting off at the mouth.

I do not like or advocate high prices for gas and I certainly do not think God has anything to do with this situation. I am making a point about how we should analyze before we accuse and criticize… especially God. Listen to what God said about Israel, which is a type of us, the Church, in Jeremiah 29:11 NAS: *"For I know the plans that I have for you, declares the Lord, plans for welfare and not calamity to give you a future and a hope."*

DAY 3

"Lord," Martha said to Jesus, "if you had been here, my brother would not have died."

JOHN 11:21, NIV

John 11:21 gives us an idea of how Martha approached Jesus when she felt anguish over her brother Lazarus' death. We often approach the Father in the same complaining way. We often start out with cursory thanks, a rehearsed phrase or two, and then get right to our "Jehovah-Do-For-Me" list. I think we have learned this approach from our culture or traditional beliefs, but it has very little to do with how the Bible teaches us to approach our Father. In fact, in all of the ways Jesus instructed us to come to the Father, that wasn't one of them.

WE CANNOT FORGET THAT PRAYER IS MORE THAN A REQUEST SESSION. PRAYER IS AN ACT OF WORSHIP.

In the Lord's Prayer (Matthew 6:9-13), Jesus models how we are to approach the Father, beginning with acknowledging God for who He is, as in "*Our Father in heaven*," giving Him precedence over any other person that we might call "father" here on earth—biological or spiritual. Verse 10 tells us to recognize His power when it says, "*your kingdom*" and "*your will*," which displays our submission to His place and His purposes. From then on, verses 11-13 speak of the power He has to feed, forgive, and lead us. Every part of this prayer is an acknowledgement that God is our source of all that is good, powerful, and sanctifying. Without Him, there is no prayer.

If you are a young believer, I encourage you to mature in your relationship with the Lord so that every time you speak to the

Father, it is not all about you. We cannot forget that prayer is more than a request session. Prayer is an act of worship. Look at Psalms 147:11 AMP, where it says: *"The Lord takes pleasure in those who reverently and worshipfully fear Him, in those who hope in His mercy and loving-kindness."* Notice that it does not say that God takes pleasure in those who complain and only call on Him when things don't go their way. Although several more verses throughout the Bible tell how to approach the Father, I think Psalm 100:4-5 NIV is really encouraging: *"Enter his gates with thanksgiving and his courts with praise; give thanks to him and praise his name. For the Lord is good and his love endures forever."*

Before I end today, I want to make clear that I am not saying that we should not make our requests known to God. God is a loving Father who cares about the needs of His children. This is what Martha must have wished she had done four days earlier. Philippians 4:6 says that we are to *"present our requests to God."*

It's all about the state of our hearts from which we approach Him; that same verse in Philippians says that our requests should be presented with a heart of thankfulness. Our prayers have no chance of being answered based on our righteousness, good deeds, or any credit that we think we have with God. As Daniel prayed, *"We do not ask because we deserve help, but because you are so merciful"* (Daniel 9:18, NLT).

When my children pray at night, they usually say "Father God…" and then begin their list of things that they want done, such as asking for a good day at school, or that no one gets into trouble with mommy or daddy, or help on a test. Then they finish with a prayer for the kids they help sponsor with World Vision. I think that their prayers are awesome and the Lord knows their hearts. But as they grow, it is my job to teach and exemplify a more mature way of drawing close to the Father. Sometimes, it's a request; sometimes it's a conversation about the day; and sometimes, I am so broken that I can say nothing and I wait for Him to do the talking.

Whatever the subject of our prayer, it should be prayed in faith with an expectant hope, because God is Yahweh (The Great I AM). He is Adonai (My Great Lord). He is Elohim (The Creator). He is El-Shaddai (The God Who Is More Than Enough). He is Jehovah-Mekaddishkem (The Lord Who Sanctifies). He is Jehovah-Shammah (The Lord Who Is There). And most importantly, we should pray in the name of Jesus Christ, His Son, who is Immanuel (God with us).

Here are a few questions to ask yourself about your prayer life:

- Do you acknowledge who God is to yourself and to the world?
- Do you spend time confessing your sins?
- Do you pray the Word of God?
- Do you pray for wisdom?
- Do you fast at times, which is a great companion of prayer?
- Do you pray for others, your least favorite people included?

For a look at some awesome models of prayer, see Ezra 9, Nehemiah 9, and Daniel 9. They are must reads.

Day 4

"Lord," Martha said to Jesus, "if you had been here, my brother would not have died."
John 11:21, niv

I think it is important for us to look at some of Martha's admirable qualities. God put people and their mistakes in the Bible for our benefit, not their judgment. So let's take a look at her more enviable attributes.

The first thing we notice about Martha is that she is hospitable; she knows how to serve people. In a culture where serving is often looked at as a bad thing, our sister Martha is a reminder of what God has called us to do to be like Him. Jesus says, *"But I am among you as one who serves"* (Luke 22:27, NIV). We see our sister Martha doing the exact same thing in Luke 10:40. The Bible says she was *"distracted with preparations."* Although her main focus had moved off of spending time with the Lord in order to serve Him, she still was the one who opened her home and served others. We also see her in John 12, after Lazarus was resurrected from the dead, doing what she does best; verse 2 NIV states, *"Martha served."*

Another attribute that Martha displayed was passion. Sometimes Christians "tuck tail" when it is time to stand for truth; they keep quiet when they should speak up. Martha shows a kind of fire that can only come from a person who is willing to risk her image in order to gain a certain result. In Luke 10, she calls her sister out for being lazy and not helping with food and other chores. I know, she was wrong, but at least she was confident and trying to make others—including Jesus—comfortable. In John 11 Martha is shown leaving her house to give Jesus a piece of her mind. I know; she was wrong again. But it takes passion and heart to speak the truth about how you really feel to someone who is in authority. How many ideas have gone to the grave because someone was afraid of what they might look like to their boss if the idea was a flop? The truth is we should be worried about being afraid.

The last attribute that I want to point out about Martha is that she was a mature believer. In view of her actions recorded in Luke 10:40 and John 11:21&29, my saying that Martha was a mature believer might seem contradictory. But when we look at John 12, where Martha, Mary and Lazarus give a dinner in Jesus' honor, verse 2 says, "*Martha served*," and that was it. After rebuke and a few bruises to her ego, Martha has learned to do what she is supposed to do and let God handle the rest. That's what I call a mature believer.

After rebuke and a few bruises to her ego, Martha has learned to do what she is supposed to do and let God handle the rest. That's what I call a mature believer.

I pray that when you read about Martha and others in the Bible who made mistakes, you will see yourself in them and find hope. But more importantly, I pray that you see how much God loves you, because He has given us so many examples to learn from so that we can become mature believers in Him.

Day 5

"Lord," Martha said to Jesus, "if you had been here, my brother would not have died."

John 11:21, NIV

Next we're going to take a look at why Martha (and Mary, her sister) would have the mettle to charge our Lord for being responsible for their brother Lazarus' death. This week, we have talked about the blame game a ton, but verse 39 gives us some insight as to why Martha was flustered with Jesus and His timing. The NIV translation shows Martha saying, *"Lord, he already stinks. It's been four days."* The first part of that statement displays her recognition of Jesus as her authority and the last part refers to Jewish customs of this period, which were instituted by God when he gave the Law to Moses.

In Martha's world, there were no sophisticated medical facilities or equipment to determine whether a person was dead, knocked unconscious, or in a coma. (Can you imagine how many people were buried alive back then?) To eliminate as many mistakes as possible, the practice was to wait three days before a person was pronounced dead. During this waiting period, people had to check on the body periodically during the day and night to look for signs of life.

Now, put yourself in Martha and Mary's shoes.

Day 1: They check several times during the day, studying the lifeless body of a man that they have loved since his birth, looking for any sign of movement, and nothing.

Day 2: They repeat the same thing, but now they are starting to look like fools; everyone knows that Lazarus is long gone.

Day 3: They go again, out of respect. All hope is gone; they are sad, confused, and mad. The sisters wonder, "Where is Jesus?"

Day 4: Martha has had enough, and she wants an explanation—and so would you.

To understand people of the Bible like Martha, it helps to learn about the culture and practices of the times in which they lived. I am not a scholar in Hebrew culture, but I have enough sense to know that it is different from P.G. County, Maryland, where I am from. When we look at Martha or anyone from the Bible from an American point of view, we miss out on a lot of what God is teaching.

Day 4: Martha has had enough, and she wants an explanation—and so would you.

I encourage you to become more familiar with Hebrew and Greek studies, because they can help you see the Bible in a whole new light. After all, Jesus (Immanuel, God with us) wasn't born a Middle Eastern man who lived in and ministered according to the Jewish culture of 2000 years ago by accident!

Day 6

"Lord," Martha said to Jesus, "if you had been here,
my brother would not have died."
John 11:21, niv

I would like to share with you a line from one of my favorite poems. I have admired this man's work for years and it has profoundly impacted my life and how I look at God's Word. The excerpt goes:

> One minute you see Jesus and He's floored,
> Next He's resurrected, cause yes, you guessed it, He's Lord,
> Yes I gotta rep' Him most def' because He soared
> Up, after coming down, just like a see-saw.

This is from a rap song (yes, rap is a form of poetry) called "Clap Your Hands" by The Ambassador. His real name is William Branch and he is a pastor at Epiphany Church in Philadelphia, Pennsylvania. He is one of the most gifted rappers I have ever heard. Every piece of music that he and others like Shai Linne, Stephen the Levite, Flame, Everyday Process, Tripp Lee, and Da Truth (and many more) write is totally committed to bringing God glory.

You may be wondering what this has to do with Martha. The answer is not a whole lot, directly, but the principle of blame is closely connected. For the past 20 years or so, our society has tried to blame (like Martha) some of the ills of our world on rap music. I will admit that most rappers produce music that is void of positive or healthy content. A lot of what our youth and some adults listen to is degrading to women, filled with filthy material, and teaches disobedience to moral values. But not all rap is the same. In fact, I love all rap music; it's the lyrics that are often troubling.

You don't have to be a Christian to know that when artists call themselves "gods" and coerce their listeners to do the same, this is wrong and there is no room for discussion. Some of our all-time favorite artists in the 1960s and 70s, who spoke out about the social climate and pointed to the injustices in our world, also wrote songs about their experiences with drugs, alcohol, and their immoral sexual behavior. No doubt these past and present artists have had a negative effect on our nation. In Ephesians 5:3-4 MSG Paul says, *"Don't allow love to turn into lust, setting off a downhill slide into sexual promiscuity, filthy practices, or bullying greed. Though tongues just love the taste of gossip, those who follow Jesus have better uses for language than that."* Don't talk dirty or silly. That kind of talk doesn't fit our style.

Truth be told, I was one who thought that I could listen to secular rap and it would have no influence on me. My wife told me otherwise. She would tell me, early in our relationship, that she could tell when I was listening to secular rap or anything that was void of content, and when I was not. In fact, I used to love to listen to Nas, Biggie Smalls, Tupac, Redman, Public Enemy, Slick Rick, Tribe Called Quest, DAS EFX, EPMD, and others. But as I started to examine myself, I concluded that she was right; listening to them *did* make me different. The way that I talked and acted when I was listening to these artists was not an example of a godly man. Luke 6:45 (NAS) explains why: "*…for his mouth speaks from that which fills his heart.*" The gateway to our heart is through our eyes, ears, and the atmosphere in which we spend our time.

I can understand the cry of some in our nation with regards to how some genres of music have had a negative effect on our youth. But when we blame and personally attack all musical artists in certain genres or styles, we throw the baby out with the bath water. Hammering musical artists with blame causes division in the church and we lose the chance to share the grace of God.

> EVERYTHING WE DO WITH OUR TALENT, MUSICAL OR NOT, SHOULD BE AN ACT OF WORSHIP, OFFERED TO GOD IN SPIRIT AND TRUTH.

Everything we do with our talent—musical or not—should be an act of worship, offered to God in spirit and truth. With regard to music, the Bible makes no mention of what style or tempo is more pleasing to God. Psalms 98:4 NIV instructs us to "*Shout for joy to the Lord, all the earth, burst into jubilant song with music*." There is no specification for rap, country, R & B, techno, or opera. What is essential is that we must be in prayer for our brothers and sisters who have a difference of opinion on how they should use their talents, while making sure we are using our own gifts and talents to glorify God. Blame and accusations only separate us.

If you're like me and love rap but want a Christian alternative, go to ChristianHipHopper.com

DAY 7

"Lord," Martha said to Jesus, "if you had been here,
my brother would not have died."
JOHN 11:21, NIV

As we begin to understand Martha and her actions toward Jesus, I think it is imperative that we take a look at the actions of her sister Mary in John 11:32. What often gets lost when we hear the story of Lazarus being resurrected from the dead is that both of the sisters accuse their Lord and Savior of not being where they thought He should be. But Martha is usually the one presented as the object of ridicule and an example of what not to do.

In John 11:32, we see that Mary is guilty of the same infraction as her sister Martha as she also said: *"Lord, if you had been here, my brother would not have died."* However, there is a significant difference in their two approaches: *"When Mary reached the place where Jesus was and saw him, she fell at his feet"* (verse 32). Before Mary spoke a word, she was in a place of humility—at the feet of Jesus in submission and reverence. This is not uncommon for Mary; for every time she is mentioned in Scripture, she is at the feet of Jesus (Luke 10:39, John 11:32, John 12:3). While Martha spent her time serving the Lord, Mary spent her time *with* the Lord. And look at the result of her actions. Mary made the exact same statement as her sister Martha but John 11:33 NIV shows Jesus having a completely different reaction to Mary; it says that Jesus was *"deeply moved in spirit and troubled."*

Neither sister knew that Jesus had already planned to go to Lazarus' dead body and wake him up (John 11:11). And I am reluctant to say that Mary's mode of pleading her case was better than Martha's, because I don't think there is a right way to accuse

God of anything, but maybe she wasn't accusing; maybe for Mary it was an honest statement reflecting her faith in the Son of God that she knew her brother would have lived if Jesus had been there. Either way, I think this is another example of how gracious our Lord is, in that He gives us what we do not deserve. Mary and Martha had myopic thinking. They knew their brother would have been alive if Jesus had been there because they knew Jesus was more powerful than death. But God had bigger plans than either of them knew. In the end of this story, not only was Lazarus resurrected, but the disciples were given another reason to believe, and Martha gave her life to Christ, perhaps for the first time, as John 11:25-27 displays.

> Mary and Martha had myopic thinking. But God had bigger plans than either of them knew.

As you look at the characters in this story, it is easy to see yourself in all of these people. We need to be encouraged from time to time, like the disciples did.

We are emotional, irrational, and passionate as well as devoted, committed and hard working like Mary and Martha—and every bit as much in need of a Savior as they were.

And we all need to be restored and brought back from the dead, just like Lazarus.

God loves us so much that He can look past our shortcomings because when He looks at us, He sees the face of His Son. But, it is important that we draw close to Him respectfully and humbly.

Week 8

"One thing you lack," he said. "Go, sell everything you have and give to the poor, and you will have treasure in heaven. Then come, follow me."

Mark 10:21, NIV

DAY 1

"One thing you lack," he said. "Go, sell everything you have and give to the poor, and you will have treasure in heaven. Then come, follow me."

MARK 10:21, NIV

I have always felt a connection with this rich young man for a number of reasons. One of them is that I was blessed with a great deal of money by playing basketball in the NBA. The other commonality was an attachment to money that took our focus off of what was and is important: family, relationships outside of family, those who needed help financially, and my relationship with God. I remember leaving my honeymoon three days early so I could get back to my house and start working on my game. I was desperately trying to get another basketball contract. I had no idea how badly that decision affected my wife until years later. It's one of those things that I regret and can never make up to her.

The funny thing about all the money, material stuff, and social recognition that came with my job is that it never could consistently keep me satisfied. Once I bought a Range Rover, then I wanted a Hummer. Once I got a house in a gated community, I was not content, so I bought one on a lake in a gated community. Over a 10-year period, I bought more than 20 brand new cars and three homes—two of those I built myself. Money can increase net worth, but it can never define your self-worth.

I'd love to tell you that a traumatic incident from childhood caused me to be so discontent, but that was not it. The truth is, I was a bad steward, plain and simple. You see, I was not secure in who I was and the "stuff" made me appear to be something that I wasn't. Psalm 35:27 NIV says, *"The Lord be exalted, who delights in the well-being of his servant.*" God wants to see us happy, but He must be exalted first—not our stuff, our goals, our money, or anything that pushes God to the back seat.

Check out Psalm 1:1-2: "*Blessed is the man who does not walk in the counsel of the wicked or stand in the way of sinners or sit in the seat of mockers. But his delight is in the law of the LORD, and on his law he meditates day and night.*" This verse says that the "blessed" (favored/happy) man/woman delights in God's Word and studies it daily. It also says that the "blessed" man does not walk in the counsel of the wicked (evil/ungodly), because they will always distract you with anything to get you to stop serving God. Here is what they will say: "That car is nice, but for $10,000 more you can get one that will start up with one push of the button and park all by itself" or "This is the neighborhood you have to live in because so and so lives there and if you get to know them, the sky is the limit." I am not against nice cars and "hot" neighborhoods (I have both), but I am against anything that keeps us from seeking the Father.

GOD WANTS TO SEE US HAPPY, BUT HE MUST BE EXALTED FIRST, NOT OUR STUFF, OUR GOALS, OUR MONEY, OR ANYTHING THAT PUSHES GOD TO THE BACK SEAT.

I think it is interesting that Jesus told this young man to sell everything, but He did not tell him to give it all away (Jesus said "*give to the poor*"). When we are focused on our "stuff," we can't even hear what the Lord is saying to us. Recent interpretations of the Bible like The Message and the New Century Version hint at how much money should be given, which I think is a great topic to discuss. Knowing Jesus, He would have probably showed this man how to multiply his wealth and, after walking with Immanuel, the money would have lost its grip on this fellow.

When that happens, you and your money become great weapons for the Kingdom of God. Proverbs 13:7 NIV adds, "*One man pretends to be rich, yet has nothing; another pretends to be poor, yet has great wealth.*"

In church circles, this man is called "the rich young ruler." Why, you may ask? Mark 10 shows him as rich, Matthew 19 displays him as "young", and Luke 18 says he is a "ruler"...add them up and you've got the rich young ruler.

Day 2

"One thing you lack," he said. "Go, sell everything you have and give to the poor, and you will have treasure in heaven. Then come, follow me."

Mark 10:21, NIV

I think it is important that we understand that money was not the only issue in Mark 10:21. The money was obviously a blessing; Deuteronomy 8:18 in the NIV says "*...it is He who gives you power to get wealth.*" This man just did not know it because he did not understand stewardship. Money magnifies your present condition. If you are generous when you have meager finances, you will be even more generous when God blesses you with more. If you have a little drinking problem when you are living paycheck to paycheck, you will become an alcoholic when you have access to more money. Again, money is not the issue. The issue is and always will be the state of our hearts.

Money is not the issue. The issue is and always will be the state of our hearts.

Money takes on the character of the person in possession of it. Some of us ought to be glad that we were not in possession of a great a deal of finances early in our journey or we might be strung out on drugs, in prison, or even dead. We all need to do a Spirit-led, Google-style search on our hearts and see what we find. If it is not Christ-centered, we need to get rid of what does not glorify God.

It is amazing that at the end of this verse, we see this man walking away from God—much like we do when things do not go according to our daily planners. You know the type. As soon as a religious leader says something that does not line up with how they want to live, they walk away from anything connected to the church. Or, if our prayer is not answered by the next day, somehow we think that God only allows others to prosper, especially those who we deem "bad" people. Yours truly has done this far too many times.

Over the years, I have had many opportunities to talk to people about why they do not like organized religion or want anything to do with the church. They usually say that they have had a bad experience or they feel that the church just wanted their money. If I can, I try to pose this scenario to them: What if you were at your favorite restaurant, and the service was bad, but you still had to pay for your food? Would that stop you from ever going out to eat again? They usually look at me and smile.

I totally understand getting upset with the Father when things do not go our way. That is what kids do. Unfortunately, we have too many kids in (and runaways from) the church. Anyone can come up with a reason to walk away from God when something does not go their way. But a mature believer trusts in the Father when they don't get their way in a certain situation. More than likely, the Father is keeping us from something that will cause us more harm than we can foresee.

Look at John 7:66-69, which says, "*From this time many of his disciples turned back and no longer followed. 'You do not want to leave too, do you?' Jesus asked the Twelve. Simon Peter answered him,* ***'Lord, to whom shall we go****? You have the words of eternal life. We believe and know that you are the Holy One of God.*" Where else will you go? Where else could the young man from Mark 10:21 go? The world will offer many options that start off fun and full of adrenaline, but they usually leave us frustrated, confused, angry, and used before we realize that we have been bamboozled. We must have a heart like Simon Peter and know that there is no other place that is safer or filled with joy and peace than God's *charis*, which is Greek for "grace."

Day 3

"One thing you lack," he said. "Go, sell everything you have and give to the poor, and you will have treasure in heaven. Then come, follow me."

Mark 10:21, niv

Have you ever seen one of those commercials where the loud-mouthed employee is going on about how he would run the company and then goes into his unflattering rendition of how the boss talks? You know what happens next: the other co-workers start to look like they are passing a stone, and Big-Mouth cannot figure out why—until he realizes too late that his boss has been standing behind him the whole time. We probably look the same way when the real us is on display in front of our authorities.

The young man in Mark 10:21 is just like Big-Mouth from the commercial. He has no idea how he looks in front of his Authority because he has no idea that He is there. Remember in verses 17 and 20 of Mark 10, this young man calls Jesus *Rabbi*, or "Teacher," just after Jesus gives him a chance to justify why he called Jesus "good." Remember, most people back then called Jesus "Teacher," especially legalists who did not want to recognize Jesus as LORD. Sound familiar?

This young man had no clue that this Man was not only the reason for his existence; He was also the reason the young man had the wealth he was so reluctant to part with. Deuteronomy 8:18 NIV says, *"But remember the Lord your God, for it is he who gives you the ability to produce wealth."* In 1 Corinthians 4:7 NLT Paul says, *"What do you have that God hasn't given you? And if all you have is from God, why boast as though you have accomplished something on your own?"* Unfortunately, this man's attitude was like a lot of church-attendees today, who think, "How can I earn or buy my salvation?" or "If it wasn't for my money, this church could not stay afloat." The young man asks, *"What **must I do** to inherit eternal life?"* (Mark 10:17)—as if he could do anything.

This kind of attitude is on display when a husband snaps at his wife on Tuesday and by Wednesday there are a dozen roses on the front porch and a larger-than-usual check in the offering plate at church on Sunday, all in an attempt to erase his guilt from Tuesday (personal experience). The truth is, the guilt can only be erased if the wife is willing to forgive the offense without any external incentives. Her forgiveness is a gift, led by grace and mercy, which comes from Christ.

The young man in Mark 10 wanted to buy a ticket to heaven. This attitude is displayed in Romans 10:3-4 NIV: *"For they being ignorant of God's righteousness, and seeking to establish their own ....For Christ is the end of the law for righteousness to everyone who believes."* It's too bad he didn't stick around to find out that the price had already been paid. He could not see this, because his wealth and, possibly, his place in society meant more to him than his place in God's Kingdom. The *Wiersbe Commentary of the New Testament* says of this man that "of all the people who ever came to the feet of Jesus, this man is the only one who went away worse than when he came." WOW! That's not a club I want join.

Does your money (or pursuit of it) get in the way of God using you for His purposes? Have you ever tried to purchase forgiveness? Has anyone tried to manipulate you with gifts, so they could feel better about themselves?

Day 4

"One thing you lack," he said. "Go, sell everything you have and give to the poor, and you will have treasure in heaven. Then come, follow me."

Mark 10:21, NIV

In 2001, I bought a brand new convertible Porsche. I just had to have this car. It was blue with tan leather interior and it was *fast*. The bottom line: it was a head turner.

The problem was, I lived in Orlando, Florida where, on most days, it was 90+ degrees and, at the time, I had a family of four. After a month, I realized that I never drove the car because I could not put the kids' seats in the rear. And to be honest, the mystique of this car had already worn off. The very next week I traded the Porsche for a SUV that was more family-friendly.

Later that next week, I got a call from Rick Godwin, my mentor. Rick wanted to know how I liked the new car and if I had broken any speeding laws in the past few weeks. I sheepishly told him that I had traded the car in, but before I could finish my sentence I got an ear-full. Rick told me that he had been watching me for the past couple of years and that he noticed that I was not really smart with my money. In his own words: "Take that checkbook and give it to your wife; you are bad with money." Then, he abruptly got off the phone before I could say a word. That conversation reminded me of a principle that Rick had taught me: We buy things we don't need, with money we don't have, to please people we don't even like.

The truth is, he was right. I was no different than the young man in Mark 10:21. We both were bad stewards who used or planned to use our money for the wrong purposes. We were both trying to purchase happiness, when Jesus is saying, "Come follow me and I will show you what 'true happiness' is." In addition, we both were solely concerned with the here and now. A quote from Rick Warren in *The Purpose Driven Life* says, "The most damaging aspect of contemporary living is short term thinking. To make the most of your life, you must keep the vision of eternity continually in your mind and the value of it in your heart."

In the Mark 10 story, Jesus explains what godly stewardship is when he says "*give to the poor.*" This principle has changed how I handle my money and what I think about purchases. I don't want to waste any more of the money that God has given me to manage. Because of this change, my wife and I have been able to give more money to ministries and people who may never know where it came from. The funny thing is, I feel so much better about sponsoring children through World Vision or St. Jude than I did when I bought a new car or a tailored suit. I cannot explain it; I just do. (See Acts 20:35.)

> I STILL HAVE AN ABUNDANCE OF NICE THINGS; THEY JUST DON'T HAVE *ME* ANYMORE.

I firmly believe that God's people should have the best, and I still have an abundance of nice things; they just don't have *me* anymore. People will tell you that money cannot buy happiness, but I disagree. Money bought me all kinds of bliss, but it could not purchase contentment, and that's what everyone is really after. There's a big difference.

The saddest part of the story in Mark 10 is that the man walked away from Jesus. He did not want to part with his wealth, which was a symptom of the pride and arrogance in his heart. For me, I equate that to where I would be if I had not had that conversation with Rick in 2001—coupled with a praying wife. I'd probably be broke.

But more importantly, I would not be able to be used to advance the Kingdom the way that my wife and I are able to now.

Listen to this quote from Henrik Ibsen: "Money may be the husk of many things, but not the kernel. It buys you food, but not appetite; medicine, but not health; acquaintances, but not friends; servants, but not loyalty; days of joy, but not peace or happiness."

Selah (pause and think about that).

Do you know God as Jehovah-Rohi?

It is a name of God that speaks of how He protects, provides, directs, leads, and cares for His people.

Go around your house and even in your closets and look for all the things that you "just had to have" and ask yourself, would my life be any better or worse without them?

Day 5

"One thing you lack," he said. "Go, sell everything you have and give to the poor, and you will have treasure in heaven. Then come, follow me."

Mark 10:21, NIV

The concept of stewardship has been an issue for me most of my adult life. I did not understand that it involved more than just money; our time and our talent need to be properly managed as well. I must admit that after reading about the rich young man in Mark 10, I would be doing you a disservice if I did not emphasize the need to pay more attention to how we manage our finances.

I would love to tell you that I have been a good steward with our finances during my wealth-producing years, but that would be a lie. But gaining some wisdom on the concept and watching other people model it before me has really made a difference in my life.

You see, over the past ten years of my life, especially after the conversation I had with Rick Godwin in 2001 about how I had mishandled my money, I have started to think about the future and what kind of legacy I was going to leave my children. I wanted them to understand what it was like to live debt-free, balance a checkbook, watch the return rates of mutual funds, avoid capital gains taxes, and many others things that I did not learn as a youth. I do not profess to be a financial expert, but I do have a lot to share with my kids so they don't make the same mistakes that I did. Because my knowledge of financial stewardship has grown, they are going to be ahead of the game.

For example, I do not like credit cards because my uncle Rob taught me how the interest from them causes you to pay more than double the principle over the long haul. And some studies say that you will spend up to 30% more when you pull out the "plastic" than you would if you were paying in cash. As a result, we try not to go crazy with the Amex card because we have to pay the bill every month, which is exactly what we have done over the past 18 years. Some months' bills are a little out of hand. But regardless of the bill, we have to pay it in full every 30 days.

As a result of our good standing with Amex, our children are going to be able to start out their adult spending lives with favor that I did not have when I began using my card to purchase things. I recently received a letter from American Express stating that because we pay our bills on time and other fees that go along with membership, all of our children will have a right to their own platinum card from Amex. You may say, "What is the big deal?" Well, when I started out using the card in the early 90s, I started out at a lower level and with less privileges (probably a blessing!) and had to prove myself to be a worthy card user. But my kids won't have to do that like I did.

> EVERYTHING WE DO AS PARENTS SHOULD BE TO EQUIP OUR CHILDREN FOR WHAT THE WORLD HAS TO THROW AT THEM, NOT HIDE THEM FROM THE STORMS THAT WILL NO DOUBT COME.

The point I am trying to make is that I have grown in this area of my life and my children are going to benefit from my growth. I have always felt that my ceiling should be my kids' floor. They should not have to deal with the same issues that I dealt with and they should be given the wisdom to handle them if they do occur. Everything we do as parents should be to equip our children for what the world has to throw at them, not hide them from the storms that will no doubt come. This is a part of prosperity that I don't think many people, including churches, teach our youth. I wish I would have received lessons like this in Sunday school, instead of only hearing about tithing and the building fund. Remember, Proverbs 22:6 NIV says, "*Train a child in the way they should go, and when he is old he will not turn from it.*" The reason we need to train our children lies in Proverbs 22:15, which says that children are born with "*folly*" in their hearts.

If you don't know a lot about finances, get with someone, learn as much as you can, and teach all you know to your kids. Most kids can speak part of a second language by the time they are 10 years old, so I am pretty sure they can learn how to balance a checkbook. Let's not be like the man in Matthew 25:25 who was afraid to do anything, and so he never gained anything. Our children or the youth that we are responsible for need us.

Don't pray that God will bring financial prosperity your way when you have not done your part in learning how to manage it. Or better yet, part with it.

DAY 6

"One thing you lack," he said. "Go, sell everything you have and give to the poor, and you will have treasure in heaven. Then come, follow me."

MARK 10:21, NIV

I must clear up a false idea that society perpetuates, which is that God is after your money. After reading our story in Mark 10, one might associate Jesus with the irresponsible clergymen seen over the years who misuse funds or use guilt and condemnation to gain them. God does challenge us in areas of our life (especially money) that get in the way of our relationship with Him. But Satan wants to deceive us into thinking that God wants us broke, using cultural trends or our emotions to get us to forget God's plan for our life. Money, or the lust of it, reveals who we are.

The greater issue in this story was the condition of this man's heart. When referring to the commandments, he tells Jesus, "*All these I have kept since I was a boy*" (Mark 10:20). This statement revealed a heart full of pride and arrogance, because we know that no one has been able to keep every commandment. Romans 3:23 NIV says, "*For all have sinned and fall short of the glory of God.*" Ironically, this man was claiming to be perfect in front of the only perfect man to ever walk the earth. The opportunity to be in right standing with God was right in front of him, but this man had no clue. He was trying to buy something that was impossible for humans to purchase. Romans 3:22 states that righteousness from God comes through faith in Jesus Christ, not from what we do or are able to buy.

After the young man showed a heart that needs repair, Jesus showed Himself to be the perfect example of grace: "*Jesus looked at him and loved him*" (Mark 10:21).What a mighty God we serve. What patience He displays with us. We gossip... He loves us. We lie... He loves us. We cheat on our taxes... He loves us. We serve other gods... He loves us. We don't tithe... He loves us.

Notice, I did not say He is pleased with us when we sin. I am saying that He never stops loving us, even when we are at our worst.

Jeremiah 9:24 NIV: "*I am the LORD, who exercises kindness, justice and righteousness on earth, for in these I delight.*"

When Jesus is listing the commandments from the Law (found in Deuteronomy 5), He only gets through six of the ten. Before He could finish, our friend from this week's verse interrupts Jesus— Wow! Imagine that. Jesus is talking and this guy is like, "Yeah, okay, that's all well and good, but I have kept all these rules and regulations... there has to be something else for me to do!"

Before you get on your moral high horse and judge him too harshly, think about this: God talks to us all the time, and we interrupt Him with the things that we consider more important to us. It usually sounds like this: "Based on my life, I believe..." or "You want me to do what with my money?" or "In my opinion, I think I should..." Sound familiar?

Day 7

"One thing you lack," he said. "Go, sell everything you have and give to the poor, and you will have treasure in heaven. Then come, follow me."

Mark 10:21, niv

I can honestly say that my lusting after money has been replaced by a thirsting after God's Word—to understand it and to apply it to my life. I still have a desire to produce wealth with the gifting that God has given me. Fortunately, my motivations are different from the past, which is one of the reasons for writing this book.

The past 15 years of my life have been tremendous with respect to accumulating wealth. My wife and I have been able to tithe large sums of money into ministries that have blessed our family, afford a lifestyle that is comfortable, and bless people that we will never meet. Yet during the past 10 years I have found myself envious of men and women who know, recall, and facilitate God's Word like they were born to do it—people like Rick Godwin, Beth Moore, John MacArthur, Creflo Dollar, Bishop T.D. Jakes, Luis Pulau, Pat Magley, John Piper, Joel Osteen (contrary to what many think), Frederick Price and many others.

Growing up, all I wanted to do was dunk like Dr. J, Michael Jordan, or Len Bias; run like Tony Dorsette and Daryl Green; catch a largemouth bass like Bill Dance; and fix a car like my stepfather Charles. I still like those things, but my envy to know the Word of God like the pastors that I listed has caused me to study the Bible, scour commentaries, and listen to teaching tapes by teachers from all over the world in an effort to know about my Father in heaven and His will.

Don't misunderstand me. I still want (at age 36) to catch a 10 pound bass, hit a draw like Tiger Woods, and coach like some of my basketball mentors, Gregg Popovich, Nat McMillian, and Doc Rivers. But this thirst for the Word is where I want my focus to remain so I can enjoy the other stuff, if it ever happens. God said to seek Him first and everything else will be added, and He decides what will be added.

> God said to seek Him first and everything else will be added, and He decides what will be added.

Unfortunately, I think this is where our friend in Mark 10:21 missed out. Jesus told him to come and follow Him, which would have led to one of the greatest journeys a man or woman could ever experience. He would have gained knowledge and understanding (wisdom) that comes from the source of all things: El Emet/ El De'ot (God of Truth/God of Knowledge).

Facilitating the Word may not be my gift, but seeking and understanding it is my choice. Look at Proverbs 1:5 AMP, which says, *"The wise also will hear and increase in learning, and the person of understanding will acquire skill and attain to sound counsel [so that he may be able to steer his course rightly]."*

Week 9

"...but as for me and my house, we will serve the Lord."
Joshua 24:15, NAS

DAY 1

"...but as for me and my house, we will serve the Lord."
JOSHUA 24:15, NAS

This verse is one of the most inspiring leadership charges in the history of mankind. "Win one for the Gipper" pales pitifully in comparison to Joshua's farewell address. This week's verse is a part of Joshua's address to the leaders of Israel as they ended their forty year journey in the wilderness (the first address can be found in Joshua 23).

I am attracted to this verse because it was an invitation to everyone in the nation of Israel, not just Joshua‘s family. Joshua had gathered all of the tribes together and challenged them to choose who they were going to serve (Joshua 24:1-15). But make no mistake about it: Joshua is speaking directly to his family—every member. Our culture is very individualistic; most of us approach life with an "all about me" mentality. Joshua's pronouncement of not only who *he* would worship and trust in but also his entire household, and hopefully his nation, stands in sharp contrast to the way we operate.

This statement was made as a proclamation of faith, not withstanding Joshua's family situation. The Bible does not give any details about Joshua's family like it does with Jacob's or David's. I think it's easy to read this verse and assume that Joshua's family was the biblical version of the Cosby's or the Brady's, but we don't know what sort of struggles they faced. In all likelihood, they were dealing with the same things many families face today (culturally relevant versions of the same things, that is; Joshua's kids probably weren't arguing for a new cell phone or more television time).

Looking at this declaration by Joshua, you get a glimpse of the strength and clarity of a man who was revered for his service to his nation's former leader, Moses. Joshua was a man who exemplified godliness; "*...Caleb...and Joshua the son of Nun, for they have followed the Lord fully*" (Numbers 32:12; NAS). He was a man who was courageous in battle (Exodus 17:9-16). He was a man who loved his family, his nation, his God.

I think it is important to point out the lack of a gray area in Joshua's statement. It does not say, "But as for me and my house, we will serve the Lord if the economy is healthy." It does not say, "We will serve the Lord if that is what my constituents want me to do." It does not say, "We will serve the Lord if we have enough money in the bank, but we'll leave our options open just in case this campaign does not work out." It does not say, "As soon as gas prices come back down, we will serve the Lord, but until then we've got to do what we've got to do."

Essentially, Joshua is saying that no matter what the rest of the nation is doing, regardless of how many religions they create to justify their lifestyles, or whether they seem to be prospering more than us, or how many people call us "Jehovah freaks," my house will trust in, submit to, seek after, obey, worship, praise, love, talk about, and honor God. Here is all of Joshua 24:15 in its entirety (NIV): "*But if serving the Lord seems undesirable to you, then choose for yourselves this day whom you will serve, whether the gods of your forefathers served beyond the River, or the gods of Amorites, in whose land you are living.* ***But as for me and my household, we will serve the LORD***." We will do this together and I will lead.

Now *that* is a man who understands how to lead his family.

A Kenyan proverb says, "Sticks in a bundle are unbreakable." Let's do whatever it takes to keep our families together.

Day 2

"…but as for me and my house, we will serve the Lord."

Joshua 24:15, NAS

Let's get something straight about leadership so we can better understand the quality of man Joshua was. It is pretty clear, from our personal experiences as well as situations we've watched from a distance, that you cannot lead if you are not an example of the things you want your followers to do. This has been one of the biggest problems in families, teams, corporations—even in the church: leaders who fail to live up to the bar they hold everyone else against. We have all seen or been part of groups that were led by individuals who would demand actions that they would not, could not, or refused to do themselves. It has been my experience that this kind of leadership breeds disdain and causes division among the ranks.

I remember playing on teams in the NBA and having our "public leader" demand maximum effort from the squad without being an example of what they expected. The sad part was, they were usually the most talented but also the least committed. This attribute revealed itself when things got tough, usually during a losing streak; they were the first ones to start blaming the other teammates for the problem, even though they were the first ones to take the credit when things went well.

Fortunately, I also had the privilege of playing alongside Patrick Ewing, Doc Rivers, Herb Williams, Derek Harper, Avery Johnson, David Robinson, Tim Duncan, Eric Snow, Grant Hill, and a few others who knew that leadership started with service. They knew that a public and private commitment to the fundamental principles of the organization was required of them, too, not just the rest of the team. My friend Eric Snow was the epitome of this leadership quality. He did whatever the team needed to win: challenged players to be their best; provided an ear for guys to talk to when they were struggling; said what needed to be said, even if meant he had to rub someone the wrong way, to make the team better and stronger.

We see these same qualities personified when we look at the life of Joshua. There are many passages that demonstrate Joshua's incredible leadership. Deuteronomy 34:9 says that Joshua was filled with the Spirit of God. Joshua 1:5 and 6:27 speak about Joshua enjoying the presence of God. Joshua 5:13-14 displays his obedience to God. Numbers 13 shows Joshua serving his country (verse 15 mentions his name being changed from Hoshea to Joshua). In Numbers 11:28 we see him as a servant of Moses, which he had been since his youth. Joshua 3:5 displays him as he inspires the people of Israel to get ready to go into the Promised Land. Joshua 4:14 shows God exalting him for doing exactly as He commanded in leading the people to their new home.

> SIR ISAAC NEWTON SAID, "IF I HAVE SEEN FARTHER THAN OTHERS, IT IS BECAUSE I WAS STANDING ON THE SHOULDERS OF GIANTS."

Because of leadership like this, the people of Israel had a perfect spearhead to follow. And their reply in Joshua 24:21 revealed their response to Joshua's charge: the people answered, *"No! We will serve the Lord."* There was no vote, not even a rebuttal…just compliance to a man who had risked and served so his people could live well. It is amazing what service to God and man can accomplish.

Sir Isaac Newton said, "If I have seen farther than others, it is because I was standing on the shoulders of giants." Joshua stood on the Lord. I encourage you to do the same.

DAY 3

"...but as for me and my house, we will serve the Lord."
JOSHUA 24:15, NAS

When Joshua speaks the words *"as for me and my house, we will serve the Lord,"* he is speaking a decree to the members of his family and his nation. By doing so, he is also setting a standard for all the youth who are within earshot—especially his.

I think this is paramount for us because of our culture. So many children are left to their own devices, forced to grow up too fast, and indirectly asked to make life changing decisions long before they are properly equipped to make them. In her article *Are Children Growing Up Too Fast?*, Kimberly Chastain discusses how we send our children to athletic, artistic, science, computer, and language camps so that their resumes will be more impressive when they try to get into college. Her question (and mine) is when did camp transition from a fun learning experience to pre-college work studies? As Chastain says, "Our society is compressing childhood more and more to where children are not children very long."

> THAT VERSE IS NOT ONLY FOR ADULTS BUT ALSO FOR CHILDREN. GOD IS INTERESTED IN EVERY DETAIL OF THEIR AMAZING LIVES, AND NOT JUST WHEN THEY GROW UP.

Joshua's declaration is not only a national address to the elders and tribal leaders of Israel, but it is a firm command to the children of *his* house that first and foremost, "*we will serve the Lord.*" This statement to a child says "I want you to serve God, make Him your desire, and He will direct your path." As Psalm 37:23 NLT says "*The steps of the godly are directed by the Lord. He delights in every detail of their lives*." That verse is not only for adults but also for children. God is interested in every detail of their amazing lives, and not just when they grow up. Joshua understands this totally and proclaims that no matter what others are doing with their kids, whether they are an experienced pianist by the age of 10, speaking a foreign language before high school starts, or traveling the world on a junior high summer break, my children "*will serve the Lord*" —first and foremost.

Please don't misunderstand me. I am all for children being involved in extracurricular activities. I know firsthand that sports can teach children many valuable lessons, as can artistic and scientific disciplines. But the Bible says in Proverbs 22:15 NIV that "*folly is bound up in the heart of a child,*" and in Proverbs 13:22 NLT that "*good people leave an inheritance even to their grandchildren…*" That inheritance is not just money; it is a legacy of serving the Lord so that the "folly" can be recognized and eradicated. As parents and guardians, we are obligated to make sure our children have a reverential view of God. Some may question the value of training children's spirituality; what if it is merely a learned behavior for them? To that I would say, as my mentor Rick Godwin taught me, to "get the habit down first, and the motivation will come."

The British poet Samuel Taylor Coleridge once had a discussion with a man who firmly believed that children should not be given formal religious instruction; he believed that they should be left to choose their own religious faith when they reached maturity. Coleridge did not disagree, but later invited the man into a neglected garden. "Do you call this a garden?" the visitor exclaimed. "Well you see," Coleridge replied, "I did not wish to infringe upon the liberty of the garden in any way. I was just giving the garden a chance to express itself."

I tell people all the time that I wasn't well versed in church activities, but I still grew up as a "drug" baby because my mother and my grandparents "dragged" me to church every Sunday. I had no clue why, but there was no room for discussion. Now that I am older, I am so thankful for the years of watching my grandfather Reverend James O. Williams Sr. preach. I am thankful that he and my grandmother Josie Mae took me all over North Carolina to vacation Bible schools. I am thankful for the times that I played tag or football outside of the church, while the older folks attended to church business. I am thankful for the chicken, cornbread, and sweet tea that were served at those church dinners, and for my mother taking me to Riverside Baptist Church where I was baptized when I was 10. But most importantly, I am thankful for the people in my family who, like Joshua, said that "we will serve the Lord."

Even when I was not walking in God's Grace, I could still remember the words, lessons, and experiences that my parents and grandparents taught me from God's Word. Someone prayed for me and believed what Paul and Silas said in Acts 16:31 NIV: *"Believe in the Lord Jesus, and you will be saved—you and your household."* I am living proof of the power in those family declarations, and I could not be more grateful for that heritage.

Day 4

"...but as for me and my house, we will serve the Lord."
Joshua 24:15, NAS

Today I want to look at the response to this verse and how it can encourage those who are not in leadership to honor those who are.

As an assistant NBA coach, I have often thought about what it would be like to be a head coach. On ESPN, we often see the glamour that goes with the job of being the leader of a pro sports team. We see the nice suits, the headsets that send plays out to the field and control the outcome of a game. We see baseball managers walk out to the mound and remove or leave a pitcher in the game. We see the power that goes with those positions, and truth be told, we are drawn to it.

But what we don't see are those same people sitting up at night watching film until two, three, sometimes four o'clock in the morning. You don't see the anguish that a coach goes through because they had to release/cut a player, knowing that the decision has just altered someone's life forever. You don't see the coach in the doctor's office beginning to have heart palpitations because of the stress. You don't see the coach driving home at night agonizing over whether or not the time away from his family is worth it. These people need support, and they need it from the people who follow their lead.

Joshua declared to the entire nation that his house "will serve the Lord." The people of Israel could very well have said "We have had enough of this travel, fighting, standing in faith." But these people believed in their leader, and more importantly, they believed in their God. In Joshua 24:21, the people of Israel proclaim, "*No! We will serve the Lord.*" They also said "*Far be it from us to forsake the Lord to serve others gods....God himself brought us and our fathers out of Egypt...He protected us on our entire journey...And the Lord drove out all the nations...*" (Joshua 24:16-18, NIV)

My friend Arto Woodley told me once that "one should never aspire to leadership; one should be called." I think the people of Israel knew their place as followers of a great man and understood that they served a vital role as God's people right where they were in life. Too often we see people connive, back bite, and manipulate so that they can be in a place of power. But sooner or later, their character and talent catches up with them and their plans crumble. God calls the people He wants to be in leadership; He also appoints those He wants to be under them. It is our job to be obedient wherever we are.

Sometimes God will put us in a place of service to prepare us for leadership, so that if we are ever promoted, we will know what the people serving us are going through. Sometimes, He puts us in a place of service simply because that is where He wants us, because He knows that we can be trusted and the person at the helm needs a man/woman like us to have their back. Everyone can't be the engine; someone has to be the oil, someone has to be the transmission, and someone has to be the spark-plug.

What about you? Can you be obedient, trustworthy, honest, and available to a leader? Can you have an attitude like Mary who was presented with the idea of being the mother of the Savior of the world at the age of 14, an unmarried virgin? Look at her reply in Luke 1:38 NIV: "*I am the Lord's servant...may it be unto me as you have said.*" This is essentially what the people of Israel said to Joshua and to the Lord: we will serve God wholeheartedly; may it be unto us as you have said.

Day 5

"…but as for me and my house, we will serve the Lord."

Joshua 24:15, NAS

Every few years, our local and national leaders bombard us with the reasons why we should trust them to lead various jurisdictions of the country—and why we shouldn't trust their opponents. For the most part, they get us excited about how they are going to fix the things that we are unhappy with. They talk about employment, the economy, better use of tax dollars, improving security and education. We usually get excited about the possibility of change. But when the election craze is over, most often we realize that our excited emotions were more powerful than our reason, and that leads to disappointment.

In Joshua 24, we see a national leader give his people hope instead of excitement. The Merriam Webster Online Dictionary defines "hope" as "to cherish with anticipation;" "to desire with expectation of obtainment;" "to expect with confidence."

What did the people of Israel hope for? For one, they needed protection from the other nations around them. In Genesis 12:7 you find the Lord's promise to give this land to Abraham's offspring. In Joshua 1:3-6, God reaffirms this promise; in verse 6 NLT, God says to Joshua *"Be strong and courageous, for you will lead my people to posses all the land I swore to give to their ancestors."* They finally have their land. Now they are in need of protection to keep it.

If you look at Joshua 12, you will find a list of the thirty-one kings that Moses defeated east of the Jordan as well as the others that Joshua defeated west of the Jordan. Those uprooted tribes of people were not just going to lie down and allow the Israelites to live in eternal bliss on their new real estate. They needed a protective covering. This is why God commanded Joshua to be "*strong and courageous*" (Joshua 1); God knew he was going to need it.

God also said to him in Joshua 1:5 NAS, "*No man will be able to stand before you all the days of your life. Just as I have been with* Moses, *I will be with you; I will not fail you or forsake you.*" Joshua understood the covenant that he was under, the covenant that had been made with Moses. This covenant (the Mosaic Covenant) was a conditional agreement, meaning you had to do something to gain something. In this case, obedience to God's Word led to protection from God's enemies (and many other blessings; you can find it in Deuteronomy 27-30).

Joshua 23:12-13 reiterates the consequences for turning your back on God. They read like this in the NAS: "*For if you ever go back and cling to these nations, these which remain among you...know with certainty that the Lord your God will not continue to drive these nations out [protection] from before you...they will be a snare and a trap to you...until you perish from off this good land which the Lord your God has given you.*"

No wonder the people of Israel, after hearing their leader's address (Joshua 23 & 24), replied with a resounding "No, but we will serve the Lord." This is an amazing example of a nation united in its commitment to God under their leader: Joshua. He gave his nation hope because he fully trusted that the God who had proven Himself to them so many times before would continue protect His chosen people if they were obedient to Him.

At the end of Ralph Waldo Emerson's poem A Nation's Strength, he writes of this kind of leader, the kind of men and women that make a nation strong. He writes:

Brave men who work while others sleep

Who dare while others fly
They build a nation's pillars deep
And lift them to the sky

Day 6

"...but as for me and my house, we will serve the Lord."

Joshua 24:15, NAS

The word "serve" is used in reference to Joshua's family commitment to Yahweh. The Hebrew word for "serve" is abad (aw-bad), meaning "to work;" "labor;" "to execute for." The Greek rendering of this word "serve" is latreuo, which *Sparkling Gems from the Greek* by Rick Renner says is a part of worship. The *MacArthur Study Bible* defines "serve" with terms like "to help" or "to work for."

> When Joshua gave this proclamation to the nation of Israel, he was essentially saying that we plan to work for the God of "all things are possible."

Joshua's mission statement to his family and the nation could have read like this: "I don't know what your plans are, but me and the people who live under this roof with my blood running through their veins will work for, worship, and try to advance the Kingdom of Jehovah...I hope that you will join us; it would be in your best interest to do so."

Jack Welch, Former chairman and CEO of General Electric, wrote in his book Winning (p.15) that "...effective mission statements balance the possible and the impossible. They give people a clear sense of direction to profitability and the inspiration to feel they are a part of something big and important." John Quincy Adams said "If your actions inspire others to dream more, learn more, do more, and become more, you are a leader."

When Joshua gave this proclamation to the nation of Israel, he was essentially saying that we plan to work for the God of "*all things are possible*" (Mark 14:36). That means it is possible to put God first and prosper. It is possible to love our spouses and be an example of a godly marriage when everyone else says that divorce is an acceptable alternative to commitment; that it's not really ok but everybody cheats so if no one knows, no one will really get hurt. It is possible to tithe, trusting God to bless your with more through 90% than you could provide for yourself with 100%. It is possible to honor your parents regardless of your past history with them, simply because we are commanded to (Deuteronomy 5:16), whether it's easy and we feel like they deserve it or not. It is possible to stay pure in a culture that evangelizes promiscuity and compromise. It is possible to teach your children to do the things that you may not have done yourself, allowing them to break the cycle of sin that has repeated itself for generations. It is possible to ______________________ (fill in the blank).

Joshua was trying to inspire a nation, but I believe that God is using Joshua to inspire us to "serve" Him with all of our hearts—simply because we are called to do so.

DAY 7

"...but as for me and my house, we will serve the Lord."

JOSHUA 24:15, NAS

Be prepared to stand alone. I repeat: be prepared... to stand... alone. When you proclaim to your co-workers, teammates, family members, your employer, your friends, that "as for me and my house, we will serve the Lord," you had better be ready to stand alone. The rest of the world will try to convince you to conform to its system, a rat race in which you would be the rat. In his book *The Puritan Pulpit*, Thomas Watson says, "How many souls have been blown into hell with the wind of popular applause?"

Throughout Scripture we see a "God-first" attitude displayed in the lives of so many—Elijah, David, Daniel, Joseph. But today I want to talk about a man who should be an inspiration to us all. His name is Stephen, and he was one of the seven leaders chosen in Acts 6 to manage distribution of food to the Jewish widows. Led by a total devotion to God, Stephen goes beyond the call of duty and challenges the Jewish leaders because they resisted the Holy Spirit. Acts 7 shows Stephen using terms like "stiff-necked" and "uncircumcised in heart and ears" when referring to these leaders. Like with Joshua, Scripture shows no one physically standing with Stephen. We have to remember that even though Stephen seemed to have been alone, God was there. God is omnipresent, which means He is everywhere all at once. What goes on in Vegas might stay in Vegas, but God is in Vegas, too.

GOD IS OMNIPRESENT, WHICH MEANS HE S EVERYWHERE ALL AT ONCE. WHAT GOES ON IN VEGAS MIGHT STAY IN VEGAS, BUT GOD IS IN VEGAS, TOO.

Stephen was stoned to death by this group of men; one of the people in the crowd was Saul of Tarsus, who later became the apostle Paul. God only knows how this event played a part in preparing Paul for his decision to follow Christ. Paul, a man who used to persecute Christians, went on to write almost 75% of the New Testament (if that doesn't make you want to praise God for His mercy and grace, not much else will).

In Stephen's final speech (Acts 7), he mentions Joseph. Just reading his story in Genesis 37-50, Joseph seemed to be in some extremely tough situations by himself. But look closely at what Stephen said about him (Acts 7:9-10, NIV): *"Because the patriarchs (Joseph's brothers) were jealous of Joseph, they sold him as a slave into Egypt. But God was with him and rescued him from all his troubles."* As He was with Joseph, He was also with Stephen. Right before he was dragged out of the city and stoned to death, Stephen was full of the Holy Spirit and he saw the glory of God (Acts 7:55). God did not leave Stephen alone.

As He was with Stephen and Joseph, He was also with Joshua—even when he proclaimed to his people, standing all alone, that his house would serve the Lord. God made a promise to Joshua at the very beginning of his time in leadership: *"I will never leave you nor forsake you"* (Joshua 1:5, NIV). I know for a fact that He tells us the same.

When we stand up and proclaim that "we will serve the Lord,"—through our words, by our lifestyle, where we spend our time, how we spend our money, how we treat others, demonstrating as much as proclaiming that we do all things by His grace and because of His mercy—He is right there with us, too.

WEEK 10

"Therefore, obey the terms of this covenant
so that you will prosper in everything you do."

DEUTERONOMY 29:9, NLT

Day 1

"Therefore, obey the terms of this covenant
so that you will prosper in everything you do."
Deuteronomy 29:9, NLT

When it comes to prosperity (success for your journey) and financial prosperity specifically, there seems to be two sides arguing about this doctrine.

One of the problems with this arguing is that it is usually done in public: in front of congregations or on television or radio. There is a side that says that Jesus was rich, or they use the wealth of Solomon, David, and Abraham to justify the lavish lifestyles that are ever present in the body. Then there is another side that claims that Jesus was poor and that we give God glory when we are broke, busted, and living in poverty—suffering for the cause, if you will. The main problem I see with regards to these prosperity doctrines is that we, the body of Christ, should not be wasting time quarreling over issues like this publicly. This causes confusion and we are losing opportunities to serve those who have dire questions about God that need answering and real needs to be met.

We are instructed about this in Titus 3:9 NLT: *"Do not get involved in foolish discussions about spiritual pedigrees or in quarrels and fights about obedience to Jewish laws."* This verse is talking about anything that keeps the "main thing" from being the "main thing"—especially publicly. A commentary from the *MacArthur Study Bible* about Titus 3:9 states: "Proclaiming truth, not arguing error, is the way to evangelize." To add to that point, we should not defame anyone, especially our brothers and sisters in the body with whom we may have a difference. James 4:11 NIV says, *"Brothers, do not slander one another. Anyone who speaks against his brother or judges him speaks against the law and judges it*." As a man who has slandered, defamed, and just plain gossiped about others, I can tell you that this is an area that we as a body of believers need to mature in—and quickly.

The second problem I see is that when we take a verse, use it out of context, isolate it, and try to use it to make a point so we can look more godly—or as my brother Pastor Jeff Ryan would say, create "justifiable Christianity"—we have moved away from truth and landed right in the middle of opinion. The Bible has 66 books; My Way and Second Opinions are not included in any translations.

If you disagree with someone in the body regarding financial prosperity, I encourage you to go to that person in private and in love. "*For anyone who does not love his brother, whom he has seen, cannot love God, whom he has not seen*" (1 John 4:20, NIV). Hopefully, you have a strong enough relationship with the person to allow you to approach them about such an issue. If you don't, then it is best to be quiet and pray that God would be all of our desire and that we would all get the Divine Help, through the Holy Spirit, that we need in every area of our lives—prosperity included.

God's Word on prosperity contains principles that can bring eternal results.

The prosperity doctrines being pushed in the church are issues, led by good intentions. God's Word on prosperity contains principles that can bring eternal results. Issues change, but God's principles last forever. As the band Third Day sings, "We gotta come together."

Day 2

"Therefore, obey the terms of this covenant
so that you will prosper in everything you do."
Deuteronomy 29:9, NLT

I thought that we would take a day to look at the various Bible translations of this week's passage. Notice the different words used for "prosper" and "covenant."

> *"So **keep** the words of this covenant to **do them**, that you may prosper in all that you do."* NAS

> *"Faithfully **obey** the terms of this **promise**. Then you will be **successful** in everything you do."* GW

> *"Keep the words of this covenant, and do them, that you may prosper in all that you do."* AKJV

> *"So keep the words of this agreement and do them, so that it may **be well** for you in everything you do."* BBE

> *"Keep therefore the words of this covenant, and fulfill them: that **you may understand** all that you do."* D-R

> *"And ye have kept the words of this covenant, and done them, so that **ye cause** all that ye do to prosper."* YLT

> *"Therefore keep the words of this covenant and do them, that you may **deal wisely and prosper** in all that you do."* AMP

I thank God for the people under the King James reign (along with William Tyndale and his pupils) during the 17th century, who took time to translate the Bible so all could understand God and His will better. I am also glad that we have a multitude of different translations to help us understand Scripture, translated so long ago.

To the many men and women who have spent countless hours making God's Word clearer: Thank you. Because of your work, we can see that words like "prosper" and "covenant" have much more depth than our traditions and culture have allowed us to know.

Meditate on these words today; ask God to give you a deeper revelation of Deuteronomy 29:9.

DAY 3

"Therefore, obey the terms of this covenant
so that you will prosper in everything you do."
DEUTERONOMY 29:9, NLT

Today I want to take a look at the word "covenant" so we can better understand what had to take place before the Israelites (and we) could prosper.

The *Webster's New World Dictionary and Thesaurus* defines covenant as a "promise." The same book says that a promise is "an agreement to do or not to do something." In the book of Deuteronomy "covenant" refers to obedience to God's Law given to Moses. The *Wiersbe Bible Commentary* states: "The secret of prosperity was the blessing of God, and the secret of receiving that blessing was obedience to God's law."

The interesting thing about a covenant is that there cannot be only one individual involved. When my wife and I were married, we entered into a covenant with each other and God. When people buy a car by way of financing, they enter a covenant with the dealership and a financial institution. Even in individual sports such as golf, covenant agreements are made between the golfer and his or her caddie. When I took the job to become an assistant coach of the Portland Trailblazers, I entered into a covenant with Nat McMillan (head coach), Kevin Pritchard (general manager), Larry Miller (president), Paul Allen (owner), the players, and—because it's Portland—the fans.

Another point about this covenant was that it was not just for the leaders or men of the tribes of Israel. Deuteronomy 29:11 NIV adds "*together with your children and your wives, and the aliens living in your camps...*" This is important, because leaders (even though this covenant was not solely for them) of any group, team, or family have to be careful about the types of covenants or promises they get into, because they have a direct effect on those who depend on them.

As a man who has been blessed with financial wealth, I am often approached with new opportunities to make more money. Most of the proposals are pretty good and have potential for lucrative returns. But as the leader of my house, I have to think about the consequences and what could happen to my family if things do not go as planned.

THE COVENANT THAT WE HAVE WITH OUR FATHER IS TIME-TESTED AND PROVEN TO BRING PROSPERITY TO THOSE WHO ENTER INTO IT WITH HIM.

That is what is so awesome about the covenant that we have with our Father; it is time-tested and proven to bring prosperity to those who enter into it with Him. Look at Psalm 37:25-26 NLT, where David says, *"I have been young and now I am old. And in all my years I have never seen the Lord forsake a man who loves him; nor have I seen the children of the godly (covenant people) go hungry. Instead, the godly are able to be generous with their gifts and loans (prosperity) to others, and their children are a blessing."*

Tomorrow we will take a deeper look at this particular covenant and how it pertains to the people in the Bible and to us.

Has a bad covenant ever put you and your family in a bad situation? What does the word "covenant" mean to you?

Day 4

"Therefore, obey the terms of this covenant
so that you will prosper in everything you do."
Deuteronomy 29:9, NLT

The covenant we are talking about in Deuteronomy 29 is different from the one previously given to Abraham (known as the Abrahamic Covenant). This covenant—the Mosaic Covenant—given on Mount Sinai to Moses was a bilateral conditional agreement, where God said: *"Now if you obey me fully and keep my covenant, then out of all nations you will be my treasured possession ...you will be for me a kingdom of priests and a holy nation"* (Exodus 19:5, NIV). The people responded together (verse 8), saying, *"We will do everything the Lord has said."*

Abraham's agreement with God was unconditional (unilateral). It was not based on the obedience of the people that were under this particular pact, as shown in Genesis 12:10-20. In this chapter, Abraham lies to Pharaoh about his marriage in order to protect himself, while risking the welfare of his wife Sarai. In the end, Abraham left Egypt with more material wealth (verse 16) than he had before he entered.

The Mosaic Covenant (given to Moses) of Deuteronomy 29 ensures that the people will prosper if they are obedient to the laws that God put in place. The blessings and curses that are related to this conditional covenant are listed in Deuteronomy 28.

Why is the covenant given to Moses so important to us thousands of years later? Because the Mosaic covenant, unlike the one given to Abraham, served the purpose of revealing our sinful nature and allowing mankind to see their need for a Savior, Jesus Christ. Our

Lord and Savior replaced the Mosaic Covenant, as He explained in Luke 22:20 NIV: "*This cup is the new covenant in my blood, which is poured out for you.*" Paul adds, "*He has made us competent as ministers of a new covenant—not of the letter but of the Spirit; for the letter kills, but the Spirit gives life*" (2 Corinthians 3:6).

Does this mean that because Christ replaced the Mosaic Covenant, we will not prosper when we are obedient? Absolutely not! Look at a New Testament application of Deuteronomy 29:9 in 3 John 2, where it says AMP, "*Beloved (you and me), I pray that you may prosper in every way and [that our body] may keep well, even as [I know] your soul keeps well and prospers.*"

DAY 5

"Therefore, obey the terms of this covenant so that you will prosper in everything you do."

DEUTERONOMY 29:9, NLT

Prosperity without peace can lead to destruction.

Believers know that our Prince of Peace is Jesus (Isaiah 9:6). Unfortunately, we also know that people are able to prosper without having a relationship with Him; as the Psalmist wrote, *"I envied the arrogant when I saw the prosperity of the wicked"* (Psalm 73:3). We see this all the time with drug cartels, corrupt lawyers and politicians, and celebrities in the entertainment industry. These people, from a worldly perspective, seem to have it all. But Proverbs 14:12 AMP says, *"There is a way which seems right to a man and appears straight before him, but at the end of it is the way of death."*

PROSPERITY WITHOUT PEACE CAN LEAD TO DESTRUCTION.

Today I want to take a brief look at the life of Howard Hughes, one of the greatest minds of the twentieth century. By the age of 12, Hughes had already built his own motorized bicycle. By the age of 14, he was taking flying lessons. By 19, he became financially independent when he inherited his father's fortune. Hughes then turned to Hollywood, where he made his mark by producing several films; one called *Two Arabian Knights* won an Academy Award.

At the age of 34, Howard Hughes bought a majority share of TWA stock and took control of the airline. In 1948, he took control of RKO, a Hollywood studio, and by 1954 he sold it for a

6.5 million dollar profit. Mr. Hughes seemed to be the definition of prosperity.

However, Mr. Hughes also became the prototype of a man who had very little peace. He was married three times. He got caught up in the Watergate scandal that rocked our nation and resulted in the resignation of President Richard Nixon. He suffered from ADHD, agoraphobia (the fear of being in an open space), and obsessive-compulsive disorder. Mr. Hughes was also addicted to codeine, valium, and other prescription drugs.

When he died in 1976, his 6'4" frame weighed only 90 lbs.; his hair was long and unkempt; his nails overgrown. The troubles in Mr. Hughes' life and his final condition can be a warning to all who are prospering and those who are seeking prosperity: you must have peace so that the prosperity won't take you out. And peace can only happen if the Holy Spirit is your guide.

One more note: 3 John 2 MSG says, "...*I pray for good fortune in everything you do, and for good health—that your everyday affairs prosper, as well as your soul!*" John is praying here for his friend Gaius that he would prosper in all that he does and in his soul and in his everyday affairs. That is total prosperity brought about by the prayer of a righteous man.

Pray for total prosperity in your life.

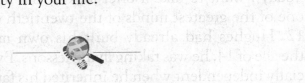

"He that is of the opinion money will do everything may well be suspected of doing everything for money." Benjamin Franklin

Day 6

"Therefore, obey the terms of this covenant
so that you will prosper in everything you do."
Deuteronomy 29:9, NLT

Many believers study the Word by reading, listening to teaching or radio, watching broadcasts on television, or going to their local Christian bookstore and purchasing limitless amounts of literature to help them prosper in their knowledge of God's Word. Unfortunately, we often have no idea of the sacrifices made so that people like you and me (and even non-believers) could have so much wealth of information about our faith and the history behind it.

Do the names Hudson Taylor and John Wycliffe ring a bell? I had no clue who these men were until I did some research about the pioneers who made it easier for the gospel to be heard all over the world. Wycliffe, for example, was one of the main figures who made it possible for the Bible to be translated into English. Long before the Protestant Reformation by Martin Luther in 1517, John Wycliffe, who was a "nonconformist" of the Catholic Church, completed the Wycliffe Bible in 1384. He is the founder of the Lollard movement, a pre-cursor to the Reformation, and is credited with single-handedly translating the Gospels of Matthew, Mark, Luke, John, and possibly the whole New Testament. His contemporaries, men like Nicholas Hereford, John Purvey, and John Trevisa, helped complete the translation of the Old Testament.

Hudson Taylor, a British missionary, spent 51 of his 73 years in China; he was the founder of China Inland Mission. While in China for those 51 years, he lost four of his children and his first wife Maria after being married for only 12 years. He was first called "the black devil" because of the outfit that he wore. Taylor paid a heavy price for taking the gospel to China. But because of his efforts and his faith in God, more than 130 million Christians in China today (probably more) prosper in the Word of God.

Listen to the Lord in Acts 13:47 NIV: "*I have made you a light for the Gentiles, that you may bring salvation to the ends of the earth.*" Men like Wycliffe, Taylor, Saint Jerome, John Chrysostom, Watchman Nee, Martin Luther, and many others from various time periods have made it possible for us and people all over the world to know about Deuteronomy 29:9, so that we can "prosper in everything" that we do.

DAY 7

"Therefore, obey the terms of this covenant
so that you will prosper in everything you do."
DEUTERONOMY 29:9, NLT

As I am constantly reminded of how prospering without God's principles as our guide can lead to destruction, I think of a man who exemplified prosperity in its totality and how it changed history. You will find his story in the book of Acts, chapter 10. His name is Cornelius.

With all that went on in the book of Acts, like Stephen becoming the first martyr, the introduction of the Holy Spirit, and Saul's Damascus road experience, it is easy to skip over Cornelius and not recognize his contribution to the history of the Body of Christ.

Cornelius was a Roman officer, one of sixty who had command of 100 men. He was a rare man among Gentiles, because pagan worship was not practiced in his house. The Scripture says he was "*one who feared God with all his household*" (Acts 10:2 NAS). It reminds me of Joshua 24:15 NIV where Joshua proclaimed, "*But as for me and my household, we will serve the Lord.*" This Roman commander was also a generous and faithful man who "*gave many alms to the Jewish people and prayed to God continually*" (Acts 10:2 NAS). In reference to this verse, *Matthew Henry's Commentary of the Whole Bible* states: "Wherever the fear of God rules in the heart, it will appear both in works of charity and of piety, and neither will excuse us from the other."

Cornelius was a man who prospered in his relationship with God, in his family's spiritual growth as they served, in his finances, in his work, in his community, and his generosity made it possible for others to prosper. The Bible says an angel told Cornelius, "*your prayers and alms have ascended as memorial before God*" (Acts 10:4 NAS). What an awesome legacy to leave future generations—to be publicly recognized by God for being faithful.

And look at his reward: Cornelius and his family were the first Gentiles to receive the Holy Spirit, as Acts 10:44-45 describes. "*While Peter was still speaking these words, the Holy Spirit came on all who heard the message... the gift of the Holy Spirit had been poured out even on the Gentiles.*"

> IF EVERYONE IS NOT SHARING IN THE PROSPERITY, THEN THERE IS NO PROSPERITY."

This story reminds me of a mission trip that I took to South Africa in 2000. I was hosted by Pastor Ray McCauley and his church, Rhema Bible Church. Pastor Ray told me that we Americans had prosperity all wrong. He said, "Prosperity was never meant for one person. If everyone is not sharing in the prosperity, then there is no prosperity."

Cornelius was faithful in being obedient. He prospered in all he did, and so did the people around him.

Did you know that Warren Buffet, whose wealth was valued at more than 40 billion dollars, donated more than 30 billion dollars to the Gates Foundation? Now that is prosperity!

Week 11

"...One thing I do know. I was blind but now I see!"

John 9:25, NIV

Day 1

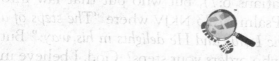

"...One thing I do know. I was blind but now I see!"

John 9:25, NIV

I love John 9:25 because it cuts right to the chase. Religious leaders and scholars are in constant debates over topics like "once saved, always saved," "end times," "speaking in tongues," "is drinking wine a sin?" and many others issues that I see as distractions from the needs of people and the power of God. Many people are answering questions that nobody is asking and using their places of power to make sure we know what they know and not necessarily what God wants us to understand—which is how much He loves us.

Our brother in John 9 had a problem. He was blind from birth and had done nothing to cause this problem: *"Neither this man or his parents sinned..."*. (John 9:3) Because he was sightless from birth, he was probably uneducated. But this man had enough common sense to know that he did not have the answer for the gift of sight that he had just received from Jesus.

> I firmly believe that "a man reaps what he sows", but who put that law into effect? God.

Think of all the blessings in your life. Now try to explain them and how they happened. Some of them you can explain (God allowed them, of course) and some have no explanation outside of His grace. You might say, "I work hard." But who gave you the ability and strength to work? God. You might even say, "I am a nice person" and that your niceness left God no choice but to bless you. But Isaiah 64:6 NAS states, "*All have become like one who is unclean, all our righteous deeds are like a filthy garment...*"

I am not trying to beat you down. I firmly believe that "*a man reaps what he sows*" (Galatians 6:7), but who put that law into effect? God. I believe in Psalm 37:23 NKJV where "*The steps of a good man are ordered by the Lord, and He delights in his way.*" But who made you good and who orders your steps? God. I believe in Luke 6:38 NIV, which says: "*Give, and it shall be given to you. A good measure, pressed down, shaken together and running over, will be poured into your lap. For with the measure you use, it will be measured to you.*" But tell me, who gave you something to give? God.

Friend, I am trying to encourage you to understand that everything good in our lives is from Elohay Elohim, the God of Gods. I truly believe that we have to have an attitude like our brother in John 9. We will never understand some of the things that God is doing and has done; we should just receive and enjoy them.

Remember Psalm 145:17 NIV: "*The Lord is righteous in all his ways and loving toward all he has made.*"

Day 2

"...One thing I do know. I was blind but now I see!"
John 9:25, NIV

I relate to this man's perspective because I was miraculously healed by God in 1990. Heart disease caused me to miss two years of my playing career at the University of Notre Dame. I know that a lot of people don't believe that God heals today the way He did back in Biblical times (even though one of His names is Jehovah-Rapha, the Lord who Heals). But I am living proof that God does heal today and will keep healing His people if we just believe, though that is a different topic for another day.

The perspective of our brother in John 9, where he chooses to just accept the gift that was given to him, is admirable. But I believe this way of thinking is alive and well, though sometimes taken to the extreme in the church. Most people are receiving blessings and miracles from God, but they do not take the time to understand more about Him and the history of our faith. The pattern goes like this: He gives... we receive... and then we walk away and forget; business as usual.

This pattern is shown in Luke 17:11-19, where Jesus heals 10 lepers of a horrible skin condition. Verse 15 says that only one came back to praise God with a "*loud voice*," while the other nine went on their way without a word of thanks. Jesus asks the man (a Samaritan) who was healed and returned to give thanks, "*Was no one found to return and give praise to God except this foreigner?*" Now that is depressing, but it is as prevalent in the church today as it was in Jesus' time.

Not all of the people who received a miracle or a healing from Jesus continued on their own way as if nothing had happened, of course—just as many follow Jesus (not just believe in Him) today. Many of the people Jesus healed decided to drop everything and follow Jesus immediately, though sometimes they were told to stay where they were and live as a witness right there (like the story of the demon possessed man in Mark 5). But the grateful, sold-out heart and the decision to follow the will of God is the key. You probably see where this is headed, but in order to follow the will of God, you have to know what it is—and *that* comes by taking the time to know Him.

> In order to follow the will of God, you have to know what it is—and *that* comes by taking the time to know Him.

Don't think I'm putting myself on a pedestal. I am not a deep person; I'm pretty average in intelligence. Yet I have in front of me five interpretations of the Bible, four commentaries, two dictionaries (told you I was average in intelligence), numerous pamphlets about Christianity and other religions, and many notes from sermons I have listened to over the years. My point is that we don't live in the dark ages anymore. The opportunity to know God better for ourselves instead of letting the media, our culture, the Discovery Channel, or National Geographic give us their version of Him, is at our fingertips. If you have a computer, you can go to BibleGateway.com and find more than 100 translations of the Bible along with studies and commentaries to enhance your knowledge of our faith so you can have a better relationship with our Father.

Look at Matthew 6:33: *"But **seek first** His kingdom and His righteousness, and all these things will be added to you."* No disrespect, but it did not say to seek Oprah, Dr. Phil, or your favorite radio disc jockey. It said to seek God's Kingdom. Many in our society have good intentions but they don't always speak with the wisdom of our Father in heaven. Even our nation's first president, George Washington, said, "It is impossible to rightly govern the world without God and the Bible."

Listen to Jesus' prayer to the Father on behalf of His disciples then and today: *"I have given them your word and the world [this system that contradicts God's Word] has hated them, for they* [the disciples and us] *are not of the world any more than I am of the world... Sanctify them by your truth; your word is truth."* (John 17:14, 17, NIV)

Day 3

"...One thing I do know. I was blind but now I see!"

John 9:25, NIV

This verse gives us a candid example of the healing power of Jesus Christ in the life of this blind man. But that is not all that happened on this occasion.

The rest of this story reveals an unexpected side of this man that emerged when he was pressured by the religious domination of the Pharisees. Our brother unloads an insightful tongue lashing that not only revealed the Pharisees' lack of Biblical knowledge, but also showed a boldness that may never have revealed itself had this man not been in the presence of Immanuel (God with us). In John 9:13-27 the Pharisees question the man about his healing. But when they begin insulting him for his belief that the healer had to be from God (John 9:28), the man answers back: "*Now that is remarkable!* [mocking them] *You don't know where he comes from, yet he opened my eyes. We know that God does not listen to sinners [basically saying, 'Don't you know the Word?']. He listens to the godly man who does His will [you and me]. Nobody has ever heard of opening the eyes of a man born blind. If this man were not from God, he could do nothing.*" (John 9:30-33, NIV)

Wow! Look at the courage, the strength, and the clarity of this man. He has gone from blind and helpless to defending the honor of our Lord. Was this characteristic always a part of this man's personality? Or was it another example of what can happen when we are in the presence of God and appreciate what He has done for us? The answer is not clear from the text. But what we *do* know is that he paid a price for his brash but needed comments; he was thrown out of the synagogue (John 9:34).

From John 9:35-38 we see the man rewarded. Jesus goes to the man and offers him the gift of salvation. The man replies, *"Lord, I believe."*

This story is not just about Jesus healing this man's eyes. We must not miss the fact that when God blesses us, He does it with a purpose in mind: advancing the Kingdom. Your big-time job and all its perks are not just for you. God blesses you so you can be a blessing. If you just had a prayer answered and keep the testimony to yourself, you have lost the opportunity to strengthen someone else's faith who might be on the cusp of walking away from God. If God promotes you to a position of power and you remain politically correct and status quo, you miss an opportunity to allow God to use you in a way that the world has never seen before (look at Tony Dungy).

If you could fill in the blanks, what would it say? "One thing I do know. I was ________________ but now I ________________."

What are you going to do now?

Reflect on what God has done for you in light of what you have seen from our brother in John 9.

Ask yourself: Have I used all that God has given me access to use, whether it is wealth, a voice, a promotion, or ability?

If so, then I praise God for you and pray that He will protect you as you stand for Him.

If not, I still praise God for you, but pray that God will give you wisdom on what, when, and how you can use the power and gifts He has given you.

Day 4

"…One thing I do know. I was blind but now I see!"

John 9:25, NIV

In October of 1990, during a preseason physical, I was diagnosed with a rare and potentially fatal heart disease called hypertrophic cardiomyopathy. At the time, I was a starting forward on the University of Notre Dame men's basketball team that was expected to win a lot of games and have a chance to play in the NCAA tournament. I also had great prospects to play in the NBA, along with teammates LaPhonso Ellis, Elmer Bennet, Damon Sweet, and Keith Tower. Unfortunately, my career—after one more trip to see a specialist and a short press conference—was over.

Permanently.

My life was rocked in a matter of a few days. Basketball and all of its perks had been my god and they were gone. I had nothing to lean on. Fortunately, by God's grace, my girlfriend Ingrid (and present wife), grew up in a Pentecostal church where they actually believe what the Bible says. She talked to me about the power that believers in Christ have when we do what the Bible says regarding healing (for more on healing, check out literature by Charles Capps). For example, look at James 5:14-15 NAS: *"Is anyone of you sick? Then he must call for the elders of the church and they are to pray over him, anointing him with oil in the name of the Lord; and the prayer offered in faith will restore the one who is sick, and the Lord will raise him up, and if he has committed sins, they will be forgiven him."*

Well, I did just that (and I had no clue what I was doing; I was just being obedient) at a church called New Wings of Faith in South Bend, Indiana. Pastor Eddie Ruiz laid hands on me and prayed a prayer of faith in agreement with the believers of that church and I was healed. The manifestation of my healing did not take place until two years later while I was undergoing testing on my heart at the National Institute of Health. It was a long two years. I kept believing and disbelieving and believing and so on. But after awhile, my faith began to grow. I stopped worrying so much about basketball and began to focus on the call of God for my life, which was tougher than fighting over screens and shooting jump shots. Then, on the day that God had already chosen, the doctors told me that I was a low risk for any kind of problems with my heart and my college career could resume. Two years later, I was drafted by the New York Knicks in the first round of the NBA draft.

It seemed unfortunate that I was drafted late in the first round of the draft, but God was working that out, too. You see, many teams passed on me because of my medical history and the liabilities that go along with a case like mine. But after playing for a number of teams over the years, I had to undergo a lot of testing to pass the routine physical. While doing so, a number of doctors told me that my heart looks better now than it did when I came out of college. NOW THAT IS GOD! In fact, I get calls every once in a while from a doctor wanting to use me in his study because he can't figure out why my heart has changed so drastically (I have the documentation to prove it). I continue to tell them all the same thing: "God healed my heart." Thank God that He healed my spiritual and emotional heart as well.

> I don't have a deep answer for you when it comes to healing. I just know that God did what the Word says He will do.

I don't have a deep answer for you when it comes to healing. I just know that God did what the Word says He will do. You don't have to believe me. I don't care about that. I know what He did for me and I am going to tell the world about it until I go on to heaven.

Day 5

"...One thing I do know. I was blind but now I see!"

John 9:25, NIV

In 2002, I signed a contract to play for the Philadelphia 76ers. It was the first time in my NBA career that I was going to be a starter from the beginning of the season. I also had the opportunity to play for Larry Brown, one of the greatest coaches and teachers of the game of basketball in the history of the NBA and NCAA.

Unfortunately, during a preseason game in Houston, I went up for a routine dunk on a fast break and came down awkwardly and twisted my knee. I left the game and was checked out by a team doctor. The diagnosis was a torn meniscus and a severe bone bruise. This moment would mark the beginning of the end of my career as a basketball player.

After two surgeries, 18 months of rehab, a number of knee drainings, seeing knee specialists, taking countless anti-inflammatory pills, wearing special shoes and a crushed spirit, my career was over. This was tough for me to accept because God had already healed my heart; my knee should have been a cinch. I prayed and prayed and prayed—but nothing. My career in Philly was over. While I was already suffering from the depression that went with not playing, I was called a quitter by some people that I really respected.

While all these things were being said about me, I remained quiet but I really wanted to retaliate. The peace of God was my guide and I still can't explain it. I just knew that God was in control, even when I was struggling to cope with the prospects of my unforeseeable future.

As I was headed back home from seeing a specialist in Birmingham, who told me that I would have to retire, I made two phone calls: one to my wife and the other to Gregg Popovich, the coach of the San Antonio Spurs. I told Gregg about my situation and we discussed my future. As we talked, I thought about being like him, and the idea of coaching came up. He told me to come by the Spurs' practice site when I got back in town, to see if I was interested in becoming a part of their staff.

I started to go to practices. All I did was go to practice and take notes and stay out of the way for three months. The Spurs' staff took me in like I was Tim Duncan; they treated me well. Six months later, I was hired as an intern, then was promoted to assistant to the player development coach, Brett Brown (what a blessing he was to me and to my way of thinking). A year later, I found myself a coach on the staff of a world championship team as we beat the Detroit Pistons in seven games, 4 to 3. A month after that, I was hired by Nat McMillan to be an assistant with the Portland Trailblazers.

Did God heal my knee? Not enough to play ball in the NBA. But had He done so, I would not be doing what I feel I was destined to do, which is serve. I get to share the gospel now like never before. As a coach, I get to serve and interact with so many people who I did not get a chance to interact with as a player. I am learning to become a better coach, but God is also using me now in a way that I never thought possible.

I thought that I had to be a popular basketball player to be used by God, and here I am: a glorified ball-boy, writing a book, and speaking all over the place about the Love of God. I know this would not have happened if I was playing basketball. My plans would have been to continue playing for six or seven more years, take my money, retire, and ride off into the sunset. By God's design (not that He caused my knee to give out, but He is using my situation for His glory), I am walking in what I feel is my purpose: serving others.

I used to think that people who served and looked after others were less than or second class citizens. I was so wrong. Look at Mark 9:35 where Jesus says, *"If anyone wants to be first, he must be the very last, and the servant of all."* That's me. As a husband, I serve my wife. As a father, I serve my children. As a coach, I serve our players. In writing this book, I am serving you.

I USED TO THINK THAT PEOPLE WHO SERVED AND LOOKED AFTER OTHERS WERE LESS THAN OR SECOND CLASS CITIZENS. I WAS SO WRONG.

If you find yourself in a situation where you have prayed and believed for a miracle from God and nothing is happening according to your plan, keep serving Him and be sensitive to His plans. Remember Mary's obedience when she was approached by an angel and told that she would give birth to a child (Jesus), even though she was an unmarried virgin. Talk about a change of plans! In Luke 1:38, Mary says, *"I am the Lord's servant... may it be to me as you have said."* Notice she did not say, "I have to get married first." She did not say, "I am not the one; go and choose someone else." She did not say "Can we wait until after the honeymoon?" She starts off with "I am the Lord's."

And so are you.

DAY 6

"...One thing I do know. I was blind but now I see!"

JOHN 9:25, NIV

Our Lord Jesus Christ healed our brother in John 9 so that he could live his life more abundantly. Regaining sight has rarely been experienced since the world began, even with the advances of modern technology. Jesus performed many such miracles because He is Jehovah-Rapha, the God who heals.

He was also no respecter of the day or season of the year, as the healing of this blind man was one of seven that took place during the Sabbath, the Jewish day of rest. By performing miracles during this holy time of the week, Jesus challenges the legalistic Jews to use the law to govern and not dominate, as 1 Timothy 1:8 teaches: *"We know that the law is good if one uses it properly."*

We know from Scripture that Jesus healed a demon-possessed man (Mark 1:21-27), Peter's mother-in-law (Mark 1:29-31), an invalid man (John 5:1-9), a man with a withered hand (Mark 3:1-6), a woman bent over (Luke 13:10-17), a man with dropsy (Luke 14:1-6), and our brother in John 9, all on the Sabbath. In doing this, Jesus proved that He was Lord of the Sabbath and not vice versa. In Mark 2:27-28 (NIV), Jesus states: *"The Sabbath was made for man, not man for the Sabbath. So the Son of Man is Lord even of the Sabbath."* This gives us freedom not to be held in bondage by laws or traditions when the work that God has put before us needs to be completed.

Can you imagine what kind of impact Jesus would have had if He told any of the people mentioned above that He could not do anything for them until after the Sabbath or the Feast of the

Passover, Pentecost, Tabernacles, Dedication, or Purim were over? That kind of thinking enslaves people, like the television evangelists who tell brothers and sisters who are sick and needy that they can be healed or rescued from their trial if they send $19.95 and receive a prayer cloth or jar of oil. If we as believers put our trust in the law or other things like shofars, palm leaves, and golden cups, we will soon focus on those things and forget about the power of God to heal, deliver, and rescue His people from any curse that originated in the fall of Adam.

When I believed for my healing in 1990, I was given a prayer cloth by my mother-in-law that she got from a healing crusade. I held on to it and it was a reminder of the power that God has and it also helped me to stay faithful in those times when I could not see anything to stay faithful about. Not one time did I ever think that the cloth had any power on its own; I also didn't think that just because Christmas or Easter was approaching, God's power was going to be stronger than it would be on Labor Day.

When Jesus was healing our friend in John 9 during the Sabbath, He was saying, "I am God and I can do what I want, when I want, for whom I want, any time I want."

Those of us who have the Holy Spirit living on the inside of us have the right to call on the power that God has given at any time. When we do this, we bring the Father glory—not objects (golden calves or prayer cloths), not times of the year (Sabbath), and especially not ourselves.

DAY 7

"...One thing I do know. I was blind but now I see!"

JOHN 9:25, NIV

If you believe in Jesus Christ as your Redeemer and Master, you, along with other saints around the world, have something in common: our present condition.

We have perfect relationship with our Father, Jehovah. Look at Revelation 21:3-4: *"Now the dwelling of God is with men, and he will live with them. They will be his people, and God himself will be with them and be their God...for the old order of things has passed away."* Because of that relationship, we are not the same as we used to be. Many of us have experienced victory in our lives over things that seemed impossible to overcome before we allowed the Holy Spirit to be our Guide. Like our brother in John 9, we have seen addictions broken (drug, alcohol, and food), generational curses canceled, relationships restored, spiritual gifts realized, miraculous healings in our bodies and emotions, and other things that God did for us that we could not do for ourselves. We are better because of the impact a Christ-centered life is having on us and the people around us.

If you are not a believer, it is not a mistake that you are reading this book. I want you to know that God loves you just the way you are, but it is against His nature to leave you in your present condition. One of God's names is Jehovah-Rohi, which means "The Lord is My Shepherd." What do shepherds do for their sheep? They provide, protect, direct, lead, and attend to their sheep and their needs—even the ones that do not want to join the herd. They all get the same care, but the ones who stay close to the shepherd seem to live a better life.

When I refer to your present condition, I am not talking about your culture, race, gender, place of residence, or anything like that, although those things can be impacted by a relationship with Elohim (The All-Powerful One). I am referring to the state of your heart. Believers remember that before we had a relationship with the Father, there were things in our hearts that were not going to bear fruit for the Kingdom. As non-Christians we were afraid of letting go of the familiar, afraid of being vulnerable to something greater than ourselves, afraid of the peer pressure we might receive, afraid that the "God thing" wouldn't work for us. But praise God for the realization that we had to change and needed help to do it, and then submitted to the call.

The truth is, we should be afraid of being afraid. Imagine if our brother in John 9 had that kind of attitude before Jesus spit on the ground, made some mud, and put it on his eyes. The man could have told Jesus to stay away from him. Having been blind his whole life, no doubt the man could have sensed Jesus approaching him. And I am confident that nobody, even back then, wanted someone to put mud on their face. What if the man had decided to say, "Hey, I have been blind all this time, I might as well finish my life this way. I am used to living like this." What if he had said, "Forget the healing stuff; just give me some change so I can 'just get by.'" What if he had said, "Never mind my eyes. Can you just give me a drink of water? This healing show never works. The witch doctor could not heal me; what makes you think you can?" Fortunately, our brother said none of these things. Instead, "*...the man went and washed, and came home seeing*" (John 9:7). This involves *submission* (went on command), *action* (washed), and *receiving* (came home seeing).

If you are a believer, I encourage you to be open about the changes that Christ has had on your heart and your life. Avoid acting like you have always been "saved and sanctified" and those who aren't saved are strange. There is power in the life of a believer when the transparency of their past life meets the integrity of their present life, showing the fingerprints of Christ all over it.

You, too, can release this power by telling the world: "*One thing I do know. I was blind but now I see.*"

WEEK 12

"For the Lord gives wisdom, and from
his mouth come knowledge and understanding."

PROVERBS 2:6, NIV

DAY 1

"For the Lord gives wisdom, and from
his mouth come knowledge and understanding."
PROVERBS 2:6, NIV

This week I want to talk about, encourage you to desire, pray that you would receive, and together with you seek after wisdom.

Proverbs 2:6 says that wisdom comes from God along with knowledge and understanding. I used to think that they were all the same thing, but they're actually distinctly different. *Strong's Exhaustive Concordance of the Bible* says that wisdom is *knowledge* guided by *understanding*. The *American Dictionary of the English Language* describes knowledge as "a clear and certain perception of that which exists, or of truth and fact." The same book says that understanding is "the faculty of the human mind by which it apprehends the real state of things presented to it." So it would be safe to say that wisdom is a God-given ability to know for sure the things that are truthful and factual. The *MacArthur Study Bible* says that wisdom is "discernment."

We believers know that wisdom comes from our Heavenly Father, Jehovah-Rohi, our Wise Shepherd, who "*leads me beside quiet waters…guides me in paths of righteousness for his name sake*" (Psalm 23:2, 3 NIV). Psalm 111:10 says "*The fear of the Lord [our Shepherd] is the beginning of wisdom; all who follow his precepts have good understanding.*"

Regarding the struggle to hear God's wisdom, the *Wiersbe Bible Commentary* states:

> "But the greatest tragedy in life isn't that people invade our privacy, get on our nerves, and help destroy our delicate hear-

> ing apparatus. The greatest tragedy is that there's so much noise that people can't hear the things they really need to hear. God is trying to get through to them with the voice of wisdom, but all they hear are the confused communications clutter, foolish voices that lead them further away from the truth."

Lastly, let's look at the apostle Paul's comments about wisdom in 1 Corinthians 2:6-7 NIV: "*We do, however, speak a message of wisdom among the mature, but not the wisdom of this age or of the rulers of this age, who are coming to nothing. No, we speak of God's secret wisdom, a wisdom that has been hidden and that God destined for our glory before time began.*" God's wisdom has been set aside just for you and me. It has been there since the beginning of time and before. You and I must go after wisdom as if our lives depended on it—because they really do.

I pray that this week and for the rest of your life you will pray for a sensitive ear to hear all that the Holy Spirit has for you. Then you can let God's wisdom be your guide and live life to the fullest.

DAY 2

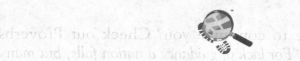

"For the Lord gives wisdom, and from
his mouth come knowledge and understanding."
PROVERBS 2:6, NIV

The University of Bad Decision Making does not discriminate against anyone who wants to enroll. I should know; I have been in their graduate program and have taken a few of their night classes! As a young 36-year-old, I am proud to say that I don't make many decisions without talking to the wise men and women God has placed around me for my benefit.

If I have to make a life decision, I talk to my wife Ingrid, Rick Godwin, Dr. Wayne Gordon, Pat Magley, Roger LeVasa, Dave Bullis, my parents, or my in-laws. If I have to make a career decision, I talk to Doc Rivers, Nat McMillan, Gregg Popovich, or my agent Steve Kauffman. When dealing in finances, I talk to Jeff Allison, my money manager, or Randy Ross, my accountant. Any questions about Scripture I refer to my wife Ingrid, Rick Godwin, Sandy Ross, or the websites of John MacArthur or Athey Creek Christian Fellowship. By now you understand that I don't make many decisions without receiving wise counsel before I move forward.

I cannot describe the anguish that I have felt and put my wife through because I made rash, emotional decisions at critical points in my life without talking things through with people wiser than me. Making crucial decisions without wise sages to help you count the cost can cause a loss of sleep, finances, relationships, and many other valuable things. I actually lost a job and more than a million dollars by making an emotional decision about my career—even after a good friend advised me differently. Talk about sleepless nights…

Need some Scripture to convince you? Check out Proverbs 11:14 NIV which says *"For lack of guidance a nation falls, but many advisers make victory sure."* How about Proverbs 15:22 NAS, which says *"Without consultation, plans are frustrated, but with many counselors they succeed."* The point is this: you did not come into this world on your own and you will definitely need the help of others if you are going to fulfill your God-given destiny.

THE POINT IS THIS: YOU DID NOT COME INTO THIS WORLD ON YOUR OWN AND YOU WILL DEFINITELY NEED THE HELP OF OTHERS IF YOU ARE GOING TO FULFILL YOUR GOD-GIVEN DESTINY.

The Greek term *adelphos* means "brothers." In his book *Sparkling Gems from the Greek*, Rick Renner refers to the idea of brothers: "You and I are brothers! We came out of the same womb of humanity. We have the same feelings; we have similar emotions; and we deal with the same problems in life. In every respect, we are truly brothers!"

The awesome thing about God is that He has put before us older and wiser *adelphos* who have been there and done that and can help us navigate this journey toward success and fruit-bearing for the Kingdom.

My mentor Rick Godwin taught me a principle that has stuck with me: "Show me your friends, and I will show you your future." Mike Freeman of Spirit of Faith Church in Temple Hills, Maryland says it this way: "stay around those who have your answer and away from those who have your problem."

Day 3

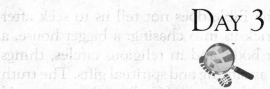

"For the Lord gives wisdom, and from
his mouth come knowledge and understanding."

Proverbs 2:6, NIV

As much as I would love to make myself look like the definition of piety, I can't. All the research and study that goes into a project like this leads me instead to a mountain of conviction, where I see where I am supposed to be in relation to where I am. I am a young man who is still fighting the lust for more money and the perks that go with it—that's just real talk.

Although I coach in the NBA making a six-figure salary, I have days when I wonder if I am making the same kind of impact that I might be able to while coaching at a local high school for less money. My desire for money has led to a lot of nice stuff, but it has never given me a consistent peace in my heart, as all things of this world are not able to do. I really believe this is why God is charging us to seek wisdom before the "stuff," because wisdom will help us put all the "stuff" in its correct place.

Many of the Proverbs emphasize the value of wisdom. Proverbs 3:13-14 NIV says "*Blessed is the man who finds wisdom, the man who gains understanding, for she is more profitable than silver and yields better returns than gold.*" In Proverbs 8:10-11 MSG Wisdom is narrating and says to "*Prefer my life-disciplines over chasing after money, and God-knowledge over lucrative career. For Wisdom is better than all the trappings of wealth; nothing you could wish for holds a candle to her.*" Proverbs 16:16 says that the pursuit of wisdom trumps the pursuit of money, as opposed to what the culture teaches us. The fact that one out of every three state lottery winners ends up broke and filing for bankruptcy proves the point.

I find it fascinating that the Bible does not tell us to seek after what our culture tries to trick us into chasing: a bigger house, a higher-paying job, a better body, and in religious circles, things like anointing and spiritual gifts. The truth is, if we had more of God's wisdom, we would be better stewards of what we *do* have.

We cannot afford to be without God's wisdom.

We are warned in Proverbs 1:32 NIV that "*the waywardness of the simple will kill them.*" Notice the Bible does not say if you are wayward you will be late for work or make a few people upset. It says that this attribute will actually kill you. The Hebrew word for "simple" is *pethiy*, meaning "foolish." The *Webster's New World Dictionary* defines the word "fool" as a "silly or stupid person" and "a victim of a trick."

We cannot afford to be without God's wisdom. A deficiency in this area has caused countless divorces, business collapses, divided countries (check 1 Kings 12), group implosions, wars, dissension in companies, and more.

Former Senator and Secretary of State (1800s) Daniel Webster wrote:

> "If there is anything in my thoughts or style to commend, the credit is due to my parents for instilling in me an early love of the Scriptures. If we abide by the principles taught in the Bible, our country will go on prospering and to prosper; but if we and our posterity neglect its instructions and authority, no man can tell how sudden a catastrophe may overwhelm us and bury all our glory in profound obscurity."

He said it better than I could.

Day 4

"For the Lord gives wisdom, and from
his mouth come knowledge and understanding."

Proverbs 2:6, NIV

Today I want to list a few promises from the Bible that come with gaining and using the wisdom that only God can provide. If you have time in your day, look up a few of them and begin to claim them by faith. God says about His Word in Jeremiah 23:28 (NIV), *"Let the prophet who has a dream tell his dream, but let the one who has my word speak it faithfully."*

Here are some of God's promises about wisdom:

Proverbs 1:3	for discipline and an effective life
Proverbs 1:5	for understanding and knowledge
Proverbs 1:10	for perseverance when tempted
Proverbs 3:2	for long life and prosperity
Proverbs 3:8	health and vitality in your body
Proverbs 3:18	for blessings (God's Favor)
Proverbs 3:23	for stability wherever you are
Proverbs 3:24	for peaceful rest
Proverbs 3:35	to gain honor
Proverbs 4:6	for protection
Proverbs 4:8	to be exalted
Proverbs 5:2	to attain discretion
Proverbs 8:14	or sound judgment
Proverbs 8:35	or favor
Proverbs 9:11	or added years to your life
Proverbs 14:8	you contemplate your ways

Ecclesiastes 7:12	for shelter and preservation of life
Ecclesiastes 7:19	for power
Isaiah 33:6	a sure foundation/stability
James 3:17	bears spiritual fruit
1 Kings 3:13	riches and honor
Micah 6:9	helps you to respect the name of God

I know this was different from my other daily devotionals. But my hope is that in reading this list, you will see the importance of seeking God's wisdom and the rewards that come from attaining it for yourself. For instance, I never thought that wisdom could give you a good night's sleep, but Proverbs 3:24 says exactly that. I hope that by looking at these promises, you can come to a better understanding about the wisdom of God.

DAY 5

"For the Lord gives wisdom, and from
his mouth come knowledge and understanding."
PROVERBS 2:6, NIV

Deuteronomy 1:17 NIV says, *"Do not show partiality in judging; hear both small and great alike."* There is so much wisdom in this statement. The *Wiersbe Bible Commentary* adds, "Throughout the law of Moses, there's an emphasis on justice and showing kindness and fairness to the poor, widows, orphans, and aliens in the land."

For us, this wisdom is a reminder to never neglect the things that our culture and past traditions would categorize as small, whether dealing with others or with issues in our lives. The Song of Songs 2:15 NLT says, *"The little foxes are ruining the vineyards. Catch them, for the grapes are all in blossom."* The NIV translates the verse this way, *"Catch for us the little foxes, the little foxes that ruin the vineyards that are in the bloom."* The "little foxes", according to the *Wiersbe Bible Commentary*, "represent those things that quietly destroy relationships." I would also add that they (the little foxes) also destroy lives.

Today let's look at the life of Samson from the book of Judges, which presents an example to us of God's wisdom in paying attention to the small details in our lives. A closer examination of the life of this mighty man reveals a few cracks in his armor that could have been repented of. Instead, they went unchecked and led to an attitude of pride and complacency that cost him his life.

As a Nazarite, Samson was to abide by three specific laws found in Numbers 6. The first of these three laws was that Nazarites were not to have any wine or strong drink (like vinegar); not even grape juice or raisins were permitted. The second law was that they could not touch or go near a carcass or dead body—not even if it was a family member. And third, a Nazarite could not shave his head until the period of consecration to the Lord was over. In Judges 14:5&9, Samson violates two of these laws and puts himself in harm's way by approaching a vineyard and scooping honey out of a dead lion.

Remember, Romans 13:14 commands us to not make any provision for the *"flesh to fulfill its lusts."* This means anything that makes us violate or think about violating God's Law should be avoided. These two infringements foreshadowed what was to come. Samson believed that his hair and the length of it were the source of his great strength (Judges 16:17). We know this is not true, because God declared (Judges 13:5) that He raised Samson up to begin the deliverance of the Israelites from the Philistines. Later in the story, we see Samson, blind and captive, praying to God to restore his strength (proving that his strength was from God, even though his hair did grow back). God answers his prayer, and Samson was still able to do the will of God by destroying many Philistines: *"Thus he killed many more when he died than while he lived"* (Judges 16:30, NIV). One can only wonder about the destiny that was not fulfilled because our brother Samson did not follow God's wisdom and take care of what seemed to him small sins.

WE SHOULD NOT NEGLECT THE "LITTLE FOXES" IN OUR LIVES THAT CAN GROW INTO UNCONTROLLABLE, FULL GROWN WOLVES.

Zechariah 4:10 NIV says, *"Who despises the day of small things?"* Meaning, God loves everything that He has created from your eyelashes to your daydreams to short prayers like "Help!" I am using hyperbole for effect, but you get the point. We should not neglect the "little foxes" in our lives that can grow into uncontrollable, full grown wolves.

Imagine if Samson had grown the attitude of the psalmist in Psalm 88:1-2 NIV: *"O Lord, the God who saves me, day and night*

I cry out before you. May my prayer come before you; turn your ear to my cry." That is the kind of prayer, I believe, that moves the heart of God to guide and advise us by the Holy Spirit. This kind of prayer takes the focus off of us and our attributes (hair, personality, economic status, job title, etc.) and puts our affections at the feet of our Lord. I know that when you think of Samson, you automatically think of Delilah. But a closer look reveals that she was just a small part of his problem.

Get wisdom, brothers and sisters—God's wisdom.

"Be faithful in small things because it is in them that your strength lies." Mother Theresa

Day 6

"For the Lord gives wisdom, and from
his mouth come knowledge and understanding."
Proverbs 2:6, NIV

Rick Godwin, my mentor and spiritual father, gave me a pearl of wisdom about twelve years ago that relates to how I choose my friends. He told me repeatedly, "show me your friends and I will show you your future." That lesson lines up with perfectly with Psalm 1:1 NIV: "*How blessed is the man who does not walk in the counsel of the wicked....*" Proverbs 2:12 NIV says, "*Wisdom will save you from the ways of wicked men.*"

Today I would like to take a quick peek at a man named Ittai and his decision to befriend and remain loyal to King David. At the time of this story, David is fugitive king; his son Absalom has rebelled and overthrown his father. Ittai, a Philistine from Gath, says to David: "*As surely as the LORD lives, and as my lord the king lives, wherever my lord the king may be, whether it means life or death, there will your servant be...*" (2 Samuel 15:2, NIV)

This is remarkable loyalty for a man who had only joined forces with his king the day before, as 2 Samuel 15:20 points out. I would love to have Ittai as a teammate. This is also amazing dedication considering David's previous situation in Gath; 1 Samuel 21:10-15 shows David acting like a lunatic when he was there. There is no doubt that Ittai at least heard about this scene.

So what was the result of Ittai's devotion to David? Look at 2 Samuel 23:29. Ittai is listed as one of a small group of men who were forever memorialized as David's bravest warriors. These men, thirty-two in all, helped David to regain his rightful throne as king.

You and I must be prayerful in all of our decisions, letting God's wisdom lead us as we choose our relationships. This is contrary to conventional wisdom, which teaches us to be led by our hearts. Unfortunately, many of us have broken hearts or hearts that have many scars from shame and rejection, which can lead to emotional decisions that are based on superficial/fleshly desires.

We know that wisdom is knowledge guided by understanding (check out Day 1 of this week). Proverbs 2:6 says that God's wisdom has so many benefits: protection, sound judgment, a solid foundation, riches, honor, peace, and many more. And in Ittai's case, the perk was an alliance with a king that had a heart comparable to God's.

Day 7

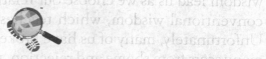

"For the Lord gives wisdom, and from
his mouth come knowledge and understanding."

Proverbs 2:6, NIV

You might think to yourself, "I am a relatively smart person; I have a college degree," or "I have always been smarter than most of the people I am around." That kind of thinking, as it relates to Proverbs 2:6, is prideful. It shows confidence in "self" instead of God. I am not devaluing a high school education, a college degree, or graduate studies. But I am making an attempt to put education in its proper place. C. S. Lewis said that "Education without values, as useful as it is, seems rather to make a man a more clever devil."

Proverbs 2:6 says that wisdom, which is knowledge guided by understanding, can only come from God. James 1:5 NIV says, "*If any of you lacks wisdom, he should ask God, who gives generously to all without finding fault, and it will be given to him.*" This is exactly what Solomon did when he became king somewhere between 15 and 19 years old (according to the *Wiersbe Bible Commentary* on 1 Kings 2). 1 Kings 3:9 says that he asked for a discerning heart to rule over the people justly. This discernment is something that cannot be attained through an institutionalized education.

Solomon's request reveals the level of trust that he had in his God (and probably, a little fear, too... hey, he was a teenager!), as he no doubt had watched his father David live a life of prayer and petition to El De'ot, the God of Knowledge. Notice, Solomon did not say "Help me to rule these people based on my sheepskin from So and So State," or "Because I was first in my class, I know that you will grant me success in my endeavors."

There is an old saying about putting the cart before the horse. In this case, wisdom must be given to us from God before we set out on any task, no matter what we think of ourselves. I believe that when we submit our human attributes, the ones given to us by God, to His will and seek His wisdom, it symbolizes how much we trust in His guidance over our lives. Submitting ourselves to God in this way will set us up for blessings that far exceed anything that we could ask for or imagine. Just check out 1 Kings 2:28; Solomon asked for wisdom and God gave it to him—along with tremendous riches and honor.

> WISDOM MUST BE GIVEN TO US FROM GOD BEFORE WE SET OUT ON ANY TASK, NO MATTER WHAT WE THINK OF OURSELVES.

Whatever situation you find yourself in, make sure that you pursue God and plead with Him for His guidance. Not seeking God for His wisdom is a sign of pride. Remember what Psalm 10:4 NIV says: "*In his pride the wicked does seek him; in all his thoughts there is no room for God.*"

WEEK 13

"Trust in the Lord with all your heart; do not depend on your own understanding. Seek his will in all you do, and he will direct your paths."

PROVERBS 3:5, NLT

DAY 1

"Trust in the Lord with all your heart; do not depend on your own understanding. Seek his will in all you do, and he will direct your paths."
PROVERBS 3:5, NLT

This verse is talking about a total commitment to God and His plan for our lives—right now and in the future. The Greek word for trust is *elpidzo* meaning "to put our hope in." But in *what*? We know that the world's ways have already failed us. That leaves us with no alternative but to place our hope in the One who should have had our affections in the first place: God.

What do you think of when the Bible tells you to trust in God? Are you one of those people who believes that you have to trust God only for the one or two prayer requests you have each week? Are you the type that thinks you only need to trust God to help you keep your job and help you get a nice bonus before Christmas? Maybe you're the kind of person who believes that trusting God means that you can have a deeper relationship with Him later in life when you have more time, because He will be there waiting whenever you are ready?

These are questions that I honestly thought I would never struggle with. God has done so many miraculous things in my life that I figured I would never have an issue trusting Him. But the storms of life have a way of taking my focus off of God and placing it square on the "world." This focus shift displays itself in the doomsday talk about the economy or how our kids will never be able to survive the next 100 years because the world is in such a bad state and Social Security will be gone.

The truth is that since the fall of Adam, life on earth has always had consequences that cause our knees to shake and our bottom lip to drop passed our waist because it, "the world," is not designed for us to trust in it. We are always going to see things that will make us think that God is not in control, things that make us blame Him for what is going on in this global rat race.

Jesus said in John 16:33 NAS, "*In the world you will have tribulation…*" This means that any system that is contrary to God's way will always be against us and try to harm us—believer and non-believer alike. But listen to the rest of John 16:33: "*…but take courage; I have overcome the world.*" The *MacArthur Study Bible* says "Christ's victory has already accomplished a smashing defeat of the whole evil rebellious system." We win, but we must trust what God has already done and is doing in the life of His people.

So what does this trust look like for us? In reference to one of the most famous "trust" passages in the Bible (Proverbs 3:5-6), The *Wiersbe Bible Commentary* says "It pictures a servant waiting for the master's command in readiness to obey, or a defeated soldier yielding himself to the conquering general."

This kind of trust means that when we believe for a healing in our bodies, we know that doctors are gifted and are doing the best they can, but our confidence is in the promises of healing that come from Jehovah-Rapha, The Lord Our Healer.

It means that when we are walking in abundance, we recognize that "*every good and perfect gift is from above*" (James 1:17, NIV).

It means that after we have done the best we know how to do and nothing seems to work, we have to believe in 1 Corinthians 16:13 NIV, which says, "*Be on guard; stand firm in the faith; be men of courage; be strong.*"

It means that every breath we take, all our decisions, our families, our careers, our country, and anything that we hold dear, must be put totally in God's Care totally.

What does trust mean to you?

What in your life have you not entrusted to God?

Has a trust been violated by a loved one that is causing you not to trust God fully?

DAY 2

"Trust in the Lord with all your heart; do not depend
on your own understanding. Seek his will in all
you do, and he will direct your paths."

PROVERBS 3:5, NLT

Trusting God with our lives is a heavy undertaking considering that most of us want to feel like we are in control of every situation—especially men. I mean, let's be honest. There are some things that we are supposed to be in control of, like the management of our time, money, our words, our whereabouts, our work ethics, and so on. But we become control freaks when we allow anything outside of God's Word to govern the management of what we have in our possession.

> WE BECOME CONTROL FREAKS WHEN WE ALLOW ANYTHING OUTSIDE OF GOD'S WORD TO GOVERN THE MANAGEMENT OF WHAT WE HAVE IN OUR POSSESSION.

For example, take average two-year-olds. They feel like they can do whatever they want all by themselves. You try to help them color a picture and they will snatch the crayon away so they can do it themselves. If you try to feed them, they will push you away and smash food in every place but their mouths. But, they are in control; thus, they are happy. Most two-year-olds are gods unto themselves with no regard for a higher authority because, in their eyes, they don't need one.

Often we act just like two-year-olds when we mismanage the things that God has placed in our care. Take finances, for an easy example. I was blown away when I started tithing because I thought I had missed out on a huge blessing. For a long time I had acted in disobedience to Malachi 3:10 NIV, which says, "*Bring the whole tithe into the storehouse, that there may be food in my house.*" I soon found out that 15% of the Church accounts for 85% of the financial giving in the body. I thought to myself, how do any churches stay open? And then I realized that we do not trust God with our money and the purpose He has for it. When we tithe, we are saying that we believe God has a plan and a purpose in giving us a stake in the advancement of the Kingdom. We are also saying that God can do more in our lives with 90% than we could ever do with a 100%. But we have to trust Him.

Another issue we have trouble with in the body is effectively sharing the love of God when leading others to Christ and allowing them to grow in God's timing. I must admit that I have failed miserably in this area because I wanted someone to grow at the same pace I was growing. In the end, I think I did more harm than I helped. The problem was that I did not trust the work of the Holy Spirit to bring the increase. I felt that I had to control the situation and maybe get the credit for someone getting "saved." Paul clearly states in 1 Corinthians 3:6-7 NIV that "*My job was to plant the seed in your hearts, and Apollos watered it, but it was God, not we, who made it grow. The ones who do the planting or watering aren't important, but God is important because he is the one who makes the seed grow.*"

This is also a trust issue for believers; if we don't see the type of results we are looking for, we quickly conclude that our brother or sister did not make a total commitment to Christ. But Romans 2:4 GW says "*Don't you realize that it is God's kindness that is trying to lead you to him and change the way you think and act?*" In the end, we try to fix them our way, but what we usually do is condemn them. They sometimes walk away confused; often times they turn to another religion or away from religion altogether. In Matthew 4:19 NIV, Jesus said, *"Come, follow me and I will make you fishers of men."* It's important to note that we must continue to follow Him, which is another way of saying that we must trust Him. He said that He would make us "fishers of men;" He never said anything about us cleaning and cooking the fish. That's His job!

There's a verse from Proverbs that I think will bring this point home. The result from obeying this command will hopefully give you some encouragement. In Proverbs 16:20 NLT, Solomon says *"Those who listen to instruction will prosper; those who trust the Lord will be happy."*

DAY 3

"Trust in the Lord with all your heart; do not depend on your own understanding. Seek his will in all you do, and he will direct your paths."

PROVERBS 3:5, NLT

Today, let's take a look at some different translations of Proverbs 3:5.

Trust in the LORD with all your heart, and do not rely on your own understanding. GW

Put all you hope in God, not looking to your reason for support. BBE

Have confidence in the Lord with all thy heart, and lean not upon thy own prudence. D-R

Confide in Jehovah with all thy heart, and lean not unto thine own intelligence. DBY

Trust unto Jehovah with all thy heart, And unto thine own understanding lean not. YLT

Lean on, trust in, and be confident in the Lord with all your heart and mind and do not rely on your own insight or understanding. (AMP)

Trust God from the bottom of your heart; don't try to figure out everything on your own. MSG

Trust in the Lord with all your heart, and do not trust in your own understanding. NLV

With all your heart you must trust the Lord and not your own judgment. CEV

I pray that the Holy Spirit would imprint this verse on your heart so that you can apply it to your life and have a more intimate relationship with our Heavenly Father.

Day 4

"Trust in the Lord with all your heart; do not depend on your own understanding. Seek his will in all you do, and he will direct your paths."

Proverbs 3:5, NLT

Today I want to talk about trusting God to lead us into proper relationships that will help us grow and keep us from the disasters that await us when we choose to make associations based on shallow motives.

Proverbs 19:4 NIV says, "*Wealth brings many friends*." In the early years of my adulthood, I had a lot of people wanting to be my "friend" because I was, in the world's eyes, an attractive commodity. I was a first round pick in the NBA, I lived in New York, and I had (I thought) a lot of money. Unfortunately, I was also pretty flimsy in my stance as Christian, especially around my so-called friends. To be honest, I cannot say that I had one person in my life at the time that I would consider a mentor (that I would listen to, anyway). My best friend, Charlie Ward, was my brother in Christ, but we were both growing together (though I thank God for his example). This weak stance as a believer was beginning to show up in areas of my life that were very vital, but I had no idea how to correct the issues that were causing me and the people I loved pain. I did not totally trust God, my marriage was a wreck, my career was going nowhere, and to top it off, I was traded to another team before the end of my second season in the NBA. You would have never known this because I had all the appearances of a good life. I had popularity, money, and really cool people who wanted to hang around me, but I was lost—and I was a guy who was "born again." A few years earlier, I had been healed of a fatal heart disease. Even after that, I still did not totally trust God.

Ingrid and I found ourselves in San Antonio to begin a new chapter. The first thing we did after finding a home was find a home church. We went to Cornerstone, where Pastor John Hagee leads a congregation of over 15,000 people. It was a lovely church and we would have stayed there, but my mother-in-law told us about a church called Eagles Nest Christian Fellowship and their pastor Rick Godwin. She said we should go there before we got settled somewhere. So we went to ENCF (now Summit Christian Center) and we fell in love with the place, the music, the fellowship, and the messages preached. I had never had a church experience like that before. Every message seemed to be aimed at "convicting Monty" and getting my attention.

But all that being said, I still did not have much of a mentor to guide me and help me apply the Word in my life properly. Then one Sunday I met Dr. Wayne Gordon (a die-hard Spurs fan), and we hit it off right away. He thought that I should meet Rick, so he introduced us.

At first I was a little hesitant to get close to a pastor, but Rick was different. I thought that he would ask me for money and tickets to the Spurs games; he never did. In fact, he and his wife Cindy became our spiritual covering, and we have never been the same. As I began to learn how to trust God with my life, the wisdom that Rick poured into me became food for every area that was in need of nourishment. I began to learn more about Christ-centered living, like biblical manhood, serving those who can't pay you back, tithing, and advancing the Kingdom, studying the Word and applying it, fulfilling my destiny, and many other critical points for maturing believers.

As I began to trust both God and Rick, others began to pour into my life, too—like Randy and Sandy Ross, whose marriage class saved my relationship with Ingrid. Dr. Gordon spent countless hours with me on the golf course. He never lectured me, but his example of godly manhood impacted me in ways that he will never know.

The point is this: had I not trusted God with my life, I would have never let myself get close to these people at ENCF. I'm from P.G. County, Maryland; where I'm from you don't trust anybody outside of your family. The violence that I saw as a kid and the masks that I put on to survive in some of those environments would not allow God to have His way in my life. I became what I thought I should look like… but it was not what God had planned for before I was formed in my mother's womb.

> Take a good look at the people that God has placed in your life.

As my life started to unravel, I realized that I had no choice but to give a God a shot. The funny thing is that as I began to trust God, the differences that I had with Rick and the ENCF family were nonexistent because I wanted what they all had: peace with God, a healthy marriage, biblical knowledge, a place to call home, and the desire to be used by God for His purposes.

What this means to you, I don't know. But I encourage you to take a good look at the people that God has placed in your life. They may not have been your first choice as associates. You may have nothing in common with them. But those differences can become the bridge to your destiny when you trust God with your future. Our Lord and Redeemer was a carpenter and He mentored a tax collector, fishermen, a wealthy physician, a political activist and many others who were so very different from Himself. Those guys changed the world.

Listen to Psalm 146:3-4 NIV: *"Do not put your trust in princes [those who have limited power], in mortal men, who cannot save. When their spirit departs, they return to the ground…"* Put your trust in Jehovah-Shammah, The Lord Who Is There, the best friend you will ever have.

Day 5

"Trust in the Lord with all your heart; do not depend on your own understanding. Seek his will in all you do, and he will direct your paths."
Proverbs 3:5, NLT

Today, I thought that we would take a look at an excerpt from *Matthew Henry's Commentary of the Whole Bible*. I have found that commentaries are a great tool to help us understand the context of a particular passage, and they are great for digging a little deeper into the "scripts" so we can understand the Word.

In reference to Proverbs 3:5, the *MHCWB* says, "…we must believe that he is able to do what he will, wise to do what is best, and good, according to his promise, to do what is best for us, if we love him, and serve." I found that statement profound in that it combines a few of God's attributes with how we can take part in His goodness if we obey His commands. The first part talks about His power when it says "he is able to do what he will," which relates to God's name Elohim, The All-Powerful One. Then the *MHCWB* says he is "wise to what is best" for us, like His name Jehovah-Rohi, The Lord is my Shepherd.

I think the most important part of this quote from the *MHCWB* is how it relates to us and what we should do. It begins with "we must believe he is able" and ends in "if we love him, and serve." Why is this the most important part? Because, these are things that we are able to do.

As an assistant coach, part of my job is to prepare guys with drills, scouting reports, film study, morale support, and other things. But I am only to assist my boss, the head coach. The head coach serves as an analogy for God, in a way. He controls the minutes, who plays, what plays are to be run, when we practice, when we leave for trips, and other things. But the one talent that I have seen in the great coaches that I have been around is that they never ask someone to do something that they can't do. As a matter of fact, some coaches have taken this a step further and have come up with creeds to emphasis this very point, like, "Do what you do" and "Stay within yourself." If a guy is trying to do too much, a coach might say "Hey—we don't need you to swing for the fences; just get on base!" (Which is another way of saying, just do your job and let the top guns make the big plays; this was usually for a role player like myself.)

GOD WILL NOT TEMPT US TO DO SOMETHING THAT WE ARE NOT ABLE TO DO.

God is doing this same thing in Proverbs 3:5 by commanding us to do what we are able to do. We are all able to trust in Him and not ourselves. By doing this, we allow Him to "swing for the fences" because He is the Top Gun (Adonai, My Great Lord).

1 Corinthians 10:1 NIV says that "*God is faithful; he will not let you be tempted beyond what you can bear. But when you are tempted, he will also provide a way out so that you can stand up under it.*" I know that some think this only pertains to God not tempting us with things like sex, drugs, lusting for money and other "big sins." But I think it also drives home the point that God will not tempt us to do something that we are not able to do. Like the last part of this verse says, He "*will also provide a way out.*"

I believe this means that when we do get into trouble with the sins of this world or when we step outside of ourselves and try to do what we are not capable of, God is always there to cover us. Nothing can happen to us without Him knowing about it. Look at Psalm 139:7-12 NLT where King David says "*I can never escape from your Spirit! I can never get away from your presence!*

If I go up to heaven, you are there; if I go down to the grave, you are there. If I ride the wings of the morning, if I dwell by the farthest oceans, even there your hand will guide me, and your strength will support me. I could ask the darkness to hide me and the light around me to become night—but even in darkness I cannot hide from you. To you the night shines as bright as day. Darkness and light are the same to you."

Trusting God is not easy in the climate we live in, but it is the only way, and we are able to do it.

Day 6

"Trust in the Lord with all your heart; do not depend on your own understanding. Seek his will in all you do, and he will direct your paths."

Proverbs 3:5, NLT

I wish that I had the wisdom of Solomon (I'm praying for it!), the courage of David, the selflessness of Andrew the disciple, the passion for truth of John the disciple, the presence of Martin Luther King Jr. or Tony Dungy, the charisma of Michael Jordan, the tirelessness of Mother Theresa, and a willingness to love the unlovable like Pat and B.J. Magley. I wish I knew Scripture like John MacArthur, Rick Godwin, Sandy Ross, and Bishop T.D. Jakes. I would love to reach the nations like Reinhard Bonnke, Billy Graham, and Luis Palau. But guess what? I don't possess many, if any, of those characteristics. To be honest, I am a pretty boring dude most days; I just happen to have a pretty exciting job (coaching in the NBA).

When I was younger, things were a little different. My parents divorced when I was 8 and I lived with my grandparents for a couple of years in the countryside of Fredericksburg, Virginia. Life was pretty laid back there. When the two years were up, I moved to P.G. County, Maryland (on the southeast side of Washington D.C.). Life was a lot different there from what it had been in Virginia. I was always a pretty good athlete, so I fit in well on the court or the field. Where I didn't fit was on the way home on the bus. I was constantly picked on about my clothing and the way I talked. Most days I got my butt whipped; then I learned how to defend myself. I was getting bigger and that led me into some pretty stupid altercations.

As I began to grow in my walk with the Lord, I realized that the senseless fighting did not go well with sharing the love of Jesus Christ. Man, was I ever tested in this area! One particular incident happened at Georgetown University, a place where a lot of NBA players would go to get some good runs in with top competition. Most days came and went with no altercations. On this particular day, I got into it with a pretty big dude—but that didn't scare me. What *did* scare me was that I knew I had to walk away. The consequences, teasing from other men, were more than I wanted to deal with.

But I walked away.

And guess what happened? I got teased. In fact, a guy who was in the gym that day became a teammate of mine later in my career; he teased me about that day for a while.

The truth is, I have been in some bad fights over some very dumb stuff. Those kinds of fights have no winner, just losers. If you have been one, you know I am telling the truth. That summer at Georgetown, I won because I trusted in the fact that I was doing what was pleasing to God, which went against my old nature. Check out Isaiah 26:3 NIV: *"You will keep in perfect peace him whose mind is steadfast, because he trusts in you."*

Trusting God, no matter what the situation, leads to *"perfect peace."*

DAY 7

"Trust in the Lord with all your heart; do not depend on your own understanding. Seek his will in all you do, and he will direct your paths."

PROVERBS 3:5, NLT

This week I talked about some people with attributes and gifting that have made them recognizable to the world. You probably have your own list of people with a talent level that makes you envy them. If you read *People* magazine or watch any of the "Rich and Famous" shows, it can make you want to live in the limelight with those people.

Over the years I have been around some of the wealthiest and most talented people in the world. I have learned from that to never compare myself to them based on the world's standards. Comparisons do two things: they make you feel inferior or they make you feel superior; there is no in-between. Thank God that He is able to take bitter, sour, sometimes rotten lemons and make amazing lemonade. 1 Corinthians 1:25 NIV says, "*For the foolishness of God is wiser than man's wisdom, and the weakness of God is stronger than man's strength.*"

Look at the life of Abraham. God called him His friend in Isaiah 41:8. In Scripture, Abraham is the only person designated as a type of God the Father, as his son Isaac is a type of Christ. Abraham is one of the few listed in the "Hall of Faith" in Hebrews 11, along with Noah, Enoch, Isaac, Jacob, Joseph, Moses, Rahab, and several others. Genesis 12:3 says that all nations of the earth will be blessed through Abraham; this promise can also be found in Galatians 3:8. If you were preparing for a sporting event and your opponent had a scouting report like Abraham's, you would be in for a long night. Look at what God said about Abraham in Genesis 18:19 NIV: *"For I have chosen him, so that he will direct his children and his household after him to keep the way of the Lord by doing what is right and just..."*

"What's your point, Monty?" The point is that none of this would have happened if Abram would have refused to trust God. By trusting God, Abram left what was known as the city of Ur and followed God into the unknown: his future and ours. Romans 4:3 NIV says, *"Abraham believed God, and it was credited to him as righteousness."* Genesis 15:6 says the same. We can safely say that Abraham trusted God and that gave him right-standing with Jehovah.

Why is this crucial? Well, Abraham and the people of his time did not have the perfect atoning blood of Jesus, by which we are justified. Abraham received his justification by trusting God.

Because he trusted God, the Abrahamic Covenant was established, providing blessing in three areas: national, personal, and universal. The Bible says that he would be the father of a great nation, that he would be blessed, and that the families of the world would be blessed through him. What's extraordinary is that Abraham never spoke a word of prophecy, never wrote a book, a song, or a law. He was just a normal nomadic dude who trusted God. God did not need him to be a tall, dark, handsome, eloquent of speech, 007-type. He just needed Abraham to be available and to trust Him.

As a closing thought, look at Jeremiah 17:7-8 NLT: *"But blessed are those who trust in the Lord and have made the Lord their hope and confidence. They are like trees planted along a riverbank, with roots that reach deep into the water. Such trees are not bothered by the heat or worried by the long months of drought."*

Blessings.

Week 14

"For the Word that God speaks is alive and full of power
[making it active, operative, energizing, and effective];
it is sharper than any two-edged sword, penetrating to
the dividing line of the breath of life [soul]
and [the immortal] spirit, and of joints and marrow
[of the deepest parts of our nature], exposing and
sifting and analyzing and judging the very
thoughts and purposes of the heart."

Hebrews 4:12, AMP

DAY 1

"For the Word that God speaks is alive and full of power [making it active, operative, energizing, and effective]; it is sharper than any two-edged sword, penetrating to the dividing line of the breath of life [soul] and [the immortal] spirit, and of joints and marrow [of the deepest parts of our nature], exposing and sifting and analyzing and judging the very thoughts and purposes of the heart."

HEBREWS 4:12, AMP

"For the word of God is quick, and powerful, and sharper than any two-edged sword, piercing even to the dividing asunder of soul and spirit, and of the joints and marrow, and is a discerner of the thoughts and intents of the heart." KJV

All Scripture is great and edifying to the soul, but this week's verse is one of my favorites. It confirms the credibility of my faith. It is the reason I so intently study the Word of God. Today we are going to look at several different translations of the first segment of this verse. I believe they will come alive to you.

"For the word of God is living and active." ASV

"For living is the word of God, and energetic." REB

"For the word of God is full of life and power." WEY

"For the word of God is living, and effectual." ABUV

"For the logos of God is a living thing, active." MOF

"For God's message is alive and full of power in action." WMS

"For the word that God speaks is alive and active." Phi

"For whatever God says to us is full of living power." TLB

These eight translations profess one thing clearly: God's Word is alive. His words bring life. They have a creative quality like nothing else. His Word can actively change our lives when we speak them. Say what He says. Speak the Word of God in any situation and it brings life. As Christian speaker Gloria Copeland writes:

> "Determine in your heart that God's Word is to your advantage and that you will act on His Word in faith, knowing that He is the God of love. The Word will only become alive to you as you accept it as truth and act upon it. Fearlessly commit yourself to the authority of God's Word. Make up your mind to walk by faith, and not by sight. Be ready to act on God's Word, even when common sense says do something else. Common means ordinary. God's Word gets you out of the ordinary and puts you into the supernatural realm of God's power!"

THESE EIGHT TRANSLATIONS PROFESS ONE THING CLEARLY: GOD'S WORD IS ALIVE.

God's Word is inextinguishable! It cannot be stopped. It is irrepressible, unquenchable, indestructible, undying, immortal, imperishable, unfailing, unceasing, enduring, everlasting, eternal, and persistent.

Day 2

"For the Word that God speaks is alive and full of power
[making it active, operative, energizing, and effective];
it is sharper than any two-edged sword, penetrating to
the dividing line of the breath of life [soul]
and [the immortal] spirit, and of joints and marrow
[of the deepest parts of our nature], exposing and
sifting and analyzing and judging the very
thoughts and purposes of the heart."

Hebrews 4:12, AMP

The Words that God speaks—especially from the pulpit on a Sunday morning—after a night out partying or after a big fight with your spouse are sure to be alive and active, piercing, discerning all your intentions and thoughts. Sometimes the preacher seems to have a direct line to God that includes a personal voicemail just for you. Only the awesome, omnipotent God is capable of knowing those hidden sins. His Words spoken can generate an immediate change. His spoken Word is very accurate and potent.

Amazingly, God's corrections make you feel more loved.

I am thankful God chooses to correct us privately (as a Father would), pulling us aside and gently—yet firmly—conveying the need for change. Amazingly, God's corrections make you feel more loved. The way He disciplines does not cause shame or embarrassment. He chooses not to condemn us and make a public display of our sin. Jesus Christ did that for us!

> *"Therefore, there is now no condemnation for those who are in Christ Jesus, because through Christ Jesus the law of the*

Spirit of life sets us free from the law of sin and death. For what the law was powerless to do, in that it was weakened by the sinful nature, God did by sending his own Son in the likeness of sinful man to be a sin offering. And so he condemned sin in sinful man, in order that the righteous requirements of the law might be fully met in us, who do not live according to the sinful nature but according to the Spirit.

Those who live according to the sinful nature have their minds set on what that nature desires; but those who live in accordance with the Spirit have their minds set on what the Spirit desires. The mind of sinful man is death, but the mind controlled by the Spirit is life and peace; the sinful mind is hostile to God. It does not submit to God's law, nor can it do so. Those controlled by the sinful nature cannot please God.

You, however, are controlled not by the sinful nature but by the Spirit, if the Spirit of God lives in you. And if anyone does not have the Spirit of Christ, he does not belong to Christ. But if Christ is in you, your body is dead because of sin, yet your spirit is alive because of righteousness. And if the Spirit of him who raised Jesus from the dead is living in you, he who raised Christ from the dead will also give life to your mortal bodies through his Spirit, who lives in you.

Therefore, brothers, we have an obligation—but it is not to the sinful nature, to live according to it. For if you live according to the sinful nature, you will die; but if by the Spirit you put to death the misdeeds of the body, you will live, because those who are led by the Spirit of God are sons of God. For you did not receive a spirit that makes you a slave again to fear, but you received the spirit of sonship. And by him we cry, "Abba, Father." The Spirit himself testifies with our spirit that we are God's children." (Romans 8:1-16, NIV)

Day 3

"For the Word that God speaks is alive and full of power [making it active, operative, energizing, and effective]; it is sharper than any two-edged sword, penetrating to the dividing line of the breath of life [soul] and [the immortal] spirit, and of joints and marrow [of the deepest parts of our nature], exposing and sifting and analyzing and judging the very thoughts and purposes of the heart."

Hebrews 4:12, AMP

"Faith comes from hearing the message, and the message is heard through the word of Christ." (Romans 10:17, NIV)

Faith comes by hearing the Word of God. Our faith is established by the spoken Word. When our faith is developed, we know the will of God because the will of God is the Word of God. If we know His will, our prayers are more effective. We will know how to prayerfully intercede for others and how to pray for ourselves. Our vocabulary will be directed by His Word. His Word + His Will = a successful and productive life.

The Lord says in Isaiah 55:10-11 AMP: *"For as the rain and snow come down from the heavens, and return not there again, but water the earth and make it bring forth and sprout, that it may give seed to the sower and bread to the eater, so shall My word be that goes forth out of My mouth: it shall not return to Me void [without producing any effect, useless], but it shall accomplish that which I please and purpose, and it shall prosper in the thing for which I sent it."* God's Word will not fail. Joshua 1:8 reminds us to keep the Word in our mouth, meditating on it day and night; pondering its precepts daily. God says our way will be prosperous and we will deal wisely and be successful if we obey this command.

I cannot stress enough the significance of the spoken Word of God as a productive tool for our lives as Christians. Faith grows by hearing His Word. As we mature, we become more like Him. Apopular saying that comes to mind is: "Association brings assimilation." In this case, I desire this principle to be true. His Word takes out the natural tendencies and inclinations and replaces the sinful nature with His nature. His Word is the only tool capable of piercing through to the dividing line of the spirit and soul, sifting and analyzing the thoughts and intents of a person. We are transformed by His Word.

Day 4

"For the Word that God speaks is alive and full of power [making it active, operative, energizing, and effective]; it is sharper than any two-edged sword, penetrating to the dividing line of the breath of life [soul] and [the immortal] spirit, and of joints and marrow [of the deepest parts of our nature], exposing and sifting and analyzing and judging the very thoughts and purposes of the heart."

Hebrews 4:12, AMP

Let's reflect upon the statement that God's spoken Word is a discerner of our thoughts and hearts. *The American Dictionary of the English Language Noah Webster 1828* defines "discerner" as: "One who sees, discovers or distinguishes; an observer. One who knows and judges; one who has the power of distinguishing. That which distinguishes; or that which causes to understand." Only God is able to distinguish our thoughts and the conditions of our heart. He is able to judge our very intentions. Our best form of response to God when His Word convicts us is humility.

David from the Old Testament was a great example. The book of Psalms is filled with his passion for righteousness. He insists that there is absolutely no way to hide from God. We may be able to mask our feelings and intentions from others, but not from God.

> *"O LORD, you have searched me and you know me. You know when I sit and when I rise; you perceive my thoughts from afar. You discern my going out and my lying down; you are familiar with all my ways. Before a word is on my tongue you know it completely, O LORD. You hem me in—behind and before; you have laid your hand upon me. Such knowledge is too wonderful for me, too lofty for me to attain."* (Psalm 139:1-6, NIV)

If we humble ourselves before God, He is quick to forgive and always desires to see us prosper: "*If my people, who are called by my name, will humble themselves and pray and seek my face and turn from their wicked ways, then will I hear from heaven and will forgive their sin and will heal their land*" (2 Chronicles 7:14, NIV). By His Word we are made perfect and complete.

By His Word we are made perfect and complete.

Receive the wholeness God has for you. Take time today to examine your heart. Listen to the quiet promptings you receive from His Word. Allow God to change your life.

> "*But he who keeps (treasures) His Word [who bears in mind His precepts, who observes His message in its entirety], truly in him has the love of and for God been perfected (completed, reached maturity). By this we may perceive (know, recognize, and be sure) that we are in Him*" 1 John 2:5, AMP

> "*You have commanded us to keep Your precepts, that we should observe them diligently. Oh, that my ways were directed and established to observe Your statutes [hearing, receiving, loving, and obeying them]!*"
> Psalm 119:4-5, AMP

DAY 5

"For the Word that God speaks is alive and full of power [making it active, operative, energizing, and effective]; it is sharper than any two-edged sword, penetrating to the dividing line of the breath of life [soul] and [the immortal] spirit, and of joints and marrow [of the deepest parts of our nature], exposing and sifting and analyzing and judging the very thoughts and purposes of the heart."

HEBREWS 4:12, AMP

The Ten Commandments are a great example of God's spoken Word being alive and active, powerful and sharper than any two-edged sword, piercing to the dividing asunder of the soul and breath of life, discerning thoughts and intents. As recorded in Exodus 20:1-17 NIV, Moses is given commandments for God's people:

And God spoke all these words: "I am the LORD your God, who brought you out of Egypt, out of the land of slavery.

"You shall have no other gods before me.

"You shall not make for yourself an idol in the form of anything in heaven above or on the earth beneath or in the waters below. You shall not bow down to them or worship them; for I, the LORD your God, am a jealous God, punishing the children for the sin of the fathers to the third and fourth generation of those who hate me, but showing love to a thousand generations of those who love me and keep my commandments.

"You shall not misuse the name of the LORD your God, for the LORD will not hold anyone guiltless who misuses his name.

"Remember the Sabbath day by keeping it holy. Six days you shall labor and do all your work, but the seventh day is a Sabbath to the LORD your God. On it you shall not do any work, neither you, nor your son or daughter, nor your manservant or maidservant, nor your animals, nor the alien within your gates. For in six days the LORD made the heavens and the earth, the sea, and all that is in them, but he rested on the seventh day. Therefore the LORD blessed the Sabbath day and made it holy.

"Honor your father and your mother, so that you may live long in the land the LORD your God is giving you.

"You shall not murder.

"You shall not commit adultery.

"You shall not steal. "You shall not give false testimony against your neighbor.

"You shall not covet your neighbor's house. You shall not covet your neighbor's wife, or his manservant or maidservant, his ox or donkey, or anything that belongs to your neighbor."

These ten words have shaped the world.

The Hebrew term for Ten Commandments literally means "ten words." These ten words have shaped the world. The words that God has spoken—the Ten Commandments—have become the benchmark for the world's standard of right and wrong. AMAZING!

DAY 6

"For the Word that God speaks is alive and full of power [making it active, operative, energizing, and effective]; it is sharper than any two-edged sword, penetrating to the dividing line of the breath of life [soul] and [the immortal] spirit, and of joints and marrow [of the deepest parts of our nature], exposing and sifting and analyzing and judging the very thoughts and purposes of the heart."

HEBREWS 4:12, AMP

Throughout the Bible, God refers to the state of the heart. God's intent in this week's Scripture is to use His spoken Word to evoke change in our hearts.

The heart is the birthplace of our emotions, will, and intellect. Therefore, it is most vulnerable. Proverbs 4:23 NIV says, "*Above all else, guard your heart, for it is the wellspring of life.*" Guarding your heart requires closely monitoring, even censoring what it is exposed to. Guarding our hearts means being cognizant of the relationships in which we engage.

Choose good and positive influences within your environment. God's Word is a great influence. Direction and wisdom come from the Word of God. When we seek Him first, our life is productive. As we allow God to work on our hearts, we become more effective in winning people to Christ.

"The poor and afflicted shall eat and be satisfied; they shall praise the Lord–they who [diligently] seek for, inquire of and for Him, and require

Him [as their greatest need]. May your hearts be quickened now and forever!" Psalm 22:26, AMP

"The humble shall see it and be glad; you who seek God, inquiring for and requiring Him [as your first need], let your hearts revive and live!" Psalm 69:32, AMP

"Do you not know that your body is the temple (the very sanctuary) of the Holy Spirit Who lives within you, Whom you have received [as a Gift] from God? You are not your own, You were bought with a price [purchased with a preciousness and paid for, made His own]. So then, honor God and bring glory to Him in your body." 1 Corinthians 6:19-20, AMP

"All who keep His commandments [who obey His orders and follow His plan, live and continue to live, to stay and] abide in Him, and He in them. [They let Christ be a home to them and they are the home of Christ.] And by this we know and understand and have the proof that He [really] lives and makes His home in us: by the [Holy] Spirit Whom He has given us." 1 John 3:24, AMP

DAY 7

"For the Word that God speaks is alive and full of power [making it active, operative, energizing, and effective]; it is sharper than any two-edged sword, penetrating to the dividing line of the breath of life [soul] and [the immortal] spirit, and of joints and marrow [of the deepest parts of our nature], exposing and sifting and analyzing and judging the very thoughts and purposes of the heart."

HEBREWS 4:12, AMP

"But this is the covenant which I will make with the house of Israel: After those days, says the Lord, I will put My law within them, and on their hearts will I write it; and I will be their God, and they will be My people. And they will no more teach each man his neighbor and each man his brother, saying, Know the Lord, for they will all know Me [recognize, understand, and be acquainted with Me], from the least of them to the greatest, says the Lord. For I will forgive their iniquity, and I will [seriously] remember their sin no more." (Jeremiah 31:33-34, AMP)

These are the words of a loving Father. He has provided a clear path to His presence and a way for all to experience His love. I passionately desire to know Him and to obey His will here on earth.

God's provision for our souls is extraordinary. My prayer is that you will earnestly desire Him with all your heart.

"[That you may really come] to know [practically, through experience for yourselves] the love of Christ, which far surpasses mere knowledge [without experience]; that you may be filled [through all your being] unto all the fullness of God [may have the richest measure of the divine Presence, and become a body wholly filled and flooded with God Himself]!" Ephesians 3:19, AMP

Week 15

"Let the words of my mouth and the meditation of my heart be acceptable in Your sight, O Lord, my [firm, impenetrable] Rock and my Redeemer."

Psalm 19:14, AMP

DAY 1

"Let the words of my mouth and the meditation of my heart be acceptable in Your sight, O Lord, my [firm, impenetrable] Rock and my Redeemer."

PSALM 19:14, AMP

Let's start out by focusing on the definitions of a few words in this week's Scripture. To attain a complete understanding of God's Word, it is best to gain clarity in the words given. The key words we are examining closely in this passage are: word, meditation, heart, and acceptable.

Word: that which is uttered or thrown out; a single component of human speech or language; living speech or oral expression.

Heart: the inner part of anything; the middle part or interior; the chief part; the vital part; the vigorous or efficaciouspart; the seat of the affections and passions; the seat of understanding; the seat of the will.

Acceptable: that which may be received with pleasure, hence pleasing to a receiver; gratifying, as an acceptable present. Meditation: close or continued thought; the turning or revolving of a subject in the mind; serious contemplation.

As you become a student of God's Word, the significance of each written word becomes very important to you. Take time today to repeat this Scripture and contemplate the definitions listed.

Day 2

"Let the words of my mouth and the meditation of my heart be acceptable in Your sight, O Lord, my [firm, impenetrable] Rock and my Redeemer."

Psalm 19:14, AMP

The first part of this passage says, "*Let the words of my mouth…*" Our words are vitally important to our quality of life. Proverbs 18:20-21 AMP says, "*A man's [moral] self shall be filled with the fruit of his mouth; and with the consequence of his words he must be satisfied [whether good or evil]. Death and life are in the power of the tongue, and they who indulge in it shall eat the fruit of it [for death or life].*"

We are created in the image and likeness of God Himself, so all that we utter from our mouth should emulate the Father. Our words should be creative and loving. In Genesis God spoke and brought forth all living things. His words are life-giving. Ours should be, too.

His words are life-giving. Ours should be, too.

Once I became a mother, I soon realized how influential my words were. All that is said in private or in frustration is shared with the world once you become a parent. Children repeat everything; even when you think they are not paying attention, they hear what you are saying. I have consciously committed to becoming more aware of and honorable with my words. I aspire to have the words of my mouth always be acceptable to God.

I have determined to fill my heart with the Word of God. This is the only sure way of taming the tongue. The Word says from the overflow of the heart the mouth speaks. If I keep Him in my heart, His love, His compassion, and His living Words will come out.

> *"He who guards his mouth and his tongue keeps himself from troubles."* Proverbs 21:23, AMP
>
> *"The wicked is [dangerously] snared by the transgression of his lips, but the [uncompromisingly] righteous shall come out of trouble. From the fruit of his words a man shall be satisfied with good and the work of a man's hands shall come back to him [as a harvest]."* Proverbs 12:13-14, AMP

Day 3

"Let the words of my mouth and the meditation of my heart be acceptable in Your sight, O Lord, my [firm, impenetrable] Rock and my Redeemer."

Psalm 19:14, AMP

"*A heart at peace gives life to the body.*" (Proverbs 14:30, NIV)

The condition of your heart is one thing that cannot be hidden. The Bible references hundreds of Scriptures concerning the condition of our hearts. Webster defines the heart as: "the seat of our understanding, will, affections, and passions." Judging by that definition, the heart is an ideal candidate for the Holy Spirit to change and make new. The heart contains a person's carnal tendencies, which need mastering. Within our hearts, we either govern our will and emotions or our will and emotions govern us. What we choose to believe and understand determines our actions. Adhering to the Word of God and surrendering our flesh to Him leads to an abundance of peace and freedom. We are made alive in Christ.

> WE EITHER GOVERN OUR WILL AND EMOTIONS OR OUR WILL AND EMOTIONS GOVERN US.

"As for you, you were dead in transgressions and sins, in which you used to live when you followed the ways of this world and of the ruler of the kingdom of the air, the spirit who is now at work in those who are disobedient. All of us also lived among them at one time, gratifying the cravings of our sinful nature and following its desires and thoughts. Like the rest we were by nature objects of wrath. But because of his great love for us, God, who is rich in mercy,

made us alive with Christ even when we were dead in transgressions—it is by grace you have been saved. And God raised us up with Christ and seated us with him in the heavenly realms in Christ Jesus, in order that in the coming ages he might show the incomparable riches of his grace, expressed in his kindness to us in Christ Jesus. For it is by grace you have been saved, through faith—and this not from yourselves, it is the gift of God—not by works, so that no one can boast." (Ephesians 2:1-9, NIV)

We cannot become legitimate and effective Christians without first securing our position with the Lord. In American society, popular culture promotes following the leading of our hearts. But in many instances, without the direction of the Holy Spirit, our hearts can lead us down a path of pain and destruction.

If you have not already dedicated your life to the Lord, ask Him now to enter into your heart and become the Lord of your life. Receive Him now as your Savior. Your life will never be the same. It will change you for the better.

"So brace up your minds; be sober (circumspect, morally alert); set your hope wholly and unchangeably on the grace (divine favor) that is coming to you when Jesus Christ (the Messiah) is revealed. [Live] as children of obedience [to God]; do not conform yourselves to the evil desires [that governed you] in your former ignorance [when you did not know the requirements of the Gospel]. But as the One Who called you is holy, you yourselves also be holy in all your conduct and manner of living. For it is written, You shall be holy, for I am holy. And if you call upon Him as [your] Father Who judges each one impartially according to what he does, [then] you should conduct yourselves with true reverence throughout the time of your temporary residence [on the earth, whether long or short]. You must know (recognize) that you were redeemed (ransomed) from the useless (fruitless) way of living inherited by tradition from [your] forefathers, not with corruptible things [such as] silver and gold. But

[you were purchased] with the precious blood of Christ (the Messiah), like that of a [sacrificial] lamb without blemish or spot. It is true that He was chosen and foreordained (destined and foreknown for it) before the foundation of the world, but He was brought out to public view (made manifest) in these last days (at the end of the times) for the sake of you. Through Him you believe in (adhere to, rely on) God, Who raised Him up from the dead and gave Him honor and glory, so that your faith and hope are [centered and rest] in God. Since by your obedience to the Truth through the [Holy] Spirit you have purified your hearts for the sincere affection of the brethren, [see that you] love one another fervently from a pure heart. You have been regenerated (born again), not from a mortal origin (seed, sperm) but from one that is immortal by the ever living and lasting Word of God. For all flesh (mankind) is like grass, and all its glory (honor) like [the] flower of grass. The grass withers and the flower drops off. But the Word of the Lord (divine instruction, the Gospel) endures forever. And this Word is the good news which was preached to you." 1 Peter 1:13-25, AMP

Day 4

"Let the words of my mouth and the meditation of my heart be acceptable in Your sight, O Lord, my [firm, impenetrable] Rock and my Redeemer."

Psalm 19:14, AMP

Meditation is sometimes regarded as non-Christian, quirky, or New Age. But the truth is that meditation on the Word of God should be a vital part of a believer's daily routine. Our society inundates the communication circuits with continuous images of fear and death via the television, the radio, music lyrics, roadside billboards, and the Internet. Our culture's marketing strategy intends to provide "close, continued thought; turning or revolving of a subject in the mind." That is how Webster defines "meditation."

Americans spend hundreds of dollars to attend silent retreat centers, attempting to turn off the meditation of society. Many take sleeping pills to turn off the meditation process. Others fall into a pit of depression and anxiety. In spite of all of the negativity in our environment, we are destined to succeed if we do as Joshua did. God gave specific instructions to Joshua as he was preparing to lead the children of Israel into the Promised Land: "*The Book of the Law shall not depart out of your mouth, but you shall meditate on it day and night, that you may observe and do according to all that is written in it. For then you shall make your way prosperous and then you shall deal wisely and have good success.*" (Joshua 1:8, AMP)

In spite of all of the negativity in our environment, we are destined to succeed if we do as Joshua did.

I was an avid nightly news watcher and newspaper reader, taking in all the current events from around the world. But I began to struggle with fear and insecurities, so I had to cut back my media intake tremendously. My mind was focusing more on the facts reported by the media systems and less on what the Word of God said. I began to fear recession, sickness and disease, child abduction and molestation. I was seeing myself as a helpless victim in a big, scary world.

"Not so!" says the Lord. He promises to protect my family and me. He promises to keep us in all our ways of obedience and service. He bore all our sins on the cross, taking sickness and disease away from us. No actual evil or calamity can come near my family. He has redeemed us from the curse. He says He will guard and keep us in perfect peace when we commit ourselves to Him. He has made us the head and not the tail. My family and I are above and never beneath. We are blessed in the city and the country. He has commanded blessing upon our storehouse and all that we undertake (Psalm 91; Galatians 3:13; Proverbs 19:23; Deuteronomy 28).

The Bible is filled with Scriptures that declare the truth about who we are in God. I realized that if I focused on His word and obeyed His commands, I had nothing to fear. I came to know the Lord personally through meditating on His Word. He is LOVE and there is no fear in love. 1 John 4:18 AMP says, "*Love turns fear out of doors and expels every trace of terror!*" I cannot and will not go back to giving first place in my life to the devil and his world system.

God has given us the key to success: meditation on His Word. His Word does not create anxiety or stress. Instead, His Word brings wisdom, direction, and peace.

Day 5

"Let the words of my mouth and the meditation of my heart be acceptable in Your sight, O Lord, my [firm, impenetrable] Rock and my Redeemer."

Psalm 19:14, AMP

This week's Scripture uses the word "acceptable." What is acceptable? We learned in Day 1 that something is acceptable when it is received with pleasure and gratification. The meditations of the heart are easily masked from others, but God sees the heart of a person. We are told in Hebrews 4:12 that God is able to discern the thoughts and purposes of a man. He is a great accountability partner! I find that contemplating His vast knowledge humbles me.

> *"How shall a young man cleanse his way? By taking heed and keeping watch [on himself] according to Your word [conforming his life to it]. With my whole heart have I sought You, inquiring for and of You and yearning for You; Oh let me not wander or step aside [either in ignorance or willfully] from Your commandments. Your words have I laid up in my heart, that I might not sin against You. Blessed are You, O Lord; teach me Your statutes. With my lips have I declared and recounted all the ordinances of Your mouth. I have rejoiced in the way of Your testimonies as much as in all riches. I will meditate on Your precepts and have respect to Your ways [the paths of life marked out by Your law]. I will delight myself in Your statutes; I will not forget Your word. Deal bountifully with Your servant, that I may live; and I will observe Your word [hearing, receiving, loving, and obeying it]. Open my eyes, that I may behold wondrous things out of Your law. I am a stranger and a temporary resident on the earth; hide not Your commandments from me. My heart is breaking with the longing that it has for Your ordinances and judgments at all times."* (Psalm 119:9-20, AMP)

God's Word makes the meditation of our hearts acceptable.

Day 6

"Let the words of my mouth and the meditation of my heart be acceptable in Your sight, O Lord, my [firm, impenetrable] Rock and my Redeemer."

Psalm 19:14, AMP

Today you are invited to meditate deeply on the words "redeem" and "rock."

Redeem: to purchase back; to ransom; to liberate or rescue from captivity or bondage, or from any obligation or liability to suffer or to be forfeited, by paying an equivalent; as, to redeem prisoners or captured goods; to redeem a pledge; to repurchase what has been sold; to regain possession of a thing alienated by repaying the value of it to the possessor.

Rock: defense, means of safety; protection; strength; asylum; a firm or immovable foundation.

*"The Lord **redeems** his servants; no one will be condemned who takes refuge in Him."* (Psalm 34:22, NIV)

*"Praise the Lord, O my soul; all my inmost being, praise his holy name. Praise the Lord, O my soul, and forget not all his benefits—who forgives all your sins and heals all your diseases, who **redeems** your life from the pit and crowns you with love and compassion, who satisfies your desires with good things so that your youth is renewed like the eagle's."* (Psalm 103:1-5, NIV)

*"This is what the Lord says—Israel's King and **Redeemer**, the Lord Almighty; I am the first and I am the last; apart from me there is no God."* (Isaiah 44:6, NIV)

*"Our **Redeemer**, He was wounded for our transgressions, He was bruised for our guilt and iniquities; the chastisement [needful to obtain] peace and well-being for us was upon Him, and with the stripes [that wounded] Him we are healed and made whole."* (Isaiah 53:5, AMP)

*"But now [in spite of past judgments for Israel's sins], thus says the Lord, He Who created you, O Jacob, and He Who formed you, O Israel: Fear not, for I have **redeemed** you [ransomed you by paying a price instead of leaving you captives]; I have called you by your name; you are Mine."* (Isaiah 43:1, AMP)

*"The Lord is my **Rock**, my Fortress, and my Deliverer; my God, my keen and firm Strength in Whom I will trust and take refuge, my Shield, and the Horn of my salvation, my High Tower."* (Psalm 18:2, AMP)

*"I will proclaim the name of the Lord. Oh, praise the greatness of our God! He is the **Rock**, His works are perfect, and all His ways are just. A faithful God who does no wrong, upright and just is He."* (Deuteronomy 32:3-4, NIV)

*"The Lord lives; blessed be my **Rock**, and exalted be God, the Rock of my salvation."* (2 Samuel 22:47, AMP)

*"For God alone my soul waits in silence; from Him comes my salvation. He only is my **Rock** and my Salvation, my Defense and my Fortress; I shall not be greatly moved."* (Psalm 62:1-2, AMP)

DAY 7

"Let the words of my mouth and the meditation of my heart be acceptable in Your sight, O Lord, my [firm, impenetrable] Rock and my Redeemer."

PSALM 19:14, AMP

As I was meditating on this verse, the Lord showed me how the words of the mouth and the meditation of the heart can be lethal. For example, self-abasing music, movies, and literature are growing in popularity, producing a thriving subculture of death and despair.

> WALKING AWAY FROM GOD IS THE WORST MISTAKE A PERSON CAN MAKE.

My younger brother was a participant in this deadly lifestyle. His life was wasted chasing a scheme drawn up by the devil. His focus became skewed by other religious beliefs contrary to Christianity. They promised a "better way," a way founded in self-preservation and the power of the inner being. The Christ factor was vehemently denied and blasphemed. His musical intake focused on death and hatred of society including all forms of authority. The words of my brother's mouth and the meditation of his heart were entirely contradictory to the Word of God. His lifestyle choices led him down a path of drugs, depression, paranoia, hatred, and self-destruction.

I share this hoping to save the lives of those experimenting with other religions and exposing themselves to perverted culture. There is no such thing as experimenting with Satan. Don't give him an open door into your soul to influence your life. I have seen numerous people get twisted up in drugs and the lifestyles that develop because of their drug abuse. I have also seen the confusion and bondage of those who have immersed themselves in other religions. Walking away from God is the worst mistake a person can make. Without God it is impossible to defeat the craftiness of Satan.

> *"For the god of this world has blinded the unbelievers' minds [that they should not discern the truth], preventing them from seeing the illuminating light of the Gospel of the glory of Christ (the Messiah), Who is the Image and Likeness of God."* (2 Corinthians 4:4, AMP)

Pray for the lives of friends and family members who are captivated by ungodly influences. We believers can pray for people who can influence the lives of our loved ones for good as well as actively represent the power of Christ before them.

> *"And Jesus went about all the cities and villages, teaching in their synagogues and proclaiming the good news (the Gospel) of the kingdom and curing all kinds of disease and every weakness and infirmity. When He saw the throngs, He was moved with pity and sympathy for them, because they were bewildered (harassed and distressed and dejected and helpless), like sheep without a shepherd. Then He said to His disciples, The harvest is indeed plentiful, but the laborers are few. So pray to the Lord of the harvest to force out and thrust laborers into His harvest."* (Matthew 9:35-38, AMP)

> *"Whenever a person turns [in repentance] to the Lord, the veil is stripped off and taken away. Now the Lord is the Spirit, and where the Spirit of the Lord is, there is liberty (emancipation from bondage, freedom)."* (2 Corinthians 3:16-17, AMP)

Passionate prayer for the lost is an effective way to change lives for Christ. Let us be diligent and obedient in our call to reach the confused and the hopeless.

Week 16

"Religion that God our Father accepts as pure and faultless is this: to look after orphans and widows in their distress and to keep oneself from being polluted by the world."

James 1:27, NIV

Day 1

"Religion that God our Father accepts as pure and faultless is this: to look after orphans and widows in their distress and to keep oneself from being polluted by the world."

James 1:27, NIV

The Amplified Bible says, "*External religion [religion as it is expressed in outward acts] that is pure and unblemished in the sight of God the Father is this: to visit and help and care for the orphans and widows in their affliction and need, and to keep oneself unspotted and uncontaminated by the world*" (James 1:27 AMP). Religion is more than society's denominations, traditions and theories. It reaches far beyond the four walls of a church. Religion can be defined as a merger between your reality and your faith. It is expressed in how we relate to and affect others. Christian religion is seen in our everyday conduct with people in our community. The world "hears" our conduct more than they hear our proclamations about God.

How do you conduct yourself in your community? How would your neighbors describe you? Christian? Or crazy? The following little survey will help you understand what I'm asking. Simply circle the one that best applies to how you appear in public:

When you are at work dealing with difficult clients: **Christian** or **Crazy**

When you are in the grocery store shopping with your kids and all of them need to use the restroom: **Christian** or **Crazy**

When you are checking into an exclusive resort for a much needed weekend getaway with your spouse and your room isn't ready: **Christian** or **Crazy**

When you are on the highway and someone cuts in front of you: **Christian** or **Crazy**

When you get pulled over by the police for speeding: **Christian** or **Crazy**

When you arrive home from a long day at work and the neighbor's dog is relieving itself in your front yard: **Christian** or **Crazy**

When you arrive at your favorite restaurant very hungry, only to hear that the reservations you made two weeks ago cannot be found: **Christian** or **Crazy**

Remember: *"You are the light of the world. A city on a hill cannot be hidden. Neither do people light a lamp and put it under a bowl. Instead they put it on its stand, and it gives light to everyone in the house. In the same way, let your light shine before men, that they may see your good deeds and praise your Father in heaven."* (Matthew 5:14-16, NIV)

Day 2

"Religion that God our Father accepts as pure and faultless is this: to look after orphans and widows in their distress and to keep oneself from being polluted by the world."
James 1:27, NIV

Our first year in Portland was very difficult. We moved from San Antonio, Texas—where the sun shines 365 days a year—to gray, dark, rainy Portland. I clung to memories of tanned skin and evenings spent swimming in a warm pool. One day during a six-week rainy stint, I was sitting at a traffic light listening to my wipers rotate back and forth across my windshield, when I suddenly felt that I was going to lose my mind. The non-stop rain and dark days had worn me down. I felt hopeless. I needed to escape.

I asked God, "Why?! Why Portland? Why all the rain?" Then I thought, "Well, I know why Portland: because my husband's job took us there. I know why the rain: because we are the Green State." Then the Holy Spirit prompted me to ask, "What?" He directed me to take the focus off of myself and find someone to serve. Because I wanted to survive the winter in Portland, I decided to get right to the task at hand.

Soon a wonderful principal at one of Portland's public schools connected me with a student whose family needed assistance. The child's mother was a young woman with no husband who had two small children and an elderly mother to care for. As I shopped for gifts and items for each person in the family, the Lord gave me specific details on what to buy.

The morning I was to deliver the items, one of the teachers from the school came along to translate because the family did not speak English. When we arrived at the house of my adopted family, the excitement was overwhelming. Everything I had purchased was an exact match. The grandmother was thrilled. In her broken English, she thanked me and blessed me. The children were very happy. Many thank you's were extended.

Upon leaving their home, the teacher who had escorted me turned to me, looked deeply into my eyes, and asked, "Who are you? Where do you come from?" I answered, "Well, my name is Ingrid and my family just moved here from Texas." She said, "No! No! I mean really, who are you? Where did you come from? People just don't do what you did for nothing." I was humbled. I told her we were Christians and we wanted to extend the love of Christ. She was moved to tears. She had never observed such generosity and love.

To see how people in our community respond to acts of true religion is a deeply moving experience. They can't help but give God praise and honor for His liberal generosity and love that we extend to them.

"As it is written: 'He has scattered abroad his gifts to the poor; his righteousness endures forever.' Now he who supplies seed to the sower and bread for food will also supply and increase your store of seed and will enlarge the harvest of your righteousness. You will be made rich in every way so that you can be generous on every occasion, and through us your generosity will result in thanksgiving to God. This service that you perform is not only supplying the needs of God's people but is also overflowing in many expressions of thanks to God. Because of the service by which you have proved yourselves, men will praise God for the obedience that accompanies your confession of the gospel of Christ, and for your generosity in sharing with them and with everyone else. And in their prayers for you their hearts will go out to you, because of the surpassing grace God has given you. Thanks be to God for his indescribable gift!" 2 Corinthians 9:9-15, NIV

DAY 3

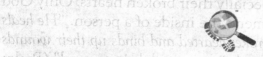

"Religion that God our Father accepts as pure and faultless is this: to look after orphans and widows in their distress and to keep oneself from being polluted by the world."
JAMES 1:27, NIV

To be a literal widow or orphan is a specifically defined, tangible condition. I have also seen many people orphaned and widowed spiritually.

For instance, a person may have natural parents and not have a relationship with one or both of them. Many children *feel* like they don't have parents; I have friends who were neglected and abandoned by their parents, and spent the entirety of their childhoods fending for themselves. There are married women who have been abandoned, both financially and physically, by their husbands. To me they could be described as widows.

God sees the heart of all people. He is able and He is willing to be the Father to the fatherless and a Husband to the widow. He is never far and is always attentive to the cry of His people.

> *"Sing to God, sing praises to His name, cast up a highway for Him Who rides through the deserts—His name is the Lord—be in high spirits and glory before Him! A father of the fatherless and a judge and protector of the widows is God in His holy habitation. God places the solitary in families and gives the desolate a home in which to dwell; He leads the prisoners out to prosperity; but the rebellious dwell in a parched land."* (Psalm 68:4-6, AMP)

In the United States, the government cares for this needy segment of our population. But our widows and orphans can be so deep in a pit of desperation and need that the government cannot completely meet their needs, especially their broken hearts. Only God can mend the inside of a person. "*He heals the brokenhearted and binds up their wounds [curing their pains and their sorrows]*" (Psalm 147:3, AMP).

Our responsibility is to be an extension of His compassionate hands, to care for those whom God places into our communities. Find a ministry in your church, or create one of your own, that specifically serves the orphans and widows. Don't wait for the foster care system or Social Security to notice a need. Initiate religion that God considers pure and faultless. Reach out!

Don't wait for the foster care system or Social Security to notice a need.

"The Lord protects and preserves the strangers and temporary residents; He upholds the fatherless and the widow and sets them upright." Psalm 146:9a, AMP

DAY 4

"Religion that God our Father accepts as pure and
faultless is this: to look after orphans and
widows in their distress and to keep oneself
from being polluted by the world."
JAMES 1:27, NIV

As a response to this week's Scripture, which encourages us to practice pure religion, I'm presenting a few suggestions to serve the orphans and widows in your community:

- ❖ Visit a nursing home or retirement community.
  - Commit to year round, not just during the holiday season.
  - Take your Bible and start a Bible study.
  - Read the Bible to an elderly person who can't see or is unable to read.
  - Take your children along. Elderly people love to touch little hands and hear their sweet, innocent voices.
- ❖ Adopt a child.
  - Many children need a loving home.
  - Consider Christian adoption agencies which are located internationally as well as in the United States.
- ❖ Volunteer.
  - Boys and Girls Club of America.
  - Church youth group.
  - Become a church deacon whose ministry is to serve the widows and orphans.
  - Find ways at your local elementary schools to extend love to a troubled child.

❖ Befriend a widow in your neighborhood.
  - Take her dinner.
  - Offer to cut the grass.
  - Take her garbage out.
  - Wash her car.
  - Clear snow off her sidewalk or driveway.

Seek ways to serve in a pure and faultless manner. As you go about your day, ask God to show you who in your community needs help or encouragement. You will be amazed at the opportunities He shows you that were right under your nose.

DAY 5

"Religion that God our Father accepts as pure and faultless is this: to look after orphans and widows in their distress and to keep oneself from being polluted by the world."
JAMES 1:27, NIV

Take time today to meditate upon these Scriptures.

"Religion that God our Father accepts as pure and faultless is this: to look after orphans and widows in their distress and to keep oneself from being polluted by the world." (James 1:27, NIV)

"External religious worship [religion as it is expressed in outward acts] that is pure and unblemished in the sight of God the Father is this: tovisit and help and care for the orphans and widows in their affliction and need, and to keep oneself unspotted and uncontaminated from the world." (James 1:27, AMP)

"Religion that pleases God the Father must be pure and spotless. You must help needy orphans and widows and not let this world make you evil." (James 1:27, CEV)

"Here are the kinds of beliefs that God our Father accepts as pure and without fault. When widows and children who have no parents are in trouble, take care of them. And keep yourselves from being polluted by the world." (James 1:27, NIRV)

"You hear, O LORD, the desire of the afflicted; you encourage them, and you listen to their cry, defending the fatherless and the oppressed, in order that man, who is of the earth, may terrify no more." (Psalm 10:17-18, NIV)

"Even to your old age and gray hairs I am he, I am he who will sustain you. I have made you and I will carry you; I will sustain you and I will rescue you." (Isaiah 46:4, NIV)

"Do not rebuke an older man harshly, but exhort him as if he were your father. Treat younger men as brothers, older women as mothers, and younger women as sisters, with absolute purity. Give proper recognition to those widows who are really in need. But if a widow has children or grandchildren, these should learn first of all to put their religion into practice by caring for their own family and so repaying their parents and grandparents, for this is pleasing to God. The widow who is really in need and left all alone puts her hope in God and continues night and day to pray and to ask God for help. But the widow who lives for pleasure is dead even while she lives. Give the people these instructions, too, so that no one may be open to blame."
(1Timothy 5:1-7, NIV)

"A father of the fatherless and a judge and protector of the widows is God in His holy habitation." (Psalm 68:5, AMP)

"For the LORD your God is God of gods and Lord of lords, the great God, mighty and awesome, who shows no partiality and accepts no bribes. He defends the cause of the fatherless and the widow, and loves the alien, giving him food and clothing." (Deuteronomy 10:17-18, NIV)

DAY 6

"Religion that God our Father accepts as pure and faultless is this: to look after orphans and widows in their distress and to keep oneself from being polluted by the world."

JAMES 1:27, NIV

It is no coincidence that God mentions caring for orphans and widows right alongside keeping ourselves from the polluted ways of the world. These two concepts are closely related. In order to reach the abandoned segment of our society, we must remain untainted by the self-centered influences in our culture. This purity is achieved by allowing our minds to be renewed by God and changed to be like Christ's. Thinking like Jesus leads us to be unselfish, compassionate, merciful, long suffering, and unconditionally loving.

> THE KEY TO PURE RELIGION IS AN ACT OF SUBMISSION TO GOD'S WAY OF THINKING AND DOING THINGS.

"Do not conform any longer to the pattern of this world, but be transformed by the renewing of your mind. Then you will be able to test and approve what God's will is—his good, pleasing and perfect will." (Romans 12:2, NIV) The NLT version of this verse says, *"Let God transform you into a new person by changing the way you think."*

The key to pure religion—allowing God to renew our minds—is an act of submission to God's way of thinking and doing things. By studying God's Word, our minds become renewed and able to figure out the will of God. Many of the world's views are contrary to God's Word. But as we renounce the destructive thinking that society, traditions, and culture have taught us, God's new way of thinking replaces the old. Our thinking and behavior change.

God wants to provide love and care for every widow's and orphan's need. He is a Father to the fatherless and a Husband to the widow. And we are to be like our Father.

"See to it that no one carries you off as spoil or makes you yourselves captive by his so-called philosophy and intellectualism and vain deceit (idle fancies and plain nonsense), following human tradition (men's ideas of the material rather than the spiritual world), just crude notions following the rudimentary and elemental teachings of the universe and disregarding [the teachings of] Christ (the Messiah)." Colossians 2:8, AMP

DAY 7

"Religion that God our Father accepts as pure and
faultless is this: to look after orphans and
widows in their distress and to keep oneself
from being polluted by the world."

JAMES 1:27, NIV

"There are many medicines and cures for all kinds of people.
But unless kind hands are given in service and
generous hearts are given in love,
I do not think there can ever be any cure for the
terrible sickness of feeling unloved.
It may happen that a mere smile, a short visit,
the lighting of a lamp, writing a letter for a blind man,
carrying a bucket of charcoal, offering a pair of sandals,
reading the newspaper for someone
—something small, very small—
may, in fact, be our love of God in action.
Listening, when no one else volunteers to listen,
is no doubt a very noble thing.
Holiness grows fast where there is kindness.
I have never heard of kind souls going astray.
The world is lost for want of sweetness and kindness.
There are many people who can do big things,
but there are very few people who will do the small things."

From *In the Heart of the World: Thoughts, Stories, and Prayers*
by Mother Teresa

Week 17

"Consequently, faith comes from hearing the message, and the message is heard through the word of Christ."

Romans 10:17, NIV

DAY 1

"Consequently, faith comes from hearing the message,
and the message is heard through the word of Christ."
ROMANS 10:17, NIV

This week's Scripture is one of the most quoted verses in Christendom. It is simple, plain, and easily attainable. Webster defines faith as: "that trust and confidence that springs from our belief in God." In Luke 17, the apostles asked Jesus to increase their faith. Jesus did not answer with a seven-step PowerPoint plan. Instead, he encouraged them to utilize the faith they already had.

Jesus compared his disciples' faith to a mustard seed. I often wondered why he used a mustard seed, until a few years ago when I chaperoned a daughter's field trip to a farm. The trip was planned during the fall season, a beautiful time of the year in Oregon. The pumpkins out in the field were bright orange; the trees were changing colors; the landscape was breath-taking. The host farmers gave a brief agricultural lesson on field corn, pumpkins, and squash. One intriguing fact they shared was how quickly *the* pumpkin seeds perish in the fields. He then explained that, unlike pumpkin seeds, the mustard seed was one of the most—if not the most— hearty seeds in existence. A mustard seed, the tiniest of all seeds, could be left unattended for as long as 200 years, yet still produce fruit when planted. One farmer never planted mustard seeds, because once they were harvested, the seed was virtually impossible to kill. AMAZING! That God would liken our faith to a mustard seed is extremely significant.

It is not the size of the seed that makes it potent, but the substance God puts into it that brings forth power. Mustard seeds cannot cross-pollinate with another plant. Just like humans, their DNA is unchangeable.

Utilize the faith you have been given. It may seem small or weak at times, but if you trust God, the results will be extraordinary.

Day 2

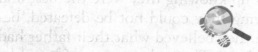

"Consequently, faith comes from hearing the message, and the message is heard through the word of Christ."
Romans 10:17, NIV

A recent television documentary on two famous tennis champion sisters, Venus and Serena Williams, described their upbringing and the relationship they had with their father. They were raised in a dangerous city in California, a place where the social climate was not conducive to many activities outside of the home. Family unity was very important to their father. He put great emphasis on family closeness—so much so that he told the girls they didn't need any friends outside of the family. They had a large family with plenty of siblings; he said that was enough.

One of the sisters interviewed for the documentary said she believed her father. Her sisters were her best friends; she had very few friends outside of her immediate family because she respected what her father had taught her. She claimed that having her sisters as her only close friends kept her from getting involved in relationships that would have influenced her negatively.

Her father also ingrained in his tennis prodigies that they were the best tennis players and no one could defeat them. He was so adamant and passionate about his views on his daughters' superiority in the field of tennis that many sports reporters called him arrogant and strange. The father coached the girls and knew their strengths and weaknesses better than anyone. He was aware of the rare tennis talent he was molding and went to great length to showcase their abilities.

From the beginning, the sisters' father insisted they have a clear sense of identity. They grew up knowing they were the best and knowing they could not be defeated, because they believed what their father had told them. Their identity was formed by repeatedly hearing their father tell them who they were.

> If we choose to believe what He says, we will become what He says.

For many years these two sisters have played at the professional level and gone undefeated. They defeat their opponents with extraordinary skill and confidence. The world has marveled at their tenacity on the courts. They are champions.

We Christians have a heavenly Father who has established our identities within the pages of a book called the Bible. His Word is the force that builds our faith. If we choose to believe what He says, we will become what He says.

Allow what God says about you to become a reality.

Day 3

"Consequently, faith comes from hearing the message,
and the message is heard through the word of Christ."
Romans 10:17, NIV

Today you are invited to meditate upon this week's verse in several different translations as well as two different quotations about faith.

> *"So then faith cometh by hearing, and hearing by the word of God."* KJV
>
> *"Consequently, faith comes from hearing the message, and the message is heard through the word of Christ."* NIV
>
> *"So faith comes by hearing [what is told], and what is heard comes by the preaching [of the message that came from the lips] of Christ (the Messiah Himself)."* AMP
>
> *"No one can have faith without hearing the message about Christ."* CEV
>
> *"So faith comes from hearing, that is, hearing the Good News about Christ."* NLT
>
> "Faith comes more quickly when you hear yourself quoting, speaking, and saying the things God said You will more readily receive God's Word into your spirit by hearing yourself say it than if you hear someone else say it." (From Charles Capps' book: *God's Creative Power Will Work for You*)
>
> "The assent of the mind to the truth of divine revelation, on the authority of God's testimony, accompanied with a cordial assent of the will or approbation of the heart; an entire confi-

dence or trust in God's character and declarations, and in the character and doctrines of Christ, with an unreserved surrender of the will to his guidance, and dependence on his merits for salvation. In other words, that firm belief of God's testimony, and of the truth of the gospel, which influences the will, and leads to an entire reliance on Christ for salvation." (*The Noah Webster Dictionary 1828 Version* definition of faith)

DAY 4

"Consequently, faith comes from hearing the message,
and the message is heard through the word of Christ."
ROMANS 10:17, NIV

Faith is developed by hearing the messages of our Savior. Being connected to a Bible-based church where the Word of God is presented is vitally important. Maturing in faith requires a consistent pursuit of His Word. Pursuing Jesus means keeping company with His Word and being surrounded with people who love Him as much as you do.

Turning from the world's ways to accept life with Jesus Christ as Lord and Savior is a big change for new believers. When a person leaves the world's sin system to become a Christian, life acquires a more purposeful focus, often changing personal goals, activities, and even friends. A new person created in Christ must first commit their mind to Him. The body will follow the intent of the mind, because it houses the will.

> *"Therefore, I urge you, brothers, in view of God's mercy, to offer your bodies as living sacrifices, holy and pleasing to God—this is your spiritual act of worship. Do not conform any longer to the pattern of this world, but be transformed by the renewing of your mind. Then you will be able to test and approve what God's will is—his good, pleasing and perfect will."* (Romans 12:1-2, NIV)

God alone is able to make us brand new. Each chapter of the Bible was written for our growth. Immerse yourself in the best book ever written.

"Every Scripture is God-breathed (given by His inspiration) and profitable for instruction, for reproof and conviction of sin, for correction of error and discipline in obedience, [and] for training in righteousness (in holy living, in conformity to God's will in thought, purpose, and action), So that the man of God may be complete and proficient, well fitted and thoroughly equipped for every good work." 2 Timothy 3:16-17, AMP

DAY 5

"Consequently, faith comes from hearing the message,
and the message is heard through the word of Christ."
ROMANS 10:17, NIV

In Hebrews 11:1, faith is defined as *"the substance of things hoped for, the evidence of things not seen."* Faith is not a tangible thing that can be held and carried. Faith is our belief, trust, and reliance on the Word of God. Faith resides in our hearts.

The logical mind is not able to make sense of faith because the five senses—taste, touch, smell, sight, and sound—are not factors in faith: *"Now faith is the assurance (the confirmation, the title deed) of the things [we] hope for, being the proof of things [we] do not see and the conviction of their reality [faith perceiving as real fact what is not revealed to the senses]."* (Hebrews 11:1, AMP)

The Christian faith is founded on the Spirit of the Living God. We become established in faith by His Word. Faith has the power to create the changes that are the evidence of things not seen. Only by God's Word are broken hearts mended. Only by His Word can a drug addict be set free from the prison of addiction. Only by His Word are sicknesses and diseases eradicated. Only by His Word can atheists become passionate crusaders for Christ.

"Now the Lord is the Spirit, and where the Spirit of the Lord is, there is liberty (emancipation from bondage, freedom). And all of us, as with unveiled face, [because we] continued to behold [in the Word of God] as in a mirror the glory of the Lord, are constantly being transfigured into His very own image in ever increasing splendor and from one degree

of glory to another; [for this comes] from the Lord [Who is] the Spirit." (2 Corinthians 3:17-18, AMP)

Jesus declared this to be His mission to the world: "*The Spirit of the Lord [is] upon Me, because He has anointed Me [the Anointed One, the Messiah] to preach the good news (the Gospel) to the poor; He has sent Me to announce release to the captives and recovery of sight to the blind, to send forth as delivered those who are oppressed [who are downtrodden, bruised, crushed, and broken down by calamity]. To proclaim the accepted and acceptable year of the Lord [the day when salvation and the free favors of God profusely abound.*" (Luke 4:18-19, AMP)

> "*For the Word that God speaks is alive and full of power [making it active, operative, energizing, and effective]; it is sharper than any two-edged sword, penetrating to the dividing line of the breath of life (soul) and [the immortal] spirit, and of joints and marrow [of the deepest parts of our nature], exposing and sifting and analyzing and judging the very thoughts and purposes of the heart.*" Hebrews 4:12, AMP

DAY 6

"Consequently, faith comes from hearing the message,
and the message is heard through the word of Christ."
ROMANS 10:17, NIV

Faith comes by hearing the Word of God repeatedly. Reading the Bible is profitable, but it is not enough. Consistently hearing the Word of God is what builds faith.

This week's Scripture reminds me of how young children are taught new concepts in grade school. In class they are surrounded by the repetition of spoken words. The ABC's are introduced to children by sight and song; manners and social skills are reinforced by their phrase repetition. Television programs introduce children to new letters and words by song and images. Foreign language teachers say the most comprehensive way to learn a new language is to become totally immersed in the culture of the language. Older students are encouraged to study abroad, where they only hear and see the images of the language they wish to learn.

CONSISTENTLY HEARING THE WORD OF GOD IS WHAT BUILDS FAITH.

Getting to know God is very similar. We must desire in our hearts to know Him and then actively pursue Him by saturating ourselves in His Word. We cannot communicate who God is to the world if we don't know Him. We must aspire to be fluent in our faith.

"Every word of God is tried and purified; He is a shield to those who trust and take refuge in Him." Proverbs 30:5, AMP

"You have been regenerated (born again), not from a mortal origin (seed, sperm), but from one that is immortal by the ever living and lasting Word of God. For all flesh (mankind) is like grass, and all its glory (honor) like [the] flower of grass. The grass withers and the flower drops off, but the Word of the Lord (divine instruction, the Gospel) endures forever. And this Word is the good news which was preached to you." 1 Peter 1:23-25, AMP

DAY 7

"Consequently, faith comes from hearing the message,
and the message is heard through the word of Christ."
ROMANS 10:17, NIV

Jesus' earthly father, Joseph, is often overlooked. Joseph came from the royal line of David. His lineage was just and upright. As a young boy, he was most likely taught the Law of the Lord by relatives. Joseph would have been familiar with the adventures of Moses, the triumphs and trials of the children of Israel, and how God had proven His faithfulness to his people for centuries; during Joseph's lifetime, the Jews were waiting for their Messiah.

Judging by Joseph's obedience to the prompting of the angel (recorded in chapters one and two of Matthew), we know he trusted God and was willing to do whatever God commanded. Since Joseph had listened to the Words of God since he was a child, his faith was firmly rooted in God. He grew up hoping for the Messiah and for the salvation of the world that the Messiah would bring. His response to God's call to be Jesus' earthly father shows how God uses ordinary men to accomplish awesome feats of faith.

Joseph's life exemplifies this Scripture: "*Faith is the substance of things hoped for, the evidence of things not seen*" (Hebrews 11:1, NKJV). Truly, there is no limit to what we can do with faith.

TRULY, THERE IS NO LIMIT TO WHAT WE CAN DO WITH FAITH.

Will you be willing to exercise your faith when God asks you to step out?

Week 18

"For as the rain and snow come down from the heavens, and return not there again, but water the earth and make it bring forth and sprout, that it may give seed to the sower and bread to the eater, So shall My word be that goes forth out of My mouth: it shall not return to Me void [without producing any effect, useless], but it shall accomplish that which I please and purpose, and it shall prosper in the thing for which I sent it."

Isaiah 55:10-11, AMP

DAY 1

"For as the rain and snow come down from the heavens, and return not there again, but water the earth and make it bring forth and sprout, that it may give seed to the sower and bread to the eater, So shall My word be that goes forth out of My mouth: it shall not return to Me void [without producing any effect, useless], but it shall accomplish that which I please and purpose, and it shall prosper in the thing for which I sent it."

ISAIAH 55:10-11, AMP

God is the author of productivity; He could be labeled a fruit farmer. His spoken Word always results in progress and multiplication. God's intentions are to bring growth in His children and in the earth. He generates this growth as He oversees all aspects of our world.

In the same way as the earth around us grows and flourishes, we are sustained and grow by His Word. He matures us in Christ and enables us to reach others with the Gospel of Jesus Christ. The Word of God is not passive or unproductive; it is alive and full of power.

THE WORD OF GOD IS NOT PASSIVE OR UNPRODUCTIVE; IT IS ALIVE AND FULL OF POWER.

As we study and meditate on His Word and allow it to change us, we become more alive! We receive more energy and become wiser. As His Word invigorates our souls, our bodies are strengthened (3 John 1:2). God's Word has the power to accomplish the tasks it was sent out to do, which always lead to life!

"And [God] Who provides seed for the sower and bread for eating will also provide and multiply your [resources for] sowing and increase the fruits of your righteousness [which manifests itself in active goodness, kindness, and charity]." 2 Corinthians 9:10, AMP

"Sow for yourselves according to righteousness (uprightness and right standing with God); reap according to mercy and loving-kindness. Break up your uncultivated ground, for it is time to seek the Lord, to inquire for and of Him, and to require His favor, till He comes and teaches you righteousness and rains His righteous gift of salvation upon you." Hosea 10:12, AMP

Day 2

"For as the rain and snow come down from the heavens, and return not there again, but water the earth and make it bring forth and sprout, that it may give seed to the sower and bread to the eater, So shall My word be that goes forth out of My mouth: it shall not return to Me void [without producing any effect, useless], but it shall accomplish that which I please and purpose, and it shall prosper in the thing for which I sent it."

Isaiah 55:10-11, AMP

The second part of this week's Scripture says, "My *Word that goes out from my mouth; it will not return to me empty but will accomplish what I desire and achieve the purpose for which I sent it*" (NIV). Throughout the Bible, the Lord is speaking. His proclamations would be very difficult to number. Thanks to God, we can take the words He declares personally. The Bible was written for us. Take in every Word and apply it to your life.

We can take the words He declares personally. The Bible was written for us.

"So everyone who hears these words of Mine and acts upon them [obeying them] will be like a sensible (prudent, practical, wise) man who built his house upon the rock. And the rain fell and the floods came and the winds blew and beat against that house; yet it did not fall, because it had been founded on the rock. And everyone who hears these words of Mine and does not do them will be like a stupid (foolish) man who built his house upon the sand. And the rain fell and the floods came and the winds blew and beat against that house, and it fell—and great and complete was the fall of it." (Matthew 7:24-27, AMP)

God encourages those who are listening to establish their lives upon His Word.

> *"Do not merely listen to the word, and so deceive yourselves. Do what it says. Anyone who listens to the word but does not do what it says is like a man who looks at his face in a mirror and, after looking at himself, goes away and immediately forgets what he looks like. But the man who looks intently into the perfect law that gives freedom, and continues to do this, not forgetting what he has heard, but doing it—he will be blessed in what he does."* (James 1:22-25, NIV)

I encourage you to seek out the answers to your life's questions from God's Word. Make the commitment to obey the truths you find in His Word. Obedience leads to success, blessing, wholeness, and righteousness. Jesus teaches in Matthew 7 that when our lives are founded on His Word, we are unscathed by the adversity and challenges which attempt to destroy our foundation. God is our Rock. He is our stabilizing force.

> *"So trust in the Lord (commit yourself to Him, lean on Him, hope confidently in Him) forever; for the Lord God is an everlasting Rock [the Rock of Ages]."* Isaiah 26:4, AMP

DAY 3

"For as the rain and snow come down from the heavens, and return not there again, but water the earth and make it bring forth and sprout, that it may give seed to the sower and bread to the eater, So shall My word be that goes forth out of My mouth: it shall not return to Me void [without producing any effect, useless], but it shall accomplish that which I please and purpose, and it shall prosper in the thing for which I sent it."
ISAIAH 55:10-11, AMP

The following Scriptures point to God's greatness. Take some time today to meditate upon Him.

"Am I a God at hand, says the Lord, and not a God afar off?" (Jeremiah 23:23, AMP)

"Show me Your ways, O Lord; teach me Your paths. Guide me in Your truth and faithfulness and teach me, for You are the God of my salvation; for You [You only and altogether] do I wait [expectantly] all the day long." (Psalm 25:4-5, AMP)

"Before the mountains were brought forth or ever You had formed and given birth to the earth and the world, even from everlasting to everlasting You are God." (Psalm 90:2, AMP)

"You will guard him and keep him in perfect and constant peace whose mind [both its inclination and its character] is stayed on You, because he commits himself to You, leans on You, and hopes confidently in You. So trust in the Lord (commit yourself to Him, lean on Him, hope confidently in Him) forever; for the Lord God is an everlasting Rock [the Rock of Ages]." (Isaiah 26:3-4, AMP)

"Have you not known? Have you not heard? The everlasting God, the Lord, the Creator of the ends of the earth, does not faint or grow weary; there is no searching of His understanding. He gives power to the faint and weary, and to him who has no might He increases strength [causing it to multiply and making it to abound]. Even youths shall faint and be weary, and [selected] young men shall feebly stumble and fall exhausted; But those who wait for the Lord [who expect, look for, and hope in Him] shall change and renew their strength and power; they shall lift their wings and mount up [close to God] as eagles [mount up to the sun]; they shall run and not be weary, they shall walk and not faint or become tired." (Isaiah 40:28-35, AMP)

"The LORD is my Shepherd [to feed, guide, and shield me], I shall not lack. He makes me lie down in [fresh, tender] green pastures; He leads me beside the still and restful waters. He refreshes and restores my life (my self); He leads me in the paths of righteousness [uprightness and right standing with Him—not for my earning it, but] for His name's sake. Yes, though I walk through the [deep, sunless] valley of the shadow of death, I will fear or dread no evil, for You are with me; Your rod [to protect] and Your staff [to guide], they comfort me. You prepare a table before me in the presence of my enemies. You anoint my head with oil; my [brimming] cup runs over. Surely or only goodness, mercy, and unfailing love shall follow me all the days of my life, and through the length of my days the house of the Lord [and His presence] shall be my dwelling place." (Psalm 23, AMP)

"And all your [spiritual] children shall be disciples [taught by the Lord and obedient to His will], and great shall be the peace and undisturbed composure of your children. You shall establish yourself in righteousness (rightness, in conformity with God's will and order): you shall be far from even the thought of oppression or destruction, for you shall not fear, and from terror, for it shall not come near you. Behold, they may gather together and stir up strife, but it is not from Me. Whoever stirs up strife against you shall fall and surrender to you. Behold, I have created the smith who blows on the fire of coals and who produces a weapon for its purpose; and I have created the devastator to destroy. But no weapon that is formed against you shall prosper, and every tongue that shall rise against you in judgment you shall show to be in the wrong. This [peace,

righteousness, security, triumph over opposition] is the heritage of the servants of the Lord [those in whom the ideal Servant of the Lord is reproduced]; this is the righteousness or the vindication which they obtain from Me [this is that which I impart to them as their justification], says the Lord." (Isaiah 54:13-26, AMP)

"Cast your burden on the Lord [releasing the weight of it] and He will sustain you; He will never allow the [consistently] righteous to be moved (made to slip, fall, or fail)." (Psalm 55:22, AMP)

"Surely His salvation is near to those who reverently and worshipfully fear Him, [and is ready to be appropriated] that [the manifest presence of God, His] glory may tabernacle and abide in our land. Mercy and loving-kindness and truth have met together; righteousness and peace have kissed each other. Truth shall spring up from the earth, and righteousness shall look down from heaven. Yes, the Lord will give what is good, and our land will yield its increase. Righteousness shall go before Him and shall make His footsteps a way in which to walk." (Psalm 85:9-16, AMP)

DAY 4

"For as the rain and snow come down from the heavens, and return not there again, but water the earth and make it bring forth and sprout, that it may give seed to the sower and bread to the eater, So shall My word be that goes forth out of My mouth: it shall not return to Me void [without producing any effect, useless], but it shall accomplish that which I please and purpose, and it shall prosper in the thing for which I sent it."
ISAIAH 55:10-11, AMP

God gives simple and applicable analogies that we can all understand, no matter what culture or era we are from. In this week's Scripture, He makes a masterful parallel between the rain and the snow from heaven and the Word that proceeds from His mouth.

Everyone will have some experience with rain or snow. Arctic areas would not encounter rain as much as they would snow. Sub-Saharan climates certainly would not have the joy of seeing white snowflakes fall from the sky, but they do have a rainy season. In each climate, the precipitation comes from heaven (the sky). Rain and snow hydrate the seeds on our miraculous planet, which then produces seed to produce food for humankind. God has ordained this truly amazing cycle.

WITHOUT SPIRITUAL WATER AND NATURAL WATER, LIFE CANNOT EXIST.

In the same way that the earth needs water for seed which produces food, we need God's Words from His mouth to hydrate our souls. His water, the living water, gives life to our soul. Jesus said, "*Whoever drinks the water I give him will never thirst. Indeed, the water I give him will become in him a spring of water welling up to eternal life*" (John 4:14, NIV). Without spiritual water and natural water, life cannot exist.

I have experienced life without God's Word and it was a barren existence. My future seemed bleak and worthless. I knew I needed a change; I knew that only God's Word could achieve it. So I committed to reading the Bible every day, I started in Genesis, and read straight through to Revelation. The Word changed my life. I will never go back to that dry and weary place again. God's Words nourished my soul and I cannot live without Him. My prayer is that you will discover the same.

"O GOD, You are my God, earnestly will I seek You; my inner self thirsts for You, my flesh longs and is faint for You, in a dry and weary land where no water is. So I have looked upon You in the sanctuary to see Your power and Your glory. Because Your loving-kindness is better than life, my lips shall praise You. So will I bless You while I live; I will lift up my hands in Your name. My whole being shall be satisfied as with marrow and fatness; and my mouth shall praise You with joyful lips when I remember You upon my bed and meditate on You in the night watches. For You have been my help, and in the shadow of Your wings will I rejoice. My whole being follows hard after You and clings closely to You; Your right hand upholds me."
Psalm 63:1-8, AMP

Day 5

"For as the rain and snow come down from the heavens, and return not there again, but water the earth and make it bring forth and sprout, that it may give seed to the sower and bread to the eater, So shall My word be that goes forth out of My mouth: it shall not return to Me void [without producing any effect, useless], but it shall accomplish that which I please and purpose, and it shall prosper in the thing for which I sent it."

Isaiah 55:10-11, AMP

In our country, many translations of the Bible's text are available. I prefer the Amplified Bible translation because it does just what its title says: it amplifies the words translated from Greek and Hebrew into English. The Greek and Hebrew languages are rich in meaning, requiring more English words for an accurate translation than we would typically use in a sentence. Once I began to study the Amplified Bible with its 4-to-1 word ratio, all other translations seemed inferior to me—less meaty.

Meditating on God's Word means reading it until it talks back to you.

All of the translations are good and we are blessed to have so many different choices available. Find one that best suits your needs. As a student of His Word, use a Bible that you can easily understand. Spend time at your local Christian book supplier to check out the many, helpful Bible study tools available. I heard a Bible teacher say one Sunday morning, "Meditating on God's Word means reading it until it talks back to you."

His Word *will* engage your soul.

"My son, if you will receive my words and treasure up my commandments within you, Making your ear attentive to skillful and godly Wisdom and inclining and directing your heart and mind to understanding [applying all your powers to the quest for it]; Yes, if you cry out for insight and raise your voice for understanding, If you seek [Wisdom] as for silver and search for skillful and godly Wisdom as for hidden treasures, then you will understand the reverent and worshipful fear of the Lord and find the knowledge of [our omniscient] God. For the Lord gives skillful and godly Wisdom; from His mouth come knowledge and understanding. He hides away sound and godly Wisdom and stores it for the righteous (those who are upright and in right standing with Him); He is a shield to those who walk uprightly and in integrity, that He may guard the paths of justice; yes, He preserves the way of His saints. Then you will understand righteousness, justice, and fair dealing [in every area and relation]; yes, you will understand every good path. For skillful and godly Wisdom shall enter into your heart, and knowledge shall be pleasant to you. Discretion shall watch over you, understanding shall keep you." Proverbs 2:1-11, AMP

"I love those who love me, and those who seek me early and diligently shall find me." Proverbs 8:17, AMP

"Because he has set his love upon Me, therefore will I deliver him; I will set him on high, because he knows and understands My name [has a personal knowledge of My mercy, love, and kindness—trusts and relies on Me, knowing I will never forsake him, no, never]." Psalm 91:14, AMP

"If any of you is deficient in wisdom, let him ask of the giving God [Who gives] to everyone liberally and ungrudgingly, without reproaching or faultfinding, and it will be given him." James 1:5, AMP

"My people are destroyed from lack of knowledge. Because you have rejected knowledge, I also reject you as my priests; because you have ignored the law of your God, I also will ignore your children." Hosea 4:6, NIV

Day 6

"For as the rain and snow come down from the heavens, and return not there again, but water the earth and make it bring forth and sprout, that it may give seed to the sower and bread to the eater, So shall My word be that goes forth out of My mouth: it shall not return to Me void [without producing any effect, useless], but it shall accomplish that which I please and purpose, and it shall prosper in the thing for which I sent it."

Isaiah 55:10-11, AMP

God's Word is simple and direct. As you pursue knowing Him, the chances for misunderstanding and confusion are diminished. God's Word is clear. He says He freely gives wisdom to the one who seeks Him: *"If any of you is deficient in wisdom, let him ask of the giving God [Who gives] to everyone liberally and ungrudgingly, without reproaching or faultfinding, and it will be given him"* (James 1:5, AMP). God wants us to pursue Him and know Him. His desire is to have a relationship with us. Knowing Him and recognizing His voice are keys to an abundant life—to the life He predestined for humankind.

GOD IS NOT IMPOSSIBLE TO UNDERSTAND.

Throughout Christianity we have allowed traditions, denominations, and ignorance to taint our views of who He is. Now is the time for a personal and intimate relationship with Him. This World is getting darker and we Christians must become brighter and more influential.

The way to dispel incorrect concepts, philosophies, and denominationalism is by developing an intimate relationship of your own with Him. God is not impossible to understand. He has given us His Word and the capacity to comprehend.

Don't waste another day without Him.

"As the deer pants for streams of water, so my soul pants for you, O God. My soul thirsts for God, for the living God." Psalm 42:1-2, NIV

"The heavens declare the glory of God; and the firmament shows and proclaims His handiwork. Day after day pours forth speech, and night after night shows forth knowledge. There is no speech nor spoken word [from the stars]; their voice is not heard. Yet their voice [in evidence] goes out through all the earth, their sayings to the end of the world. Of the heavens has God made a tent for the sun, which is as a bridegroom coming out of his chamber; and it rejoices as a strong man to run his course. Its going forth is from the end of the heavens, and its circuit to the ends of it; and nothing [yes, no one] is hidden from the heat of it. The law of the Lord is perfect, restoring the [whole] person; the testimony of the Lord is sure, making wise the simple. The precepts of the Lord are right, rejoicing the heart; the commandment of the Lord is pure and bright, enlightening the eyes. The [reverent] fear of the Lord is clean, enduring forever; the ordinances of the Lord are true and righteous altogether. More to be desired are they than gold, even than much fine gold; they are sweeter also than honey and drippings from the honeycomb. Moreover, by them is Your servant warned (reminded, illuminated, and instructed); and in keeping them there is great reward. Who can discern his lapses and errors? Clear me from hidden [and unconscious] faults. Keep back Your servant also from presumptuous sins; let them not have dominion over me! Then shall I be blameless, and I shall be innocent and clear of great transgression. Let the words of my mouth and the meditation of my heart be acceptable in Your sight, O Lord, my [firm, impenetrable] Rock and my Redeemer." Psalm 19, AMP

Day 7

"For as the rain and snow come down from the heavens, and return not there again, but water the earth and make it bring forth and sprout, that it may give seed to the sower and bread to the eater, So shall My word be that goes forth out of My mouth: it shall not return to Me void [without producing any effect, useless], but it shall accomplish that which I please and purpose, and it shall prosper in the thing for which I sent it."

Isaiah 55:10-11, AMP

Allow the living water of these words to soak into you today, and be changed.

"Rain and snow fall from the sky. But they don't return without watering the earth that produces seeds to plant and grain to eat. That's how it is with my words. They don't return to me without doing everything I send them to do." (CEV)

"I don't think the way you think. The way you work isn't the way I word." God's Decree: *"For as the sky soars high above earth, so the way I work surpasses the way you work, and the way I think is beyond the way you think. Just as rain and snow descend from the skies and don't go back until they've watered the earth, Doing their work of making things grow and blossom, producing seed for farmers and food for the hungry, So will the words that come out of my mouth not come back empty-handed. They'll do the work I sent them to do; they'll complete the assignment I gave them."* (MSG)

"For as the rain and the snow come down from heaven and do not return there but water the earth, making it bring forth and sprout, giving seed to the sower and bread to the eater, so shall my word be that goes out from my mouth; it shall not return to me empty, but it shall accomplish that which I purpose, and shall succeed in the thing for which I sent it." (ESV)

Week 19

"He sends forth His word and heals them and rescues them from the pit and destruction."

Psalm 107:10, AMP

Day 1

"He sends forth His word and heals them and rescues them from the pit and destruction."
Psalm 107:10, AMP

"He sent His word and healed them, and delivered them from their destructions."
Psalm 107:20, KJV

God's Word has the ability to heal and rescue us from devastating circumstances. In Genesis' story of creation, the power of His Word is clearly outlined. By His Word, God created everything.

Psalm 107:10 refers to the words *"the pit and destruction,"* which describe conditions of desperation that require aid from an outside source. God sent His Word to rescue us from the devastation of the pit and destruction.

The "Word" referred to in this week's Scripture points is twofold. First, Jesus is the Word: *"In the beginning [before all time] was the Word (Christ), and the Word was with God, and the Word was God Himself. He was present originally with God. All things were made and came into existence through Him; and without Him was not even one thing made that has come into being"* (John 1:1-3 AMP).

> His Word points us in the direction of His will.

Second, the "Word" represents God's Word in printdform—the Bible. God has created a path for us to take that leads us away from destruction. His Word points us in the direction of His will. His will is His Word and His Word is life. God never intended for us to function in a state of brokenness and despair. He has repeatedly confirmed in His Word a life of wholeness through Jesus Christ (the Word).

Christians never need to settle for a wretched life or believe God wants us to remain broken. Our verse says, "*...He sent His Word and healed them and delivered them from their destructions* KJV." To believe anything less denies God's plan for salvation and all that Christ accomplished for us at the cross.

Day 2

"He sends forth His word and heals them and rescues them from the pit and destruction."
Psalm 107:10, AMP

During challenging times, having Scriptures memorized or written down for meditation gives us an advantage. Meditating on God's Word is part of His success formula. Meditating means more than simply reading the words on the page; it means fixing your mind on the Word so deeply that you do what it teaches. Knowing what God's Word says about you is crucial to living a successful life. God has said in Jeremiah 1:12b AMP: *"For I am alert and active, watching over My word to perform it."* His Word is life and health to our body.

> Meditating means more than simply reading the words on the page; it means fixing your mind on the Word so deeply that you do what it teaches.

If we actively live out His precepts and His commands, we experience the peace and success God planned for us. In Joshua 1:8 (AMP) God instructs Joshua and all of us: *"This Book of the Law shall not depart out of your mouth, but you shall meditate on it day and night, that you may observe and do according to all that is written in it. For then you shall make your way prosperous, and then you shall deal wisely and have good success."*

Pondering the Word of God builds faith and faith comes by hearing His Word. As you meditate on His Word, you will begin to see yourself as God sees you—one of His own. He has taken extreme measures to show you He loves you and wants to save you. Receive Him today!

"For we are God's [own] handiwork (His workmanship) ,recreated in Christ Jesus, [born anew] that we may do those good works which God predestined (planned beforehand) for us [taking paths which He prepared ahead of time], that we should walk in them [living the good life which He prearranged and made ready for us to live]." Ephesians 2:10, AMP

Day 3

"He sends forth His word and heals them and rescues them from the pit and destruction."
Psalm 107:10, AMP

Take some time today to soak in what God claims about His very own Words.

"BLESS (affectionately, gratefully praise) the Lord, O my soul; and all that is [deepest] within me, bless His holy name! Bless (affectionately, gratefully praise) the Lord, O my soul, and forget not [one of] all His benefits—Who forgives [every-one of] all your iniquities, Who heals [each one of] all your diseases, Who redeems your life from the pit and corruption, Who beautifies, dignifies, and crowns you with loving-kindness and tender mercy; Who satisfies your mouth [your necessity and desire at your personal age and situation] with good so that your youth, renewed, is like the eagle's [strong, overcoming, soaring]! The Lord executes righteousness and justice [not for me only, but] for all who are oppressed." (Psalm 103:1-6, AMP)

"I am alert and active, watching over My words to perform it." (Jeremiah 1:12b, AMP)

"So then faith cometh by hearing, and hearing by the word of God." (Romans 10:17, KJV)

"For as the rain and snow come down from the heavens, and return not there again, but water the earth and make it bring forth and sprout, that it may give seed to the sower and bread to the eater, So shall My word be that goes forth out of My mouth: it shall not return to Me void [without producing any effect, useless], but it shall accomplish that which I please and purpose, and it shall prosper in the thing for which I sent it." (Isaiah 55:10-11, AMP)

"Man shall not live and be upheld and sustained by bread alone, but by every word that comes forth from the mouth of God." (Matthew 4:4, AMP)

"Every Scripture is God-breathed (given by His inspiration) and profitable for instruction, for reproof and conviction of sin, for correction of error and discipline in obedience, [and] for training in righteousness (in holy living, in conformity to God's will in thought, purpose, and action), So that the man of God may be complete and proficient, well fitted and thoroughly equipped for every good work." (2 Timothy 3:16-17, AMP)

"I will lift up my eyes to the hills [around Jerusalem, to sacred Mount Zion and Mount Moriah]—From whence shall my help come? My help comes from the Lord, Who made heaven and earth. He will not allow your foot to slip or to be moved; He Who keeps you will not slumber. Behold, He who keeps Israel will neither slumber nor sleep. The Lord is your keeper; the Lord is your shade on your right hand [the side not carrying a shield]. The sun shall not smite you by day, nor the moon by night. The Lord will keep you from all evil; He will keep your life. The Lord will keep your going out and your coming in from this time forth and forevermore." (Psalm 121, AMP)

DAY 4

"He sends forth His word and heals them and rescues them from the pit and destruction."

PSALM 107:10, AMP

"When Jesus had entered Capernaum, a centurion came to him, asking for help. 'Lord,' he said, 'my servant lies at home paralyzed and in terrible suffering.' Jesus said to him, 'I will go and heal him.' The centurion replied, 'Lord, I do not deserve to have you come under my roof. But just say the word, and my servant will be healed. For I myself am a man under authority, with soldiers under me. I tell this one, "Go"' and he goes; and that one, "Come," and he comes. I say to my servant, "Do this," and he does it.' When Jesus heard this, he was astonished and said to those following him, 'I tell you the truth, I have not found an one in Israel with such great faith. I say to you that many will come from the east and the west, and will take their places at the feast with Abraham, Isaac and Jacob in the kingdom of heaven. But the subjects of the kingdom will be thrown outside, into the darkness, where there will be weeping and gnashing of teeth.' Then Jesus said to the centurion, 'Go! It will be done just as you believed it would.' And his servant was healed at that very hour." (Matthew 8:5-13, NIV)

THE WORD OF GOD HAS THE POWER IN ITSELF TO HEAL, DELIVER, AND SET FREE.

The centurion recognized the power of Jesus' words, for he had been following Jesus and observing the disciples for some time. As a distinguished leader in his regiment, the centurion was familiar with the order of command for those in power. He had spent many days observing Jesus and listening to His messages, becoming a believer in someone who his culture and the Roman army opposed. Seeing the miracles and hearing the wisdom of this man they called King of the Jews changed the centurion's life. His understanding and belief in Jesus' power was astonishing to Jesus; the Lord remarked that He had not found anyone in Israel with such faith.

Jesus sent forth His Word and healed and rescued two people in this story. The centurion received Jesus' Words and believed them. He developed faith in the power of the God of Israel by hearing the Words and seeing the actions of Christ, which led to his rescue from the pit and destruction of the Roman Empire. And the servant of the centurion was healed of sickness by the power of the Word.

The Word of God has the power in itself to heal, deliver, and set free. The power of God's Word never changes. What the Word did for the centurion centuries ago can be done for you today!

Day 5

"He sends forth His word and heals them and rescues them from the pit and destruction."

Psalm 107:10, AMP

When I was pregnant with my third child, I started having labor pains prematurely. We lived in Orlando, Florida, far away from all of our family and close friends. During a routine exam, the OBGYN discovered I was having regular contractions, and recommended I immediately go to the hospital to check in for monitoring. My heart started to race and so did my thoughts; having a premature baby was never a part of the plan. I quickly felt overcome by emotions. I gathered myself, scooped up my two children, and drove to the hospital. Monty was a player for the Orlando Magic at the time and I was unable to contact him at the practice site. The children and I sat in the lobby of the hospital until he came to get them.

I checked into the triage area, only to be treated as another number; this hospital is one of the busiest in the country. I was directed to sit in a small waiting room with other pregnant women until a bed opened up. I could not believe this was happening. The longer I sat in the waiting area, the stronger the labor pains became. I remember thinking, "I'm all alone. No husband. No family. No friends."

Finally, a bed opened up and I was moved into a common labor area equipped with several beds separated by hospital curtains. The nurses started an IV and hooked me up to a monitor to observe the contractions. I remember the nurse looking through me and not really at me. She was doing her job, but it was clear that, to her, I was one of thousands of women in and out of this hospital. She did not have time to console me or attend to my emotional needs.

I felt such despair that fear gripped my mind. I knew this sweet baby growing inside of me was special and I knew God cared, but this entire situation had caught me off guard. I desperately needed someone to stand strong for me. Then the nurses gave me news of more contractions and informed me of all the health risks of delivering a premature baby. My fear grew even larger.

Then, suddenly, the phone rang. It was Monty. He had called our pastor in San Antonio and my Bible teacher to ask for prayer. Knowing that people were interceding on behalf of my baby provided me some relief. Within moments after Monty and I finished talking; our pastor from San Antonio called. He did not ask how I was doing. He did not make small talk. He immediately went into a prayer of authority and he proclaimed the Word of the Lord over my baby and my body. PRAISE GOD! He blessed me and hung up. Shortly thereafter my Bible teacher called and declared a Word from the Lord for my child. I felt overjoyed. Immediately my condition changed—the contractions stopped.

After the hospital staff was assured of my stability, I was discharged. Two months later I delivered a healthy baby girl. To God be the Glory! His Word was sent to heal and deliver us from the pit and from destruction. His Word changed my life.

Day 6

"He sends forth His word and heals them and rescues them from the pit and destruction."
Psalm 107:10, AMP

Personal fear can be a pit. Most of our society's media news coverage is filled with fear. I find television news reports very disturbing; they are virtually impossible for me to watch, especially now that I have children. I have to keep my mind focused on God's Words in order to combat the barrage of fearful images in our media, especially as they pertain to children. If I let my imagination wander, I can become a trembling wreck. The reports of serial rapists, child molesters, child abductions, and Amber Alerts promote many insecurities and fear in me.

I don't deny that this information is pertinent to the public for catching criminals and recovering lost children. But a daily intake of all of these overwhelming facts produces fear. God has *absolutely not* created us to be afraid. 2 Timothy 1:7 AMP describes a spirit of fear as: "*cowardice, craven, cringing, fawning*." God has created us with a spirit of love, along with a calm mind that is well-balanced with discipline and self-control.

God has absolutely not created us to be afraid.

God has assured us in His Word of His continuous protection and uncompromising ability to deliver us from every evil. Not only do we have assurance of His presence, but nothing evil or wicked can come near us. He has given us a covenant of protection. Psalm 91 NIV is full of our covenant promises:

He who dwells in the shelter of the Most High
will rest in the shadow of the Almighty.
I will say of the LORD, "He is my refuge and my fortress,
my God, in whom I trust."
Surely he will save you from the fowler's snare
and from the deadly pestilence.
He will cover you with his feathers,
and under his wings you will find refuge;
his faithfulness will be your shield and rampart.
You will not fear the terror of night,
nor the arrow that flies by day,
nor the pestilence that stalks in the darkness,
nor the plague that destroys at midday.
A thousand may fall at your side,
ten thousand at your right hand,
but it will not come near you.
You will only observe with your eyes
and see the punishment of the wicked.
If you make the Most High your dwelling—
even the LORD, who is my refuge—
then no harm will befall you,
no disaster will come near your tent.
For he will command his angels concerning you
to guard you in all your ways;
they will lift you up in their hands,
so that you will not strike your foot against a stone.
You will tread upon the lion and the cobra;
you will trample the great lion and the serpent
"Because he loves me," says the LORD, "I will rescue him;
I will protect him, for he acknowledges my name.
He will call upon me, and I will answer him;
I will be with him in trouble,
I will deliver him and honor him.
With long life will I satisfy him
and show him my salvation."

God has delivered us from the pit of fear that leads to destruction. He has created a place for us in Him and it is called the secret place. Will you come and experience His peace?

"Fear not [there is nothing to fear], for I am with you; do not look around you in terror and be dismayed, for I am your God. I will strengthen and harden you to difficulties, yes, I will help you; yes, I will hold you up and retain you with My [victorious] right hand of rightness and justice." Isaiah 41:10, AMP

"The eyes of the Lord are toward the [uncompromisingly] righteous and His ears are open to their cry." Psalm 34:15, AMP

"For You, Lord, will bless the [uncompromisingly] righteous [him who is upright and in right standing with You]; as with a shield You will surround him with goodwill (pleasure and favor)." Psalm 5:12, AMP

"Don't be afraid. I am with you. Don't tremble with fear. I am your God. I will make you strong, as I protect you with my arm and give you victories." Isaiah 41:10, CEV

"No [actual] evil, misfortune, or calamity shall come upon the righteous, but the wicked shall be filled with evil, misfortune, and calamity." Proverbs 12:21, AMP

"The reverent worshipful fear of the Lord leads to life, and he who has it rests satisfied; he cannot be visited with (actual) evil." Proverbs 19:23, AMP

DAY 7

"He sends forth His word and heals them and rescues them from the pit and destruction."

PSALM 107:10, AMP

"God is not a man, that He should tell or act a lie, neither the son of man, that He should feel repentance or compunction [for what He has promised]. Has He said and shall He not do it? Or has He spoken and shall He not make it good?" (Numbers 23:19, AMP)

The declarations of wholeness in God's Word are true and never-failing. 2 Timothy 3:16 (AMP) says, "*Every scripture is God-breathed.*" We can confidently believe the Word of the Lord. God cannot lie. There just isn't anything false in Him.

The plans of the father of lies and deception—Satan—are always to kill, steal, and destroy. Our God is committed to bringing us into wholeness and restoration.

Believe God when He says that He sends forth His Word to heal and deliver us from destruction. Take time to find Scriptures that apply to your specific needs. Then believe what God says.

Week 20

"In your anger, do not sin; when you are on your beds,
search your hearts and be silent. Selah.
Offer right sacrifices and trust in the Lord."

Psalm 4:4-5, NIV

Day 1

"In your anger, do not sin; when you are on your beds,
search your hearts and be silent. Selah.
Offer right sacrifices and trust in the Lord."

Psalm 4:4-5, NIV

This week's Scripture verses have been instrumental in my crusade for righteous living. I have been challenged to release my cares to the Lord. In times past, I often felt frustrated and provoked by circumstances which led to anger that controlled me. When anger is our pilot, we only arrive at destinations of sin and destruction.

WHEN ANGER IS OUR PILOT, WE ONLY ARRIVE AT DESTINATIONS OF SIN AND DESTRUCTION.

Our adversary, the devil, loves to see Christians living outside of the will of God and deep in sin. I've learned that life cannot be controlled by human abilities. Without God, it is impossible to navigate through life's challenges. He truly gives clear direction and peace that goes beyond what the mind can understand.

"Therefore humble yourselves [demote, lower yourselves in your own estimation] under the mighty hand of God, that in due time He may exalt you, Casting the whole of your care [all your anxieties, all your worries, all your concerns, once and for all] on Him, for He cares for you affectionately and cares about you watchfully. Be well balanced

(temperate, sober of mind), be vigilant and cautious at all times; for that enemy of yours, the devil, roams around like a lion roaring [in fierce hunger], seeking someone to seize upon and devour." 1 Peter 5:6-8, AMP

"Many are the sorrows of the wicked, but he who trusts in, relies on, and confidently leans on the Lord shall be compassed about with mercy and with loving-kindness. Be glad in the Lord and rejoice, you [uncompromisingly] righteous [you who are upright an in right standing with Him]; shout for joy, all you upright in heart!" Psalm 32:10-11, AMP

"Lean on, trust in, and be confident in the Lord with all your heart and mind and do not rely on your own insight or understanding. In all your ways know, recognize, and acknowledge Him, and He will direct and make straight and plain your paths." Proverbs 3:5-6, AMP

"Blessed be the Lord, because He has heard the voice of my supplications. The Lord is my Strength and my [impenetrable] Shield; my heart trusts in, relies on, and confidently leans on Him, and I am helped; therefore my heart greatly rejoices, and with my song will I praise Him." Psalm 28:6-7, AMP

DAY 2

"Be angry [or stand in awe] and sin not; commune with
your own hearts upon your beds and
be silent (sorry for the things you say in your hearts).
Selah [pause, and calmly think of that]!
Offer just and right sacrifices; trust (lean on
and be confident) in the Lord."

PSALM 4:4-5, AMP

The middle section of this scripture encourages us to stop and be silent. I love this part of the verse: BE SILENT!

We certainly cannot hear what the Holy Spirit is telling us if we are being controlled by our speech and feelings. Being silent means calming your body and your mind. When I have heard my elders speak of this silence, they say it means quieting your spirit, not talking, not moving, not thinking; just being still. This is when God is able to speak to us.

To arrive at this kind of silence before God takes maturity. In an age that emphasizes productivity, silence is rare, yet imperative in our relationship with the Father.

Strive to arrive at a place of silence with Him.

"This is what the Sovereign LORD, the Holy One of Israel, says: In repentance and rest is your salvation, in quietness and trust is your strength." Isaiah 30:15a, NIV

"Great peace have they who love Your law; nothing shall offend them or make them stumble." Psalm 119:165, AMP

DAY 3

"In your anger, do not sin; when you are on your beds,
search your hearts and be silent. Selah.
Offer right sacrifices and trust in the Lord."
PSALM 4:4-5, NIV

The following Scriptures focus on anger. Take some time today to reflect on them.

"He who is slow to anger is better than the mighty, he who rules his spirit than he who takes a city." (Proverbs 16:32, AMP)

"A soft answer turns away wrath, but a harsh word stirs up anger." (Proverbs 15:1, AMP)

"For God did not give us a spirit of timidity (of cowardice, of craven and cringing and fawning fear), but [He has given us a spirit] of power and of love and of calm and well-balanced mind and discipline and self-control." (2 Timothy 1:7, AMP)

"An angry man stirs up strife, and a furious man abounds in transgression." (Proverbs 29:22, NKJV)

"The discretion of a man makes him slow to anger, and his glory is to overlook a transgression." (Proverbs 19:11, NKJV)

"Do not hasten in your spirit to be angry, for anger rests in the bosom of fools." (Ecclesiastes 7:9, NKJV)

"But now put away and rid yourselves [completely] of all these things: anger, rage, bad feeling toward others, curses and slander, and foulmouthed abuse and shameful utterances from your lips!" (Colossians 3:8, AMP)

"Understand [this], my beloved brethren. Let every man be quick to hear [a ready listener], slow to speak, slow to take offense and to get angry. For man's anger does not promote the righteousness God [wishes and requires]." (James 1:19-20, AMP)

"Don't sin by letting anger control you. Think about it overnight and remain silent. Interlude. Offer sacrifices in the right spirit, and trust the Lord." (Psalm 4:4-5, NLT)

"But each of you had better tremble and turn from your sins. Silently search your heart as you lie in bed. Offer the proper sacrifices and trust the LORD." (Psalm 4:4-5, CEV)

"Be angry [or stand in awe] and sin not; commune with your own hearts upon your beds and be silent (sorry for the things you say in your hearts). Selah [pause, and calmly think of that]! Offer just and right sacrifices; trust (lean on and be confident) in the Lord." (Psalm 4:4-5, AMP)

Day 4

"In your anger, do not sin; when you are on your beds,
search your hearts and be silent. Selah.
Offer right sacrifices and trust in the Lord."

Psalm 4:4-5, NIV

Learning how to control our anger and become free of anger issues is part of the maturing process for Jesus' followers. He has made us light for the world and encourages us to: *"Let your light so shine before men that they may see your moral excellence and your praiseworthy, noble, and good deeds and recognize and honor and praise and glorify your Father who is in heaven."* (Matthew 4:16, AMP)

If we conduct our affairs like those who don't know God in times of stress or conflict, then our heavenly Father is not represented correctly. We cannot mirror the ungodly responses in our society. James 1:20 NIV explains: *"For man's anger does not bring about the righteous life that God desires."* Anger does not promote righteousness; it's simply the result of an emotional takeover. God should be the only conductor in our lives. For our benefit, He can dissolve any and all anger problems by His Word. He disintegrates anger issues by the power of His Word.

Take time today to meditate on three Scriptures regarding anger in order to encourage your faith. Applying His Word to your situation will bring change.

Yesterday I presented 11 verses to ponder. Which of them apply to your own personal circumstances?

Day 5

"In your anger, do not sin; when you are on your beds,
search your hearts and be silent. Selah.
Offer right sacrifices and trust in the Lord."

Psalm 4:4-5, NIV

Today let's reflect upon definitions of anger rendered by the Latin language.

- Latin: n. *ango*: "to choke, strangle, vex; whence anger, vexation, anguish, the quinsy (inflammation of the throat), angina (to choke)."

- Anger: "to strangle; a violent passion of the mind excited by a real or supposed injury; usually accompanied with a propensity to take vengeance or to obtain satisfaction from the offending party. This passion however varies in degrees of violence, and in ingenious minds, may be attended only with a desire to reprove or chide the offenders. Anger is also excited by an injury offered to a relation, friend or party to whom one is attached; and more degrees of it may be excited by cruelty, injustice or oppression offered to those with whom one has no immediate connection, or even to the community of which one is a member. Nor is it unusual to see something of this passion roused by gross absurdities in others, especially in controversy or discussion. Anger may be inflamed till it rises to rage and temporary delirium." *(From the American Dictionary of the English Language Noah Webster 1828 version)*

I find it most interesting that in both Latin and Hebrew, "anger" is defined as "to strangle." Strangle is defined as: "to choke, to suffocate; to destroy life by stopping respiration; to suppress, to hinder from birth or appearance."

In Genesis 2:7 AMP, Scripture states, "*Then the Lord God formed man from the dust of the ground and breathed into his nostrils the breath or spirit of life, and man became a living being.*" In Psalm 33:6 AMP we are taught that, "*By the Word of the Lord were the heavens made and all their host by the breath of His mouth.*" God Himself is the one "*Who gives life and breath and all things to all people*" (Acts 17:15, AMP).

ANGER-OVERLOAD IS A DEATH TRAP.

If the definition of anger is "to strangle," which is to stop breath, that can mean that our anger stops the very life force of who we are. Anger that is tolerated and allowed to govern our lives can inhibit God from using us for His glory. We stop being productive Christians when we give way to anger. Anger-overload is a death trap. BEWARE!

"*But every person is tempted when he is drawn away, enticed and baited by his own evil desire (lust, passions). Then the evil desire, when it has conceived, gives birth to sin, and sin, when it is fully matured, brings forth death. Do not be misled, my beloved brethren. Every good gift and every perfect (free, large, full) gift is from above; it comes down from the Father of all [that gives] light, in [the shining of] Whom there can be no variation [rising or setting] or shadow cast by His turning [as in an eclipse]. And it was of His own [free] will that He gave us birth [as sons] by [His] Word of Truth, so that we should be a kind of first fruits of His creatures [a sample of what He created to be consecrated to Himself]. Understand [this], my beloved brethren. Let every man be quick to hear [a ready listener], slow to speak, slow to take offense and to get angry. For man's anger does not promote the righteousness God [wishes and requires].*" James 1:14-20, AMP

Day 6

"In your anger, do not sin; when you are on your beds,
search your hearts and be silent. Selah.
Offer right sacrifices and trust in the Lord."

Psalm 4:4-5, NIV

"But now you must rid yourselves of all such things as these: anger, rage, malice, slander, and filthy language from your lips. Do not lie to each other, since you have taken off your old self with its practices and have put on the new self, which is being renewed in knowledge in the image of its Creator. Here there is no Greek or Jew, circumcised or uncircumcised, barbarian, Scythian, slave or free, but Christ is all, and is in all. Therefore, as God's chosen people, holy and dearly loved, clothe yourselves with compassion, kindness, humility, gentleness and patience. Bear with each other and forgive whatever grievances you may have against one another. Forgive as the Lord forgave you. And over all these virtues put on love, which binds them all together in perfect unity. Let the peace of Christ rule in your hearts, since as members of one body you were called to peace. And be thankful. Let the word of Christ dwell in you richly." (Colossians 3:8-16, NIV)

Anger is not a quality we should boast about. We should strive to rid ourselves of any and all things that encourage angry responses. Each day as we draw closer to God, study His Word, and commit to obeying what we read, our minds are being renewed. The old way of functioning is being replaced with His way.

God graciously extends mercy to us. His love is unconditional and His patience toward us never ends. Christian speaker Gloria Copeland writes: "Read the Bible with the knowledge that God had it written for your benefit—not for His. He is already quite successful." The Bible equips us to move forward in Him.

Try to live out the insight you receive from His Word.

"Understand [this], my beloved brethren. Let every man be quick to hear [a ready listener], slow to speak, slow to take offense and to get angry. For man's anger does not promote the righteousness God [wishes and requires].So get rid of all uncleanness and the rampant outgrowth of wickedness, and in a humble (gentle, modest) spirit receive and welcome the Word which implanted and rooted [in your hearts] contains the power to save your souls. But be doers of the Word [obey the message], and not merely listeners to it, betraying yourselves [into deception by reasoning contrary to the Truth]. For if anyone only listens to the Word without obeying it and being a doer of it, he is like a man who looks carefully at his [own] natural face in a mirror; For he thoughtfully observes himself, and then goes off and promptly forgets what he was like. But he who looks carefully into the faultless law, the [law] of liberty, and is faithful to it and perseveres in looking into it, being not a heedless listener who forgets but an active doer [who obeys], he shall be blessed in his doing (his life of obedience)." James 1:19-25, AMP

Day 7

"In your anger, do not sin; when you are on your beds,
search your hearts and be silent. Selah.
Offer right sacrifices and trust in the Lord."

Psalm 4:4-5, NIV

Make Me an Instrument of Your Peace

(Prayer of St. Francis of Assisi)

Lord, make me an instrument of your peace.
Where there is hatred, let me sow love;
Where there is injury, pardon;
Where there is doubt, faith;
Where there is despair; hope;
Where there is darkness, light;
Where there is sadness, joy.
O divine Master, grant that I may not so
much seek to be consoled, as to console;
To be understood, as to understand;
To be loved, as to love.
For it is in giving that we receive;
It is in pardoning that we are pardoned;
And it is in dying that we are born to eternal life.

WEEK 21

"For wherever there is jealousy (envy) and contention (rivalry and selfish ambition), there will also be confusion (unrest, disharmony, rebellion) and all sorts of evil and vile practices."

JAMES 3:16, AMP

DAY 1

"For wherever there is jealousy (envy) and contention
(rivalry and selfish ambition), there will also be
confusion (unrest, disharmony, rebellion)
and all sorts of evil and vile practices."
JAMES 3:16, AMP

This week's verse brings to mind family gatherings I have attended over the years. Unfortunately, our extended families are impaired by jealousy and contention. My husband and I have made a conscious effort to stop any and all beginnings of self-ambition with our immediate family. Our children have been taught that no one and nothing will or should separate our family.

Our philosophy has been encapsulated in the story of the original family. God created the heavens and the earth and all was declared "good." No problems, no evil; just a lush life. Trouble began with that lying coward Lucifer. He was banished from heaven because of his selfish ambition. He desired to be God. He wanted to be worshiped. His jealousy and selfishness got him expelled from the best life he could have ever had. Unfortunately, his actions triggered a downward spiral for mankind. Lucifer influenced Adam and Eve to make decisions which were disharmonious with God, just as he does with our families today.

We are thankful that our sovereign God provided a way back into relationship with Him through Jesus Christ. Today we can choose not to allow our emotions and selfishness to control our lives. We can choose not to have a divided family.

"[Let your] love be sincere (a real thing); hate what is evil [loathe all ungodliness, turn in horror from wickedness], but hold fast to that which is good. Love one another with brotherly affection [as members of one family], giving precedence and showing honor to one another." Romans 12:9-10, AMP

"Finally, brethren, farewell (rejoice)! Be strengthened (perfected, completed, made what you ought to be); be encouraged and consoled and comforted; be of the same [agreeable] mind one with another; live in peace, and [then] the God of love [Who is the Source of affection, goodwill, love, and benevolence toward men] and the Author and Promoter of peace will be with you." 2 Corinthians 13:11, AMP

DAY 2

"For wherever there is jealousy (envy) and contention (rivalry and selfish ambition), there will also be confusion (unrest, disharmony, rebellion) and all sorts of evil and vile practices."
JAMES 3:16, AMP

The following Scriptures highlight the importance of not having envy and strife in your life.

"A hot-tempered man stirs up strife, but he who is slow to anger appeases contention." (Proverbs 15:18, AMP)

"A calm and undisturbed mind and heart are the life and health of the body, but envy, jealousy, and wrath are like rottenness of the bones." (Proverbs 14:30, AMP)

"He who loves strife and is quarrelsome loves transgression and involves himself in guilt; he who raises high his gateway and is boastful and arrogant invites destruction." (Proverbs 17:19, AMP)

"It is an honor for a man to cease from strife and keep aloof from it, but every fool will quarrel." (Proverbs 20:3, AMP)

"Let us live and conduct ourselves honorably and becomingly as in the [open light of] day, not in reveling (carousing) and drunkenness, not in immorality and debauchery (sensuality and licentiousness), not in quarreling and jealousy. But clothe yourself with the Lord Jesus Christ (the Messiah), and make no provision for [indulging] the flesh [put a stop to thinking about the evil cravings of your physical nature] to [gratify its] desires (lusts)." (Romans 13:13-14, AMP)

"So be done with every trace of wickedness (depravity, malignity) and all deceit and insincerity (pretense, hypocrisy) and grudges (envy, jealousy) and slander and evil speaking of every kind. Like newborn babies you should crave (thirst for, earnestly desire) the pure (unadulterated) spiritual milk, that by it you may be nurtured and grow unto [completed] salvation, since you have [already] tasted the goodness and kindness of the Lord." (1 Peter 2:1-3, AMP)

"Love endures long and is patient and kind; love never is envious nor boils over with jealousy, is not boastful or vainglorious, does not display itself haughtily. It is not conceited (arrogant and inflated with pride); it is not rude (unmannerly) and does not act unbecomingly. Love (God's love in us) does not insist on its own rights or its own way, for it is not self-seeking; it is not touchy or fretful or resentful; it takes no account of the evil done to it [it pays no attention to a suffered wrong]. It does not rejoice at injustice and unrighteousness, but rejoices when right and truth prevail. Love bears up under anything and everything that comes, is ever ready to believe the best of every person, its hopes are fadeless under all circumstances, and it endures everything [without weakening]. Love never fails [never fades out or becomes obsolete or comes to an end]." (1 Corinthians 13:4-8, AMP)

For the desires of the flesh are opposed to the [Holy] Spirit, and the [desires of the] Spirit are opposed to the flesh (godless human nature); for these are antagonistic to each other [continually withstanding and in conflict with each other], so that you are not free but are prevented from doing what you desire to do. But if you are guided (led) by the [Holy] Spirit, you are not subject to the Law. Now the doings (practices) of the flesh are clear (obvious): they are immorality, impurity, indecency, idolatry, sorcery, enmity, strife, jealousy, anger (ill temper), selfishness, divisions (dissensions), party spirit (factions, sects with peculiar opinions, heresies), Envy, drunkenness, carousing, and the like. I warn you beforehand, just as I did previously, that those who do such things shall not inherit the kingdom of God. But the fruit of the [Holy] Spirit [the work which His presence within accomplishes] is love, joy (gladness), peace, patience (an even temper, forbearance), kindness, goodness (benevolence), faithfulness, gentleness (meekness, humility), self-control (self-restraint, continence). Against such things there is no law [that can bring a charge]. And those who belong to Christ Jesus (the Messiah) have crucified the flesh (the godless human nature) with its passions and appetites and desires. If we live by the [Holy] Spirit, let us also walk by the Spirit. [If by the Holy Spirit we have our life in God, let us go forward walking in line, our conduct controlled by the Spirit.] Let us not become vainglorious and self-conceited, competitive and challenging and provoking and irritating to one another, envying and being jealous of one another." (Galatians 5:17-26, AMP)

Take time today to hear the voice of the Lord. He can show you how these words apply to you. We all have areas in our lives that need attention. Will you consider His quiet promptings to improve your life?

Enjoy the journey! Receive the goodness God has waiting for you.

DAY 3

"For wherever there is jealousy (envy) and contention (rivalry and selfish ambition), there will also be confusion (unrest, disharmony, rebellion) and all sorts of evil and vile practices."
JAMES 3:16, AMP

The rebellion of Korah is recorded in the book of Numbers (chapter 16). This story is a powerful example of how envy and selfish ambition create anarchy within the camp of the Lord. Korah and a group of his followers (in Numbers 16:2 they are called "*men well known and of distinction*") vehemently challenged the leadership God put over His people, having determined that Moses and Aaron were not fit leaders. They started complaining and demanding a change of leadership. In the end, they lost their lives—and so did their family members.

Moses had been divinely chosen by God from birth. I'm sure the entire camp was aware of his miraculous escape from Pharaoh at birth and how he was raised in the king's palace before fulfilling the plan of the Lord to lead His people out of slavery and into the Promised Land. In fact, in Numbers 12:6-8 AMP, God says:

> *"Hear now My words: If there is a prophet among you, I the Lord make Myself known to him in a vision and speak to him in a dream. But not so with My servant Moses; he is entrusted and faithful in all My house. With him I speak mouth to mouth [directly], clearly and not in dark speeches; and he beholds the form of the Lord. Why then were you not afraid to speak against My servant Moses?"*

> *"When Moses entered the tent, the pillar of cloud would descend and stand at the door of the tent, and the Lord would talk with Moses. And all the people saw the pillar of cloud stand at the tent door, and all the*

people rose up and worshiped, every man at his tent door. And the Lord spoke to Moses face to face, as a man speaks to his friend." (Exodus 33:9-11, AMP)

Moses was unquestionably part of God's plan for this journey through the wilderness. It is completely astonishing to think that anyone would doubt the capability of Moses' (and Aaron's) leadership. But this scenario happens every Sunday at many churches across America. One member of the church will persuade some members of the trustee board or some deacons to slander and usurp the leadership of the pastor.

Use Korah and his friends as an example of what not to do when you become discouraged in the wilderness, when life's circumstances are not what you expected or planned. Don't question the competency of your pastor with the people of influence in the church. Go before the Lord in humble submission. If your pastor needs to be corrected, let God be God. Nine times out of ten, our own insecurities and frailties are what draw us to a place of discontentment towards our leaders.

Use Korah and his friends as an example of what not to do when you become discouraged in the wilderness, when life's circumstances are not what you expected or planned.

Seek Him. Only the Lord can keep us from destroying ourselves and those around us.

"*It is better to trust and take refuge in the Lord than to put confidence in man.*" Psalm 118:8, AMP

"*Let not mercy and kindness [shutting out all hatred and selfishness] and truth [shutting out all deliberate hypocrisy or falsehood] forsake you; bind them about your neck, write them upon the tablet of your heart. So shall you find favor, good understanding, and high esteem in the sight [or judgment] of God and man. Lean on, trust in, and be confident in the Lord with all your heart and mind and do not rely on your own insight or understanding. In all your ways know, recognize, and acknowledge Him, and He will direct and make straight and plain your paths."* Proverbs 3:3-6, AMP

"All the ways of a man are pure in his own eyes, but the Lord weighs the spirits (the thoughts and intents of the heart). Roll your works upon the Lord [commit and trust them wholly to Him; He will cause your thoughts to become agreeable to His will, and] so shall your plans be established and succeed. The Lord has made everything [to accommodate itself and contribute] to its own end and His own purpose—even the wicked [are fitted for their role] for the day of calamity and evil. Everyone proud and arrogant in heart is disgusting, hateful, and exceedingly offensive to the Lord; be assured [I pledge it] they will not go unpunished." Proverbs 16:2-5, AMP

DAY 4

"For wherever there is jealousy (envy) and contention (rivalry and selfish ambition), there will also be confusion (unrest, disharmony, rebellion) and all sorts of evil and vile practices."

JAMES 3:16, AMP

I visualize this week's verse as an equation: IF—THEN.

IF you have:

- Envy
- Jealousy
- Contention
- Rivalry
- Selfish Ambition

THEN you have:

- Confusion
- Unrest
- Disharmony
- Rebellion
- Vile (mean, hateful, base) Practices

When I examine situations where many "THEN" factors are present, this equation—without exception—is true. For instance, during times of disharmony in my marriage, I was struggling with selfish ambition. In my family growing up, sibling rivalry, rebellion, and confusion were constantly present. When jealousy has arisen between friends, evil responses reared their ugly heads. Even jealousy towards a person we don't really know (like a neighbor, a celebrity, or someone at the local gym) can evoke mean and hateful actions toward them.

As you meditate on this week's Scripture, let the Holy Spirit reveal instances in the past or present where you may have been a factor in the IF—THEN equation. It really is that simple. Acknowledge how emotions and insecurities can affect the present and the future.

"The foolishness of man subverts his way [ruins his affairs]; then his heart is resentful and frets against the Lord." Proverbs 19:3, AMP

"He who is of a greedy spirit stirs up strife, but he who puts his trust in the Lord shall be enriched and blessed." Proverbs 28:25, AMP

Day 5

"For wherever there is jealousy (envy) and contention (rivalry and selfish ambition), there will also be confusion (unrest, disharmony, rebellion) and all sorts of evil and vile practices."

James 3:16, AMP

An essential factor to maturing in Christ is being willing to change. God is awesome, because He is faithful to us and His promises help us change. He reveals an area of sin in our life and then gives us ample opportunity to come to Him and humbly surrender it to Him. And He is able to mend broken hearts and restore damaged relationships.

Jesus Christ came to give us hope; not to condemn us.

"The Lord is close to those who are of a broken heart and saves such as are crushed with sorrow for sin and are, humbly and thoroughly penitent." (Psalm 34:18, AMP)

"He heals the brokenhearted and binds up their wounds [curing their pains and their sorrows]." (Psalm 147:3, AMP)

Jesus Christ came to give us hope; not to condemn us. His life forever established our victory over sin. When we became Christians and dedicated our lives to God, everything changed. We became new individuals, yielding our lives to a way based on love—not attaining a higher status based on our own success.

"For the law of the Spirit of life [which is] in Christ Jesus [the law of our new being] has freed me from the law of sin and of death. For God has done what the Law could not do, [its power] being weakened by the flesh [the entire nature of man without the Holy Spirit]. Sending His own Son in the guise of sinful flesh and as an offering for sin, [God] condemned sin in the flesh [subdued, overcame, deprived it of

its power over all who accept that sacrifice], so that the righteous and just requirement of the Law might be fully met in us who live and move not in the ways of the flesh but in the ways of the Spirit [our lives governed not by the standards and according to the dictates of the flesh, but controlled by the Holy Spirit]." (Romans 8:2-4, AMP)

Through Jesus Christ, we are capable of overcoming debilitating choices based on emotions. Living a life of peace and happiness is the plan God has for us. This is not to say temptations will not come to lure us back into our old ways of living. But it does mean that when situations arise that used to lead us into chaos, confusion, and disharmony, we are equipped with the Spirit of the Lord to resist. God has given us His personal armor to defeat the wiles of the enemy:

"Put on the full armor of God so that you can take your stand against the devil's schemes. For our struggle is not against flesh and blood, but against the rulers, against the authorities, against the powers of this dark world and against the spiritual forces of evil in the heavenly realms. Therefore put on the full armor of God, so that when the day of evil comes, you may be able to stand your ground, and after you have done everything, to stand. Stand firm then, with the belt of truth buckled around your waist, with the breastplate of righteousness in place, and with your feet fitted with the readiness that comes from the gospel of peace. In addition to all this, take up the shield of faith, with which you can extinguish all the flaming arrows of the evil one. Take the helmet of salvation and the sword of the Spirit, which is the word of God. And pray in the Spirit on all occasions with all kinds of prayers and requests. With this in mind, be alert and always keep on praying for all the saints." (Ephesians 6:11-18, NIV)

Use God's weapons: the Word of God (which is alive and active, sharper than any two-edged sword); the truth (which maintains freedom); our righteousness (received through our identity in Jesus Christ); peace (which signifies the presence of God); our faith (established by believing the Word of God); salvation (a free gift); the Holy Spirit (our comforter).

Do not be afraid of your past sins and the schemes of Satan. He is powerless. God has made us His own. He has given us everything we need to be victorious and unscathed by the enemy.

Day 6

"For wherever there is jealousy (envy) and contention (rivalry and selfish ambition), there will also be confusion (unrest, disharmony, rebellion) and all sorts of evil and vile practices."

James 3:16, AMP

Moving on after someone has hurt or offended us in some way is not always easy, and it's not what we usually want to do. Our natural tendency is to call two or three people and talk about the situation, to run over every minor detail replaying the hurt again and again. But this unproductive response does not encourage healing. The Bible encourages us to move forward in forgiveness.

> *"Be gentle and forbearing with one another and, if one has a difference (a grievance or complaint) against another, readily pardoning each other; even as the Lord has [freely] forgiven you, so must you also [forgive]. And above all these [put on] love and enfold yourselves with the bond of perfectness [which binds everything together completely in ideal harmony. And let the peace (soul harmony which comes) from Christ rule (act as umpire continually) in your hearts [deciding and settling with finality all questions that arise in your minds, in that peaceful state] to which as [members of Christ's] one body you were also called [to live]. And be thankful (appreciative), [giving praise to God always]."* (Colossians 3:13-15, AMP)

> *"For if you forgive people their trespasses [their reckless and willful sins, leaving them, letting them go, and giving up resentment], your heavenly Father will also forgive you. But if you do not forgive others their trespasses [their reckless and willful sins, leaving them, letting them go, and giving up resentment], neither will your Father forgive you your trespasses."* (Matthew 6:14-16, AMP)

If you are the one who created the offense, simply humble yourself before God. Ask Him to forgive you. Then offer an apology to the other person(s) and let God heal the relationship. God is quick to forgive you and will restore the relationship. As author Dr. Chuck Lynch writes in his book *I Should Forgive, But…*,

> "Withholding forgiveness until an offender understands or acknowledges the emotional pain they have inflicted is a subtle form of revenge. Why? Because it's hoping that the offender would hurt a little, too, in order to understand. But this type of revenge robs you of your freedom and allows the offender to keep control of you."

> *"Strive to live in peace with everybody and pursue that consecration and holiness without which no one will [ever] see the Lord."* Hebrews 12:14, AMP

> *"Repay no one evil for evil, but take thought for what is honest and proper and noble [aiming to be above reproach] in the sight of everyone. If possible, as far as it depends on you, live at peace with everyone. Beloved, never avenge yourselves, but leave the way open for [God's] wrath; for it is written, Vengeance is Mine, I will repay (requite), says the Lord. But if your enemy is hungry, feed him; if he is thirsty, give him drink; for by so doing you will heap burning coals upon his head. Do not let yourself be overcome by evil, but overcome (master) evil with good."* Romans 12:17-21, AMP

Day 7

"For wherever there is jealousy (envy) and contention (rivalry and selfish ambition), there will also be confusion (unrest, disharmony, rebellion) and all sorts of evil and vile practices."

James 3:16, AMP

"*Let us walk honestly, as in the day; not in rioting and drunkenness, not in chambering and wantonness, not in strife and envying. But put ye on the Lord Jesus Christ, and make not provision for the flesh, to fulfill the lusts thereof.*" (Romans 13:13-14, KJV)

Whenever I detect an "emotional takeover" rise up inside me, I immediately retreat to a private place and renounce any incorrect thoughts I may be having. This may seem silly to you, but it's a very necessary practice for me. "*Inasmuch as we] refute arguments and theories and reasonings and every proud and lofty thing that sets itself up against the [true] knowledge of God; and we lead every thought and purpose away captive into the obedience of Christ (the Messiah, the Anointed One).*" (2 Corinthians 10:5, AMP)

When the Christ-like thinking of our minds is challenged, we need the Word of God to wield as our weapon.

I proclaim the Word of God that pertains to the situation out loud so my whole being can hear it. This is one of the reasons why we need to study the Word and know what it says about who we are in Christ. When the Christ-like thinking of our minds is challenged, we need the Word of God to wield as our weapon (Ephesians 6).

For years now I have written scriptures on 3x5 cards and read them repeatedly until I memorized them. My box of Scripture cards have been a life line many times over. I encourage you to start a method of memorizing Scripture that works for you.

"You will guard him and keep him in perfect and constant peace whose mind [both its inclination and its character] is stayed on You, because he commits himself to You, leans on You, and hopes confidently in You." Isaiah 26:3, AMP

Week 22

"The fear of the LORD tendeth to life: and he that hath it shall abide satisfied; he shall not be visited with evil."

Proverbs 19:23, KJV

DAY 1

"The fear of the LORD tendeth to life: and he that hath it shall abide satisfied; he shall not be visited with evil."
PROVERBS 19:23, KJV

Let's start this week by meditating on several translations of our verse.

> *"The fear of the LORD leads to life: Then one rests content, untouched by trouble."* NIV

> *"Fear of the Lord leads to life, bringing security and protection from harm."* NLT

> *"Fear-of-God is life itself, a full life, and serene—no nasty surprises."* MSG

> *"The reverent, worshipful fear of the Lord leads to life, and he who has it rests satisfied; he cannot be visited with [actual] evil."* AMP

In the *American Dictionary of the English Language*, "fear" is defined as: "the worship of God, reverence; respect; due regard; to have a reverential awe; to venerate." To fear God does not mean to be afraid, shrinking, or trembling. It means to show God our deepest respect and honor, our highest regard and esteem. We show God our fear of Him through many acts of worship and reverence, such as: studying His Word, obeying His Word, and living a life governed by His Word.

I could make a long list of do's and don'ts on how to fear God and how not to. But any advice can be condensed into three simple commands: Study. Obey. Do.

"Worship the Lord your God and serve him only." Matt 4:10, NIV

"We know [positively] that we are of God, and the whole world [around us] is under the power of the evil one. And we [have seen and] know [positively] that the Son of God has [actually] come to this world and has given us understanding and insight [progressively] to perceive (recognize) and come to know better and more clearly Him Who is true; and we are in Him Who is true—in His Son Jesus Christ (the Messiah). This [Man] is the true God and Life eternal. Little children, keep yourselves from idols (false gods)—[from anything and everything that would occupy the place in your hear due to God, from any sort of substitute for Him that would take first place in your life]. Amen (so let it be)." 1 John 5:19-21, AMP

DAY 2

"The fear of the LORD tendeth to life: and he that hath it shall abide satisfied; he shall not be visited with evil."

PROVERBS 19:23, KJV

When we accept our identity that was sacrificially arranged for us by Jesus Christ, we cannot help but revere God, fear Him, and honor Him. Christ came to give us a new beginning, a new birth date, a new identity. When we accept Him into our lives, we become a part of His family. We gain His lineage, His bloodline, even His character. All of His family traits and rights become ours when we become Christians. To deny all that Jesus Christ accomplished for us on the cross is utterly disrespectful, dishonorable, and insulting.

> *"For he chose us in him before the creation of the world to be holy and blameless in his sight. In love he predestined us to be adopted as his sons through Jesus Christ, in accordance with his pleasure and will—to the praise of his glorious grace, which he has freely given us in the One he loves. In him we have redemption through his blood, the forgiveness of sins, in accordance with the riches of God's grace that he lavished on us with all wisdom and understanding. And he made known to us the mystery of his will according to his good pleasure, which he purposed in Christ, to be put into effect when the times will have reached their fulfillment—to bring all things in heaven and on earth together under one head, even Christ. In him we were also chosen, having been predestined according to the plan of him who works out everything in conformity with the purpose of his will, in order that we, who were the first to hope in Christ, might be for the praise of his glory. And you also were included in Christ when you heard the word of truth, the gospel of your salvation. Having believed, you were marked in him with a seal, the promised Holy Spirit, who is a*

deposit guaranteeing our inheritance until the redemption of those who are God's possession—to the praise of his glory." (Ephesians 1:4-19, NIV)

We have to remember that God *chose us*. He adopted us, taking us from our sin-filled lives to one of godliness. We are no longer stuck in identities that were formed by our culture, tradition, or ethnic background. We are *His*. Honor God by believing and receiving your new identity. We are Christians, above any other identity.

WE HAVE TO REMEMBER THAT GOD CHOSE US.

"The body is a unit, though it is made up of many parts; and though all its parts are many, they form one body. So it is with Christ. For we were all baptized by one Spirit into one body—whether Jews or Greeks, slave or free—and we were all given the one Spirit to drink." (1 Corinthians 12:12-13, NIV)

In the *Archaeological Study Bible*, a footnote under 1 Corinthians 12:12 reads: "The believers in Corinth, and elsewhere in the ancient world, came from diverse ethnic and socioeconomic backgrounds. But in Christ there is no ethnic, cultural or social distinction."

We are *His*!

Day 3

"The fear of the LORD tendeth to life: and he that hath it shall abide satisfied; he shall not be visited with evil."

Proverbs 19:23, KJV

This week's Scripture speaks of life. The following verses tell us even more about the kind of life the Lord wants for us. I encourage you to meditate on these Scriptures today.

"Even to your old age I am He, and even to hair white with age will I carry you. I have made, and I will bear; yes, I will carry and will save you." (Isaiah 46:4, AMP)

"He who dwells in the secret place of the Most High shall remain stable and fixed under the shadow of the Almighty [Whose power no foe can withstand]. I will say of the Lord, He is my Refuge and my Fortress, my God; on Him I lean and rely, and in Him I [confidently] trust. For [then] He will deliver you from the snare of the fowler and from the deadly pestilence. [Then] He will cover you with His pinions, and under His wings shall you trust and find refuge; His truth and His faithfulness are a shield and a buckler. You shall not be afraid of the terror of the night, nor of the arrow (the evil plots and slanders of the wicked) that flies by day, Nor of the pestilence that stalks in darkness, nor of the destruction and sudden death that surprise and lay waste at noonday. A thousand may fall at your side, and ten thousand at your right hand, but it shall not come near you. Only a spectator shall you be [yourself inaccessible in the secret place of the Most High] as you witness the reward of the wicked. Because you have made the Lord your refuge, and the Most High your dwelling place, there shall no evil befall you, nor any plague or calamity come near your tent. For He will give His angels [especial] charge over you to accompany and defend and preserve you in all your ways [of obedience and service].

They shall bear you up on their hands, lest you dash your foot against a stone. You shall tread upon the lion and adder; the young lion and the serpent shall you trample underfoot. Because he has set his love upon Me, therefore will I deliver him; I will set him on high, because he knows and understands My name [has a personal knowledge of My mercy, love, and kindness—trusts and relies on Me, knowing I will never forsake him, no, never]. He shall call upon Me, and I will answer him; I will be with him in trouble, I will deliver him and honor him. With long life will I satisfy him and show him My salvation." (Psalm 91, AMP)

"*I am the Good Shepherd. The Good Shepherd risks and lays down His [own] life for the sheep.*" (John 10:11, AMP)

"*The steps of a [good] man are directed and established by the Lord when He delights in his way [and He busies Himself with his every step]. Though he falls, he shall not be utterly cast down, for the Lord grasps his hand in support and upholds him. I have been young and now am old, yet I have not seen the [uncompromisingly] righteous forsaken or their seed begging bread. All day long they are merciful and deal graciously; they lend, and their offspring are blessed.*" (Psalm 37:23-26, AMP)

"*The reverent, worshipful fear of the Lord leads to life, and he who has it rests satisfied; he cannot be visited with [actual] evil.*" (Proverbs 19:23, AMP)

"*Blessed (Happy, fortunate, to be envied) is everyone who fears, reveres, and worships the Lord, who walks in His ways and lives according to His commandments. For you shall eat [the fruit] of the labor of your hands; happy (blessed, fortunate, enviable) shall you be, and it shall be well with you. Your wife shall be like a fruitful vine in the innermost parts of your house; your children shall be like olive plants round about your table. Behold, thus shall the man be blessed who reverently and worshipfully fears the Lord. May the Lord bless you out of Zion [His sanctuary], and may you see the prosperity of Jerusalem all the days of your life; Yes, may you see your children's children. Peace be upon Israel!*" (Psalm 128:1-6, AMP)

"*Whoso hearkens to me [Wisdom] shall dwell securely and in confident trust and shall be quiet, without fear or dread of evil.*" (Proverbs 1:33, AMP)

"He hides away sound and godly Wisdom and stores it for the righteous (those who are upright and in right standing with Him); He is a shield to those who walk uprightly and in integrity, that He may guard the paths of justice; yes, He preserves the way of His saints." (Proverbs 2:7-8, AMP)

"For the Lord God is a Sun and Shield; the Lord bestows [presents] grace and favor and [future] glory (honor, splendor, and heavenly bliss)! No good thing will He withhold from those who walk uprightly. O Lord of hosts, blessed (happy, fortunate, to be envied) is the man who trusts in You [leaning and believing on You, committing all and confidently looking to You, and that without fear or misgiving]!" (Psalm 84:11-12, AMP)

"The eyes of the Lord are toward the [uncompromisingly] righteous and His ears are open to their cry." (Psalm 34:15, AMP)

"I sought (inquired of) the Lord and required Him [of necessity and on the authority of His Word], and He heard me, and delivered me from all my fears. They looked to Him and were radiant; their faces shall never blush for shame or be confused." (Psalm 34:4-5, AMP)

"Let your character or moral disposition be free from love of money [including greed, avarice, lust, and craving for earthly possessions] and be satisfied with your present [circumstances and with what you have]; for He [God] Himself has said, I will not in any way fail you nor give you up nor leave you without support. [I will] not, [I will] not, [I will] not in any degree leave you helpless nor forsake nor let [you] down (relax My hold on you)! [Assuredly not!] So we take comfort and are encouraged and confidently and boldly say, The Lord is my Helper; I will not be seized with alarm [I will not fear or dread or be terrified]. What can man do to me?" (Hebrews 13:5-6, AMP)

"[For then it will be that] the Lord has taken away the judgments against you; He has cast out your enemy. The King of Israel, even the Lord [Himself], is in the midst of you; [and after He has come to you] you shall not experience or fear evil any more. In that day it shall be said to Jerusalem, Fear not, O Zion. Let not your hands sink down or be slow and listless. The Lord your God is in the midst of you, a Mighty One, a Savior [Who saves]! He will rejoice over you with joy; He will rest [in silent satisfaction] and in His love He will be silent and make no mention [of past sins, or even recall them]; He will exult over you with singing." (Zephaniah 3:15-17, AMP)

Day 4

"The fear of the LORD tendeth to life: and he
that hath it shall abide satisfied; he shall
not be visited with evil."

Proverbs 19:23, KJV

Throughout this devotional book, numerous verses that describe righteousness also include references to peace, love, happiness, and success. One of those Scriptures is Proverbs 21:21 NIV: *"He who pursues righteousness and love finds life, prosperity and honor."* The Lord intends for us to live triumphantly, functioning successfully here on earth as representatives of a creative, all-powerful, victorious, good God. We need to reflect Jesus. Then, when non-Christians observe our lives, they will see the goodness of God. Jesus stated in John 10:10 AMP: *"The thief comes only in order to steal and kill and destroy. I came that they may have and enjoy life, and have it in abundance (to the full, till it overflows)."* Overflowing, abundant lives become the standards of excellence and vitality in communities; they speak without words that God's plan for us is good and not evil.

I have encountered an unprecedented amount of disbelief regarding the concept of abundant life. The adversary, Satan, has blinded the eyes of many unsuspecting people. If he can get a person to not receive the Word of God, he cleverly snags them with persecution, doubt, tradition, and unbelief. He tries everything within his power to keep the Word of God from entering into the hearts of people. He endeavors to keep us stagnant and broken. He is a thief. His purpose is to kill, steal, and destroy (John 10:10).

My prayer is that you will truly believe the gospel and receive the freedom it provides. I want everyone to live in peace and openly—unashamedly—receive every benefit declared in the Word of God. We see what God hopes for us when Jesus informs the disciples of His purpose here on earth: "*To preach the good news (the Gospel) to the poor; He has sent Me to announce release to the captives and recovery of sight to the blind, to send forth as delivered those who are oppressed [who are downtrodden, bruised, crushed, and broken down by calamity], to proclaim the accepted and acceptable year of the Lord [the day when salvation and the free favors of God profusely abound].*" (Luke 4:18b-19, AMP)

"*For whoever finds me [Wisdom] finds life and draws forth and obtains favor from the Lord.*" Proverbs 8:35, AMP

"*The reverent and worshipful fear of the Lord prolongs one's days, but the years of the wicked shall be made short.*" Proverbs 10:27, AMP

"*Reverent and worshipful fear of the Lord is a fountain of life, that one may avoid the snares of death.*" Proverbs 14:27, AMP

Day 5

"The fear of the LORD tendeth to life: and he that hath it shall abide satisfied; he shall not be visited with evil."
Proverbs 19:23, KJV

God has given us many promises concerning the kind of life we are to live. Let's look at several of them below.

> *"No actual evil, misfortune, or calamity shall come upon the righteous, but the wicked shall be filled with evil, misfortune, and calamity."* (Proverbs 12:21, AMP)
>
> *"Even to your old age I am he, and even to hair white with age will I carry you. I have made, and I will bear; yes, I will carry and will save you."* (Isaiah 46:4, AMP)
>
> *"Who is the man who reverently fears and worships the Lord? Him shall He teach in the way that he should choose. He himself shall dwell at ease, and his offspring shall inherit the land. The secret [of the sweet, satisfying companionship] of the Lord have they who fear (revere and worship) Him, and He will show them His covenant and reveal to them its [deep, inner] meaning."* (Psalm 25:12-14, AMP)
>
> *"This is the covenant I will make with the house of Israel after that time, declares the Lord, I will put my laws in their minds and write them on their hearts. I will be their God, and they will be my people. No longer will a man teach his neighbor, or a man his brother, saying, "Know the Lord,' because they will all know me, from the least of them to the greatest. For I will forgive their wickedness and will remember their sins no more."* (Hebrews 9:10-12, NIV)
>
> *"For we are God's [own] handiwork (His workmanship), recreated in Christ Jesus, [born anew] that we may do those good works which*

God predestined (planned beforehand) for us [taking paths which He prepared ahead of time], that we should walk in them [living the good life which He prearranged and made ready for us to live]." (Ephesians 2:10, AMP)

As the preceding Scriptures show, God plans wholeness and goodness for us through Jesus Christ. Honor the Lord with your time and attention, because He longs for a relationship with you. Study what the Word says about your life. Then, receive it into your heart so that you can become deeply rooted in Him. Know that God adores you and desires greatness for you.

Like Paul, I pray this prayer for you and your life in Christ:

"That you may have the power and be strong to apprehend and grasp with all the saints [God's devoted people, the experience of that love] what is the breadth and length and height and depth [of it]; [That you may really come] to know [practically, through experience for yourselves] the love of Christ, which far surpasses mere knowledge [without experience]; that you may be filled [through all your being] unto all the fullness of God [may have the richest measure of the divine Presence, and become a body wholly filled and flooded with God Himself]! Now to Him Who, by (in consequence of) the [action of His] power that is at work within us, is able to [carry out His purpose and] do superabundantly, far over and above all that we [dare] ask or think [infinitely beyond our highest prayers, desires, thoughts, hopes, or dreams]." Ephesians 3:18-20, AMP

DAY 6

"The fear of the LORD tendeth to life: and he that hath it shall abide satisfied; he shall not be visited with evil."
PROVERBS 19:23, KJV

As I sat down each day to write an entry for this devotional, I felt humbled by the immensity of the task. Many times I asked the Lord, "How am I—a person who has so little writing experience—going to communicate Your truth?" On each occasion He told me: "Just write My Word. My Word will reach My people. It alone has the power within it to bring life to those seeking. It will direct them which way to go. The Holy Spirit will do the rest."

TAKE GOD'S WORD FOR WHAT IT SAYS. DON'T ADD TO IT AND DON'T QUESTION ITS VALIDITY. USE IT AS YOUR PLUMB LINE FOR TRUTH.

I can testify that God is faithful to His Word and has been faithful to me. The Bible is simple and clear. As you study Proverbs 19:23 this week, as well as the other Scriptures presented, take God's Word for what it says. Don't add to it and don't question its validity. Use it as your plumb line for truth. Put all traditional beliefs and life experiences aside. Receive His Word as personal promises to you. Believe Him.

"Blessed (Happy, fortunate, to be envied) are the undefiled (the upright, truly sincere, and blameless) in the way [of the revealed will

of God], who walk (order their conduct and conversation) in the law of the Lord (the whole of God's revealed will). Blessed (happy, fortunate, to be envied) are they who keep His testimonies, and who seek, inquire for and of Him and crave Him with the whole heart. Yes, they do no unrighteousness [no willful wandering from His precepts]; they walk in His ways. You have commanded us to keep Your precepts, that we should observe them diligently. Oh, that my ways were directed and established to observe Your statutes [hearing, receiving, loving, and obeying them]! Then shall I not be put to shame [by failing to inherit Your promises] when I have respect to all Your commandments. I will praise and give thanks to You with uprightness of heart when I learn [by sanctified experiences] Your righteous judgments [Your decisions against and punishments for particular lines of thought and conduct]. I will keep Your statutes; O forsake me not utterly. How shall a young man cleanse his way? By taking heed and keeping watch [on himself] according to Your word [conforming his life to it]. With my whole heart have I sought You, inquiring for and of You and yearning for You; Oh, let me not wander or step aside [either in ignorance or willfully] from Your commandments. Your word have I laid up in my heart, that I might not sin against You. Blessed are You, O Lord; teach me Your statutes. With my lips have I declared and recounted all the ordinances of Your mouth. I have rejoiced in the way of Your testimonies as much as in all riches. I will meditate on Your precepts and have respect to Your ways [the paths of life marked out by Your law]. I will delight myself in Your statutes; I will not forget Your word. Deal bountifully with Your servant, that I may live; and I will observe Your word [hearing, receiving, loving, and obeying it]. Open my eyes, that I may behold wondrous things out of Your law." Psalm 119:1-18, AMP

Day 7

"The fear of the LORD tendeth to life: and he that hath it shall abide satisfied; he shall not be visited with evil."

Proverbs 19:23, KJV

Make a commitment today to receive the promised life God has prepared for you. Choose to live a holy life, fearfully worshiping the Lord. Meditate upon the truth in His Word about your identity in Christ. Don't go another day without the assurance of His divine care for you.

I encourage you to pray this prayer to God today: "Father, I choose to accept all that you have for me. I choose to believe Your Word. May my life be a living testament of Your goodness and faithfulness. I will passionately seek You and find You. May your Word be the spiritual DNA of my soul. May the eyes of my heart never grow tired of seeking Your truth. You are my standard. I am Yours. I am a blood-bought covenant child of God, adopted into the Creator's family. I enthusiastically accept my identity. I will walk with you all the days of my life."

"THE LORD is my Shepherd [to feed, guide, and shield me], I shall not lack. He makes me lie down in [fresh, tender] green pastures; He leads me beside the still and restful waters. He refreshes and restores my life (my self); He leads me in the paths of righteousness [uprightness and right standing with Him—not for my earning it, but] for His name's sake. Yes, though I walk through the [deep, sunless] valley of the shadow of death, I will fear or dread no evil, for You are with

me; Your rod [to protect] and Your staff [to guide], they comfort me. You prepare a table before me in the presence of my enemies. You anoint my head with oil; my [brimming] cup runs over. Surely or only goodness, mercy, and unfailing love shall follow me all the days of my life, and through the length of my days the house of the Lord [and His presence] shall be my dwelling place." Psalm 23, AMP

Week 23

"Let the peace of Christ rule in your hearts, since as members of one body you were called to peace. And be thankful."

Colossians 3:15, NIV

Day 1

"Let the peace of Christ rule in your hearts, since as members of one body you were called to peace. And be thankful."

Colossians 3:15, NIV

I'd like to start this week by meditating on our Scripture, particularly focusing on its theme of peace in Christ.

> *"Let the peace of Christ rule in your hearts, since as members of one body you were called to peace. And be thankful."* (Colossians 3:15, NIV)
>
> *"And let the peace (soul harmony which comes) from Christ rule (act as umpire continually) in your hearts [deciding and settling with finality all questions that arise in your minds, in that peaceful state] to which as [members of Christ's] one body you were also called [to live]. And be thankful (appreciative), [giving praise to God always]."* (Colossians 3:15, AMP)
>
> *"And let the peace that comes from Christ rule in your hearts. For as members of one body you are called to live in peace. And always be thankful."* (Colossians 3:15, NLT)
>
> *"Let the peace that the Christ gives decide all doubt within your hearts for you also were called to the enjoyment of peace as members of one Body and show yourselves thankful."* (Colossians 3:15, TCNT)

DAY 2

"Let the peace of Christ rule in your hearts, since as
members of one body you were called to peace.
And be thankful."
COLOSSIANS 3:15, NIV

Noah Webster defines "peace" as "a state of quiet or tranquility; freedom from disturbance or agitation; applicable to society, to individuals, or to the temper of the mind." The psalmist tells us how to get peace: "*Great peace have they who love your law, and nothing can make them stumble*" (Psalm 119:165, NIV). The "law" Psalm 119 refers to is the Word of God and His commandments. When we fervently study the Scriptures, God's Words are absorbed into our mind and heart and body and spirit, creating peace and a sense of safety.

WHEN WE ALLOW CHRIST TO RULE IN OUR LIVES, WE CAN REST.

By continually living out the principles learned through study of the Word of God, our lives will begin to reflect peace and harmony with others. We will naturally live our lives in ways that align with God's will and His purpose. David understood this: "*I will keep Your law continually, forever and ever [hearing, receiving, loving, and obeying it]. And I will walk at liberty and at ease, for I have sought and inquired for [and desperately required] Your precepts.*" (Psalm 119:44-45, AMP)

The Amplified Bible translation of Colossians 3:15a states: "*Let the peace (soul harmony which comes) from Christ rule (act as umpire continually) in your hearts [deciding and settling with finality all questions that arise in your minds, in that peaceful state].*"

When we allow Christ to rule in our lives, we can rest. He is the Prince of Peace, the anointed peacemaker. We can trust Him. When we relinquish our old ways of handling life, He replaces them with His righteous ways. We become new, living a life that is pleasing to the Father. And, in return, a spirit of peace and tranquility grows within us.

Christ's peace is attainable, even in this world of chaos and con-fusion. Pursue peace by meditating on God's Word and by turning over every aspect of your life to Jesus. His righteousness will lead you into a peace-filled life.

"And the effect of righteousness will be peace [internal and external], and the result of righteousness will be quietness and confident trust forever. My people shall dwell in a peaceable habitation, in safe dwellings, and in quiet resting-places." Isaiah 32:17-18, AMP

"The LORD gives strength to his people; the LORD blesses his people with peace." Psalm 29:11, NIV

"Come, my children, listen to me; I will teach you the fear of the LORD. Whoever of you loves life and desires to see many good days, keep your tongue from evil and your lips from speaking lies. Turn from evil and do good; seek peace and pursue it." Psalm 34:11-14, NIV

"A heart at peace gives life to the body, but envy rots the bones." Proverbs 14:30, NIV

"Though the mountains be shaken and the hills be removed, yet my unfailing love for you will not be shaken, nor my covenant of peace be removed," says the LORD, who has compassion on you." Isaiah 54:10, NIV

"Whoever would love life and see good days must keep his tongue from evil and his lips from deceitful speech. He must turn from evil and do

good; he must seek peace and pursue it. For the eyes of the Lord are on the righteous and his ears are attentive to their prayer, but the face of the Lord is against those who do evil." 1 Peter 3:10-12, NIV

"[After all] the kingdom of God is not a matter of [getting the] food and drink [one likes], but instead it is righteousness (that state which makes a person acceptable to God) and [heart] peace and joy in the Holy Spirit. He who serves Christ in this way is acceptable and pleasing to God and is approved by men. So let us then definitely aim for and eagerly pursue what makes for harmony and for mutual upbuilding (edification and development) of one another." Romans 14:17-19, AMP

"Strive to live in peace with everybody and pursue that consecration and holiness without which no one will [ever] see the Lord." Hebrews 12:14, AMP

DAY 3

"Let the peace of Christ rule in your hearts, since as members of one body you were called to peace. And be thankful."
COLOSSIANS 3:15, NIV

"Judas, not Iscariot, asked Him, Lord, how is it that You will reveal Yourself [make Yourself real] to us and not to the world? Jesus answered, If a person [really] loves Me, he will keep My word [obey My teaching]; and My Father will love him, and We will come to him and make Our home (abode, special dwelling place) with him. Anyone who does not [really] love Me does not observe and obey My teaching. And the teaching which you hear and heed is not Mine, but [comes] from the Father Who sent Me. I have told you these things while I am still with you. But the Comforter (Counselor, Helper, Intercessor, Advocate, Strengthener, Standby), the Holy Spirit, Whom the Father will send in My name [in My place, to represent Me and act on My behalf], He will teach you all things. And He will cause you to recall (will remind you of, bring to your remembrance) everything I have told you. Peace I leave with you; My [own] peace I now give and bequeath to you. Not as the world gives do I give to you. Do not let your hearts be troubled, neither let them be afraid. [Stop allowing yourselves to be agitated and disturbed; and do not permit yourselves to be fearful and intimidated and cowardly and unsettled.]" (John 14:22-27, AMP)

GOD TEACHES US STANDARDS IN HIS WORD THAT WILL LEAD US INTO LIVES OF PEACE.

The Greek word for "peace" in the preceding Scripture is *eirene*, which means: "to join, peace by implied prosperity, one, peace quietness, rest." We are joined to God's peace. We become one with the peace of Christ when we make the choice to live by His Word. Jesus prefaces the joining of peace with one condition: *"If a person really loves Me, he will keep* My *Word [obeying* My *teaching] and* My *Father will love him."* Obedience is mandatory in order for Christ's peace and tranquility to enter our lives.

Unfortunately, some Christians rebel against God's principles for our protection and prosperity, though they still expect to experience peace. But God teaches us standards in His Word that, if followed by the help of the Holy Spirit, will lead us into lives of peace in Him.

Life is an open book test. Choose to live by His Word.

Day 4

"Let the peace of Christ rule in your hearts, since as members of one body you were called to peace. And be thankful."

Colossians 3:15, NIV

"But the Comforter (Counselor, Helper, Intercessor, Advocate, Strengthener, Standby), the Holy Spirit, Whom the Father will send in My name [in My place, to represent Me and act on My behalf], He will teach you all things. And He will cause you to recall (will remind you of, bring to your remembrance) everything I have told you. Peace I leave with you; My [own] peace I now give and bequeath to you. Not as the world gives do I give to you. Do not let your hearts be troubled, neither let them be afraid. [Stop allowing yourselves to be agitated and disturbed; and do not permit yourselves to be fearful and intimidated and cowardly and unsettled.]" (John 14:26, AMP)

Jesus told his disciples that they would be joined by the Holy Spirit after He returned home to the Father. As John 14:26 teaches, the Spirit's purpose is to guide, assist, and minister to us throughout life.

Since Monty and I married in 1994, we have lived a nomadic life, moving every couple of years. I have enjoyed every move and look forward to new friends and new assignments from the Lord. But moving from one city to another requires a significant amount of help from the Holy Spirit, if the goal is to have a peaceful transition.

Monty and I have committed to relying totally on the Lord when it comes to moving. By His grace (praise God!), we have had drama-free moves each time. God faithfully gives us clear directions on how to efficiently move; how, when, and what to pack; where to look for homes; where to enroll the children in school—the list goes on and on.

When we wait and seek the direction of the Holy Spirit, life is much simpler, stress-free!

God has always been faithful in making our paths straightforward. Our rule is: if we don't have peace about a decision, we don't make one. I'm referring to that peace the Amplified Bible describes in Colossians 3:15 as: *"an umpire continually deciding and settling with finality all questions that arise in our minds."* When we wait and seek the direction of the Holy Spirit, life is much simpler—stress-free! The Holy Spirit gives supernatural knowledge and insight into circumstances we would not naturally have the wisdom to handle.

Sadly, when we have not listened to the Holy Spirit and followed our own thinking and natural knowledge instead, the end results are not desirable. Moving forward without the assurance and confidence of the Holy Spirit is disastrous.

"Now we have not received the spirit [that belongs to] the world, but the [Holy] Spirit Who is from God, [given to us] that we might realize and comprehend and appreciate the gifts [of divine favor and blessing so freely and lavishly] bestowed on us by God." 1 Corinthians 2:12, AMP

Day 5

"Let the peace of Christ rule in your hearts, since as members of one body you were called to peace. And be thankful."
Colossians 3:15, NIV

Letting the peace of Christ rule in our hearts is exemplified by the woman whose doctor finds a lump in her breast during her annual physical exam. Upon learning the information, she doesn't hysterically call three people to broadcast the news. She doesn't even tell her husband or children. She calmly and confidently chooses to go before the Lord, reminding Him of His promises of wholeness: nothing missing, nothing broken.

The woman takes time every day for two weeks to meditate on healing Scriptures and verses containing her blood-bought rights through Jesus Christ. She petitions the Holy Spirit for wisdom and insight on her request. She is careful not to allow any talk of death to enter her mind or mouth, but only the Word of God.

At the end of two weeks, the woman returns to the doctors' office to see the radiologist. Her disposition is cheerful and strong as a scan of her body is run to measure abnormalities. The doctors are astonished at the results: no trace of any growths, praise God! She tells the doctors, "I knew all along My God healed me of all sickness and disease. My body is free and will continue to be free of all brokenness."

This woman allowed the peace of Christ to rule her heart. She is like the woman with the issue of blood who knew of a Savior who could heal her, too:

"And there was a woman who had had a flow of blood for twelve years, And who had endured much suffering under [the hands of] many physicians and had spent all that she had, and was no better but instead grew worse. She had heard the reports concerning Jesus, and she came up behind Him in the throng and touched His garment, For she kept saying, If I only touch His garments, I shall be restored to health. And immediately her flow of blood was dried up at the source, and [suddenly] she felt in her body that she was healed of her [distressing] ailment. And Jesus, recognizing in Himself that the power proceeding from Him had gone forth, turned around immediately in the crowd and said, Who touched My clothes? And the disciples kept saying to Him, You see the crowd pressing hard around You from all sides, and You ask, Who touched Me? Still He kept looking around to see her who had done it. But the woman, knowing what had been done for her, though alarmed and frightened and trembling, fell down before Him and told Him the whole truth. And He said to her, Daughter, your faith (your trust and confidence in Me, springing from faith in God) has restored you to health. Go in (into) peace and be continually healed and freed from your [distressing bodily] disease." (Mark 5:25-34, AMP)

The woman with the issue of blood pressed through a large crowd of people, risking her life to touch the Savior's garment. The woman in our modern day story also knew that if she remained in God's presence, her deliverance was guaranteed. She did not believe her doctors' expectations or seek the help of friends or family. Both women knew Jesus was the only answer. In Him they found their peace. By Him they were healed.

"Surely He has borne our griefs (sicknesses, weaknesses, and distresses) and carried our sorrows and pains [of punishment], yet we [ignorantly] considered Him stricken, smitten, and afflicted by God [as if with leprosy]. But He was wounded for our transgressions, He was bruised for our guilt and iniquities; the chastisement [needful to obtain] peace and well-being for us was upon Him, and with the stripes [that wounded] Him we are healed and made whole." Isaiah 53:4-5, AMP

DAY 6

"Let the peace of Christ rule in your hearts, since as members of one body you were called to peace. And be thankful."
COLOSSIANS 3:15, NIV

This Scripture's encouragement to *"Let the peace of Christ rule in your hearts"* is certainly applicable to marriage. I have meditated on this verse numerous times through the course of my marriage. Whenever two people are in a relationship, a significant amount of effort is made towards compromise and harmony. The devil loves to see Christian marriages in strife, since his purpose is to kill, steal, and destroy (John 10:10). But Christians have something much greater and more influential than him; we have the peace of Christ. We are capable of having peaceful marriages by the help of the Holy Spirit. Jesus says (in the latter part of John 10:10, AMP): *"I came that they may have and enjoy life, and have it in abundance (to the full, till it overflows)."*

EVERY TIME THE HOLY SPIRIT HAS BEEN INVOLVED IN OUR PROBLEMS, THE ISSUES WERE SUPERNATURALLY RECTIFIED.

I trust in the ability of the Holy Spirit. On those occasions when a resolution between Monty and me cannot be reached, I ask the Holy Spirit to intercede. First I humble myself in prayer and repent of any wrongs on my part in order to align myself with the love of God. Otherwise, I could be an obstacle that is prohibiting the movement of God.

"Therefore, as God's chosen people, holy and dearly loved, clothe yourselves with compassion, kindness, humility, gentleness and patience.

Bear with each other and forgive whatever grievances you may have against one another. Forgive as the Lord forgave you. And over all these virtues put on love, which binds them all together in perfect unity. Let the peace of Christ rule in your hearts, since as members of one body you were called to peace. And be thankful." (Colossians 3:12-15, NIV)

The Holy Spirit lives in my husband and the Holy Spirit lives in me. If we cannot naturally resolve a disagreement, I am assured the Holy Spirit in both of us can bring about any change needed for resolution. Every time the Holy Spirit has been involved in our problems, the issues were supernaturally rectified.

I would encourage you to do the same. The next time you and your husband (or you and anyone, for that matter) reach a stalemate, do not allow your emotions or pride to destroy the relationship. Turn to the Holy Spirit, whose job is to help us move the obstacles out of our lives.

DAY 7

"Let the peace of Christ rule in your hearts, since as members of one body you were called to peace. And be thankful."

COLOSSIANS 3:15, NIV

The last part of this week's Scripture admonishes us to be thankful for the peace God has given us through the help of the Holy Spirit. As we examine some of the titles given to the Holy Spirit in 1 John 5:7-11 and John 14:26 (in the Amplified Bible translation), we will understand the great gift God has given us by providing us with the Holy Spirit's presence even more.

Helper: aids and assists us, furnishes or administers remedies; making it easier for someone to do something by offering one's services.

Intercessor: act of intervening on behalf of another, for us.

Advocate: publicly supports us; recommends particular causes or policies.

Strengthener: makes us stronger, enables or encourages us to act or move more vigorously or effectively.

Standby: ready, alert, and waiting for duty or immediate deployment.

Counselor: trained to give guidance on personal, social, or psychological problems.

Comforter: provides comfort after a loss or disappointment.

Witness to Christ's coming: He was present before creation, witnessing the coming of Christ.

Truth: an extension of the Father.

How can we not be grateful?! God has provided all that we need for our well-being. By allowing the Holy Spirit to do His work within you, you will gain peace.

Week 24

"Praise the LORD, O my soul; all my inmost being, praise his holy name. Praise the LORD, O my soul, and forget not all his benefits—who forgives all your sins and heals all your diseases, who redeems your life from the pit and crowns you with love and compassion, who satisfies your desires with good things so that your youth is renewed like the eagle's."

Psalm 103:1-5, NIV

Day 1

"Praise the LORD, O my soul; all my inmost being, praise his holy name. Praise the LORD, O my soul, and forget not all his benefits—who forgives all your sins and heals all your diseases, who redeems your life from the pit and crowns you with love and compassion, who satisfies your desires with good things so that your youth is renewed like the eagle's."

Psalm 103:1-5, NIV

In Psalm 103, David expresses a great amount of honor and gratitude to God. He eloquently lists the benefits of life with God: sins forgiven, diseases removed, a life redeemed, compassion, love, dreams fulfilled, and youth renewed.

Living life strong and in full abundance describes the life of King David. I enjoy reading the Psalms he wrote. I imagine him as a man of two worlds: in one world he is required to be austere and intimidating; in the other, he sits humbly and quietly before the Lord. I admire David's character and commitment to God. King David is accurately described as a man after God's own heart.

Unlike David, there have been times in my life when I felt so overcome with gratitude towards God that I could not find the words to express my heart. Some of these moments include:

- after the births of my children,
- after each of my children's decision to dedicate their life to Christ,
- after Monty's heart doctors confirmed that his heart was completely healed,

- after the many times my children were protected from injury,
- after the news of Monty's job promotion, and
- after each time I ponder the weight of sin from which I have been released.

The list could go on forever.

God has been and will continue to be faithful to His Word. I openly receive all His benefits and will never forget them. I could never give honor to another source for what God has done in my life. Take time today to thank God for His goodness in your life.

DAY 2

"Praise the LORD, O my soul; all my inmost being, praise his holy name. Praise the LORD, O my soul, and forget not all his benefits—who forgives all your sins and heals all your diseases, who redeems your life from the pit and crowns you with love and compassion, who satisfies your desires with good things so that your youth is renewed like the eagle's."

PSALM 103:1-5, NIV

The Lord tells us that He will forgive our wickedness and remember our sins no more (Jeremiah 31:34). Hebrews 10:17 NIV repeats this promise: "*Their sins and lawless acts I will remember no more.*" Scripture also teaches us that: "*He has rescued us from the dominion of darkness and brought us into the kingdom of the Son he loves, in whom we have redemption, the forgiveness of sins*" (Colossians 1:13-14 NIV). It goes on to say, "*Blessed are they whose transgressions are forgiven, whose sins are covered. Blessed is the man whose sin the Lord will never count against him.*" (Romans, 4:7-8 NIV)

KNOWING YOUR IDENTITY THROUGH CHRIST IS TRULY EMPOWERING.

Through Christ—the Messiah, the Anointed One—we have been set free. We have a new identity. In 2 Corinthians 5:20 we are called "*ambassadors.*" God made the Messiah, who was sinless, to be sin for us, so that in Jesus we might become the righteousness of God. This truth is foundational for Christians. Knowing your identity through Christ is truly empowering. We are no longer dirty sinners, habitually going about our day sinning against God. He created salvation for us through the cross, an act which cleans us of all our wrong-doing. We become a new creation.

"In Him also you were circumcised with a circumcision not made with hands, but in a [spiritual] circumcision [performed by] Christ by stripping off the body of the flesh (the whole corrupt, carnal nature with its passions and lusts). [Thus you were circumcised when] you were buried with Him in [your] baptism, in which you were also raised with Him [to a new life] through [your] faith in the working of God [as displayed] when He raised Him up from the dead. And you who were dead in trespasses and in the uncircumcision of your flesh (your sensuality, your sinful carnal nature), [God] brought to life together with [Christ], having [freely] forgiven us all our transgressions, Having cancelled and blotted out and wiped away the handwriting of the note (bond) with its legal decrees and demands which was in force and stood against us (hostile to us). This [note with its regulations, decrees, and demands] He set aside and cleared completely out of our way by nailing it to [His] cross. [God] disarmed the principalities and powers that were ranged against us and made a bold display and public example of them, in triumphing over them in Him and in it [the cross]." (Colossians 2:11-15, AMP)

"Therefore if any person is [ingrafted] in Christ (the Messiah) he is a new creation (a new creature altogether); the old [previous moral and spiritual condition] has passed away. Behold, the fresh and new has come! But all things are from God, Who through Jesus Christ reconciled us to Himself [received us into favor, brought us into harmony with Himself] and gave to us the ministry of reconciliation [that by word and deed we might aim to bring others into harmony with Him]. It was God [personally present] in Christ, reconciling and restoring the world to favor with Himself, not counting up and holding against [men] their trespasses [but cancelling them], and committing to us the message of reconciliation (of the restoration to favor). So we are Christ's ambassadors, God making His appeal as it were through us. We [as Christ's personal representatives] beg you for His sake to lay hold of the divine favor [now offered you] and be reconciled to God. For our sake He made Christ [virtually] to be sin Who knew no sin, so that in and through Him we might become [endued with, viewed as being in, and examples of] the righteousness of God [what we ought to be, approved and acceptable and in right relationship with Him, by His goodness]." (2 Corinthians 5:17-22, AMP)

Our new nature is Christ-like, God-like. Our new identity is one of the benefits of adoption into the Christian family. The devil no longer has control over our bodies and minds. We have been forgiven. Shame disappears. Jesus Christ's sacrifice was complete. He never needs to be crucified again. What He did was enough, once and for all.

"O Praise the Lord, O my soul, all my inmost being, praise his holy name. Praise the Lord, O my soul and forget not all his benefits, who forgives all your sins!"

"He personally bore our sins in His [own] body on the tree [as on an altar and offered Himself on it], that we might die (cease to exist) to sin and live to righteousness. By His wounds you have been healed." 1 Peter 2:24, AMP

"For Christ [the Messiah Himself] died for sins once for all, the Righteous for the unrighteous (the Just for the unjust, the Innocent for the guilty), that He might bring us to God. In His human body He was put to death, but He was made alive in the spirit." 1 Peter 3:18, AMP

"BLESSED (HAPPY, fortunate, to be envied) is he who has forgiveness of his transgression continually exercised upon him, whose sin is covered. Blessed (happy, fortunate, to be envied) is the man to whom the Lord imputes no iniquity and in whose spirit there is no deceit." Psalm 32:1-2, AMP

"Who gave (yielded) Himself up [to atone] for our sins [and to save and sanctify us], in order to rescue and deliver us from this present wicked age and world order, in accordance with the will and purpose and plan of our God and Father." Galatians 1:4, AMP

"For the grace of God (His unmerited favor and blessing) has come forward (appeared) for the deliverance from sin and the eternal

salvation for all mankind. It has trained us to reject and renounce all ungodliness (irreligion) and worldly (passionate) desires, to live discreet (temperate, self-controlled), upright, devout (spiritually whole) lives in this present world, Awaiting and looking for the [fulfillment, the realization of our] blessedhope, even the glorious appearing of our great God and Savior Christ Jesus (the Messiah, the Anointed One), *Who gave Himself on our behalf that He might redeem us (purchase our freedom) from all iniquity and purify for Himself a people [to be peculiarly His own, people who are] eager and enthusiastic about [living a life that is good and filled with] beneficial deeds."* Titus 2:11-14, AMP

Day 3

"Praise the LORD, O my soul; all my inmost being, praise his holy name. Praise the LORD, O my soul, and forget not all his benefits—who forgives all your sins and heals all your diseases, who redeems your life from the pit and crowns you with love and compassion, who satisfies your desires with good things so that your youth is renewed like the eagle's."

Psalm 103:1-5, NIV

In this week's Scripture we read that God *"heals all your diseases."* God's care is the best health care plan available—all diseases are healed!

God said He would take sickness from us. Some believe that sickness and disease are from God to strengthen us or to teach us a lesson, but His Word does not say that. In James 1:17 (KJV), we find that: "*Every good gift and every perfect gift is from above, and cometh down from the Father of lights, with whom is no variableness, neither shadow of turning.*" God is consistent.

Some believe that sickness and disease are from God to strengthen us or to teach us a lesson, but His Word does not say that.

Two thousand years ago, God humbled Himself and came to this fallen earth in human form to save the lives of all humankind. Jesus came to give us life. He came so that we could have forgiveness of our sins and physical wholeness. Jesus Christ, our Messiah, openly, publicly, and triumphantly defeated the powers that rage against us (Colossians 2:15). As a result of the cross, we are free to receive our blood-bought benefits, including healing and wholeness.

"If you will diligently hearken to the voice of the Lord your God and will do what is right in His sight, and will listen to and obey His commandments and keep all His statutes, I will put none of the diseases upon you which I brought upon the Egyptians, for I am the Lord Who heals you." Exodus 15:26, AMP

"When evening came, many who were demon-possessed were brought to him, and he drove out the spirits with a word and healed all the sick. This was to fulfill what was spoken through the prophet Isaiah: "He took up our infirmities and carried our diseases." Matthew 8:16-17, NIV

"He sent forth his word and healed them; he rescued them from the grave." Psalm 107:20, NIV

"He gives strength to the weary and increases the power of the weak. Even youths grow tired and weary, and young men stumble and fall; but those who hope in the LORD will renew their strength. They will soar on wings like eagles; they will run and not grow weary, they will walk and not be faint." Isaiah 40:29-31, NIV

"So do not fear, for I am with you; do not be dismayed, for I am your God. I will strengthen you and help you; I will uphold you with my righteous right hand." Isaiah 41:10, NIV

"Christ redeemed us from the curse of the law by becoming a curse for us, for it is written: 'Cursed is everyone who is hung on a tree." Galatians 3:13, NIV

"God made him who had no sin to be sin for us, so that in him we might become the righteousness of God." 2 Corinthians 5:21, NIV

"The thief comes only in order to steal and kill and destroy. I came that they may have and enjoy life, and have it in abundance (to the full, till it overflows)." John 10:10, AMP

"Surely He has borne our griefs (sicknesses, weaknesses, and distresses) and carried our sorrows and pains [of punishment], yet we

[ignorantly] considered Him stricken, smitten, and afflicted by God [as if with leprosy]. But He was wounded for our transgressions, He was bruised for our guilt and iniquities; the chastisement [needful to obtain] peace and well-being for us was upon Him, and with the stripes [that wounded] Him we are healed and made whole." Isaiah 53:4-5, AMP

"And these attesting signs will accompany those who believe: in My name they will drive out demons; they will speak in new languages; They will pick up serpents; and [even] if they drink anything deadly, it will not hurt them; they will lay their hands on the sick, and they will get well." Mark 16:17-18, AMP

"And if the Spirit of Him Who raised up Jesus from the dead dwells in you, [then] He Who raised up Christ Jesus from the dead will also restore to life your mortal (short-lived, perishable) bodies through His Spirit Who dwells in you." Romans 8:11, AMP

"So let us seize and hold fast and retain without wavering the hope we cherish and confess and our acknowledgement of it, for He Who promised is reliable (sure) and faithful to His word." Hebrews 10:23, AMP

"Jesus Christ (the Messiah) is [always] the same, yesterday, today, [yes] and forever (to the ages)." Hebrews 13:8, AMP

"Is anyone among you sick? He should call in the church elders (the spiritual guides). And they should pray over him, anointing him with oil in the Lord's name. And the prayer [that is] of faith will save him who is sick, and the Lord will restore him; and if he has committed sins, he will be forgiven." James 5:14-15, AMP

"And this is the confidence (the assurance, the privilege of boldness) which we have in Him: [we are sure] that if we ask anything (make any request) according to His will (in agreement with His own plan), He listens to and hears us. And if (since) we [positively] know that He listens to us in whatever we ask, we also know [with settled and absolute knowledge] that we have [granted us as our present possessions] the requests made of Him." 1 John 5:14-15, AMP

Day 4

"Praise the LORD, O my soul; all my inmost being, praise his holy name. Praise the LORD, O my soul, and forget not all his benefits—who forgives all your sins and heals all your diseases, who redeems your life from the pit and crowns you with love and compassion, who satisfies your desires with good things so that your youth is renewed like the eagle's."

Psalm 103:1-5, NIV

Our Scripture refers to *"being redeemed from the pit."* To me, the pit describes a place of total desperation. This condition is usually the result of either depending on others for life instruction instead of trusting in God, or by making decisions based solely on our emotions.

Proverbs 14:21 AMP warns us: *"There is a way which seems right to a man and appears straight before him, but at the end of it is the way of death."* No way out. No hope. Stuck. This pit can also be described as sin.

But in God's mercy and kindness, He hears our cry when we humble ourselves, repent, and yield our circumstances to Him. God's divine intervention is the only thing that can rescue us from ourselves. His compassion and love are unconditional and undeserving. He chooses to set us back on the track that leads us to intimacy with Him.

Instead of keeping a record of all our wrong-doings, God extends His hand to rescue us from the pit (Psalm 34:22). Redemption occurred when Jesus took the punishment for our sin and the grief for our sorrows upon Himself. In exchange for our despair, God offers us compassion and love. In exchange for weariness and death, He gives us good things that renew us. In God we have salvation. In Him we have rest, peace, and life.

DAY 5

"Praise the LORD, O my soul; all my inmost being, praise his holy name. Praise the LORD, O my soul, and forget not all his benefits—who forgives all your sins and heals all your diseases, who redeems your life from the pit and crowns you with love and compassion, who satisfies your desires with good things so that your youth is renewed like the eagle's."

PSALM 103:1-5, NIV

Monty and I met twenty years ago at Notre Dame: freshmen year, first week of school, and first day on campus at a minority welcome banquet. His skinny, tall frame and strong East Coast accent amazed me. I had never encountered a man like him before. It wasn't love at first sight, but I was intrigued. We became friends and a few months later started dating. Our conversations rarely touched on sports. In fact, I had no idea that he was an All American, All National Team member, a nationally and internationally recognized high school player, most recruited player of the year, or even an awesome basketball player!

At the beginning of every school year at Notre Dame, football dominates the campus; basketball is not a big focus. Monty told me he played basketball and was on scholarship at the school. I thought, "Oh! That's nice. Free tuition. Free room and board. Wish I could get a scholarship." I asked Monty if he could dunk a ball and, hesitantly, he answered "No." I figured as much. With those skinny legs and his slow walking, I couldn't imagine him being all that good. When I finally attended one of his games, I was dumbfounded. This skinny, slow-walking guy with whom I had spent so much time was a basketball prodigy. How we laugh today at my ignorance!

I soon realized that basketball was his life. Since Monty was a little boy, a career in basketball had been his life dream. God had given him a unique, athletic gift. He was good at it and he loved it.

But one year later, Monty came to my dorm to tell me he was no longer allowed to play basketball—*ever*. The team doctors had found an abnormal heart rhythm during routine physicals. Monty was diagnosed with a rare heart abnormality that would not allow him to participate in any sports for the rest of his life. This news was unfathomable, life-shattering. He was too young for such a final declaration.

We decided to pray. I can't tell you how many walks we took around our campus, as Monty sought God concerning the gift He had placed in Monty. We knew God was the Healer. Monty believed his basketball career was not over. He still wanted to play in the NBA and win championships.

Two years later Monty received another heart examination, this time at the National Institute of Health in Bethesda, Maryland. They ran every test imaginable. The amount of running, sweating, and stress the body is put through during these tests makes even the people watching them feel exhausted. This time Monty received a good report. No abnormalities. No extra rhythms. Monty was released to play basketball again.

"Praise the Lord, O my Soul and all my inmost being, praise his holy name. Praise the Lord, O my soul and forget not all His benefits."

Monty went on to play two more years at Notre Dame, graduated, and later was drafted in the first round as the number 24 pick with the New York Knicks.

God heals all our diseases.

DAY 6

"Praise the LORD, O my soul; all my inmost being, praise his holy name. Praise the LORD, O my soul, and forget not all his benefits—who forgives all your sins and heals all your diseases, who redeems your life from the pit and crowns you with love and compassion, who satisfies your desires with good things so that your youth is renewed like the eagle's."
PSALM 103:1-5, NIV

Proverbs 13:12 AMP says, "*Hope deferred makes the heart sick, but when the desire is fulfilled, it is a tree of life.*" Psalm 37:4-5 AMP encourages us to, "*Delight yourself also in the Lord and he will give you the desires and secret petitions of your heart. Commit your way to the Lord [roll and repose each care of your load on Him]; trust (lean on, rely on and be confident) also in Him and he will bring it to pass.*" The Lord knows our every desire and passion. He encourages us to trust Him with every care.

What I mean by trust is to confer with Him about everything that matters to you. Align your desires with the Word of God. Take time to listen to the voice of the Holy Spirit regarding your dreams. Make God a factor in every aspect of your life.

One of my teachers once said that in his twenties, he would work up a plan for his life and never think to ask God about it. In his forties, he would conjure up dreams and elaborate plans for his life and then ask God to bless it. Then, in his sixties, after years of unfulfilled dreams and plans, the truth dawned on him. Before planning or dreaming or working up anything, he asked God what plans God had for his life so that he could successfully bring glory to God. After this humble approach, my teacher made good life decisions and became very successful.

God wants us to enjoy life, to live life wide open. Our pocket-sized plans are small compared to what God can do. His ways are so much higher and complex than ours. I would much rather align myself with one of His plans than to create one of my own and ask Him along. Ephesians 3:20b AMP tells us: *"He is able to [carry out His purpose and] do superabundantly, far over and above all that we [dare] ask or think [infinitely beyond our highest prayers, desires, thoughts, hopes, or dreams]."*

GOD WANTS US TO ENJOY LIFE, TO LIVE LIFE WIDE OPEN.

Putting God first eliminates stress and worry, which drain us of life and contribute to early aging and depression. We can eliminate turmoil by consulting God first. He is well-qualified for the job.

DAY 7

"Praise the LORD, O my soul; all my inmost being, praise his holy name. Praise the LORD, O my soul, and forget not all his benefits—who forgives all your sins and heals all your diseases, who redeems your life from the pit and crowns you with love and compassion, who satisfies your desires with good things so that your youth is renewed like the eagle's."

PSALM 103:1-5, NIV

Meditate upon these various translations of this week's Words of life.

"Praise the LORD, O my soul; all my inmost being, praise his holy name. Praise the LORD, O my soul, and forget not all his benefits—who forgives all your sins and heals all your diseases, who redeems your life from the pit and crowns you with love and compassion, who satisfies your desires with good things so that your youth is renewed like the eagle's." NIV

"With all my heart I praise the LORD, and with all that I am I praise his holy name! With all my heart I praise the LORD! I will never forget how kind he has been. The LORD forgives our sins, heals us when we are sick, and protects us from death. His kindness and love are a crown on our heads. Each day that we live, he provides for our needs and gives us the strength of a young eagle." CEV

"O my soul, bless God. From head to toe, I'll bless his holy name! O my soul, bless God, don't forget a single blessing! He forgives your sins—every one. He heals your diseases—every one. He redeems you from hell—saves your life! He crowns you with love and mercy—a paradise crown. He wraps you in goodness—beauty eternal. He renews your youth—you're always young in his presence." MSG

"BLESS (affectionately, gratefully praise) the Lord, O my soul; and all that is [deepest] within me, bless His holy name! Bless (affectionately, gratefully praise) the Lord, O my soul, and forget not [one of] all His benefits—Who forgives [every one of] all your iniquities, Who heals [each one of] all your diseases, Who redeems your life from the pit and corruption, Who beautifies, dignifies, and crowns you with loving-kindness and tender mercy; Who satisfies your mouth [your necessity and desire at your personal age and situation] with good so that your youth, renewed, is like the eagle's [strong, overcoming, soaring]!" AMP

Week 25

"Praise the LORD. Blessed is the man who fears the LORD, who finds great delight in his commands. His children will be mighty in the land; the generation of the upright will be blessed. Wealth and riches are in his house, and his righteousness endures forever. Even in darkness light dawns for the upright, for the gracious and compassionate and righteous man."

Psalm 112:1-4, NIV

DAY 1

"Praise the LORD. Blessed is the man who fears the LORD, who finds great delight in his commands. His children will be mighty in the land; the generation of the upright will be blessed. Wealth and riches are in his house, and his righteousness endures forever. Even in darkness light dawns for the upright, for the gracious and compassionate and righteous man."

PSALM 112:1-4, NIV

Studying Scripture in numerous versions helps us understand the Word more clearly. For your meditation, this week's verses are offered below in five different translations.

"Praise Ye the Lord. Blessed is the man that feareth the Lord, that delighteth greatly in His commandments. His seed shall be mighty upon earth: the generation of the upright shall be blessed. Wealth and riches shall be in his house: and his righteousness endureth forever. Unto the upright there ariseth light in the darkness: he is gracious, and full of compassion, and righteous." KJV

"Praise the Lord! (Hallelujah!) Blessed (happy, fortunate, to be envied) is the man who fears (reveres and worship) the Lord, who delights greatly in His commandments. His [spiritual] offspring shall be mighty upon earth; the generation of the upright shall be blessed. Prosperity and welfare are in his house, and his righteousness endures forever. Light arises in the darkness for the upright, gracious, compassionate, and just [who are in right standing with God]." AMP

"Praise the LORD. Blessed is the man who fears the LORD, who finds great delight in his commands. His children will be mighty in the land; the generation of the upright will be blessed. Wealth and riches are in his house, and his righteousness endures forever. Even in darkness light dawns for the upright, for the gracious and compassionate and righteous man." NIV

"Shout praises to the LORD! The LORD blesses everyone who worships him and gladly obeys his teachings. Their descendants will have great power in the land, because the LORD blesses all who do right. They will get rich and prosper and will always be remembered for their fairness. They will be so kind and merciful and good, that they will be a light in the dark for others who do the right thing." CEV

"Praise the Lord! How joyful are those who fear the Lord and delight in obeying his commands. Their children will be successful everywhere; an entire generation of godly people will be blessed. They themselves will be wealthy, and their good deeds will last forever. Light shines in the darkness for the godly. They are generous, compassionate, and righteous." NLT

DAY 2

"Praise the LORD. Blessed is the man who fears the LORD, who finds great delight in his commands. His children will be mighty in the land; the generation of the upright will be blessed. Wealth and riches are in his house, and his righteousness endures forever. Even in darkness light dawns for the upright, for the gracious and compassionate and righteous man."

PSALM 112:1-4, NIV

This particular Scripture passage confirms the goodness of God's plan for our lives. As I have studied this passage, examining every word, my soul has been encouraged. I have hope that my children will become more than I have imagined because Monty and I delight in God's commandments. I am uniquely aware each day of how our commitment to God affects our children. It is refreshing to know that they will reap royal benefits because of our obedience to Him.

> *"I was young and now I am old, yet I have never seen the righteous forsaken or their children begging bread."* (Psalm 37:25, NIV)
>
> *"But from everlasting to everlasting the LORD's love is with those who fear him, and his righteousness with their children's children—with those who keep his covenant and remember to obey his precepts."* (Psalm 103:17-18, NIV)

Our relationship with God is not just an investment in our lives but also in the lives of our children and grandchildren. I have seen firsthand how a godly grandparent's or parent's relationship with God has established a good life for the grandchild or child. Investing in a relationship with God is similar to financially investing for a secure future for your family. Many go to great lengths to create a comfortable lifestyle for their families. How much more do you think God does for His children?!

God promises to bless us because of the obedience and adoration we have towards Him. We are promised temporal as well as eternal security. Monty and I are establishing a legacy of righteousness for our family. Our grandchildren and children will know us as living memorials to the goodness and faithfulness of God.

> *"The [uncompromisingly] righteous shall flourish like the palm tree [be long-lived, stately, upright, useful and fruitful]; they shall grow like a cedar in Lebanon [majestic, stable, and incorruptible]. Planted in the house of the Lord, they shall flourish in the courts of our God. [Growing in grace] they shall still bring forth fruit in old age; they shall be full of sap [of spiritual vitality] and [rich in the] verdure [of trust, love and contentment]. [They are living memorials] to show that the Lord is upright and faithful to His promises; He is my Rock and there is no unrighteousness in Him."* Psalm 92:12-15, AMP

Day 3

"Praise the LORD. Blessed is the man who fears the LORD, who finds great delight in his commands. His children will be mighty in the land; the generation of the upright will be blessed. Wealth and riches are in his house, and his righteousness endures forever. Even in darkness light dawns for the upright, for the gracious and compassionate and righteous man."

Psalm 112:1-4, NIV

I want you to remember that the Word of God applies to us today. From the beginning, God's Word has been a creative tool. They are also our source of strength. God's Word is consistently true for us. Incorporate it into your life.

"For as the rain and snow come down from the heavens, and return not there again, but water the earth and make it bring forth and sprout, that it may give seed to the sower and bread to the eater, so shall My word be that goes forth out of My mouth: it shall not return to Me void [without producing any effect, useless], but it shall accomplish that which I please and purpose, and it shall prosper in the thing for which I sent it. For you shall go out [from the spiritual exile caused by sin and evil into the homeland] with joy and be led forth [by your Leader, the Lord Himself, and His word] with peace; the mountains and the hills shall break forth before you into singing, and all the trees of the field shall clap their hands. Instead of the thorn shall come up the cypress tree, and instead of the brier shall come up the myrtle tree; and it shall be to the Lord for a name of renown, for an everlasting sign [of jubilant exaltation] and memorial [to His praise], which shall not be cut off." (Isaiah 55:10-13, AMP)

"Light is sown for the [uncompromisingly] righteous and strewn along their pathway, and joy for the upright in heart [the irrepressible

joy which comes from consciousness of His favor and protection]." (Psalm 97:11, AMP)

"If you set your heart aright and stretch out your hands to [God], If you put sin out of your hand and far away from you and let not evil dwell in your tents; Then can you lift up your face to Him without stain [of sin, and unashamed]; yes, you shall be steadfast and secure; you shall not fear. For you shall forget your misery; you shall remember it as waters that pass away. And [your] life shall be clearer than the noonday and rise above it; though there be darkness, it shall be as the morning. And you shall be secure and feel confident because there is hope; yes, you shall search about you, and you shall take your rest in safety. You shall lie down, and none shall make you afraid; yes, many shall sue for your favor. But the eyes of the wicked shall look [for relief] in vain, and they shall not escape [the justice of God]; and their hope shall be to give up the ghost." (Job 11:13-20, AMP)

"BLESSED (HAPPY, *fortunate, to be envied) is everyone who fears, reveres, and worships the Lord, who walks in His ways and lives according to His commandments."* (Psalm 128:1, AMP)

"For You, Lord, will bless the [uncompromisingly] righteous [him who is upright and in right standing with You]; as with a shield You will surround him with goodwill (pleasure and favor)." (Psalm 5:12, AMP)

"BLESSED (HAPPY, *fortunate, to be envied) are the undefiled (the upright, truly sincere, and blameless) in the way [of the revealed will of God], who walk (order their conduct and conversation) in the law of the Lord (the whole of God's revealed will). Blessed (happy, fortunate, to be envied) are they who keep His testimonies, and who seek, inquire for and of Him and crave Him with the whole heart. Yes, they do no unrighteousness [no willful wandering from His precepts]; they walk in His ways."* (Psalm 119:1-3, AMP)

"Who is the man who reverently fears and worships the Lord? Him shall He teach in the way that he should choose. He himself shall dwell at ease, and his offspring shall inherit the land. The secret [of the sweet, satisfying companionship] of the Lord have they who fear (revere and worship) Him, and He will show them His covenant and reveal to them its [deep, inner] meaning." (Psalm 25:12-14, AMP)

DAY 4

"Praise the LORD. Blessed is the man who fears the LORD, who finds great delight in his commands. His children will be mighty in the land; the generation of the upright will be blessed. Wealth and riches are in his house, and his righteousness endures forever. Even in darkness light dawns for the upright, for the gracious and compassionate and righteous man."

PSALM 112:1-4, NIV

"...Light arises in the darkness for the upright..."

God's light makes us different from the world. The light He raises for us illuminates the route He has established for us; *"Your word is lamp to my feet and a light for my path"* (Psalm 119:105 NIV). God's way is sure to make us successful and prosperous in all that we do (Deuteronomy 28:1-14). The light God provides for us keeps us from wandering, worrying, and searching for a purpose in life. An existence without a relationship with God is not life at all—without Him, we are empty and void. God gives us life, along with a sense of direction and purpose, by the light of His Word.

> *"Arise, shine, for your light has come and the glory of the Lord rises upon you. See, darkness covers the earth and thick darkness is over the peoples, but the Lord rises upon you and his glory appears over you. Nations will come to your lights and kings to the brightness of your dawn."* (Isaiah 60:1-3, NIV)

When we walk in the light, we reflect Him. When people see us, they see the light of the Lord shining from the inside out.

"You are the light of the world. A city set on a hill cannot be hidden. Nor do men light a lamp and put it under a peck measure, but on a lamp stand, and it gives light to all in the house. Let your light so shine before men that they may see your moral excellence and your praiseworthy, noble, and good deeds and recognize and honor and praise and glorify your Father Who is in heaven." (Matthew 5:14-16, AMP)

You may have heard such comments made to you as: "There is something different about you." "Did you get your teeth whitened?" "Your smile is so bright! You just light up the room when you enter." These comments are not because you are such a great person or because you have accomplished a great feat. People are drawn to you because Jesus Christ is dwelling on the inside, shining through you. Praise God! I tell my girls that when people stare at you and compliment your beauty, it's not you they see, but Jesus; so smile back and say "hello," or "thank you."

BE KIND AND ALLOW THE HOLY SPIRIT TO WORK THROUGH YOU TO BLESS SOMEONE.

Be kind and allow the Holy Spirit to work through you to bless someone. This world is dark and lonely. But thanks to God, we can be ambassadors for Christ and become an extension of who He is: loving, kind, gentle, merciful, compassionate, benevolent, wise, trustworthy—the list could go on forever.

Just remember that when you are in the grocery store or gas station or riding in your car on the highway: You are walking in the light of the Lord. You know where you are going because God's word is your guide. People are drawn to you. Be Christ for someone who doesn't know Him.

DAY 5

"Praise the LORD. Blessed is the man who fears the LORD, who finds great delight in his commands. His children will be mighty in the land; the generation of the upright will be blessed. Wealth and riches are in his house, and his righteousness endures forever. Even in darkness light dawns for the upright, for the gracious and compassionate and righteous man."

PSALM 112:1-4, NIV

The Bible is a book of truth that never leaves the reader bored or without inspiration. I absolutely love the Word of God; each day I encounter something new. It is alive and active, generating changes inside the soul of the reader. God patiently and compassionately gives us countless chances to comprehend His truth.

The last part of verse four in today's Scripture describes the blessed man as *"gracious, full of compassion, and righteous"*—two qualities God shows us on a daily basis. In Exodus 34:6 NIV God describes Himself as: *"The LORD, the LORD, the compassionate and gracious God, slow to anger, abounding in love and faithfulness."*

Webster's dictionary defines the words "gracious" and "compassionate" as follows:

- Gracious: courteous, polite, civil, chivalrous, well-mannered, mannerly, tactful, diplomatic; kind, benevolent, considerate, thoughtful, obliging, accommodating, indulgent.
- Compassionate: compassionate concern for the victims, sympathetic, empathetic, understanding, caring, solicitous, sensitive, warm, loving; merciful, lenient, tolerant, consid ate, kind, humane, charitable, big-hearted.

Throughout the Bible, God is referred to as compassionate and loving. When we become spiritually born anew, we are able to take on His characteristics. We can choose to be like Him. Some would say, "Well, *I* can't. He is God and the people I have to deal with here on earth are impossible. I'm not God!" It's true that you can't, but God can. He has given us a wonderful example. Two thousand years ago a man walked the earth exemplifying God perfectly. His name is Jesus Christ, the Messiah. His ministry with the disciples actively moved by virtue of compassion: *"When he saw the crowds, he had compassion on them, because they were harassed and helpless, like sheep without a shepherd"* (Matthew 9:36, NIV). *"When Jesus landed and saw a large crowd, he had compassion on them and healed their sick"* (Matthew 14:14, NIV).

We are able, with the help of the Lord, to serve others and show the love of Christ. He equips us and commands us to do so. Our actions should mimic that of our Heavenly Father. He lavishly bestows love and compassion on us, and we can do the same.

We are blessed to be a blessing. Find someone in your community to whom you can show the love of Christ.

"Be kind and compassionate to one another, forgiving each other, just as in Christ God forgave you." Ephesians 4:32, NIV

"Therefore, as God's chosen people, holy and dearly loved, clothe yourselves with compassion, kindness, humility, gentleness and patience." Colossians 3:12, NIV

"The end of all things is near. Therefore be clear-minded and self-controlled so that you can pray. Above all, love each other deeply, because love covers over a multitude of sins. Offer hospitality to one another without grumbling. Each one should use whatever gift he

has received to serve others, faithfully administering God's grace in its various forms. If anyone speaks, he should do it as one speaking the very words of God. If anyone serves, he should do it with the strength God provides, so that in all things God may be praised through Jesus Christ. To him be the glory and the power forever and ever. Amen." 1 Peter 4:7-11, NIV

"Finally, all of you, live in harmony with one another; be sympathetic, love as brothers, be compassionate and humble. Do not repay evil with evil or insult with insult, but with blessing, because to this you were called so that you may inherit a blessing." 1 Peter 3:8-9, NIV

Day 6

"Praise the LORD. Blessed is the man who fears the LORD, who finds great delight in his commands. His children will be mighty in the land; the generation of the upright will be blessed. Wealth and riches are in his house, and his righteousness endures forever. Even in darkness light dawns for the upright, for the gracious and compassionate and righteous man."

Psalm 112:1-4, NIV

"The LORD had said to Abram, 'Leave your country, your people and your father's household and go to the land I will show you. I will make you into a great nation and I will bless you; will make your name great, and you will be a blessing. I will bless those who bless you, and whoever curses you I will curse; and all peoples on earth will be blessed through you." (Genesis 12:1-3, NIV)

This week's passage is similar to the call given in Genesis 12. God's call to Abram parallels the call He gives to us today. Hebrew rabbinical commentary on the traditional first five books of the Old Testament (the Torah, or Chumash) explains, "God assured Abraham that he would not suffer detrimental consequences commonly resulting from extended travel; its rigors make it harder to bear children [which must have been of particular concern to the childless Abraham and Sarah], they diminish one's wealth; and they harm one's reputation. In this verse, God told him that he would not suffer in any of these ways."

Similarly, Psalm 112 assures us of provision, protection, and success when we are in relationship with God. When we obey the call of the Lord, we have to step out of our familiar world. Cultural and familial identities change. Abram and Sarai took a risk. In their culture, leaving the homeland was not common, especially if the couple did not have children of their own. Abram chose God over a life he knew from generations past. He trusted God: "*Abraham believed in (trusted in) God, and it was credited to his account as righteousness (right living and right standing with God)*." (Romans 4:3 AMP)

James 2:23 tells us that God called Abraham His friend. Later, after the call, the Lord confirmed His faithfulness to Abram and cut covenant with him. In Genesis 17 God changed Abram's name to Abraham (and Sarai to Sarah), declaring him to be a father of many nations at the age of ninety-nine years old. He is proof that it is never too late to obey the Lord.

LIFE WITH THE LORD IS FAR FROM UNEVENTFUL.

God is able to do anything. He is looking for willing participants—people who desire a change from the old familiar, from a life of sin or from mediocrity. I guarantee you that life with the Lord is far from uneventful.

Read the Bible. You will see He has an exciting and blessed life for His followers. Won't you choose Him? Step out and live passionately for Him!

Day 7

"Praise the LORD. Blessed is the man who fears the LORD, who finds great delight in his commands. His children will be mighty in the land; the generation of the upright will be blessed. Wealth and riches are in his house, and his righteousness endures forever. Even in darkness light dawns for the upright, for the gracious and compassionate and righteous man."

Psalm 112:1-4, NIV

On this last day for our week in Psalm 112, I am reminded of our concept for this book—*look again*. The Lord has impressed upon me to take a second look at my life and the impact I am making on the places of influence He has placed me in:

- First, my husband and marriage.
- Second, my children and motherhood.
- Third, my community as a Christian.

In each of these relationships, I ask the following questions:

- Am I a blessing to those around me?
- Am I walking in love and obedience to His word?
- Am I representing the Father?

Each morning I encourage my daughters to take a second look in the mirror and ask themselves, "Do I look the best I can look today? Am I accurately representing my Father?" If they can answer "Yes," then it's time to begin the day. If they take that second look and decide a better dress would be more fitting or a different hairstyle would be better suited for the day, then it's time to reassess and redress. My purpose is to teach them two things: the importance of showing the world that excellence comes from serving God and the importance of our family identity.

People who don't know Jesus should be able to observe our excellence in dress, behavior, and manners, noticing a difference in our disposition because of who our Father is. We also represent our earthly fathers. Monty and I believe our children should have a sense of pride in who they are when they leave the house. They should also know that their father, by way of the blessings from our Heavenly Father, is a great provider.

I encourage you to look again at your life and ask yourself, "*Am I the best I can be for the Lord today?* When people see me, do they see my Father?" If the answer is "No," then reassess and redress. Take time to hear the Holy Spirit's promptings towards change. Seek God for direction in the areas that need a change. Search through the Word to find verses that apply to you. Let His Word change you. If the answer is "Yes," become the world-changer you were created to be.

Let your light shine!

Week 26

"Blessed is the man who trusts in the Lord, whose confidence is in Him. He will be like a tree planted by the water that sends out its roots by the stream. It does not fear when heat comes; its leaves are always green. It has no worries in a year of drought and never fails to bear fruit."

Jeremiah 17:7-8, NIV

DAY 1

"Blessed is the man who trusts in the Lord, whose confidence is in Him. He will be like a tree planted by the water that sends out its roots by the stream. It does not fear when heat comes; its leaves are always green. It has no worries in a year of drought and never fails to bear fruit."

JEREMIAH 17:7-8, NIV

I want to start off by looking at this week's verse from four different translations to get a wider point of view. I encourage you to meditate on it and let it soak into your heart.

"[Most] blessed is the man who believes in, trusts in, and relies on the Lord, and whose hope and confidence the Lord is. For he shall be like a tree planted by the waters that spreads out its roots by the river; and it shall not see and fear when heat comes; but its leaf shall be green. It shall not be anxious and full of care in the year of drought, nor shall it cease yielding fruit." AMP

"But blessed is the man who trusts me, God, the woman who sticks with God. They're like trees replanted in Eden, putting down roots near the rivers—Never a worry through the hottest of summers, never dropping a leaf, Serene and calm through droughts, bearing fresh fruit every season." MSG

"But blessed are those who trust in the Lord and have made the Lord their hope and confidence. They are like trees planted along a riverbank, with roots that reach deep into the water. Such trees are not bothered by the heat or worried by long months of drought. Their leaves stay green, and they never stop producing fruit." NLT

Day 2

"Blessed is the man who trusts in the Lord, whose
confidence is in Him. He will be like a tree planted by
the water that sends out its roots by the stream.
It does not fear when heat comes; its leaves are always
green. It has no worries in a year of drought
and never fails to bear fruit."

Jeremiah 17:7-8, NIV

What does the word "blessed" actually mean? *The American Dictionary of the English Language* (Noah Webster 1828 version) defines the word as "made happy or prosperous; extolled; pronounced happy; prosperous in worldly affairs; enjoying spiritual happiness and the favor of God; enjoying heavenly felicity."

Psalm 5:12 AMP teaches us that a person who trusts in the Lord is a person of great success and favor: "*For You, Lord, will bless the [uncompromisingly] righteous [him who is upright and in right standing with You]; as with a shield You will surround him with goodwill (pleasure and favor).*" The "righteous" in this verse refers to believers who trust in, adhere to, and rely on the Word of God as their vital necessity in all aspects of their lives.

Once Monty and I became parents, we began to see how little we knew and how desperately we needed to be in relationship with God. We realized the weightiness of our responsibilities as parents. Deep within, we knew we did not have the wisdom we needed to properly raise these precious gifts from God. We were never ones to read parenting help books; thankfully, the Lord impressed upon us that the wisdom for parenting is found in His Word.

Each of our children has been given a unique personality and unusual gifts for the advancement of His kingdom. The Lord has faithfully provided us with wisdom and grace for each child. We are convinced that He is blessing our parenting because we have completely trusted in His wisdom concerning the children. We don't fear the teenage years. We don't worry about financial stability throughout our years as a growing family. We are choosing to believe what God says about His "righteous."

In a personal way, we have taught the children one of the promises found in Jeremiah 33:9 AMP: *And [Jerusalem]* The Williams Family *shall be to Me a name of joy, a praise and a glory before all the nations of the earth that hear of all the good I do for it, and they shall fear and tremble because of all the good and all the peace, prosperity, security, and stability I provide for it.*

We want our children to know that God is real and that the wisdom in His Word is the key to every part of our lives. We consult Him about everything and we impress upon them the importance of doing the same.

"Blessed (happy, fortunate, to be envied) is the man who makes the Lord his refuge and trust, and turns not to the proud or to followers of false gods. Many, O Lord my God, are the wonderful works which You have done, and Your thoughts towards us; no one can compare with You! If I should declare and speak of them, they are too many to be numbered. Sacrifice and offering You do not desire, nor have You delight in them; You have given me the capacity to hear and obey [Your law, a more valuable service than] burnt offerings and sin offerings [which] You do not require." Psalm 40:4-6, AMP

"I sought (inquired of) the Lord and required Him [of necessity and on the authority of His Word], and He heard me, and delivered me from all my fears. The Angel of the Lord encamps around those who fear Him [who revere and worship Him with awe] and each of them He delivers. O taste and see that the Lord [our God] is good!

Blessed (happy, fortunate, to be envied) is the man who trusts and takes refuge in Him. O fear the Lord, you His saints [revere and worship Him]! For there is no want to those who truly revere and worship Him with godly fear. The young lions lack food and suffer hunger, but they who seek (inquire of and require) the Lord [by right of their need and on the authority of His Word], none of them shall lack any beneficial thing." Psalm 34:4, 7-10, AMP

Day 3

"Blessed is the man who trusts in the Lord, whose confidence is in Him. He will be like a tree planted by the water that sends out its roots by the stream. It does not fear when heat comes; its leaves are always green. It has no worries in a year of drought and never fails to bear fruit."

Jeremiah 17:7-8, NIV

Trees are instrumental in good water quality. By filtering hazardous, underground chemicals with their roots, trees protect water consumed by animals and people. Trees play a part in stream energy as well. The roots dissipate the stream energy which results in less erosion and a redirection in flood damage. Trees are vitally significant in the durability of the stream and to all of the surrounding terrain.

God is presenting an important comparison when He likens those who trust Him to trees planted by a stream. The relationship trees have to the water system surrounding them is very similar to our role as Christians in modern society. We are the stabilizing force in our communities. As we flourish and grow in His Word, our influence becomes greater—financially, spiritually, physically, and emotionally. We efficiently impact our communities with the truth and light of Jesus. When we are deeply rooted and established in the Word of God, we are able to influence those around us and come out successful in diverse times.

God is presenting an important comparison when He likens those who trust Him to trees planted by a stream.

In our generosity and in serving our communities, God will be glorified. In 2 Corinthians 9:12-14 AMP we are told: "*For the service that the ministering of this fund renders does not only fully supply what is lacking to the saints (God's people), but it also overflows in many [cries of] thanksgiving to God. Because at [your] standing of the test of this ministry, they will glorify God for your loyalty and obedience to the Gospel of Christ which you confess, as well as for your generous-hearted liberality to them and to all [the other needy ones]. And they yearn for you while they pray for you, because of the surpassing measure of God's grace (His favor and mercy and spiritual blessing which is shown forth) in you.*"

> *"Blessed is the man who does not walk in the counsel of the wicked or stand in the way of sinners or sit in the seat of mockers. But his delight is in the law of the Lord, and on his law he meditates day and night. He is like a tree planted by steams of water, which yields its fruit in season and whose leaf does not wither. Whatever he does prospers."*
> Psalm 1:1-3, NIV

> *"The righteous will flourish like a palm tree, they will grow like a cedar of Lebanon; planted in the house of the Lord, they will flourish in the courts of our God. They will still bear fruit in old age, they will stay fresh and green, proclaiming, "The LORD is upright; he is my Rock, and there is no wickedness in him."* Psalm 92:12-15, NIV

DAY 4

"Blessed is the man who trusts in the Lord, whose confidence is in Him. He will be like a tree planted by the water that sends out its roots by the stream. It does not fear when heat comes; its leaves are always green. It has no worries in a year of drought and never fails to bear fruit."

JEREMIAH 17:7-8, NIV

Oregon has some of the most beautiful natural landscapes in the United States. When we first moved here from Texas, I was completely taken by the vast beauty of this region—particularly the trees and the rivers. The terrain is truly breathtaking. Portland, where we live, has two major rivers that run through the heart of the city. We are fortunate to have many parks and walkways situated along the river fronts. During the summer months, we go on long family walks and take in the magnificent landscape. I have on many occasions stopped to ponder the awesomeness of God's handiwork. The trees so tall and majestic, full of flowers and brightly colored leaves; the rivers bulging along the bank, refreshing the air with a clean crisp fragrance. There is undoubtedly no way anyone could deny the presence of our Creator and His goodness for us. He surrounds us with beauty.

Jeremiah 17:7-8 compares the blessed man to a tree planted by the stream. As I read this verse, I visualize Christians being a intriguing as the bountiful Oregon landscape. Tourists come from all parts of our nation to vacation and experience the richness of the land in this state. As a Christian, I aspire to influence the world by spreading the Gospel to all people. In order to reach people who don't know the Lord, there has to be something about me that attracts them to me; that factor is the character of God inside of me. As I put my confidence in Him and trust that His Word is true, developing my faith, I will be like the strong majestic, powerful trees of Oregon, acting as a refuge and an ambassador of hope for the lost. Let's allow others to see God inside of us.

DAY 5

"Blessed is the man who trusts in the Lord, whose
confidence is in Him. He will be like a tree planted by
the water that sends out its roots by the stream.
It does not fear when heat comes; its leaves are always
green. It has no worries in a year of drought
and never fails to bear fruit."

JEREMIAH 17:7-8, NIV

> "*...a tree planted by the water that sends out its roots by the stream... shall not see or fear when heat comes but its leaf shall be green...*" AMP

Symbolically, the tree represents the righteous, us, and the stream is the living water, the Lord. Daily I am comforted by the confidence I have from knowing God. Knowing Him demands intimacy and a consistent commitment to His precepts. I would equate it to a marriage covenant: *"This is the covenant which I will make with the house of Israel: After those days, says the Lord, I will put My law within them, and on their hearts will I write it; and I will be their God, and they will be My people. And they will no more teach each man his neighbor and each man his brother, saying, Know the Lord, for they will all know Me [recognize, understand, and be acquainted with Me], from the least of them to the greatest, says the Lord. For I will forgive their iniquity, and I will [seriously] remember their sin no more."* (Jeremiah 31:33-34, AMP)

Throughout Biblical history and still to this day, God has sought the heart of man. His love for us has been an unfailing factor since creation. Reading the Scriptures often reminds me of a love letter between two passionate people. He lavishes His unconditional love on us without measure.

God repeatedly declares His desire to have us as His own. He considered our well-being centuries before we knew there was a need. His Word is full of declarations of commitment and protection without end. As I have come to know Him more intimately, I have come to know that He loves me. He promises to never leave me or forget about me. I have a life-long companion and I would definitely say I have "married up." I am in covenant with the God Most High, Possessor of Heaven and Earth!

"Behold, I have indelibly imprinted (tattooed a picture of) you on the palm of each of My hands; [O Zion] your walls are continually before Me." Isaiah 49:16, AMP

"For He [God] Himself has said, I will not in any way fail you nor give you up nor leave you without support. [I will] not, [I will] not, [I will] not in any degree leave you helpless nor forsake nor let [you] down (relax My hold on you)! [Assuredly not!] So we take comfort and are encouraged and confidently and boldly say, The Lord is my Helper; I will not be seized with alarm [I will not fear or dread or be terrified]. What can man do to me?" Hebrews 13:5b, 6, AMP

"The Lord is my Shepherd [to feed, guide, and shield me] I shall not lack. He makes me lie down in [fresh, tender] green pastures; He leads me beside the still and restful waters. He refreshes and restores my life (my self); He leads me in the paths of righteousness [uprightness and right standing with Him—not for my earning it, but] for His name's sake. Yes, though I walk through the [deep, sunless] valley of the shadow of death, I will fear or dread no evil, for You are with me; Your rod [to protect] and Your staff [to guide], they comfort me. You prepare a table before me in the presence of my enemies. You anoint my head with oil; my [brimming] cup runs over. Surely [only] goodness, mercy, and unfailing love shall follow me all the days of my life, and through the length of my days the house of the Lord (and His presence] shall be my dwelling place." Psalm 23, AMP

DAY 6

"Blessed is the man who trusts in the Lord, whose confidence is in Him. He will be like a tree planted by the water that sends out its roots by the stream. It does not fear when heat comes; its leaves are always green. It has no worries in a year of drought and never fails to bear fruit."

JEREMIAH 17:7-8, NIV

"Cast your burden on the Lord [releasing the weight of it] and He will sustain you; He will never allow the [consistently] righteous to be moved (made to slip, fall, or fail)." (Psalm 55:22, AMP)

"Fear not [there is nothing to fear], for I am with you; do not look around you in terror and be dismayed, for I am your God. I will strengthen and harden you to difficulties, yes, I will help you; yes, I will hold you up and retain you with My [victorious] right hand of rightness and justice." (Isaiah 41:10, AMP)

"Casting the whole of your care [all your anxieties, all your worries, all your concerns, once and for all] on Him, for He cares for you affectionately and cares about you watchfully." (1Peter 5:7, AMP)

"Do not fret or have any anxiety about anything, but in every circumstance and in everything, by prayer and petition (definite requests), with thanks-giving, continue to make your wants known to God. And God's peace [shall be yours, that tranquil state of a soul assured of its salvation through Christ, and so fearing nothing from God and being content with its earthly lot of whatever sort that is, that peace] which transcends all understanding shall garrison and mount guard over your hearts and minds in Christ Jesus." (Philippians 4:6-7, AMP)

The Scriptures above are just a few of the passages that confirm God's intent to sustain us. We must not allow fear and anxiety to affect us. The Word encourages us to release all of our cares to Him because He cares for us.

It's in our best interest not to worry or fear; our bodies are simply not equipped to tolerate the stress. Doctors have proven that numerable physical malfunctions are related to stress. Our culture feeds anxiety to us through all sources of media. To maintain a peaceful mindset, you have to make a conscious decision not to give your attention to the fear, stress, and anxiety offered by our society, but instead to concentrate on the promises of the Lord.

I once heard a teacher describe his battle with fear as a test of the will. When fear attempted to grip his thinking, he would remember what the Word says in Psalm 23:4 NASB, "*Even though I walk through the valley of the shadow of death I will fear no evil for You are with me.*" He said defeating fear is not about denying fear's presence. Defeating fear is about choosing *not* to fear.

DEFEATING FEAR IS NOT ABOUT DENYING FEAR'S PRESENCE.

Don't choose fear. Fear must not be an optional response for us. Instead, make a decision to choose the Word rooted in your heart. Choosing not to fear is simply choosing God's Word. Take time to meditate on verses that declare the protection and love of God. Simply say NO to fear. Fear is the root of stress, anxiety, anger, lust, hatred, and all evil things—none of which are love-based. These emotions do not come from God, because God is *LOVE*. And where there is love, there cannot be fear (1 John 4:18).

God has established us as His own; by His Word we are assured of His constant presence and protection. Receive His peace. Choose not to fear, but to believe.

DAY 7

"Blessed is the man who trusts in the Lord, whose confidence is in Him. He will be like a tree planted by the water that sends out its roots by the stream. It does not fear when heat comes; its leaves are always green. It has no worries in a year of drought and never fails to bear fruit."
JEREMIAH 17:7-8, NIV

"*...its leaves are always green...and never fails to bear fruit...*"

This week we have seen many verses that support God's ability to keep us undamaged and productive in harsh times. When we choose to trust Him, He maintains our vitality by the power of His Word. What a testament to the faithfulness of God!

Everything I've presented to you this week boils down to this: put all your confidence in God. Rely on His wisdom, His provision, His promises, His Word. People are unable to substitute for God. When hard times come, a thousand phone calls to a thousand friends cannot provide the amount of relief one conversation with God can bring. Our relationship with God is the most effective relationship we have against the devil's plans to destroy us.

"*As for God, His way is perfect! The word of the Lord is tested and tried; He is a shield to all those who take refuge and put their trust in Him.*" Psalm 18:30, AMP

"*The Lord is my Strength and my [impenetrable] Shield; my heart trusts in, relies on, and confidently leans on Him, and I am helped; therefore my heart greatly rejoices, and with my song will I praise Him. The Lord is their [unyielding] Strength, and He is the Stronghold of salvation to [me] His anointed."* Psalm 28:7-8, AMP

"I will bless the Lord at all times; His praise shall continually be in my mouth. My life makes its boast in the Lord; let the humble and afflicted hear and be glad. O magnify the Lord with me, and let us exalt His name together. I sought (inquired of) the Lord and required Him [of necessity and on the authority of His Word], and He heard me, and delivered me from all my fears. They looked to Him and were radiant; their faces shall never blush for shame or be confused. This poor man cried, and the Lord heard him, and saved him out of all his troubles. The Angel of the Lord encamps around those who fear Him [who revere and worship Him with awe] and each of them He delivers. O taste and see that the Lord [our God] is good! Blessed (happy, fortunate, to be envied) is the man who trusts and takes refuge in Him. O fear the Lord, you His saints [revere and worship Him]! For there is no want to those who truly revere and worship Him with godly fear. The young lions lack food and suffer hunger, but they who seek (inquire of and require) the Lord [by right of their need and on the authority of His Word], none of them shall lack any beneficial thing. Come, you children, listen to me; I will teach you to revere and worshipfully fear the Lord. What man is he who desires life and longs for many days, that he may see good? Keep your tongue from evil and your lips from speaking deceit. Depart from evil and do good; seek, inquire for, and crave peace and pursue (go after) it! The eyes of the Lord are toward the [uncompromisingly] righteous and His ears are open to their cry. The face of the Lord is against those who do evil, to cut off the remembrance of them from the earth. When the righteous cry for help, the Lord hears, and delivers them out of all their distress and troubles. The Lord is close to those who are of a broken heart and saves such as are crushed with sorrow for sin and are humbly and thoroughly penitent. Many evils confront the [consistently] righteous, but the Lord delivers him out of them all."
Psalm 34:1-19, AMP

HURRY UP

It would be pointless for us to spend so much time and so many resources on this project without challenging you to give your life to Christ if you have not done so, and to encourage those who are followers of Jesus to be diligent in sharing God's love with those who don't know Him.

Revelation 19:14 says, "*The armies of heaven were following him, riding on white horses and dressed in fine linen, white and clean.*" This event takes place during the second coming of Christ after the "rapture" of millions of Christians, dead and alive. The armies are those of us who believe in and spend our lives following Jesus. "White" and "clean" represent our new condition based on what Christ did to remove the stain of sin.

We have no idea when or how God plans to take us home with Him, just like we have no idea when the second coming will take place. We are simply commanded to watch and be ready (Matthew 24:42). Matthew 24:36 says, "*No one knows about the day or hour, not even the angels in heaven, nor the Son, but only the Father*" knows when these events will take place.

Often we think that the cleverest trick up Satan's sleeve is to get people thinking that he does not exist, that things like the rapture were mythological tales. But that is not necessarily true. There's a story in *Jon Courson's Application Commentary New Testament* of a meeting between Satan and three of his demons:

> One demon said, "I've got a plan. Let's whisper in people's ears that there is no God."
>
> "No," Satan said, "creation declares the reality of God. People are too smart to deny His existence. A few idiots might be sucked in, but not the masses."

> "I've got it," a second demon said. "We'll say there's no hell."
>
> "No," said Satan. "People innately understand the need for retribution and judgment. People won't buy that."
>
> A third demon said, "Let me suggest how we might trick them. Instead of saying 'No God' or 'No Hell,' we'll just say 'No Hurry.'"
>
> "That's it!" Satan said gleefully.
>
> And he commissioned his demons to go throughout the world whispering, "No hurry."

It's so tempting to believe that time is on our side, that we have enough of it to get our lives together…after just a little more fun. It's so easy to get distracted and not take our eternal relationship with God seriously. But if you are honest with yourself, you know that there is no way that you can get yourself together, regardless of your accomplishments or success, regardless of how much you have acquired so far in your life. There is still a need for redemption, for being made right before God.

If you have any questions or doubts lingering about eternity, please go to our "Do You Know Jesus" page and take this opportunity to make Jesus the Savior of your life. If you have already chosen him as your Savior, it's time to get serious about making Him Lord of every part of your life.

Don't miss your chance to be a part of His army.

Week 27

"No one here has more authority than I do. He has held back nothing from me except you, because you are his wife. How could I do such a wicked thing? It would be a great sin against God."

Genesis 39:9, NLT

DAY 1

"No one here has more authority than I do. He has held
back nothing from me except you, because you are
his wife. How could I do such a wicked thing?
It would be a great sin against God."

GENESIS 39:9, NLT

The word "Genesis" means beginning. And the book of Genesis contains the start of just about everything—creation, humanity, sin, culture, and industry. We also see the beginning of God's divine plan for redemption through the offspring of Noah, Abraham and Sarah, Isaac, and Jacob.

Joseph was the eleventh son of Jacob, but the firstborn of his favorite wife Rachel. For this reason, Joseph had a special place in his dad's heart. Besides being his father's favorite son, Joseph had other issues with his brothers. The biggest conflict resulted from him sharing his dream that they would all bow down to him one day. His jealous brothers plotted to kill him, but decided at the last moment to sell him into slavery instead. So, they threw him into a pit until they could get rid of him. After Joseph was gone, they brought their father Joseph's torn and blood-stained, multi-colored coat (a gift from his father and a catalyst to their jealousy) to make him believe his son was dead.

Joseph showed up in Egypt working for Potiphar, the captain of Pharaoh's guard. God gave Joseph success in everything he did. Potiphar recognized the skill and favor on Joseph and put him in charge of everything he had, including his house. As he worked in Potiphar's house, Potiphar's wife tried to seduce him. It is right at this point of the story where this week's verse lands.

Joseph fled from the advances of Potiphar's wife. She then proceeded to have him framed for rape and thrown in prison. While in prison, Joseph interpreted the dreams of two other prisoners. He later had the opportunity to interpret Pharaoh's dreams. Joseph's interpretations saved Egypt and gained him a lofty promotion. He became second in command in all of Egypt and oversaw the survival plan and food distribution during the seven years of famine that he predicted.

During the seven years of famine, Joseph's brothers came back into the picture. They were forced to make the journey to Egypt for grain. The brothers did not recognize him, but after testing them a few times, Joseph revealed his identity to them and they were reunited. Joseph's whole family moved to Egypt. Joseph's father Jacob eventually dies after blessing his sons.

Even in the middle of bad things happening in Joseph's life, God was with him. Joseph allowed God to work through him during the whole process. Though Joseph's father did not know what really happened to his son, God did. He had an irrevocable plan for Joseph's life, despite the many difficulties Joseph faced. In fact, it was exactly those difficulties that prepared him for living out that plan. God has a plan and a purpose for you, too!

Joseph went from the pit, to the prison, to the palace before his God-given vision became a reality. Never give up on your dream, regardless of what happens to you. When your dream is from God, it will come to pass if you stay faithful.

DAY 2

"No one here has more authority than I do. He has held back nothing from me except you, because you are his wife. How could I do such a wicked thing? It would be a great sin against God."

GENESIS 39:9, NLT

Author Napoleon Hill said, "The path of least resistance is what makes rivers and men crooked." Where do you draw the line? How can you be a person with godly standards?

The root word of "standards" is "stand." Stand means to take up and maintain a specified position. You need to decide what makes you stand. Shadrach, Meshach, and Abednego stood up when everyone else bowed down. Daniel continued to pray even though a lions' den was promised to those who did. Even when she knew it might seal her fate, Esther went to the king to save her people.

IT'S OKAY TO BE UP AND DOWN WITH GOD, BUT IT'S NOT OKAY TO BE IN AND OUT.

Long before each took their stand, they decided on their standards. They resolved to never sacrifice a principle for an immediate gain. Matthew 10:28 NLT says, *"Don't be afraid of those who want to kill your body; they cannot touch your soul. Fear only God, who can destroy both soul and body in hell."* They maintained the position that it was far better to honor God and accept man's punishment than to lower their standards and face God's discipline.

Lowering your standards might gain the "A," the job, the promotion, or the girl. You may get out of trouble or in with the crowd. But it will come at great cost. If you don't stand for something, you will fall for anything. It's okay to be up and down with God, but it's not okay to be in and out. Inconsistency will kill your testimony.

Joseph was not drawing a new line in the sand when he said, "*How could I do such a wicked thing?*" He was reminding himself of a line he had already drawn in the sand and had resolved never to cross. Don't wait until the situation is upon you before you determine what your response will be.

A wise, old saying teaches that "sin will always take you farther than you want to go, keep you longer than you want to stay, and charge you more than you are willing to pay." But having godly standards will put you in a position where God can bless your life, make you rise higher than you expected, and guarantee you the best life possible.

Day 3

"No one here has more authority than I do. He has held back nothing from me except you, because you are his wife. How could I do such a wicked thing? It would be a great sin against God."

Genesis 39:9, NLT

Nobody is fireproof! Even the most mature believer has a weakness in their spiritual armor that leaves them exposed to the fiery darts of the enemy (Ephesians 6:16).

The ancient Greeks told of a warrior named Achilles. His mother was warned that he would one day be wounded and die, so when he was a baby she dipped him in the river Styx, which was supposed to make him invincible. But as she dipped him in, she held him by one heel, which meant that the protective waters didn't cover the place where her hand was. And it was in that heel that he was fatally wounded.

What is your Achilles' heel? Where could the enemy fatally wound you? Pride? Money? Anger? Impatience?

"If you think you are standing strong, be careful not to fall" (1 Corinthians 10:12, NLT). You need to know what might make you fall. Temptation can be a brief impulse or a powerful urge. Temptation is anything that is opposed to what God approves.

Joseph is in his early twenties. His sex drive is fully at work, just like any other young adult his age. Potiphar's wife is in close contact with him daily, pressuring him to go to bed with her (Genesis 39:7-10). He is facing extreme temptation. Your greatest strength is to know your weakness, and learn from it. Perhaps Joseph had seen other men fall prey to Potiphar's wife's seduction. Maybe he saw the devastation that giving into temptation caused in these men's personal lives, professions, marriages, and families. 1 Corinthians 10:13b NLT says that, "*When you are tempted, he will show you a way out so that you can endure.*" Joseph realized that this woman could take him down. Are there things in your life that could take you down, too? To be a person with godly standards, you need to identify and recognize the things that could make you fall.

> To be a person with godly standards, you need to identify and recognize the things that could make you fall.

Once you know the things that can make you fall, those are the same things from which you need to run. In Genesis 39:12, Joseph is resisting Potiphar's wife, but she grabs him by the coat and gives one more request for him to go to bed with her. The story says he left his coat in her grip and ran out of the house.

Notice that in running, he had to give up something he valued and left it behind. For example, if lust is what makes you fall, then remove, filter, or get some accountability for your Internet and cable usage. If gossip is your Achilles' heel, you need to stop spending so much time around that friend, even if it means no longer walking in the mornings, going out for coffee dates, or instant messaging with them.

If you are ever going to do something great for God, it will cost you something. Proverbs 16:17 NLT states, "*The path of the virtuous leads away from evil; whoever follows that path is safe.*" Joseph was victorious over temptation because he made up his mind to obey God and make no provisions for his flesh to walk on the path of sin.

DAY 4

"No one here has more authority than I do. He has held back nothing from me except you, because you are his wife. How could I do such a wicked thing? It would be a great sin against God."
GENESIS 39:9, NLT

Someone once said that life is ten percent what happens to you and ninety percent what you make of it. What does this mean? It means that your life is not determined by what happens, but by your response after it happens.

YOUR LIFE IS NOT DETERMINED BY WHAT HAPPENS, BUT BY YOUR RESPONSE AFTER IT HAPPENS.

Joseph was sold into slavery by his own brothers. He was framed and thrown into prison for rape. He was forgotten by a former fellow inmate. If Joseph sat in that prison cell bitterly plotting his revenge on his brothers, or if he had let down his guard when Potiphar's wife pressured him for sex, he would have had to forfeit his dream.

But Joseph didn't focus on the pain; he only envisioned the possibilities. Prosperity and promotion often come during the most difficult times. Never give up on your dream, regardless of the circumstances. If it's from God, He will arrange it to happen if you stay faithful.

Scripture says, "*Therefore, my beloved brethren, be firm, immovable, always abounding in the work of the Lord, knowing and being continually aware that your labor in the Lord is not futile*" (1 Corinthians 15:58, AMP). Nothing you experience is wasted time or energy. It took twenty-two years for Joseph's dream—a dream that came from God to help guide him—to become reality. As a slave and prisoner, Joseph learned the language and culture of Egypt. This experience would be needed years later in order for him to fulfill his purpose. God allowed Joseph to be falsely accused and cast into prison. But not just any prison; this prison was for political prisoners. Joseph was put in charge of people like the king's butler and baker. From these people, he learned the protocol needed to be a high-ranking government official.

The way you reach your dream may not turn out to be what you expected, but your labor is never wasted. It all has a purpose. You can't have a testimony without a test. You may have experienced a setback, but get ready for the comeback. What you see as your biggest problem right now may produce your greatest advantage in the future. See every adversity as an opportunity in disguise.

God has been preparing you all of your life for what you are just about to do.

DAY 5

"No one here has more authority than I do. He has held back nothing from me except you, because you are his wife. How could I do such a wicked thing? It would be a great sin against God."

GENESIS 39:9, NLT

Today you are invited to relate to this passage with the Ignatian Meditation method. This way to meditate is adapted from Ignatius of Loyola, a spiritual leader who would invite people to use their imaginations to recreate a story in the Bible. This exercise can help you get face-to-face with the scriptures and with Jesus.

Step 1 - Read the entire Bible passage: Genesis 39:1-23.

Step 2 - Read the entire Bible passage again, but this time choose a new viewpoint in which to engage the story. Here are four different ways to engage with a passage. Choose one before reading the Scripture the second time through:

- **Go there!** Imagine yourself somewhere in the story, observing it as it unfolds. Where do you see yourself? Who are you standing or sitting next to? What would you have seen if you had been in Potiphar's house? What do you hear? Who is there with you? What are people saying? What do you think?

- **Be there!** Use the rest of your senses to experience the scene—touch, smell, listen, and feel.

- **Become a character in the story!** What do they see? How does the character feel?

- **Be you!** Enter the story as yourself. How would you feel if you were there?

Step 3 - Record the thoughts that God, through the Holy Spirit, is dropping into your heart as you reread the passage from one of the four perspectives mentioned above. Use an extra piece of paper, or your own personal journal.

Suggestions:

- Start with prayer. God, through the Holy Spirit, can drop suggestions into your heart and mind.
- Ask a question such as, "God, what truth are you trying to communicate to me?"
- Write a letter to God.
- Make notes about what you're learning.
- Compose a prayer.
- Draw a picture of your praise.

Day 6

"No one here has more authority than I do. He has held back nothing from me except you, because you are his wife. How could I do such a wicked thing? It would be a great sin against God."

Genesis 39:9, NLT

Joseph is often called "the Dreamer." God gave Joseph a vision for his life and he never let go of it. Joseph's decisions were driven by his dream.

He must have had his dream in mind when he refused Potiphar's wife: "How could I do this? I've come so far and God's seen me through so much already. His plans for my life are bigger than one moment of sin with you." The way Joseph responded to what life threw at him gives us some keys to making our dreams a reality.

A dreamer is "one who has ideas or conceives projects regarded as impractical" *(Merriam-Webster's Dictionary)*. As you pursue your dream, don't be surprised when other people do not believe in your dream. God sees your potential before your parents, friends, or anyone else. Joseph's brothers attacked him and threw him in a pit, saying, "We'll see what becomes of his dreams!" Your family and friends may get jealous and even attack you, because you dare to live with purpose. Why? Because the vision is yours, not theirs.

When Joseph's brothers said, *"Hey, here comes the dreamer!"* (Genesis 37:19), the word that they use for "dreamer" really means "lord, possessor, or owner of dreams." God didn't give anyone else your dream; you own it. You can't let a dream snatcher's lack of excitement for your vision steal it away from you. George

Bernard Shaw wrote, "Some men see things as they are and say, 'Why?' I dream of things that never were and say, 'Why not?'" Others might not see it ever coming to pass, but you have the 20/20 vision.

God says, *"I know what I'm doing. I have it all planned out—plans to take care of you, not abandon you, plans to give you the future you hope for"* (Jeremiah 29:11b NLT. You may have dreams for your future. You may have hope of achieving lofty goals. Keep in mind that just because the vision has not been realized, there is no reason to think that it's over. Joseph's dream led him to the pit and to prison before it was ever fulfilled in the palace. But everywhere he went he knew the Lord was with him. Listen to what Joseph said to his brothers in Genesis 50:20 NLT, *"You intended to harm me, but God intended it all for good. He brought me to this position so I could save the lives of many people."* Trust God. He knows what He's doing. He's with you all the way.

> God didn't give anyone else your dream; you own it. You can't let a dream snatcher's lack of excitement for your vision steal it away from you.

Take another look at what happened to Joseph's family when he held fast to his dreams. His family was blessed. Joseph's dream saved their lives! Joseph never lost sight of his dream, no matter what happened.

You must always stay focused on the vision and dream in front of you. Live on purpose. The Lord will bless you and everyone around you when you are a dreamer.

DAY 7

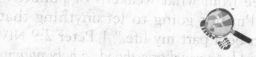

"No one here has more authority than I do. He has held back nothing from me except you, because you are his wife. How could I do such a wicked thing? It would be a great sin against God."

GENESIS 39:9, NLT

Imagine the most pure lake possible: crystal blue water with sunlight shining on the surface, tiny ripples dancing. As you soak in its splendor, you're awestruck by its beauty.

Now imagine a trickling stream of sewage making its way into that beautiful lake. Over time, what was once a magnificent sight will turn into a muddy, murky mess.

In one sense, this happens more often than you think. We live in a culture that bombards us each day with images of beauty, love, and romance. These images influence our thoughts, attitudes, and behavior. They tell us that appearance matters, that we have to perform to a certain level to be loved, and that we can spend years playing games with relationships without doing damage to our marriages. The same way sewage taints a clear lake, these lies taint God's plan for purity.

"Who may climb the mountain of the Lord? Who may stand in his holy place? Only those whose hands and hearts are pure" (Psalm 24:3-4, NLT). Joseph was pursuing purity when he ran from Potiphar's wife and avoided her from that point on. Because Joseph made a decision to have clean hands and a pure heart, he experienced God's constant presence and help. His future family was blessed. What's pure is always what's best.

Purity is about more than just sex. Pure means "free from corruption, unmixed, being free from what weakens or pollutes." Pursuing purity is saying, "I'm not going to let anything that doesn't belong in God's plan be a part my life." 1 Peter 2:9 NIV says, "*But you are a chosen people, a royal priesthood, a holy nation, a people belonging to God, that you may declare the praises of him who called you out of darkness into his wonderful light*." You are called to be different and separate from the world.

Why do a lot of believers want to know "How far is too far?" (Translated: "How close to the world's standards can I get before I fall in?") That kind of questioning reveals a flawed thought process going on in their heart. If someone took you to the Grand Canyon, how close to the edge of the cliff would you do a dance and still be safe? Five feet? One foot? Three inches? Instead of "How far is too far?", you should be asking, "How pure can I stay?" (Translated: "How close to God's standards can I remain and receive all of His blessing?")

If you want God's best, you must live by God's principles. You must stop judging yourself by the standards of this world and start living by the standards of our God. Purity is a direction—a persistent, determined pursuit of righteousness. The real question, when it comes to purity, is, "What are the best choices for my life, my relationship with God, and my future?"

God cares about your future. Jeremiah 29:11 NLT says, "*For I know the plans I have for you, says the Lord. They are plans for good and not for disaster, to give you a future and a hope*." God didn't come to take away your fun. He came to take away your pain!

Care enough about your life to ask the right questions. Pursue purity. Make it a goal. Purity will put you in a place where God can use you.

WEEK 28

Look here, you who say, "Today or tomorrow we are
going to a certain town and will stay there a year.
We will do business there and make a profit."
How do you know what your life will be like tomorrow?
Your life is like the morning fog—it's here a
little while, then it's gone.
What you ought to say is, "If the Lord wants us to,
we will live and do this or that."
Otherwise you are boasting about your own plans,
and all such boasting is evil.
Remember, it is sin to know what you ought to
do and then not do it.

JAMES 4:13-17, NLT

DAY 1

Look here, you who say, "Today or tomorrow we are going to a certain town and will stay there a year. We will do business there and make a profit." How do you know what your life will be like tomorrow? Your life is like the morning fog—it's here a little while, then it's gone. What you ought to say is, "If the Lord wants us to, we will live and do this or that." Otherwise you are boasting about your own plans, and all such boasting is evil. Remember, it is sin to know what you ought to do and then not do it.
JAMES 4:13-17, NLT

A few years ago I was trying to avoid traffic delays caused by road work in my neighborhood. I decided to take a shortcut through a local cemetery (you would've had to been there to understand). As I was driving through the graveyard—besides wondering, "What I am doing?"—I started looking at all of the tombstones. Some had epitaphs with some personal information inscribed onto them, and some were really simple in detail. They were all different sizes. Some were erect and some lay flat. But what they all had in common was a "born on" date and a "died on" date, with a dash separating those two significant dates. I thought to myself, "That little dash represents the sum total of each of these people's lives—every decision, success, failure, dream. Everything thereever was about them is summed up by one, little punctuation mark—a dash!"

The decisions you make every day influence your future and create your past. Who you are today is a direct result of the decisions you have made up to this point in life. Galatians 6:7 NLT says, *"You will always harvest what you plant."* That means that the quality of your planting today will directly affect the quality of your harvesting tomorrow. As the saying goes, "Sow a thought, reap an action. Sow an action, reap a habit. Sow a habit, reap a lifestyle. Sow a lifestyle, reap a destiny."

Notice that destiny begins with what you purpose in your heart and mind to pursue. In Acts 13:22 NIV we read what was spoken about David's life, *"He testified concerning him: 'I have found David son of Jesse a man after my own heart; he will do everything I want him to do.'"* What an epitaph!

> You are, today, a result of your decisions yesterday. Tomorrow your life will be a result of your decisions today.

Our passage this week is very reflective and invites us to take a long, hard look at our own lives. You are, today, a result of your decisions yesterday.And tomorrow your life will be a result of your decisions today. What will your dash represent? The choice is yours.

Decisions that determine your destiny begin in your heart and mind today.

DAY 2

Look here, you who say, "Today or tomorrow we are
going to a certain town and will stay there a year.
We will do business there and make a profit."
How do you know what your life will be like tomorrow?
Your life is like the morning fog—it's here a
little while, then it's gone.
What you ought to say is, "If the Lord wants us to,
we will live and do this or that."
Otherwise you are boasting about your own plans,
and all such boasting is evil.
Remember, it is sin to know what you ought to
do and then not do it.

JAMES 4:13-17, NLT

If you are reading this today, I have good news for you: you are alive!

That is something to be thankful for and to never take for granted. Ecclesiastes 8:15 (NLT) says that we should *"have fun, because there is nothing better for people in this world than to eat, drink, and enjoy life."* People should live life to its fullest potential.

Other translations of James 4:14 ask the reader the question, "What is your life?" The verse then goes on to describe our lives with metaphors like mist, vapor, and fog. There's always that moment, soon after summer ends, when we emerge from our homes in the morning and we can once again see our warm breath as it hits the cold air and then vanishes. Fall has arrived and we realize that more time has passed. James says that our lives are like that. They are like the steam from a tea kettle or an early morning fog that soon disappears.

What is your life? The first thing I visualize when I think of my life is a number line with a zero on the far left and a much larger number on the far right. Psalm 90:10 NLT says, "*Seventy years are given to us! Some even live to eighty.*" I hope to live longer, Lord willing, but let's say my number on the far right is actually 80. If I were going to place an "X" on that line to represent where I see myself right now, it would be somewhere left of center. Where might you place yours?

There are many people who have their security in the plans that they have for tomorrow, next week, next month, next year, and into the future. They convince themselves that success in education, work, marriage, family, and retirement rests in the right formula, as if their life were in their own hands.

A few years ago I was hospitalized with pneumonia. I thought I was just really sick; later on I learned that during my hospitalization, the doctors told my wife that I was closer to death than life. I was in my mid-thirties. I thought that my "X" was still a little bit left of center, but in reality it was almost as far to the right as it could go. I was dying and I had no idea. I believe that God miraculously healed me and restored my health. But the whole process changed me. It forced me to really evaluate my life, my time, and my priorities. I began to seriously consider the impact I was or was not making.

Scripture says, "*Teach us to number our days and recognize how few they are; help us to spend them as we should*" (Psalm 90:12, TLB). James simply poses the question "What is your life?" to get us to reevaluate what it means that we are even here. Let me repeat the good news. If you are reading this devotional today, that means that you have been given life and breath by God. He has a plan to prosper you. He has a divine will for your life. He has a purpose for you that no one else can fulfill. Have a deep sense of joy that your every breath is an undeserved gift from above!

Live each new day with that truth on your mind. You have been given the gift of now!

Ask God to help you live it to its fullest potential.

DAY 3

Look here, you who say, "Today or tomorrow we are going to a certain town and will stay there a year. We will do business there and make a profit." How do you know what your life will be like tomorrow? Your life is like the morning fog—it's here a little while, then it's gone. What you ought to say is, "If the Lord wants us to, we will live and do this or that." Otherwise you are boasting about your own plans, and all such boasting is evil. Remember, it is sin to know what you ought to do and then not do it.

JAMES 4:13-17, NLT

Today we are taking a closer look at James 4:15: "*Instead, you ought to say, 'If it is the Lord's will, we will live and do this or that.'*" Did you know that God has a plan and a purpose for your life that no one else can fulfill? Other places in His Word say that He is mindful of us, and that His thoughts about us are so many they cannot be numbered.

Think about this for a moment. God looked across the corridors of time and placed people exactly where He wanted them to be so they could accomplish specific purposes at specific moments. He said, "David, you will kill that giant, and be a king. Esther, you will rise to royalty to rescue my people. I have called you for such a time as this. Moses, you will lead my people out of slavery in Egypt." Scripture says every day of our lives—right down to the moment—was laid out before a single one of them had happened yet (Psalm 139). Throughout history, God has foreknown exactly who He was going to use as His champions.

It is no mistake that you are living your dash right here, right now. I've heard parents go down the line introducing their children, "This is Johnny, this is Suzy, this is Timmy, and this is our little accident." Let me make this clear: with God there are no mistakes. It's not like God is all of a sudden saying, "Thanks a lot, mom and dad. Now what am I supposed to do with this one? I guess I better come up with a new eternal plan that includes one more." No, God said *"before I formed you, I knew you."* There are no accidents. You are here on purpose. God has a will for your life.

If you found a $20 bill on the ground, you would want it. If the bill was used, dirty, crumpled, and torn on the edges, you would still want it. If in the past the $20 had changed hands in a drug deal, had been used to pay for a prostitute or an abortion, you would still pick it up and put it in your pocket. This is a very valuable lesson. No matter what had happened to the money, you still wanted it because it did not decrease in value. It was still worth $20. Many times in our lives we are dropped, crumpled, and ground in the dirt by the wrong decisions we make and the circumstances that come our way. We feel as though we are worthless. But no matter what has happened, you will never lose your value in God's eyes. To Him, dirty or clean, crumpled or finely creased, you are still priceless.

> IT IS NO MISTAKE THAT YOU ARE LIVING YOUR DASH RIGHT HERE, RIGHT NOW.

Luke 15:3-7 tells us that God will pursue us if we lose sight of our purpose and get lost. He celebrates and throws a party each time He brings a lost one home. God knows you have the goods. He believes in you. You are priceless to God.

Pursue the Lord's will and keep praying for opportunities to open up for you to fulfill His purposes.

Day 4

Look here, you who say, "Today or tomorrow we are
going to a certain town and will stay there a year.
We will do business there and make a profit."
How do you know what your life will be like tomorrow?
Your life is like the morning fog—it's here a
little while, then it's gone.
What you ought to say is, "If the Lord wants us to,
we will live and do this or that."
Otherwise you are boasting about your own plans,
and all such boasting is evil.
Remember, it is sin to know what you ought to
do and then not do it.

James 4:13-17, NLT

Today, take some time to read and think through some additional scriptures related to James 4:13-17, then journal your thoughts on a separate sheet of papers or in your own personal journal.

Don't brag about tomorrow, since you don't know what the day will bring. (Proverbs 27:1, NLT)

You can make many plans, but the Lord's purpose will prevail. (Proverbs 19:21, NLT)

...When someone has been given much, much will be required in return; and when someone has been entrusted with much, even more will be required. (Luke 12:48, NLT)

...What do you have that God hasn't given you? And if everything you have is from God, why boast as though it were not a gift? (1 Corinthians 4:7, NLT)

And so, God willing, we will move forward to further understanding. (Hebrews 6:3, NLT)

And this world is fading away, along with everything that people crave. But anyone who does what pleases God will live forever. (1 John 2:17, NLT)

Suggestions:

- Prayerfully reflect on these verses and record the thoughts that God, through the Holy Spirit, is dropping into your heart.
- Ask a question, such as "God, what truth are you trying to communicate to me?"
- Write a letter to God.
- Take notes about what you're learning.
- Compose a prayer.
- Draw a picture of your praise.

Day 5

Look here, you who say, "Today or tomorrow we are
going to a certain town and will stay there a year.
We will do business there and make a profit."
How do you know what your life will be like tomorrow?
Your life is like the morning fog—it's here a
little while, then it's gone.
What you ought to say is, "If the Lord wants us to,
we will live and do this or that."
Otherwise you are boasting about your own plans,
and all such boasting is evil.
Remember, it is sin to know what you ought to
do and then not do it.
James 4:13-17, NLT

A young girl went for a walk on the beach. In the distance on the sand, she saw what looked like thousands of shells. As she got closer, she realized that the shells were actually thousands of starfish that had washed up on the shore. When the ocean had turned from high tide to low tide, the starfish got stuck on the beach. They couldn't survive out of the ocean until the tide came back in. When the little girl realized this, she began to quickly pick up starfish and throw them, one by one, back into the salt water. A man saw what was going on and he yelled towards the girl, "What do you think you are trying to do? There are thousands of starfish and this beach goes on for miles. You could never save all of them!" The young girl considered what the man said, but then picked up a starfish and said, "You are correct. But I can save this one." And she tossed it as far as she possibly could into the water.

This famous story has been adopted by a ministry called Royal Family Kids Camps (RFKC) for which I have had the privilege of volunteering. RFKC is the nation's leading network of camps for abused, neglected, and abandoned children. Volunteers give up weeks of vacation to invest and make a difference in the lives of more than three million children in America —one child at a time.

> You can't do everything, but you can do a lot more than you think you can.

James 4:17 says that there are good things that you should be doing. Your life has value to others. You can't do everything, but you can do a lot more than you think you can. And God will take what you do, bless it, and multiply it—just like he did with a little boy's lunch beside the Sea of Galilee. A great miracle occurred when Jesus took five loaves of bread and two fish and fed more than 5,000 people. But the miracle would not have happened if one little boy was not willing to first share what he had. He could have said, "Look at all these people. There is no way my measly lunch could make a dent in feeding them.Why bother?" Instead, he took what he had to Jesus. Jesus then made the lunch grow into enough to feed everyone—one person at a time.

As followers of Christ, you ought to do good with your life. When you combine your will with God's power, there is no limit to the good that can be done for others. Stop looking at the size of the job and just do what you know is right to do today. God is looking for people who will seek His will and not their own.

So find a starfish, pick it up, and throw it back in the ocean. That's all God wants you to do. He'll do the rest.

DAY 6

Look here, you who say, "Today or tomorrow we are
going to a certain town and will stay there a year.
We will do business there and make a profit."
How do you know what your life will be like tomorrow?
Your life is like the morning fog—it's here a
little while, then it's gone.
What you ought to say is, "If the Lord wants us to,
we will live and do this or that."
Otherwise you are boasting about your own plans,
and all such boasting is evil.
Remember, it is sin to know what you ought to
do and then not do it.

JAMES 4:13-17, NLT

"Look here, you who say, 'Today or tomorrow we are going to a certain town and will stay there a year. We will do business there and make a profit.'" This was the practice for merchants in ancient times. Businessmen travelled from city to city, carrying their goods. They would set up shop and trade their goods for a length of time and then move on to the next stop. Life was about making money and moving on to make more. Very little consideration was given to God's divine will and providence. No one said, "We will do everything for God's glory to further His Kingdom." Their highest ambition was to make a profit and gain earthly wealth for themselves. "We will do this—ourselves."

That wasn't just a character issue of ancient merchants. Today, people say things like "I've got my plans all figured out. My portfolio is in place and my future is secure. I am going to work at this company for 20 years and then retire on my 401K and investments. After I retire, I will then move to Florida with my wife and collect shells on the beach." But when asked if they are going to church this weekend, they say, "I don't know; I might be busy." The *Jon Courson New Testament Application Commentary* says, "We have it backwards! We should be saying, 'I may go skiing next week if God wills.' Or, 'I may go on vacation in July if that's what the Lord has for me.' But as for going to church on Sunday (as for feeding the poor, as for reaching the lost, as for being in the Word and prayer)? 'I will be there absolutely!'"

If acquiring money and possessions are a person's entire focus, it can be easy for God to be left out of the picture. That's what Jesus meant when He said, "*No one can serve two masters. Either he will hate the one and love the other, or he will be devoted to the one and despise the other. You cannot serve both God and Money*" (Matthew 6:24, NIV). Do you just have money or does money have you?

In this passage, James is not trying to tell us that planning for our future is wrong, but that the attitudes that drive our planning may be wrong. How much of your future happiness depends on the promises you make yourself today? He asks, "*How do you know what your life will be like tomorrow?*" As I write this devotion, the United States economy is in turmoil. The stock market is volatile and many good people are losing their jobs due to cutbacks. And what about our own mortality? Charles Spurgeon said, "All men count all men mortal but themselves." (Interesting note: Charles Spurgeon died the very week his sermon on James 4:13-17—which contained this quote—was published.)

HOW MUCH OF YOUR FUTURE HAPPINESS DEPENDS ON THE PROMISES YOU MAKE YOURSELF TODAY?

Have you left room for God to interrupt your life should He choose to do so? *Matthew Henry's Whole Bible Commentary* states:

"How vain a thing it is to look for anything good in futurity, without the concurrence of Providence."

Don't buy into a system that says life is about doing and acquiring. Instead, set your heart on things above. If you will

- make *"God's Kingdom come, God's will be done"* your highest ambition,
- use the resources He makes you a steward over to help make it happen, and
- get your priorities in line with the Word and the will of God,

then you will be more fulfilled and your life more marked with success than you could ever imagine.

DAY 7

Look here, you who say, "Today or tomorrow we are going to a certain town and will stay there a year. We will do business there and make a profit."
How do you know what your life will be like tomorrow? Your life is like the morning fog—it's here a little while, then it's gone.
What you ought to say is, "If the Lord wants us to, we will live and do this or that."
Otherwise you are boasting about your own plans, and all such boasting is evil.
Remember, it is sin to know what you ought to do and then not do it.

JAMES 4:13-17, NLT

Did you realize that sin isn't just something we shouldn't do? Sin is also something we *don't* do that we *should* do. The sin of omission is the failure to do what we ought to do.

My Dad used to come to my basketball games. He was a great fan of basketball. I remember shooting free throws at a very critical point of one game. Making the shots would secure victory and missing would mean defeat. The pressure was on. Our home crowd was silent. Just as I began to go into my shooting motion my dad called out loud to me, "You can be a hero, or you can be a zero!" No matter how poor his timing, it was still true: this was a time either to shine or to shrink.

Scripture tells us that we are all created to do good works in Christ. We shine when we do good works, and God gets glory through our lives. We also shrink when we pass up the opportunities God brings our way and God receives no glory. James says, "*It is sin to know what you ought to do and then not do it.*" With every divine opportunity to do good, we can choose to be a hero or a zero for God.

Years ago I heard the following story.

> One night at a small church in Georgia, a man shared how he had become a Christian while in Sydney, Australia. "I was at the street corner in Kings Cross, when I felt a tug on my sleeve. Turning, I found myself face to face with a street bum. The man simply asked me, 'Mister, if you were to die tonight, where would you spend eternity?' That question troubled me over the next three weeks. I had to find an answer, and I ended up giving my life to Christ." The pastor was amazed. But imagine his amazement when, three years later, another man came to his church and told an almost identical story. He had been in Sydney when a derelict pulled on his sleeve and then asked him, "If you were to die tonight, where would you spend eternity?" Haunted by the street bum's question, he eventually sought and found an answer in Jesus. Shortly after hearing the second story, the pastor had to be in Sydney for a missions conference. He went to Kings Cross to see if he could find the man mentioned at his church two different times. Pausing on a street-corner, he felt a tug at his jacket. He turned, and before the old man could say anything, the pastor blurted out, "I know what you're going to say! You're going to ask me if I were to die tonight, where would I spend eternity?" The old man was stunned. "How did you know that?" The pastor told him the whole story. When he finished, the man started to cry. "Mister," he said, "ten years ago I gave my life to Jesus, and I wanted to do something for him. But a man like me can't do much of anything. So I decided I would just hang out on

> GOD WILL NOT ONE DAY SAY, "WELL DONE, GOOD AND SUCCESSFUL SERVANT." HE WILL SAY, "WELL DONE, GOOD AND FAITHFUL SERVANT."

> this corner and ask people that simple question. I've been doing that for years, mister, but tonight is the first time I ever knew it did anybody any good."

God will not one day say, "Well done, good and successful servant." He will say, "Well done, good and *faithful* servant." Stop worrying about the future. Instead, remember to do the good you know you ought to do. When you share Christ's love, or help a person in need, you aren't responsible for the outcome. He will take care of that.

Take advantage of the divine appointments He has for you today. Ask God to give you His eyes for the world around you. Obey God's prompting, even if you can't see whether it does anybody any good.

Week 29

"He has showed you, O man, what is good. And
what does the LORD require of you?
To act justly and to love mercy and to
walk humbly with your God."

Micah 6:8, NIV

Day 1

"He has showed you, O man, what is good. And
what does the LORD require of you?
To act justly and to love mercy and to
walk humbly with your God."

Micah 6:8, NIV

Our verse comes at the end of the book of Micah, where after disciplining and restoring His people (first five chapters), God begins to reconcile Israel back to Himself. The scene in chapter six is that of a courtroom. The witnesses are the mountains and the foundations of the earth. Israel is on trial for opposing their covenant with God.

"What do you want from us? Should we sacrifice our eldest sons?" Israel's childish defense argument was that there are too many requirements for them to observe in order to please God and make up for their sins. But the people knew very well what God wanted from them. God had made it crystal clear. They knew that sacrifice was only acceptable if it came from the right heart attitude. They chose to ignore God every time He expressed His desire for an intimate relationship with them. Instead, they brought their sacrifices and offerings to try to appease Him and try to make Him forget the ugliness of the sins that they were committing. The people tried to convince themselves that meaningless practice of routine was all that God required. They tried to replace relationship with ritual. Samuel once said the same thing to Saul, *"Does the LORD delight in burnt offerings and sacrifices as much as in obeying the voice of the LORD? To obey is better than sacrifice, and to heed is better than the fat of rams"* (1 Samuel 15:22, NIV).

Micah speaks God's rebuttal when he says that there is nothing new that God requires of them. God had already made plain and clear the three things that He required and considered good. The Hebrew word used in this passage for "requires" means "commands." Literally, "These three things are what the Lord commands you to do." Two requirements had to do with their approach toward others and the other one had to do with their approach toward God:

- "*Act justly*" meant that they were to defend and look out for the rights of the helpless.
- "*Love mercy*" meant "loyal love" in Hebrew. They were to love each other with committed love like that of a husband and wife or a parent and child.
- "*Walk humbly*" meant submit to and follow God's will. It meant remembering who God is and not to live recklessly.

In the New Testament, Jesus comes on the scene and breaks these three commands down to just two: love God and love others (Mark 12).

And if that seems overwhelming, then just focus on a single word: love.

Day 2

"He has showed you, O man, what is good. And
what does the LORD require of you?
To act justly and to love mercy and to
walk humbly with your God."

Micah 6:8, NIV

Most people have felt the pressure to perform. Performance is an outward action motivated by an inward desire to please. Children work to pull good grades at school and be on their best behavior for their parents. Athletes try to live up to their coach's expectations and deliver in the clutch. Employees stay productive to earn a profit for their company. When our performance meets or exceeds expectation, everyone is pleased. It's a beautiful thing!

In the Old Testament Law there were more than six hundred requirements given for Israel to observe. Unable to live up to the do's and don'ts of the law, Israel comes belly-aching to the prophet Micah, saying (in a martyr's tone), "What are we supposed to do to please God? What does He want from us?"

Isn't that just like you and me? When our performance does not meet expectation, instead of taking responsibility, we project the blame onto someone (or something) else: "My boss doesn't understand what it's like to actually work." "My parents expect me to be perfect all the time." "My coach is so cruel; he made me run all practice just because I was late." "What next, God, my firstborn son?"

In Micah 6:8, we see that Micah takes the more than six hundred requirements of the law and reduces them down to three: do what is right, love mercy, and walk humbly. Now, even I can do three things. In the New Testament, Jesus takes these three things and reduces them down to two: love God and love others. There is great blessing for those who obey God. His ways work. But, if you want God's best, you will give Him your best.

Here's the deal: God *wants* you to have His best! So, He does not change or lower His requirements; He simplifies. Can you see God's love and kindness all over this passage?

No human but Jesus has ever lived up to God's standards, but God makes a way for us. When we put our faith in Christ, the Holy Spirit empowers us to live up to the ideal that God requires. With God's help we begin to do what is right, to love mercy, and to walk humbly more and more every day. Our outward actions grow from an inward attitude to please God more and more all the time.

Who do you try to please? If you just listen to the people around you and try to dance to their tune, you will always be frustrated. If you place too high a value on the opinions and criticisms of others, you will end up burdened with feelings of guilt and inadequacy. If you are just out to please yourself, you will selfishly think the world revolves around you. That's why we be-lievers seek to please God, not other people. Our ultimate accountability is to God. "*We are not trying to please men but God, who tests our hearts.*" (1 Thessalonians 2:4, NIV}

GOD WANTS YOU TO HAVE HIS BEST!

Ask God to help you do what He requires today. Let the Spirit of God go to work inside you. You'll find yourself wanting to please God in every way.

God wants you to have His best. You do not have to settle for anything less.

DAY 3

"He has showed you, O man, what is good. And what does the LORD require of you? To act justly and to love mercy and to walk humbly with your God."
MICAH 6:8, NIV

We live in a time of relativism, in a world that says, "What's right for you may not be what's right for me." In an interview on *Good Morning America*, Duchess Sarah Ferguson said, "I'd like to know who makes the rules, who sets the rules."

Culture tries to convince that the only absolute is that "there are no absolutes." (Do you get the irony—absolutely no absolutes?) No right. No wrong. Just do whatever the situation determines. "It's all good."

"To act justly" means "to do what is right." God is saying, "I want you to do the right thing in every situation." But who sets the rules? Who determines what's right and what's wrong? It's a question worth exploring. After all, Isaiah 5:20 NIV has some pretty strong words on the subject, *"Woe (or, as good as dead) to those who call evil good and good evil."* It definitely is not *all* good.

Some people think they can set their own rules. "As long as I am not hurting anyone else, it's OK." Have you ever been convinced that you were absolutely right about something? In your heart and mind you knew that you knew that you knew you were right? But in the end, you turned out to be absolutely wrong? Isaiah 55:8-9 (NIV) says, *"For my thoughts are not your thoughts, neither are your ways my ways," declares the LORD. "As the heavens are higher than the earth, so are my ways higher than your ways and my thoughts than your thoughts.*" The truth is that we do not know everything, because we do not have all of the facts. Living solely by what we think is right is faulty reasoning.

THE TRUTH IS THAT WE DO NOT KNOW EVERYTHING, BECAUSE WE DO NOT HAVE ALL OF THE FACTS.

A second group of people are in the "majority rules" camp. Francis Schafer calls it "the dictatorship of the fifty-one percent." If most people say something is right or wrong for themselves, then it becomes right or wrong for everyone. I used to teach high school math. Before I left the teaching profession, I heard of one school district experimenting with a new instructional method where students would get together in groups to do their math assignments. Whatever answer the majority of the students came up with became the right answer for their group. I mean no disrespect to the educational system intended there, but no matter how many people tell me that 2+2=5, I will still know that the answer is absolutely 4! There are laws that are passed and policies that are put into practice that will remain absolutely wrong even though they receive fifty-one percent or more of the votes. What's popular these days seldom seems to be what's right. Letting the majority decide is an unreliable way to distinguish right from wrong.

Another group of people would say, "I let my conscience be my guide. If my conscience is clear, then I did nothing wrong." But the Bible doesn't teach that we should live by our consciences. Jiminy Cricket was the one who taught us (in the animated movie *Pinocchio*), "Take the straight and narrow path and if you start to slide, give a little whistle, give a little whistle. And always let your conscience be your guide." But Walt Disney certainly doesn't determine the rules! 1 Timothy 4:2 says that in the last days mans' conscience will be seared, unable to determine right from wrong. Paul states, *"My conscience is clear, but that does not make me innocent. It is the Lord who judges me"* (1 Corinthians 4:4, NIV). Paul was a spiritual giant, yet he was not going to leave it up to his conscience to decide if he was in the right.

I want you to look again at Micah 6:8, *"What does the LORD require of you?"* Micah doesn't ask: "What do you think is right? What is the majority opinion? What is your conscience telling you?" He doesn't even ask, "What does your priest, bishop or pastor teach?" Micah says, "This is God's standard!" Jesus had the same frame of reference as Micah and Paul for meeting God's requirements. He said, *"I always do the things that are pleasing to Him"* (John 8:29, NIV).

Make the decision to act justly today. Whatever God says, do it! Don't cut corners or sacrifice principles for immediate gain. Stay in God's Word and you will train yourself to distinguish good from evil. Listen to the discernment of the Holy Spirit. If you are going to do what's right, you will need to walk with integrity in every area. Remember that God is on your side. Stand up for righteousness even if no man stands with you. You will be rewarded for your faithfulness.

DAY 4

"He has showed you, O man, what is good. And
what does the LORD require of you?
To act justly and to love mercy and to
walk humbly with your God."
MICAH 6:8, NIV

While I was growing up, I used to play a game called *Mercy* with my friends. We would lock fingers and try to bend each others' hands back until someone would shout out "Mercy!" because they could not take the pain any longer and needed relief.

The word "mercy" means to show kindness. One thing that God requires from us is to show kindness to each other. Yet, mercy is not a quality we expect to see much of these days. You've probably seen the bumper sticker that encourages readers to "Practice random acts of kindness and senseless beauty." Why does kindness seem random to the world? Mercy is admired, but isn't practiced nearly enough.

When a person walks justly, something else can easily creep into the picture. That "something else" is judgment. We say things like "God, I am so thankful that I am not like her." "Can't he go one Sunday morning without smoking in front of the church?" "Look at that offensive shirt that kid is wearing!" Look at what God requires here: "Do the right things, yes, but to others I want you to show mercy." Understand that God prefers to change a heart before He changes a shirt. Mercy always triumphs over judgment.

So what about payback? We are not generally a society that lets a matter slide when we've been wronged. In Matthew 18, Jesus tells a parable about a servant who owed a million dollars to a king. His wife and kids were to be sold to repay all that he owed. The servant threw himself before the king and shouted, "Mercy!" The king showed him kindness, canceled the debt, and set him free. But that servant went immediately to one of his fellow servants who owed him just a few dollars and demanded payback. "Mercy!" shouted the se ond servant. Instead of granting mercy, the first servant had the poor man thrown into prison until he could pay him back. The king heard about all that had happened. Angered, he called the unmerciful servant to him and said, "You wicked man! You asked for mercy and I gave it to you. You should have shown the same mercy to your fellow servant." The king threw him into prison to be tortured until he could pay back all he owed. Jesus finished this story by saying, "This is how the Father will treat each of you unless you forgive from the heart."

Judge and you will be judged. Show mercy and forgiveness, and other people will do the same for you. Matthew 5:7 NASB tells us, *"Blessed are the merciful, for they shall receive mercy."* The world shouts back, "But that's not fair! You don't know how much they've wronged me. You don't know the pain I've been through." If we are going to talk about fairness, we only get as far as a perfect man named Jesus who experienced pain, abuse, injustice, and a humiliating death He didn't deserve as He cancelled our debt. We are forgiven because He took the fall for us, which is anything but fair. Fair says that each of us should have been on the cross. Mercy says it's been taken care of. Do you want payback or do you want mercy? Do you want fair or do you want God's blessing? In *Hamlet*, Shakespeare wrote, "Use every man after his desert, and who shall scape whipping?...the less they deserve, the more merit is in your bounty."

I love to be around people who love mercy. Do you want that quality in your own life? Be slow to judge and quick to forgive. Ask God for divine opportunities to show mercy. Begin to love and practice kindness at every opportunity and it will begin to seem less "random" to the world.

Day 5

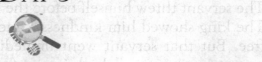

"He has showed you, O man, what is good. And
what does the LORD require of you?
To act justly and to love mercy and to
walk humbly with your God."

Micah 6:8, NIV

There is no one I would rather take a walk with than my wife. When I think about walking, I think about spending time with her. I think about the relationship we have. We walk on beaches, around malls, and through neighborhoods. We share stories, we laugh, we cry, we work things out; we do life together. She truly is the best friend I have in this life.

Micah 6:8 says that God wants His creation to walk through life with Him like that. He desires to spend time with us and do life together with us. As we walk with God, He wants us to be mindful that He's in control. No one who has a personal experience with God will ever come out of it with any illusion of their own grandeur. When Isaiah saw a vision of God, he said, "*Woe is me. For I am undone*" (Isaiah 6:5, NKVJ). After Daniel's vision, he said, "*So I was left alone to see this grand vision. I had no strength left in me. My face turned deathly pale, and I was helpless.*" (Daniel 10:8, GW)

I have a novelty t-shirt a friend of mine picked up for me when he was on vacation. It has a picture of a hand with two fingers crossed and pointed upward. The message on the t-shirt says, "Me and God are like this (*crossed fingers*). He's the taller one." That simple gesture has become the metaphor I use to visualize the kind of relationship I have with God. We're close, but He's definitely bigger and knows a lot more than me.

To walk humbly simply means to walk in total dependency. Our regular conversation should be "Lord, which direction do you want me to go? What things do you want me to do? How can I serve you today?" I see prayer all over this kind of relationship. I don't mean the rambling on and on kind of prayer, but the being silent and listening to His voice kind of prayer.

> It's impossible to walk humbly with God if you're not inviting Him to come along.

If you desire to let God call the shots, then you have got to be someone who prays. Lack of prayer, lack of waiting and listening for God's direction is like saying, "Lord, I got this one. I can make this journey on my own." It's impossible to walk humbly with God if you're not inviting Him to come along.

Don't settle for a weekend-to-weekend relationship with God. Do life together with God each day. Totally depend on the Lord and you'll see your relationship with Him come alive in you. Make it a point each morning to ask God to come on the day's journey. Then, before heading out, stop and ask Him where He'd like to take you. Remember, He's the taller one.

DAY 6

"He has showed you, O man, what is good. And what does the LORD require of you? To act justly and to love mercy and to walk humbly with your God."

MICAH 6:8, NIV

Today you are invited to read some additional scriptures related to Micah 6:8 and then journal your thoughts on a sheet of paper or in your journal.

"*A light shines in the dark for honest people, for those who are merciful and kind and good. It is good to be merciful and generous. Those who are fair in their business will never be defeated. Good people will always be remembered.*" (Psalm 112:4-6, NCV)

"*The Lord is more pleased when we do what is right and just than when we offer him sacrifices.*" (Proverbs 21:3, NLT)

"*Learn to do good. Seek justice. Help the oppressed. Defend the cause of orphans. Fight for the rights of widows.*" (Isaiah 1:17, NLT)

"*And you must love the Lord your God with all your heart, all your soul, all your mind, and all your strength.' The second is equally important: 'Love your neighbor as yourself.' No other commandment is greater than these.*" (Mark 12:30-31, NLT)

"*Instead, be kind to each other, tenderhearted, forgiving one another, just as God through Christ has forgiven you.*" (Ephesians 4:32, NLT)

"*Finally, all of you should be of one mind. Sympathize with each other. Love each other as brothers and sisters. Be tenderhearted, and keep a humble attitude. Don't repay evil for evil. Don't retaliate with insults when people insult you. Instead, pay them back with a blessing. That is what God has called you to do, and he will bless you for it.*" (1 Peter 3:8-9, NLT)

Suggestions:

- Start with prayer. God, through the Holy Spirit, can drop suggestions into your heart and mind.
- Ask a question such as, "God, what truth are you trying to communicate to me?"
- Write a letter to God.
- Make notes about what you're learning.
- Compose a prayer.
- Draw a picture of your praise.

DAY 7

"He has showed you, O man, what is good. And
what does the LORD require of you?
To act justly and to love mercy and to
walk humbly with your God."

MICAH 6:8, NIV

As I sat drinking my bottle of Ethos Water at Starbucks this morning and studying about how God requires justice, I felt like God was showing me a correlation between my water, our verse, and the ever-growing focus on social justice in religion. Although hard to completely and concisely describe, a decent definition of social justice could be "efforts to secure a world that affords individuals and groups fair treatment and an impartial share of the benefits of society." Social justice can also refer to the distribution of advantages and disadvantages within a society.

This brings me back to my water bottle. I was reading on their website that "Ethos Water is a brand with a social mission: helping children around the world get clean water and raising awareness of the World Water Crisis." According to *Merriam-Webster's Dictionary*, *ethos* means "the distinguishing character, sentiment, moral nature, or guiding beliefs of a person, group, or institution."

The social mission of this bottled water company reminds me of one of the three commands God gave Israel. He told them (Micah 6:8) to do justice; to defend and look out for the rights of the helpless. Almost all of Jesus' teachings revolved around social justice. He preached good news to the poor, release to the captives, sight to the blind, and freedom to the oppressed. James 1:27 MSG says, "*Real religion, the kind that passes muster before God the Father, is this: Reach out to the homeless and loveless in their plight, and guard against corruption from the godless world."* Social justice seems to be a guiding belief and distinguishing character-istic—*ethos*—of following Christ.

Let's go back to the water bottle again. Water is mentioned 722 times in the Bible. The first mention of water is in Genesis 1:2 NLT: *"The earth was formless and empty, and darkness covered the deep waters. And the Spirit of God was hovering over the surface of the waters."* The last mention of water is in Revelation 22:17 NLT: *"The Spirit and the bride say, 'Come.' Let anyone who hears this say, 'Come.' Let anyone who is thirsty come. Let anyone who desires drink freely from the water of life."* Water has great spiritual significance.

Thinking about the spiritual significance of water leads us to a well; Jesus sat by a well with a Samaritan woman to talk to her about thirst. *"Whoever drinks of the water I give him will never thirst. Indeed the water I give him will become in him a spring of water welling up to eternal life"* (John 4:14, NIV). The God of living water has always pursued the thirsty in the heat of the desert. Jesus came to offer the eternal stream of God's water to the broken and thirsty. The water of Jesus brought life to the Samaritan. The water that Jesus offered held no judgment for the misfits and outcasts. These were the very people that Jesus went out of His way to find. God's water is for anyone who wants to drink. To the Samaritan woman, Jesus exposed her unhealthy pattern of broken relationships. He exposed her "broken cisterns and showed her the way of living water" (from www.followtherabbi.com).

Jesus showing the Samaritan woman the way of living water brings us back to social justice. Jesus came to give the world justice and peace and the pathway that leads to eternal life. When you receive Christ, your spiritual thirst is quenched and the Living Water now inside of you wells up into a spring that flows out to the broken around you. For the believer, social justice and evangelism are as non-negotiable as they are inseparable.

Week 30

But he gives us even more grace to stand against such evil desires. As the Scriptures say, "God opposes the proud but favors the humble."

James 4:6, NLT

DAY 1

But he gives us even more grace to stand against such evil desires. As the Scriptures say, "God opposes the proud but favors the humble."
JAMES 4:6, NLT

The book of James was written 1500 years ago, but it speaks to problems that are still common today. People are fighting, cheating, killing, and warring with each other to get what they don't have. Selfish pride has put them into survival mode. "You gotta' look out for number one;" "God helps those who help themselves;" "The most important thing is getting ahead." Sound familiar?

You might ask, "What's wrong with trying to get ahead?" The answer is nothing. There is nothing wrong with getting ahead. God wants his children to be blessed. The first half of Deuteronomy 28 tells about God's blessings for obedience; it is full of statements like these: *"I am the head and not the tail," "I am above only and not beneath," "I will lend and not borrow."*

THE ISSUE IS NOT IN THE TRYING TO GET AHEAD, IT IS IN THE WAY WE DO THE TRYING.

God wants us to have His best. The issue is not in the trying to get ahead, it is in the way we do the *trying*. The way we receive God's best is to first have a heart to give Him our best through humble obedience. It's a cause–effect type of guarantee that God makes to us. God promises, "If you will obey, then I will bless."

The book of Daniel starts with a story about some Israelite teenagers being captured and brought to the palace of Babylon.

They were supposed to eat the king's food and drink the king's wine—which was an awesome privilege for foreign captives—while being educated in the language and customs of their captors. We learn that four of those young men decided to stubbornly live according to God's law instead of following the culture of Babylon. They had every opportunity to gain position, power, and influence if they would compromise and fall in line like everyone else, but they refused to sacrifice their principles for an immediate gain.

Here's the kicker of this story: in the end, these four guys were found to be ten times better and more skilled than everyone else in appearance, health, and "*in every matter of wisdom and understanding*" (Daniel 1:20, HCSB). Daniel says that God gave them favor with leadership and with their peers. Because these four chose God, God chose them.

God wants to help you learn how to live in love and at peace with the people in your life. He wants to lift you up to live in His blessings and favor.

Humility will move you from a life of survival into a life of significance.

DAY 2

But he gives us even more grace to stand against such evil desires. As the Scriptures say, "God opposes the proud but favors the humble."
JAMES 4:6, NLT

Today I want to take a closer look at some of the key words used in James 4:6.

The first word we are singling out is the word "*humble*." Noah Webster defines humility as "a spirit of submission." We'll come back to this in a little while but I wanted to start with this fresh in your mind.

The second word is "*favor*." Webster defines favor as "aid, assistance, or effort in one's behalf." You know about favorites—the favorite child, the teacher's pet, the favorite to win. They're the ones who get all the breaks, the rewards, the full attention, and the privileges. That's what favor is. My siblings jokingly call me "The Golden Child," because people always like me and things always seem to work out well for me. But I know that all of this favor is not coincidence—and it's not because I'm prefect. It's because God is working behind the scenes, showering my life with His grace. God is giving me His aid and assistance. He is blessing me for obedience.

The New King James Version of James 4:6 reads, "*God resists the proud, but gives grace to the humble*." The original word used for "resists" means "to rage in battle against." If you have ever played Risk, you have a good frame of reference for that concept. The goal of the game is to set up armies in such a way as to control all the territories—to conquer the world—through the strategic elimination of the other players during battles. The word "resists" carries imagery that is a lot like this game. It's a picture of God setting Himself in a battle arrayed against those who are proud. Simply put, the proud resist God: God's truth, God's laws, and God's divine guidance. It's no wonder that God sets Himself against the proud. We need to guard against the pride in our hearts if we do not want God to resist us.

Back to James 4:6. The original word used for "grace" means "joy, pleasure, delight, sweetness, charm, thanks, benefits, or reward." Grace, as opposed to disgrace, is honor. So in other words, God gives honor to the humble.

Let's be clear: true humility does not lead to disgrace. True humility will lead to honor. You can have confidence that God is working behind the scenes on your behalf. You will get the break. You will get the job or the promotion. Your children will serve the Lord. You will be accepted into that college.

I want to close with some of Matthew Henry's thoughts on grace:

> *"Wherever God gives true grace, He will give more. He will especially give more grace to the humble, because they see their need of it, will pray for it, and be thankful for it; and such shall have it. For this reason, we are taught to submit ourselves entirely to God."*

DAY 3

But he gives us even more grace to stand against such evil desires. As the Scriptures say, "God opposes the proud but favors the humble."

JAMES 4:6, NLT

God opposes the proud.

Think about that for a moment. Pride actually causes God to choose sides.

I played basketball all the way through college. In each game I was assigned to guard the player on the other team who was considered the biggest threat to our objective: winning. I made it my personal mission to nullify that player's contribution to the game. In other words, I opposed that player.

Take a look at a few words that describe how God feels about pride: "detests" (Proverbs 16:5, NLT), "hates," and "abomination" (Proverbs 6:16-17, NKJV). That doesn't leave any room here for us to ask, "How do You *really* feel about that, God?"

So why such strong words? Why does God oppose pride so much? Isaiah 14:12-15 refers to Satan, his rebellion against God, and fall from heaven. Verses 13 and 14 in the Amplified Bible say: *"And you said in your heart, I will ascend to heaven; I will exalt my throne above the stars of God; I will sit upon the mount of assembly in the uttermost north. I will ascend above the heights of the clouds; I will make myself like the Most High." Scofield Reference Notes* makes this comment about these verses: "This tremendous passage marks the beginning of sin in the universe. When Lucifer said, 'I will,' sin began."

After that, Satan came to Adam and Eve in the Garden of Eden and tempted them with this same idea of becoming *"like God"* (Genesis 3:5) and they gave in. Sin entered mankind and we were cut off from the intimate relationship God intends. Sin, and our consequent separation from God, has its origins in pride.

Pride will always try to dethrone or usurp God in your heart.

In athletics there is always an opponent trying to dethrone the champ. In the same way, pride will always try to dethrone or usurp God in your heart. God is always the victor. Isaiah 42:13 NKJV says, *"He shall prevail against his enemies."*

God always comes out on top. And if you live for God, you become a champion, too.

In every decision you make and every task you perform today, pray that God would be on the throne. Ask Him to call the shots.

If you do, you'll see yourself rising higher and going farther than you ever dreamed.

Day 4

But he gives us even more grace to stand against such evil desires. As the Scriptures say, "God opposes the proud but favors the humble."
James 4:6, NLT

Today you are going to read a few additional scriptures related to pride and humility. Then, use an extra piece of paper or a personal journal to write down your thoughts.

When pride comes, then comes shame; but with the humble is wisdom. (Proverbs 11:2, NKJV)

And whoever exalts himself will be humbled, and he who humbles himself will be exalted. (Matthew 23:12, NKJV)

Then he said, "I tell you the truth, unless you turn from your sins and become like little children, you will never get into the Kingdom of Heaven. So anyone who becomes as humble as this little child is the greatest in the Kingdom of Heaven. (Matthew 18:3-4, NLT)

Don't push your way to the front; don't sweet-talk your way to the top. Put yourself aside, and help others get ahead. Don't be obsessed with getting your own advantage. Forget yourselves long enough to lend a helping hand. (Philippians 2:3-4, MSG)

Therefore humble yourselves under the mighty hand of God, that He may exalt you in due time, casting all your care upon Him, for He cares for you. (1 Peter 5:6-7, NKJV)

For the world offers only a craving for physical pleasure, a craving for everything we see, and pride in our achievements and possessions. These are not from the Father, but are from this world. And this world is fading away, along with everything that people crave. But anyone who does what pleases God will live forever. (1 John 2:16-17, NLT)

Suggestions:

- Start with prayer. God, through the Holy Spirit, can drop suggestions into your heart and mind.
- Ask a question such as, "God, what truth are you trying to communicate to me?"
- Write a letter to God.
- Make notes about what you're learning.
- Compose a prayer.
- Draw a picture of your praise.

DAY 5

But he gives us even more grace to stand against such evil desires. As the Scriptures say, "God opposes the proud but favors the humble."

JAMES 4:6, NLT

Pride is like a flagpole. Humility is like an elevator.

I was given that word picture years ago and I have never forgotten it.

When you're climbing the flagpole of pride, you call the shots. You are in control, and you make the decisions. Once we climb a flagpole and reach the top, there is only one thing left to do: slide down!

When we get on our knees and humble ourselves before God, it's like being on an elevator. You get on, you kneel down, and your position never changes. But the next thing you know, God has pushed the button and you're on the 25th floor. God promoted you without you having to do it yourself. How high you rise, how fast you get there, and what floors you stop at on the way is totally under His control and up to His will. The door opens and God simply tells you to "step out."

1 Peter 5:6-7 NLT says, "*Humble yourselves, therefore, under God's mighty hand,* ***that he may lift you up in due time.*** *Cast all your anxiety on him because he cares for you.*" See? Humility is like an elevator.

It's humbling to admit that we need help and have no idea where we are going—like guys asking for directions when they get lost. "I don't need someone to tell me where to go. I can get there on my own. Stopping will only slow me down." But God asks us to cast our anxieties on Him and ask for the right direction for our lives. It's amazing how often we just take a pass on the privilege to pray. "No thanks, God. I'll go it alone on this one."

The *Jon Courson New Testament Application Commentary* on James 4:6 equates an unwillingness to pray with the sin of pride: "Who is the proud person? Barometers predict storms by measuring air pressure. Prayer-ometers indicate pride by measuring prayer pressure." Choosing not to pray indicates pride in our hearts. It is our pride that says, "I don't need someone to tell me where to go. I can get there on my own. Stopping will only slow me down." Lack of prayer will always indicate the presence of pride.

Climb down from the flagpole of pride and step onto the elevator of humility. The door is open. Humble yourself and kneel down in prayer, because your posture precedes your position. Let God push the buttons. Seek first His Kingdom. And then?

Welcome His guidance. God can lift you higher than you could even dream of going on your own.

Start trusting God today to lift you up in His time.

DAY 6

But he gives us even more grace to stand against such evil desires. As the Scriptures say, "God opposes the proud but favors the humble."

JAMES 4:6, NLT

Did you catch the first part of this verse? It talks about grace as undeserved divine assistance. Essentially, grace is the work of the Holy Spirit in us.

We experience God's initial grace at salvation. The Holy Spirit immediately begins to show us that we are to live righteously, but anyone who has walked with God for more than five minutes knows that we are still prone to stray from Him to follow our old, evil desires. That's when this greater grace kicks in to help us resist sin and to draw us back when we wander away.

In the Old Testament, God gave the Ten Commandments to the Israelites. God said, "Here are the rules. Here's what is right. Here's what is wrong. Now obey. Just say 'no'." History reveals the repeated failure of Israel to live up to those expectations. And truthfully, believers today aren't doing any better at living up to the Law.

The "Just Say No" to drugs campaign was supposed to educate children and discourage them from getting involved in recreational drug use. The problem with that campaign was that the drug use issue in America was underestimated. As a result, the "Just Say No" campaign has been reduced to not much more than a catch phrase.

While just saying no is a solid, practical solution to an individual drug problem, there are no physical solutions to spiritual problems. We cannot simply say "no" to sin and maintain a right relationship with God by external abstinence alone. However, we have a helper living on the inside. Titus 2:11-12 says that grace teaches us to say "no" to ungodliness. The word "teaches" means to mold character by reproof, as a father would correct or discipline a son.

The Holy Spirit not only convicts us of sin and compromise, but also enables us to serve God as we should.

Just think about that. The Holy Spirit who dwells in us not only convicts us of sin and compromise, but also enables us to serve God as we should. If you listen to what the world is saying, you become worldly-minded. If you will listen to what the Spirit says, you can become spiritually-minded. On your own, it is impossible for you to be sinless, but the Spirit will teach you to sin less and less all the time.

You see, following Christ is not as much about overcoming sin as it is about letting Jesus overcome *you*!

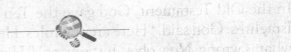

Do you realize that God has your well-being in mind?

Today, when the Spirit of grace speaks to your heart, you can listen, trust, and obey.

Make an adjustment, eliminate that unproductive activity, spend more time growing in the Word and prayer.

If you do, you will see yourself growing stronger and receiving more of God's grace and blessing.

Day 7

But he gives us even more grace to stand against such evil desires. As the Scriptures say, "God opposes the proud but favors the humble."
James 4:6, NLT

An Old Testament Jewish guy named Uzziah was 16 years old when he became the King of Judah. 2 Chronicles 26:4-5 NIV says, *"He did what was right in the eyes of the LORD…As long as he sought the LORD, God gave him success."* Notice that Uzziah did not do what he thought was right in his own eyes; he did what was right in the Lord's eyes. His character test was to determine if God would approve of his actions. As long as he sought God, he had God's favor.

I wish this story had a happy ending for King Uzziah. In 2 Chronicles 26:16 we learn that *"after Uzziah became powerful, his pride led to his downfall."* Uzziah began to take his relationship with God for granted. He lost the fear of the Lord and stopped seeking God. He forgot whose shoulders he was standing on. Pride is becoming more confident in your own abilities than in the ability of God.

Success sometimes leads us to believe that we are responsible for it. We forget the virtues that brought us to that place and how we got them in the first place. Pride has its greatest opportunity when you are having your highest success. Abraham Lincoln said, "If you want to determine the greatness of a man, give him power, not poverty. You will find out more about an individual when they are given power. A lot of people can endure hardship, but can't handle power."

I love how many professional Christian athletes are using their platform and the favor God has given them through televised sports. During their post-game interviews, instead of the usual braggadocios sound-bite about the game, their audience hears them giving glory to Jesus first and foremost. But some people, who do not give God the glory before they become well-known, foolishly pray, "God, if you make me famous, rich, and a star athlete, I will use my position and popularity to tell others about Christ." If you can't tell them now, you'll never be able to when you're famous. Seek first the Kingdom and everything else will be added.

When you finally reach the mountain's peak, whose flag will you stick in the ground at the summit?

When you succeed, will you continue to stay faithful to God, or will you forget about Him? When you finally reach the mountain's peak, whose flag will you stick in the ground at the summit? To whom will you give the glory for your accomplishments? Many people achieve their goals and forget how they got there.

Remember to keep an attitude of humility. It's not a matter of *if* God will give you His favor, raise you to new heights and cause you to be successful.

The question is this: will you give Him the glory when He does?

Week 31

"And if anyone forces you to go one mile,
go with him two [miles]."

Matthew 5:41, AMP

Day 1

"And if anyone forces you to go one mile,
go with him two [miles]."
Matthew 5:41, AMP

Close to 50 years after Jesus went up into heaven, one of his disciples, Matthew, began to write about the life of Christ the King. Matthew was a tax collector before becoming one of the disciples. Tax collectors were not popular with Jewish people in those days for two reasons: most of them were dishonest (they collected more money than the tax required and pocketed it for themselves), and their job was to collect money for a foreign empire that they didn't want in their country in the first place.

Jesus, a good Jewish man, walks up to this social outcast one day, says *"Follow me,"* and Matthew immediately gets out of his tax-collecting booth, leaving his profession to follow Jesus (Mark 2:13-14). Right after Matthew begins to follow Jesus, we see Matthew inviting his tax collector friends and all the other disreputable people he knew over to his house so they can meet Jesus. The religious people were outraged that Jesus spent time with Matthew and his friends, but Jesus simply reinforced the fact that He came to save people like this. I love the parenthetical phrase in Mark 2:15 (NLT) that reads, *"There were many people of this kind among Jesus' followers."*

This week's scripture lands right in the middle of the Sermon on the Mount. Jesus gave this sermon on a mountain close to Capernaum (hence the clever name). With crowds gathering and His disciples sitting around Him, Jesus sat down and began to speak. In that culture, being seated suggested authority, so rabbis would usually sit when teaching. This sermon, the most famous one that Jesus ever preached, included the Lord's Prayer, the Golden Rule, and the Beatitudes. With thousands of people standing around, quietly listening to what He had to say, these were the topics that Jesus chose to talk about. It must have been very important to Jesus that all the people (including us) would hear and know this teaching.

The entire Sermon on the Mount is contained in chapters 5 through 7 of Matthew and is divided into several parts: comforting verses that emphasize what we are supposed to do, the relationship of Jesus to the Old Testament law, our relationship with God, and our relationship with other people.

Our verse for this week is part of the section where Jesus teaches about the true intent of the Law. In this part of the Sermon on the Mount, Jesus often says, "*You have heard…, but I say…*" People had been taught to observe every detail of the Law God gave Moses, but over the centuries the emphasis had been placed on outward obedience instead of the inward motivation—the heart of God behind the laws. Jesus taught that the true intent (or spirit) of the Law is to bring us into the right relationship with God and with the people in our lives; He emphasized the thoughts and acts that lead to obedience.

We will spend the rest of the week looking at Matthew 5:41 and an attitude of "second mile service." But the Sermon on the Mount is a must read for those who want to follow Christ completely.

If you've never read all of Matthew 5, 6, and 7 or if it has been awhile since you did, take some time to read (and maybe re-read) through those three chapters this week.

DAY 2

"And if anyone forces you to go one mile,
go with him two [miles]."
MATTHEW 5:41, AMP

Have you ever gone the extra mile for someone?

This is where that statement came from. Here in Matthew 5:41, Jesus makes a very simple statement that has been used around the world in sports, business, and many other fields. Jesus said, *"If someone forces you to go one mile, go with him two miles"* NIV. He is saying, "Go the extra mile."

People repeat this phrase all the time without knowing what Jesus was talking about. In that day, Judea and Galilee were under Roman rule. According to the Roman aw, a Roman soldier could stop you at any time, tap you on the shoulder with his spear, and ask you to carry his pack, luggage, or armor for up to one mile. A Roman mile was a thousand paces: 1520 yards; 4560 feet. A task like that was humiliating for a Jew—being forced to work for a soldier of the hated Roman Empire. You can imagine the typical response once the 1,000th step was reached; drop the pack to the ground and walk off, right? It's probably the response a Roman soldier would have come to anticipate and expect: "...997, 998, 999, 1000! See ya! Wouldn't wanna be ya!"

JESUS SAYS, "SURPRISE YOUR ENEMIES BY GOING ANOTHER MILE WITH THEM."

Jesus says, "Surprise your enemies by going another mile with them." Look at what Romans 12:20-21 NIV also tells us to do,

"On the contrary: If your enemy is hungry, feed him; if he is thirsty, give him something to drink. In doing this, you will heap burning coals on his head. Do not be overcome by evil, but overcome evil with good." No, the heaping of burning coals on their heads does not mean that you get to torch your enemies or that your good deed will smolder in them and avenge you for what you put up with. Fire was the only way to keep a house warm in those days. No fire meant no heat for a household and no way to cook the meals. Every morning, one person from the town would put hot coals in a clay jar and carry it around on their head so that every house could restart any fires that went out over night. The idea of heaping coals is for us go above and beyond to serve and bless our enemies. The result is that our enemies are changed; when you heap coals on their heads in that way, you have given them something useful that they'll be carrying around to share with other people—and evil is overcome because good has taken its place.

You can overcome evil just by doing good for someone else. How different would our world look today if evil were overcome? Jesus' challenge is for you to be different! He says, "Don't just do what's expected or required—the minimum. I don't want you to give the typical one mile service. What I want from you is second mile service."

Think about the opportunities available for you to influence people for God's Kingdom as you walk with them in the second mile today.

DAY 3

"And if anyone forces you to go one mile,
go with him two [miles]."
MATTHEW 5:41, AMP

Just picture a Roman soldier's face, when one of the Jews he had pressured for the one-mile leg of his journey takes step number 1000, and then 10001, 1002, 1003...without dropping the whole load to the ground and turning around to walk away. Can you imagine the conversations that would have taken place in mile two after the servant would say, "Hey, do you mind if I carry your armor another mile?" The soldier may say, "Why are you doing this? The law says you could have been done way back there. What makes you different from everyone else I've ever asked before to do this?" The relationship would go from servant to friend during that extra mile. The servant would be able to tell the soldier that he was just trying to follow the teachings of Jesus and the soldier would be much more open to hearing the story than he was during the first mile.

"DEFINING CHRISTIANITY IS PORTRAYED NOT IN THE FIRST MILE OF SERVICE, BUT IN THE SECOND."

Jesus knows that there are realities of witness and character that can only be experienced in the realm of "above and beyond" service. Oswald Chambers said, "Defining Christianity is portrayed not in the first mile of service, but in the second." The first mile is walked because of man's law, but the second mile is walked because of God's love. The first mile is walked because you are obeying a person, but the second mile is walked because you are obeying God. The first mile is walked to fulfill an obligation, but the second mile is walked to earn the right to witness.

When someone else has the authority, you most likely have no say during mile one. They have the sword, they give out the paycheck, they control the playing time, they set your curfew, or they determine your grades. So what do you do? You carry their gear.

But, in the second mile, God's love takes control. By going the extra mile, you say, "The sword, the paycheck, the playing time, the curfew, and the report card are not my highest motivation. And, if you will walk with me for another mile, I'll tell you what my motivation is."

When you not only yield your rights to serve your enemies, but also double your service to them, as Christ teaches us here, God will be free to use you to bring about the supernatural results that He wants. Love goes on when your obligation ends.

What second mile does God want you to walk today?

DAY 4

"And if anyone forces you to go one mile,
go with him two [miles]."
MATTHEW 5:41, AMP

Take some time today to read a few additional scriptures related to Matthew 5:41. Then, journal your thoughts in your personal journal or on a separate sheet of paper.

Whoever wants to be a leader among you must be your servant, and whoever wants to be first among you must be the slave of everyone else. For even the Son of Man came not to be served but to serve others and to give his life as a ransom for many. (Mark 10:43-45, NLT)

But if your enemy is hungry, feed him; if he is thirsty, give him drink; for by so doing you will heap burning coals upon his head. Do not let yourself be overcome by evil, but overcome (master) evil with good. (Romans 12:20-21, AMP)

For you, brethren, have been called to liberty; only do not use liberty as an opportunity for the flesh, but through love serve one another. (Galatians 5:13, NKJV)

Share each other's burdens, and in this way obey the law of Christ. If you think you are too important to help someone, you are only fooling yourself. You are not that important. (Galatians 6:2-3, NLT)

Don't look out only for your own interests, but take an interest in others, too. You must have the same attitude that Christ Jesus had. Though he was God, he did not think of equality with God as something to cling to. Instead, he gave up his divine privileges; he took the humble position of a slave and was born as a human being. (Philippians 2:4-7, NLT)

Suggestions:

- Prayerfully reflect on these verses and record the thoughts that God, through the Holy Spirit, is dropping into your heart.
- Ask a question such as, "God, what truth are you trying to communicate to me?"
- Write a letter to God.
- Take notes about what you're learning.
- Compose a prayer.
- Draw a picture of your praise

Day 5

"And if anyone forces you to go one mile,
go with him two [miles]."
Matthew 5:41, AMP

Going the second mile is a great way to communicate God's love and your love to others. But something happens that you may not expect when you put Jesus' Sermon on the Mount teachings into practice. You go from being under control to being *in* control.

Mahatma Gandhi was tired of the exploitation of the people of India (Britain occupied India for many years—like the Romans were occupying Israel in Jesus' time). He began to look for a way to end the injustice. Gandhi was not a believer, but it was during this time that he picked up a Bible and read Jesus' Sermon on the Mount. As he read it, he found principles that influenced him: Turn the other cheek…Give your shirt and your coat, too…Go an extra mile…Give to anyone who asks without expecting something back…Resist evil with good…The meek will inherit the earth…

Gandhi mobilized the nation of India in an unprecedented campaign of nonviolent resistance. History books record that he told his people, "Now it's possible to resist evil; this is your first responsibility; never adjust to evil, resist it. But if you can resist it without resorting to violence or to hate, you can stand up against it and still love the individuals that carry on the evil system." They would be beaten, shot, cursed, and some would even die, but they would not fight back.

And it worked. The British morale became bruised; they knew they could never defeat the millions who had united to follow these teachings of Jesus. Here is an amazing thing about this story: to this day, there is no greater friendship between two nations than the one between the people of Britain and the people of India, simply because Gandhi's followers decided to resist evil with good.

Jesus' teachings removed the limitations of the Law. The Jews had been taught *"an eye for an eye and a tooth for a tooth, a burn for a burn, a wound for a wound, a bruise for a bruise, a life for a life"* (Exodus 21:24-25, GW). Those ways satisfied the offense, but did not satisfy God's higher law of love.

Are you ready to give up your rights and take control? Practice the teachings of Christ at your job, in your family, or at your school. Resist evil with good.

The one who goes the second mile really *does* control the conditions.

DAY 6

"And if anyone forces you to go one mile,
go with him two [miles]."

MATTHEW 5:41, AMP

I would like to take a quick look today at a story from Genesis 24 that shows going the second mile in action: the story of Isaac and Rebekah.

Back then, fathers were responsible for choosing a wife for their children. When Isaac was 40 years old, his father, Abraham, sent a servant to go find a wife for Isaac. When the servant reached the land where he was sent, he stopped to water his camels. It just happened to be the time of day when the young women from the town were also coming to draw water from the well for their homes. Abraham's servant prayed that he would know who to choose by asking one of the women for a drink and that her response would be to say, *"Not only you, but all of the camels as well."* He asked a woman named Rebekah to get him a drink and after she gave him a drink, she said, *"I'll draw water for your camels, too, until they have had enough to drink."* The servant chose Rebekah to be Isaac's wife.

Good story, right? Let's more clearly visualize what really went on there at the well. The servant had ten camels with him—camels who had just walked a long way across the desert. A camel can drink up to 30 gallons of water. That's 300 gallons of water! And it wasn't like she could just turn on the faucet and wait for the water to come out. Rebekah not only had to refill her jug over and over, but she also had to retrieve the water out of the well each time. Imagine how sore her arms would be after hauling 300 gallons of water, let alone how much of her day she spent doing that for a stranger. She had no idea who this man was, but it was just part of her character to go above and beyond. That's second mile service in action.

What Rebekah did not foresee in all of this were the blessings that would be coming back her way for going the extra mile.

***She* was blessed.** Rebekah was given a gold ring for her nose and large gold bracelets for her wrists, she got a husband, and she was going to marry into an extremely wealthy family. When you give yourself for that extra mile, you will receive the extra blessing. You really can't out-give God.

SHE HAD NO IDEA WHO THIS MAN WAS, BUT IT WAS JUST PART OF HER CHARACTER TO GO ABOVE AND BEYOND.

***Her* family was blessed.** Rebekah's family was given expensive gifts. Being a servant at school, at your job, on your team, or at your church opens the door for your family to be blessed. Going the extra mile can change your family.

***It opened the door* for even more remarkable things.** Rebekah becoming Isaac's wife also put her in the lineage of Jesus, the Messiah. In Rebekah's case, going two miles instead of one (or none) put her in the family tree of the One who came to save the world.

Going the second mile will unlock doors of blessing, favor, and advancement that you could never see coming.

DAY 7

"And if anyone forces you to go one mile,
go with him two [miles]."

MATTHEW 5:41, AMP

It takes a pretty specific attitude to go the second mile—to ask your supervisor for extra work when you've completed your assignment; to clean up a mess you didn't make before anyone asks you to; to take out the trash, and also pick up the garbage that is spilling out on the ground around the trash can; to finish an important task at work on your own time, after punching out and without getting paid. Attitude is an outward expression of an inward feeling. Tell a typical teenager to clean their room before they are allowed to go to a friend's house and you will most likely see an outward expression of an inward feeling.

Philippians 2:5 NLT is the key to the kind of attitude it takes to provide second-mile service: *"You must have the same attitude that Christ Jesus had."* And what was His attitude? Philippians 2 describes Jesus as humble, unselfish, thoughtful of others above Himself, not trying to impress, caring about what other people were concerned about, and serving people. A second-mile attitude is an outward expression of a *Jesus* feeling.

A SECOND-MILE ATTITUDE IS AN OUTWARD EXPRESSION OF A JESUS FEELING.

Some translations of Philippians 2 say that Jesus *"made himself of no reputation."* Other translations say that *"he made himself nothing."* That phrase in the Greek language literally means that Jesus *"emptied himself"* (theology books call it *kenosis*).

This means that Jesus, though He remained divine, set aside the privileges of deity and did everything as a servant-man who was empowered by the Holy Spirit.

The significance of this for us is huge! To have a second-mile attitude—the same attitude as Christ—we need to be willing to become completely emptied of ourselves. But we also have to be completely filled with and directed by God's Spirit of power, love, and compassion for the world.

Are you willing to be made "nothing"? Are you ready to have the mind of Christ and enact outward expressions of Jesus feelings for this world?

If you have the attitude that goes the second mile for people, you will always have friends and your life will always have meaning and purpose.

Week 32

"In the same way, the tongue is a small thing that makes grand speeches. But a tiny spark can set a great forest on fire. And the tongue is a flame of fire. It is a whole world of wickedness, corrupting your entire body. It can set your whole life on fire, or it is set on fire by hell itself."

James 3:5-6, NLT

DAY 1

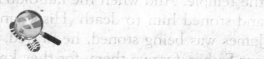

"In the same way, the tongue is a small thing that makes grand speeches. But a tiny spark can set a great forest on fire. And the tongue is a flame of fire. It is a whole world of wickedness, corrupting your entire body. It can set your whole life on fire, or it is set on fire by hell itself."

JAMES 3:5-6, NLT

The author of the book of James in the New Testament was not James the "Son of Thunder" who was the brother of John and the disciple of Jesus. The James who wrote this intense letter was the son of Mary and Joseph and the half brother of Jesus.

James grew up in the same house with Jesus, but he did not grow up believing that Jesus was the Messiah (or the Christ) for whom his people had been waiting. In fact, he may have even thought his brother was a bit crazy: *"When his family heard what was happening, they tried to take him away. 'He's out of his mind,' they said"* (Mark 3:21, NLT). Not until after the resurrection did James believe that Jesus was who He was. Maybe an appearance by Jesus specifically to James (1 Corinthians 15:7) played a role in James' conversion. What we know for sure is that James opens his epistle 30 years later by humbly saying, *"James, a servant of God and the Lord Jesus Christ."*

Shortly after James wrote these verses, he was martyred. The Jewish historian Josephus wrote that James was accused and condemned to be stoned. Eusebius, another historian, wrote that the religious leaders took James to the temple and "demanded that he should renounce the faith of Christ before all the people." Instead, he confessed to the crowd that "Jesus was the Son of God, our Savior and Lord." When he said this, James was thrown from the top of the temple. And when the fall didn't kill him, they went down and stoned him to death. Historian Hegesippus wrote that as James was being stoned, he prayed, "I entreat thee, Lord God our Father, forgive them, for they know not what they do [thus following his brother's example to the last]."

Which brings us around to this week's theme: the power of our tongue.

Scripture says in Romans 10:9-10 NLT, "*If you confess with your mouth that Jesus is Lord and believe in your heart that God raised him from the dead, you will be saved. For it is by believing in your heart that you are made right with God, and it is by confessing with your mouth that you are saved.*" Why does James say that such a small part of your body has so much power? Because even your eternal destination is determined by what you speak and confess. With your tongue you can use your words to agree with the enemy's lies and establish his words and schemes in your heart. Or you can use your words to agree with God, establish His plans in your heart, and be saved.

For the first part of his life, James did not believe that his half-brother was really the Son of God. But seeing Him crucified and resurrected was an experience that changed his life. James now understood that Jesus had given His life for him. At the end of his own life, James confidently used his words to confess his unwavering faith in the One he had spoken against. Someone once said that maybe James' memory of the unkind words he said about Jesus before coming to faith inspired him to write "one of the most insightful passages about the tongue in all literature."

Don't ever underestimate the power of your words! Find out what God's Word says about life, about others, and about you. Meditate on those truths in prayer and then use your words to agree with what God says, establishing His words in your heart.

DAY 2

"In the same way, the tongue is a small thing that makes grand speeches. But a tiny spark can set a great forest on fire. And the tongue is a flame of fire. It is a whole world of wickedness, corrupting your entire body. It can set your whole life on fire, or it is set on fire by hell itself."

JAMES 3:5-6, NLT

The problem of having control over the tongue actually begins in childhood. Remember the things we used to say when we were little?

Mine!

I'm telling!

Tattle-tale, tattle-tale…

Liar, liar, pants on fire…

Sticks and stones may break my bones, but words will never hurt me…

In 1 Corinthians 13:11 NLT Paul says, "*When I was a child, I spoke and thought and reasoned as a child. But when I grew up, I put away childish things.*" Careless words, though never okay, are almost expected from children. But we are not children anymore, and we need to learn the power of the words we allow out of our mouths. Sticks and stones *do* break bones, but words have the power to hurt, too.

James 3:5 says our small tongues like to make "*grand speeches*," and boy was he right. Have you ever had one of those moments when you suddenly realize that you may have just said too much? I know I have. I reason in my head, "Did I just think that, or did I actually say it?"

Take a quick look at Proverbs 10:19 NIV: "*When words are many, sin is not absent, but he who holds his tongue is wise.*" What is the author trying to say? He's saying the wiser you get, the fewer words you are going to use. We need to use our mouths to say less more often. Publius, the Greek sage, said, "I have often regretted my speech; never my silence."

Scripture tells us that Jesus was oppressed, afflicted, and led to the slaughter, yet He did not open His mouth (Isaiah 53:7). He could have cut them all down with a single word. Do you think that Jesus ever regretted His silence? I don't think so. In Hebrews 12:2 NIV, Paul writes, "*who for the joy set before him endured the cross, scorning its shame, and sat down at the right hand of the throne of God.*" Jesus held His tongue because He had a greater purpose—our salvation—joyfully on His mind.

If you will commit to having that same kind of Kingdom mentality, you will find yourself using your words more purposefully. You will find yourself holding words back when the Holy Spirit reveals to you that speaking those words would not serve God's greater purposes for someone else. Instead of using your words to tear people down, you will begin using them to build people up. Allowing the Holy Spirit to control your words will open up more opportunities to be a witness.

You know, by now, that your words have the power to not only hurt, but to destroy. Many of you may carry around a broken heart because of words that were spoken in the past by friends, family, coaches, bosses, or coworkers. The good news is that the heart Maker is also the heart Healer. If time hasn't healed all wounds, God promises that He will.

Teach your tongue to be obedient to God's Word. If you do, then, when you need to open your mouth to speak, words of blessing will come out from the overflow of your heart (Matthew 12:34).

DAY 3

"In the same way, the tongue is a small thing that makes
grand speeches. But a tiny spark can set a great
forest on fire. And the tongue is a flame of fire.
It is a whole world of wickedness, corrupting your
entire body. It can set your whole life on fire,
or it is set on fire by hell itself."

JAMES 3:5-6, NLT

Garbage in, garbage out.

Just a few verses beyond James 3:5 NLT, he writes: "*Does a spring of water bubble out with both fresh water and bitter water? Does a fig tree produce olives, or a grapevine produce figs? No, and you can't draw fresh water from a salty spring.*" James is saying that a person's tongue will reveal who they are.

Jesus said, "*For whatever is in your heart determines what you say. A good person produces good things from the treasury of a good heart, and an evil person produces evil things from the treasury of an evil heart.*" (Matthew 12:34-35, NLT) Your words will come out sounding like whatever is really stored up inside of you.

People can become really good at making the outside look great in order to hide what is going on inside them. They can have a good name and reputation. People around them can even sing their praises. But the tell-tell sign of who they really are is how that person talks and the substance of their conversation. You will learn more about who someone is by what they are saying about others than by what others are saying about them. Your words reveal who you are.

Start turning the bitter waters inside of you into fresh, sweet waters.

How?

Stop hanging around negative people and begin to talk about how good God has been to you and how good He will be to others. Refuse to listen to gossip and begin to speak graciously about others. "The polluted puddles of put-downs and pettiness (in your heart) will start to become pools of purity and praise" (*The Jon Courson New Testament Commentary*).

Grace in, grace out.

Day 4

"In the same way, the tongue is a small thing that makes grand speeches. But a tiny spark can set a great forest on fire. And the tongue is a flame of fire. It is a whole world of wickedness, corrupting your entire body. It can set your whole life on fire, or it is set on fire by hell itself."

James 3:5-6, NLT

Today is dedicated to reading some additional scriptures related to the power of words. At the end, journal your thoughts.

All day long you plot destruction. Your tongue cuts like a sharp razor; you're an expert at telling lies. You love evil more than good and lies more than truth. You love to destroy others with your words, you liar! (Psalm 52:2-4, NLT)

The tongue can bring death or life, those who love to talk will reap the consequences. (Proverbs 18:21, NLT)

For whatever is in your heart determines what you say. A good person produces good things from the treasury of a good heart, and an evil person produces evil things from the treasury of an evil heart. (Matthew 12:34-35, NLT)

The words you say will either acquit you or condemn you. (Matthew 12:37, NLT)

When I was a child, I spoke and thought and reasoned as a child. But when I grew up, I put away childish things. (1 Corinthians 13:11, NLT)

Do not let any unwholesome talk come out of your mouths, but only what is helpful for building others up according to their needs, that it may benefit those who listen. And do not grieve the Holy Spirit of God, with whom you were sealed for the day of redemption. Get rid of all bitterness, rage and anger, brawling and slander, along with every form of malice. Be kind and compassionate to one another, forgiving each other, just as in Christ God *forgave you.* (Ephesians 4:29-32, NIV)

Finally, brothers, whatever is true, whatever is noble, whatever is right, whatever is pure, whatever is lovely, whatever is admirable—if anything is excellent or praiseworthy—think about such things. (Philippians 4:8, NIV)

Suggestions:

- Prayerfully reflect on these verses and record the thoughts that God, through the Holy Spirit, is dropping into your heart. Ask God a question such as, "God, what truth are you trying to communicate to me?"
- Write a letter to God.
- Make notes about what you're learning.
- Compose a prayer.
- Draw a picture of your praise.

DAY 5

"In the same way, the tongue is a small thing that makes grand speeches. But a tiny spark can set a great forest on fire. And the tongue is a flame of fire. It is a whole world of wickedness, corrupting your entire body. It can set your whole life on fire, or it is set on fire by hell itself."

JAMES 3:5-6, NLT

In a careful reading of this week's verses, you'll notice that James says that the tongue corrupts *your* body and can set *your* whole life on fire.

Think about this for a moment. Taming your tongue is not only about bringing blessings and not curses to the lives of the people around you. According to James, the words you choose to speak will either bless or burn you, too.

In Luke 6:38 NLT, Jesus said: "*Give, and you will receive. Your gift will return to you in full—pressed down, shaken together to make room for more, running over, and poured into your lap. The amount you give will determine the amount you get back.*" Paul said: "*Whoever sows sparingly will also reap sparingly, and whoever sows generously will also reap generously*" (2 Corinthians 9:6, NIV). This principle of sowing and reaping has withstood the test of time, and it applies to your words, too.

The words you speak will eventually come back to you in the same manner as they were spoken. When people find out someone has been criticizing them or gossiping behind their back, their natural reaction is to look outward instead of inward. If they act in the flesh, they might criticize or gossip about them right back. They snap, they tear down, they hurt—"*corrupting your entire body… setting your whole life on fire.*"

Your first response to criticism or gossip should be to reevaluate yourself, because you only get back what you give out. When you live by the Spirit, you go directly to God and ask Him who you may have been criticizing or gossiping about. When He reveals something to you, be quick to make adjustments.

A story is told about an angry little boy who ran around his village shouting, "I hate you! I hate you!" No one knew quite how to respond to him. Eventually the little boy ran to the edge of a steep cliff and shouted into the valley, "I hate you! I hate you!" Back from the valley came an echo: "I hate you! I hate you!" Startled at this, the boy ran home. With tears in his eyes, he told his mother that there was a mean little boy in the valley who shouted at him, "I hate you! I hate you!" His mother took the boy back to the cliff and told him to shout, "I love you! I love you!" When he did, back came the reply: "I love you! I love you!" From that day on, the little boy wasn't angry anymore. What you say to others and say about others, whether curses or blessings, will come back to you like an echo.

> YOUR LIFE IS MEASURED BY WHAT YOU REAP, BUT IT IS DETERMINED BY WHAT YOU SOW.

Your life is measured by what you reap, but it is determined by what you sow. You get out of life what you put into it. Make a point to speak only words of life, faith, and blessing. You will stop the fires before they get set and guarantee a harvest of life, faith, and blessing in your life as well.

DAY 6

"In the same way, the tongue is a small thing that makes grand speeches. But a tiny spark can set a great forest on fire. And the tongue is a flame of fire. It is a whole world of wickedness, corrupting your entire body. It can set your whole life on fire, or it is set on fire by hell itself."
JAMES 3:5-6, NLT

When I was driving through Deschutes National Forest in Central Oregon this past fall, I saw thousands of brush piles blazing. The fires were purposely set to eliminate the fuel that feeds wildfires. Forestry crews thinned trees and brush to reduce hazardous fuels where human activity.

James says that there is another human activity that can set a great forest on fire: our words. What can you do to keep your tongue from igniting fires? The answer is simple: remove the fuel.

WHAT CAN YOU DO TO KEEP YOUR TONGUE FROM IGNITING FIRES? THE ANSWER IS SIMPLE: REMOVE THE FUEL.

What are some fuels that can ignite fires? Here are three big ones:

- **Gossip.** Gossip consists of slander, lies, and defamation which all feed contention the same way wood fuels a fire. Proverbs 26:20 NLT says that, *"Fire goes out without wood, and quarrels disappear when gossip stops."* Here is a good life principle: Never believe anything bad about a person unless you know it's absolutely true;

never tell it unless it's absolutely necessary; and, remember to fear God, because He is listening while you tell it.

- **Lies.** Jesus, talking about the devil, said, *"He was a murderer from the beginning, not holding to the truth, for there is no truth in him. When he lies, he speaks his native language, for he is a liar and the father of lies"* (John 8:44, NIV). When you lie you are speaking hell's language. Every time you lie, you put yourself and others into bondage. The truth will set you free.

- **Harsh Words.** When we hear a word, the sound waves activate 24,000 tiny nerves in our ears. The activity makes the pituitary gland release hormones. Our whole body reacts to words! Studies show that when a person hears harsh words, the physical-chemical reaction takes 72 hours to subside. 1 Peter 3:9 (NIV) instructs, *"Do not repay evil with evil or insult with insult, but with blessing, because to this you were called so that you may inherit a blessing."* You might say, "That's not fair! What they did really hurt me." You may be right, but do you want fair, or do you want blessing?

The brush in the forest was a fire hazard because it had died. It had fallen to the ground and dried up because it could no longer take in the water and nutrients from the trees. Listen to what Scripture says to you about staying connected to your source of life: *"Yes, I am the vine; you are the branches. Those who remain in me, and I in them, will produce much fruit. For apart from me you can do nothing. Anyone who does not remain in me is thrown away like a useless branch and withers. Such branches are gathered into a pile to be burned."* (John 15:5-6, NLT)

Stay connected to the Living Water. He's your source of spiritual life and vitality. Allow God to burn away the choking underbrush of gossip, lies, and harsh words in your life daily. Use your words to pray, to lift up praises, and to be a witness. Ask God to help you speak only words that will bring healing and restoration.

Don't just let your silence be golden; let your speech be golden, too.

DAY 7

"In the same way, the tongue is a small thing that makes grand speeches. But a tiny spark can set a great forest on fire. And the tongue is a flame of fire. It is a whole world of wickedness, corrupting your entire body. It can set your whole life on fire, or it is set on fire by hell itself."

JAMES 3:5-6, NLT

Words. When used carelessly, they will set your life on fire (James 3:6). But when used correctly, they will move mountains: *"For assuredly, I say to you, whoever says to this mountain, 'Be removed and be cast into the sea,' and does not doubt in his heart, but believes that those things he says will be done, he will have whatever he say."* (Mark 11:23, NKJV)

> FAITH HAS NO FALL-BACK PLAN. FAITH ALWAYS TAKES ACTION AND FAITH ALWAYS INVOLVES A RISK.

Notice that Jesus did not tell us to pray and ask God to remove the obstacle in our path. He didn't tell us to read the Word more to overcome the problem. He said have faith in God and speak to the mountain; tell it to be gone. He says you will have what you say. It is what you say that counts.

Paul said to use your mouth to confess that Jesus is Lord (Romans 10:9-10). Hebrews 13 says we should confidently speak out His promises. Why is expressing things in words so important to faith? Sure, you can have a quiet confidence that God will make the mountain move. Then, if nothing happens, no one will ever know. But where is the faith in that? Faith has no fall-back plan. Faith always takes action and faith always involves a risk. Faith changes things and makes things happen.

During the battle of Jericho recorded in Joshua, Joshua told the Israelites not to talk for six days (Joshua 6:10). He did not want them feeding off of each others' words. If they had been allowed to speak, can you imagine the possible conversations on the first day alone? "This is so stupid! What a waste of time!" The complaints and grumbling would probably have been at full scale by day six and they might not have gained the victory that God had in store for them.

Do you say words like, "I am just sure I will catch that terrible illness that's been going around"? Or do you declare, "*By His wounds I am healed*"? Do you utter, "My life has been one setback after another; I'll never accomplish my dreams"? Or do you proclaim, "*I can do all things through Christ who gives me strength!*"? Is it, "I don't think I'll ever be free from this addiction;" or "*Who the Son sets free is free indeed!*"?

If you want to live a life of faith, your words are going to have to be consistent with the Word of God.

Don't underestimate the clout your words carry. Whether it's concern about health, economy, marriage, or children, put the power of faith-filled words to work on your mountain. Say, "*Be removed and cast into the sea.*" Announce to the world that you agree with what God says about you and declare His truth over your life.

If you do, you will see continual victory over your mountains.

Week 33

"But when you are praying, first forgive anyone you are holding a grudge against, so that your Father in heaven will forgive your sins, too."

Mark 11:25, NLT

Day 1

"But when you are praying, first forgive anyone you are holding a grudge against, so that your Father in heaven will forgive your sins, too."
Mark 11:25, NLT

Church people love to quote Mark 11:22-24 NLT where Jesus explains that faith can move mountains: *"I tell you the truth, you can say to this mountain, 'May you be lifted up and thrown into the sea,' and it will happen. But you must really believe it will happen and have no doubt in your heart. I tell you, you can pray for anything, and if you believe that you've received it, it will be yours."* Simply put, if you have the faith to believe, you receive. That is a promise Jesus makes to anyone willing to deny themselves, take up their cross, and follow Him.

We need to realize just how closely faith and forgiveness are related.

But if we're not careful, we might skip right over verse 25, which says that lack of forgiveness in our hearts will short-circuit our prayers and leave us powerless.

We need to realize just how closely faith and forgiveness are related. Jesus makes this connection between faith and forgiveness in Mark 11:25 and again in Matthew 6:15. We can't hold a grudge and expect to have our prayers answered at the same time.

The big question is: "Why?" The answer comes down to an underlying principle of love.

A person who will not forgive does not truly love and will continue to hurt themselves and other people. God loves us so much that He will confront us with our sin of unforgiveness in order to bring about repentance and restoration. A forgiving spirit is an indicator that you are a child of the Most High God—entitled to everything your Father has at His disposal.

Paul says that faith expresses itself in love (Galatians 5:6). When you release the people who have done you wrong, you remove the faith barrier and experience the power that can move the mountains in your life.

Have you been praying for something big, but you're not getting the results you are looking for? Ask God to reveal to you by His Holy Spirit if there is any hidden unforgiveness in your heart. Remove any obstacles to faith.

Then begin to speak to the mountain, *"be lifted up and thrown into the sea,"* and it will happen.

DAY 2

"But when you are praying, first forgive anyone you are holding a grudge against, so that your Father in heaven will forgive your sins, too."
MARK 11:25, NLT

Greek philosophy teaches that "forgiveness" means "an act of pardon; to cease blame." One of the first things President Ford did after assuming office in 1974 was to give President Nixon a full pardon for the Watergate scandal. The charges of crime against him ceased. President Ford wiped the slate clean. The past could not be held against Nixon—it was as if he had never done anything wrong. That is one power of forgiveness.

However, in Aramaic the word for forgiveness is more of an internal, self-healing tool. Proverbs 23:7 NIV tells us that as a man "*thinks in his heart, so is he.*" Harboring unforgiveness in our heart can cause us to reproduce the very things we detest, such as envy, hatred, strife, and bitterness. For example, more than 93% of child abusers were abused by their parents. There is truth in the old saying; "hurt people hurt people."

Unforgiveness is like a cancer that is easily treated or removed in the early stages, but will cause deterioration and possible loss of life when left untreated. Talking about his father in an interview in the January 2004 issue of Vibe Magazine, Jay-Z said, "That first time he left, that was my biggest and only heartbreak in life. I've had long-term relationships with beautiful women who loved me to death, but I had always been holding back. I had never been in love, because my heart was still broken from my father." Unforgiveness has the potential to destroy you, your relationships, your life, and your future.

Forgiving is not always about the other party. What if the person who wronged you never says they are sorry? Will you let them continue to control the quality of your life indefinitely? If they are the ones with the problem, why are you the one in pain?

> Forgive; every time you remember, choose to forgive again.

The root meaning of the Aramaic word for forgiveness is to "untie or let loose." Forgiveness is not letting someone off the hook for their offenses and calling what happened "OK." You untie, let loose, or let go so that you can be OK, even though the thing that happened wasn't OK. A famous quote goes as follows: "To forgive is to set a prisoner free and discover the prisoner was you."

You've heard the phrase, "I will forgive, but I won't forget." Don't buy into that system. Forgive; every time you remember, choose to forgive again. How many times? Jesus told Peter to forgive 490 times (Matthew 18:22). Since there are one thousand four hundred forty minutes in a twenty- four-hour day, you would need to forgive the same individual every three minutes.

When you forgive over and over, something begins to change on the inside. God's supernatural power at work within you enables you to move on.

Forgive until you forget. Let it go so God can change your life and set you free.

DAY 3

"But when you are praying, first forgive anyone you are holding a grudge against, so that your Father in heaven will forgive your sins, too."

MARK 11:25, NLT

First things first. Dinner before dessert. Practice before perfection. A foundation before a roof. When it comes to our prayers being powerful and effective, Jesus says forgiveness comes first.

Jesus set the example for us in many of His prayers. When He delivered the great Sermon on the Mount in the book of Matthew, He taught the people there to pray *"and forgive us our sins, as we have forgiven those who sin against us."* One time when the disciples were alone with Jesus, they asked Jesus to teach them how to pray (Luke 11:4). Jesus again instructed them, *"Forgive us our sins, as we forgive those who sin against us."* Finally, while hanging on the cross suffering torture and torment, Jesus prayed, *"Father, forgive them, for they don't know what they are doing"* (Luke 23:34).

Leonardo da Vinci painted *The Last Supper* in a church in Milan. A very interesting story is associated with this painting. At the time he was painting the famous fresco, he had an enemy who was another painter. He had had a heated argument with this man and resented him. When he painted Judas Iscariot's face at the table with Jesus, he used the face of his enemy so that he would appear as the man who betrayed Jesus. He took great satisfaction in knowing that others would see the face of his enemy on Judas for many years to come.

As he worked, he often tried to paint the face of Jesus, but couldn't make any progress. He felt frustrated and confused. Eventually, he realized the problem. His bitterness for the other painter was interfering with his ability to finish Jesus' face. Only after he made peace with his enemy and repainted the face of Judas was he able to paint the face of Jesus and complete the masterpiece.

Forgiveness removes a hindrance from God hearing and answering your prayers.

In the same way, if you choose to forgive your enemies, just as God has chosen to forgive you, you will be able to see the face of Jesus in your life. Forgiveness removes a hindrance from God hearing and answering your prayers. Jesus forgave in the moment of the greatest pain, anguish, and injustice of His life. He forgave, so that we can be forgiven. The next time you stand, sit, or kneel to pray, forgive. This will open the door for God to pour His supernatural blessings into your situation.

First things first.

DAY 4

"But when you are praying, first forgive anyone you are holding a grudge against, so that your Father in heaven will forgive your sins, too."
MARK 11:25, NLT

One of the first and biggest reasons people refuse to forgive is because they were unquestionably wronged. What another person did to them was terrible. It *did* hurt. It was *not* right. People in this circumstance say, "I have a right to be angry!" And they do. But it only brings them more pain.

In 1960, Adolph Coors III of the famous Coors family was kidnapped and held for ransom. Months later, his body was found on a hillside; he had been shot to death. Adolph Coors IV, his son, was 14 years old. Adolph not only lost his father, but also his best friend. The son was filled with hatred for Joseph Corbett, the man who murdered his dad. Fifteen years later, Adolph Coors IV accepted Christ and left the family business, but he was still harboring a deep hatred for his father's killer.

Years later, Coors said, "From long exposure I had learned that hatred hurts the hater even more than the one being hated." In 1977, he went to the Colorado State penitentiary where Joseph Corbett was serving the life sentence for killing Adolph Coors III.

"He wouldn't see me," Coors said, "so I sent him a letter asking him to forgive me for the hatred I had been cherishing for 17 years. I also told him that I had forgiven him. As I walked from the prison, I felt the fullness of God's love and forgiveness. That day I became a free man!"

Adolph Coors IV and his son, Adolph Coors V, now lead a ministry that helps individuals and families develop personal relationships with Christ.

What Coors suffered was terrible. It hurt. It was not right. And he felt he had a right to be angry. But God was able to show him that even the worst of offenses can and should be forgiven. God took what the enemy intended for destruction and used it for good.

Paul wrote in Romans 12:14 that we should bless the people who persecute us and pray that God would bless them. Michael W. Smith sings a song called "Above All." It is about how our sins and offenses put Christ on the cross, how He endured all the pain and "took the fall" for us so that we could be forgiven. The lyrics to the chorus of the song say:

> Crucified, laid behind the stone
> You lived to die rejected and alone
> Like a rose trampled on the ground
> You took the fall and thought of me
> Above all

Jesus, the Rose of Sharon (Song of Solomon 2:1), allowed Himself to be trampled and crushed in order to release the aroma of forgiveness and grace into the world. Perhaps this is what Mark Twain was referring to when he wrote: "Forgiveness is the fragrance that the violet sheds on the heel that has crushed it."

Scripture says, "*But thanks be to God, Who in Christ always leads us in triumph [as trophies of Christ's victory] and through us spreads and makes evident the fragrance of the knowledge of God everywhere*" (2 Corinthians 2:14, AMP). You may be crushed, but you have not been abandoned. You may have experienced a setback, but be ready for the comeback. Take what the enemy intended for your demise, and use it for your advantage.

Spread the victorious aroma of Christ to this world.

DAY 5

"But when you are praying, first forgive anyone you are holding a grudge against, so that your Father in heaven will forgive your sins, too."
MARK 11:25, NLT

Drivers come up with some far-fetched excuses when they try to talk their way out of a ticket. A newspaper printed a few sample excuses from actual police reports: "Coming home, I drove into the wrong house and collided with a tree I don't have." "The guy was all over the road. I had to swerve a number of times before I hit him." "An invisible car came out of nowhere, struck my vehicle, and vanished." "The indirect cause of this accident was this really little guy in a small car with a big mouth."

Instead of saying, "Please excuse me," these guys should be saying, "Please forgive me."

This brings up another reason people refuse to forgive others: inability to accept the responsibility for our own failure. People with this frame of mind always say, "I didn't do anything! It was all their fault." Here are some other excuses people make: "It's the teacher's fault I didn't pass the class; she didn't tell us everything we had to study." "My parents made me this way; they were never involved in my life." "If she wasn't always on my case about something, I would spend more time and be more involved at home." "I am so mad at God; He caused all of this to happen to me."

One of the pastors at a church I attended once asked his little boy, "Who pooped your diaper?" The toddler proceeded to point to someone else in the room and said, "They did." We laugh at that toddler's story because it's so ridiculous, but people do that in every area of their life. And when people allow themselves to stay in a "they-pooped-my-diaper" mode, those feelings of resentment will take root way down deep in their heart.

I heard a story told about a set of identical twin boys. They were raised together in the same less-than-ideal family environment. Years later, one was convicted of a crime and sent to prison. When interviewed about his situation, he said, "With the way I was raised, with what I saw and had to go through as a child, what other choice did I have?" The second twin had become the head of a large corporation. When interviewed about his rise to the top, he said, "With the way I was raised, with what I saw and had to go through as a child, what other choice did I have?" Forgiveness comes down to a decision.

A little boy was mad at his best friend, Andrew. They got into a fight and he told his mother, "I hate Andrew, I never want to see him again—and I hope his dog dies!" The next day he was going out to play and his mother said, "Where are you going?" He said, "I'm going to play with Andrew." She said, "I thought you never wanted to see him again and hoped his dog died?" He said, "Yeah, I said that about Andrew, but me and Andrew are good forgetters."

Recognize your part in the forgiveness process. The word forgiving comes from two words "forth" (which means forward) and "giving." Forgiving literally means forward giving. Do you see what that means? Forgiveness is an exercise of your faith, not your feelings.

God may be asking you to initiate the first move of forgiveness—by faith, give it forward! If you just ignore the wound, it will not go away. Make the decision to give forgiveness and make things right as far as it depends on you.

Then, be prepared to receive the promise that when you give love and forgiveness, it will be given back to you in good measure, pressed down, shaken together, and running over (Luke 6:38).

DAY 6

"But when you are praying, first forgive anyone you are holding a grudge against, so that your Father in heaven will forgive your sins, too."

MARK 11:25, NLT

What about a victim mentality? This is the mindset that says, "I am the only one who has been wronged. Woe is me. This and that happened to me." Victimization is some of the most fertile soil for unforgiveness.

During my 11-year tenure in youth ministry, I talked with hundreds of students who had been victimized by friends or family, like a 16-year-old girl who was raped and became pregnant as a result. She was a victim. Most people would agree that she had every right to harbor bitterness and hatred towards her attacker. But instead of allowing unforgiveness and shame to settle in—feelings that could lead her to suicide or abortion—she allowed the Lord to heal her body and her emotions. During that process, she realized that the baby inside of her had done nothing wrong. This child was also a victim. She chose to forgive her attacker and not pass on her anger and resentment to another innocent life. She chose to see her adversity as an opportunity in disguise. The girl came out of a big mess with a big message.

Think about Joseph's life (Genesis 37-50). He was a victim. He was sold into slavery, falsely accused of rape, and sent to prison. When he did favors for people by interpreting their dreams, they forgot about him. But Joseph would never have attained his dreams if he had lived in the past and not forgiven or pardoned those who did him wrong. The way he handled his test left him with quite a testimony.

A victim mentality will keep a person in a losing posture, thinking that they will forever be at the mercy of their unfortunate circumstance. Scripture tells us in John 16:33 that trouble will happen, but it then says, "*be of good cheer*" because Christ has overcome the world. Romans 8:37 AMP says, "*Yet amid all these things [suffering, affliction, tribulation, calamity, distress, persecution, hunger, destruction, peril, or sword] we are more than conquerors and gain a surpassing victory through Him Who loved us*." Listen to what God says! God uses language like overcome, victory, and conqueror.

FORGIVENESS IS GIVING UP THE POSSIBILITY OF A BETTER PAST AND EMBRACING THE REALITY OF AN INCREDIBLE FUTURE.

Jeremiah 29:11 tells us of God's plan to prosper you and not to harm you. He plans to give you a hope and a future. Forgiveness is giving up the possibility of a better past and embracing the reality of an incredible future. Learn to live in God's incredible blessings today by forgiving others for the wrongs you have suffered. As preachers often say, "God wants you to be a victor and not a victim."

DAY 7

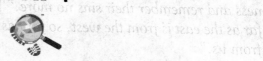

"But when you are praying, first forgive anyone you are holding a grudge against, so that your Father in heaven will forgive your sins, too."

MARK 11:25, NLT

Three longtime friends were out fishing on a boat. After a couple hours without a nibble, they started to get bored.

"I've got an idea," the first man said. "Let's be totally honest with each other and confess our worst sins. I'll go first. I have a big problem with the sin of lust. I've been cheating on my wife for over a year. I just can't seem to control myself."

The second man said, "As long as we're being honest with each other, I'll tell you what my problem is. It's the sin of greed. I just can't get enough money, so I've been embezzling funds from my company for years. I just can't seem to control myself."

The third man said, "Well, my problem is the sin of gossip. Not only can't I control myself, I can't wait to get home!"

How does God respond to our sins? Some people view God as the cop-around-the-corner who can't wait to lay down the law the moment they step out of line, like the third guy in the story who can't wait to go broadcast their failures to the world. But that's exactly the opposite of what God says in His Word that He will do.

Look at the last part of Mark 11:25 NIV: *"your Father in heaven will forgive your sins…"* Isaiah 43:25 says NIV, "*I, even I, am he who blots out your transgressions, for my own sake, and remembers your sins no more.*" Jeremiah 31:34 says NIV, "*I will forgive their wickedness and remember their sins no more.*" Psalms 103:12 says NIV, "*As far as the east is from the west, so far has he removed our transgressions from us.*"

You have been forgiven by God. He gives you a new life through Jesus Christ, so stop looking back on the past. Beating yourself up over past sins and failures is like letting the garbage man haul off your trash, then feeling so bad for creating such a mess that you drive down to the dump, load it all up in your car, and bring it back to your room. It is even worse if you haul it all back because you miss the garbage.

When you come to Jesus, He takes all of the garbage of your old life and throws it into the depths of the sea (Micah 7:19). Then He puts up two signs: one that says, "No fishing!" and one that says, "No swimming or diving!" He forgave you; now forgive yourself. Let it go and do not look back. Don't run away from God when your life gets off track. Run to Him. Ask for forgiveness, and get right back on.

Remember to thank God today that He "*will forgive your sins, too.*"

Week 34

"Confess your sins to each other and pray for each other so that you may be healed. The earnest prayer of a righteous person has great power and produces wonderful results."

James 5:16, NLT

DAY 1

"Confess your sins to each other and pray for each other so that you may be healed. The earnest prayer of a righteous person has great power and produces wonderful results."
JAMES 5:16, NLT

Dynamite is dangerous stuff. But when used properly, it produces powerful results. Construction workers use dynamite to demolish old, worn-out buildings in order to make room for new, state-of-the-art structures. Dynamite is used to reach gold and precious stones buried deep within a mountain. It's also used to blast tunnels and cut paths for highways. Just like dynamite, our prayers have the power to demolish strongholds, protect from harm, and make a way where there seems to be no way.

Daniel interpreted dreams and spent a miraculous night uneaten in a den full of starving lions. The book of Acts mentions that sick people were healed when Peter walked by and his shadow passed over them. Luke talks about miracles happening when Paul's sweatbands would be laid on the sick or demon-possessed. In our minds, we say these men are "way up there" and we are "way down here." We think we're nothing special like that to God.

Not so! James 5:16 says, "*The earnest prayer of a righteous person has great power and produces wonderful results*." Did you catch what that means? It says a good person has great power in prayer. God will use the plain, old, ordinary, good people's prayers in powerful and effective ways.

Right after this verse, James talks about another one of the Heroes of the Faith: Elijah. Elijah prayed down fire from heaven. He prayed and the rain stopped for three and a half years. He prayed again and the rain came back. Do you know what verse 17 of James 5 says about Elijah? "*Elijah was a man just like us*." God answered the prayer of a man who was just like us. Elijah had all the moral weaknesses we do and he didn't have any superpowers.

You don't need to be a spiritual superhero for God to answer your prayer. An ordinary person with an extraordinary faith has the same capacity to be used as Elijah, Peter, Paul, Daniel, or anyone else. Your ability is not nearly as important as your availability.

You are playing with dynamite! And with great power comes great responsibility.

DAY 2

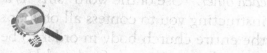

"Confess your sins to each other and pray for each other so that you may be healed. The earnest prayer of a righteous person has great power and produces wonderful results."

JAMES 5:16, NLT

James 5:16 tells us to *"Confess your sins to each other."* Back up a few verses and you will see a few instructions for prayer. James 5:13 says, *"Is any among you afflicted? Let him pray."* James 5:14 then says, *"Is any sick among you? Let him call for the elders of the church; and let them pray over him."*

According to the *Matthew Henry Commentary*, there are three types of effective prayers prescribed to us in these three verses: ministerial, social, and secret. The 13th verse directs people to pray for themselves. The 14th directs people to seek the prayers of ministers. And the 16th directs Christians to pray privately for one another. Let's take a moment to unpack each one.

Pray for yourself: The affliction that James refers to in this verse is suffering hardship. Many of the people who would be reading James' letter had escaped the persecution of Acts 8:1-4, so he was most likely addressing prayer as a way of bringing healing to mental, spiritual, and emotional hurts. The cure for hardship is prayer. James says that the responsibility of the afflicted person is to pray for themselves first.

Pray with elders: People who are sick are instructed to call upon the elders of the church. "*Sick*" not only refers to a physical weakness but to a spiritual or emotional powerlessness as well. And the person who is ill is supposed to take the initiative for prayer.

Pray with others: This verse tells us to "*Confess your sins to each other.*" Use of the word "sins" is a bit misleading. James is not instructing you to confess all of your sins to a priest, pastor, or to the entire church body in order to be forgiven. We are supposed to confess our sins to God and He is faithful and just to forgive us. A better translation would be "confess your faults or trespasses." James urges anyone who has wronged a brother or sister to go to the one they trespassed against and seek forgiveness and reconciliation.

Prayer is our great weapon in times of adversity, physical weakness, emotional powerlessness, and conflict. God promises to hear you when you pray in faith. Jonathan Edwards said, "That which God abundantly makes the subject of His promises, God's people should abundantly make the subject of their prayers." For your prayers to carry their greatest impact and produce the extraordinary results that James talks about, you must pray within the context of the Word of God.

Let God's great power flow through you today. Pray effectively and with great faith. If you do, you can expect wonderful results.

Day 3

"Confess your sins to each other and pray for each other so that you may be healed. The earnest prayer of a righteous person has great power and produces wonderful results."
James 5:16, NLT

We are God's kind of people!

When you take your prayers to God on a continual basis, you are fulfilling one of the basic purposes for your life; you were created for intimate relationship with God. Passion for God and vision for people are two ingredients for a productive and fulfilling life.

Your prayers do not have to be complicated or lengthy. In fact, you will do better if you strive to keep it simple. Martin Luther said, "The fewer the words, the better the prayer." The key is for you to just make sure you are spending time praying.

Why? Because "Love" is spelled T-I-M-E (you get the point). I have seen hundreds of students whose parents made the mistake of thinking that giving them money and things equaled love. But if you talk to those same kids who are feeling lonely and unsatisfied, they will tell you that they would rather be given their parents' time.

Any good habit requires time—*quality* time, not just whatever time is leftover when everything else is taken care of. Just like a marriage or parenting relationship, your prayer relationship with God requires your time, effort, and attention. 1 Timothy 4:7 NLT tells us to "*train yourself to be godly.*" Becoming godly is a choice;

it takes continual spiritual discipline. No one becomes godly by accident. James uses the word "*earnest*" to describe the prayers that are powerful and produce results. "Earnest" means "a serious and intent mental state; a considerable or impressive degree or amount."

The quality and the quantity of your hang-time with God will affect everything you do. "He who runs from God in the morning will scarcely find Him the rest of the day," John Bunyan wrote. Earnestly spending time with God in prayer enables you to see your life, school, work, relationships, health, finances, attitudes, and reactions—good *and* bad—from God's perspective.

Let God lead and guide you in your prayers. Let Him open up your eyes to what you and the others around you really need.

If you spend time finding out the will of God in your life, your prayers will take on a whole new power and effectiveness every day.

DAY 4

"Confess your sins to each other and pray for each other so that you may be healed. The earnest prayer of a righteous person has great power and produces wonderful results."

JAMES 5:16, NLT

Today let's read some different translations of James 5:16 to gain a better understanding of the passage. At the end you can journal your thoughts on a blank sheet of paper or in your personal journal.

Therefore confess your sins to each other and pray for each other so that you may be healed. The prayer of a righteous man is powerful and effective. NIV

Therefore, confess your sins to one another, and pray for one another so that you may be healed. The effective prayer of a righteous man can accomplish much. NASB

Make this your common practice: Confess *your sins to each other and pray for each other so that you can live together whole and healed. The prayer of a person living right with* God *is something powerful to be reckoned with.* MSG

Confess to one another therefore your faults (your slips, your false steps, your offenses, your sins) and pray [also] for one another, that you may be healed and restored [to a spiritual tone of mind and heart]. The earnest (heartfelt, continued) prayer of a righteous man makes tremendous power available [dynamic in its working]. AMP

Confess your trespasses to one another, and pray for one another, that you may be healed. The effective, fervent prayer of a righteous man avails much. NKJV

If you have sinned, you should tell each other what you have done. Then you can pray for one another and be healed. The prayer of an innocent person is powerful, and it can help a lot. CEV

Suggestions:

- Prayerfully reflect on these verses and record the thoughts that God, through the Holy Spirit, is dropping into your heart. Ask a question such as, "God, what truth are you trying to communicate to me?"
- Write a letter to God.
- Make notes about what you're learning.
- Compose a prayer.
- Draw a picture of your praise.

DAY 5

"Confess your sins to each other and pray for each
other so that you may be healed. The earnest
prayer of a righteous person has great power
and produces wonderful results."
JAMES 5:16, NLT

Are you adventuresome enough to pray? Do you have the intestinal fortitude to make your requests known to God? Are you willing to step out of your comfort zone and experiment with an explosive mindset?

A righteous person's prayers make them a real "dynamo." Today we are going to look at some of the most dangerous prayers we can pray. Dangerous because, when prayed, they can do a lot of positive damage in you and for the Kingdom of God.

"God, enlarge me." Isaiah 54:2 NIV says, "*Enlarge the place of your tent, stretch your tent curtains wide, do not hold back, lengthen your cords*." Your prayer should be for God to stretch your vision and enlarge your impact for Him. Just like a rubber band, we do not fulfill our intended purpose until we are stretched by hands that see a greater potential for us. You may experience some discomfort for a while, but in the end you will stretch farther and accomplish more for God than you ever thought possible.

"God, renew me." Psalm 51:10 NIV says, "*Create in me a pure heart,* O God, *and renew a steadfast spirit within me*." Are you willing to allow God into your heart's home; to go into every room and closet of your life? Psalm 139:23-24 NIV says, "*Search me,* O God, *and know my heart; test me and know my anxious thoughts*.

See if there is any offensive way in me, and lead me in the way everlasting." Are you willing to look at what He finds there?

"God, direct me." Proverbs 3:5-6 AMP says, "*Lean on, trust in, and be confident in the Lord with all your heart and mind and do not rely on your own insight or understanding. In all your ways know, recognize, and acknowledge Him, and He will direct and make straight and plain your paths.*" Are you willing to not only know God's direction, but also to trust, believe, and follow it?

"God, break me." Prayer like this is asking God to break us of habits, hang-ups, or hand-me-downs. It's asking God to break any hardness in our heart and to bring us back to our first love, which is Christ. Hosea 10:12 NKJV says, "*Break up your fallow ground for it is time to seek the LORD*"

"God, send me." Luke 10:2 NIV says, "*He told them, 'The harvest is plentiful, but the workers are few. Ask the Lord of the harvest, therefore, to send out workers into his harvest field.'*" The workers Jesus speaks of are not just missionaries in other lands. You are a worker who is called into that harvest field, too! Are you courageous enough to pray that God would send you to minister to people who need His touch every day? Isaiah 6:8 NIV says, "*Then I heard the voice of the Lord saying, 'Whom shall I send? And who will go for us?' And I said, 'Here am I. Send me!'*"

The Greek word *dunamis* is often used in conjunction with the activity of the Holy Spirit in the life of a believer. *Dunamis* means "power" or "force," and it is the root for our words: dynamic, dynamite, and dynamo.

Are you ready for some powerful results? Pray these dangerous prayers and let the dynamite activity of the Holy Spirit go to work through you.

DAY 6

"Confess your sins to each other and pray for each other so that you may be healed. The earnest prayer of a righteous person has great power and produces wonderful results."

JAMES 5:16, NLT

If anyone ever knew how to pray effectively, it was Jesus.

The disciples must have realized that there was power in effective prayer. They watched Jesus preach with authority, feed crowds, walk on water, heal the sick, cast out demons, and bring people back from the dead. Even though they were present when all of this happened, they still asked Jesus to teach them how to pray: *"One day Jesus was praying in a certain place. When he finished, one of his disciples said to him, 'Lord, teach us to pray, just as John taught his disciples'"* (Luke 11:1, NIV).

This scenario with the disciples and Jesus reminds me of a story about a young boy learning to pray.

> Five year old Johnny asked his daddy for a baby brother and offered to do whatever he could to help. His dad thought for a moment and said, "I'll tell you what. If you pray every day for two months, I guarantee that God will give you a brother!"
>
> Johnny took his dad's challenge to heart and began praying for a baby brother. He prayed every night for a month, but he began to lose faith when nothing was happening. He asked around and found out that what he was hoping for had never occurred in the history of the whole neighborhood. "You just don't pray for two months and then get a new baby brother," he was told. So, Johnny quit praying.

After another month, Johnny's mother went to the hospital. When she came back home, Johnny's parents called him into the bedroom.

He walked in, not expecting to find anything. He noticed a blanket next to his mother. He pulled it back to reveal not just one baby brother but two! His mother had twins.

Johnny's dad said, "Now aren't you glad you prayed?"

Johnny hesitated a little and then looked up and said, "Yes, but aren't you glad I quit when I did?"

Johnny's dad already knew his son's prayers would be answered. Your heavenly Father also knows in advance whether or not our prayers will be answered. He can see the future. And the Bible also tells us that God knows our wants and needs, even before we ask. So why pray? Because God wants us to participate in the process—among other things, by demonstrating our faith in and dependence on Him.

Prayer doesn't change God; it changes things.

God's hand is moved by our prayers. Someone once said that prayer is more than a wish; it is the voice of faith directed to God. Prayer doesn't change God; it changes *things*. God knows that you need things before you ever ask. He knows exactly when you need your prayers answered, too. But He says to pray anyway! When you pray you are bringing yourself into submission with what God already wills and has planned for your life.

Don't forfeit your right to influence your future in this way. Life change, direction, and provision are in His hand and they are just an earnest prayer away.

DAY 7

"Confess your sins to each other and pray for each other so that you may be healed. The earnest prayer of a righteous person has great power and produces wonderful results."

JAMES 5:16, NLT

Some people say, "I tried prayer once and it didn't work." They were left with questions like "Is God really there? And, if He is, does He even care about me?" We need to realize that God answers every prayer, but sometimes His answer is "No!"

Jesus taught his disciples to pray this way: *"Your will be done."* If you are going to pray God's will, you have to be ready for some "yes" answers and some "no" answers. And you have to be ready to be okay with it.

I heard this story of a little boy named Jimmy who wanted to be a cowboy. He spent a lot of time watching old western movies and television shows.

When he was seven, Jimmy said, "Dad, I want to be a cowboy when I grow up. Will you help me?"

"Sure, son," said his dad.

Jimmy grew into a fine young man. And, as you might expect, he outgrew his childhood fantasy of becoming a cowboy, and turned instead to girls, sports, studying, and preparing for a career in business.

One day, Jimmy went to his father and said, "Dad, I want to go to college. Will you help me?"

His dad said, "College? Son, you can't go to college. When you were seven, you said you wanted to be a cowboy. So I bought you a ranch in Texas with 50 head of cattle! There's no money left for college. And, you need to take care of your ranch."

Jimmy replied, "But, Dad! I was just a child when I said that! I didn't know then what I know now! I don't want a ranch! I want an education!"

Sometimes we are kind of like Jimmy; we don't know what's best for us. Sometimes we ask with the wrong motives. Sometimes we ask things that are the will of God, but not the right time. Sometimes we just don't have enough perspective to know that we are still growing and that we won't always want the same things we want now. We need to be ready for a "yes" or a "no" and be thankful for whatever answer He gives, trusting that God's wisdom and perspective are much better than ours.

Our heavenly Father knows exactly what we need (even when we don't) and we should be thankful that God doesn't answer our prayers according to our will. Who knows what we would wind up with? Instead of grumbling about prayers going unanswered, learn to be grateful.

When you pray "Your will be done," God is released to work behind the scenes for your advantage.

When you pray *"Your will be done,"* God is released to work behind the scenes for your advantage. In Romans 8 the Bible teaches that the Holy Spirit will pray for us, because we do not always know what to ask. If you will pray like Jesus taught the disciples, you will be able to rest at ease, knowing that whatever happens will be according to God's will.

James says that it is the *"righteous person"* whose prayers get answered. You not only need to pray God's will be done, but you'd better also be doing God's will if you expect results. God's first priority, after all, is your spiritual condition. 2 Chronicles 7:14-15 NIV says, "*If my people, who are called by my name, will humble themselves and pray and seek my face and turn from their wicked ways, then will I hear from heaven and will forgive their sin and will heal their land. Now my eyes will be open and my ears attentive to the prayers offered in this place.*" God does not answer the prayers of those who have no commitment to do His will. At the same time, our obedience and loyalty to God results in our heard and quickly-answered prayers.

I want to leave you with a few prayers that always get answered. These prayers are really the very heartbeat of our Heavenly Father: "Save me." "Forgive me." "Change me." "Use me." "Save them." The reason these prayers always get answered is because they fall in line with truths in the scriptures.

When you approach God with Spirit-inspired prayer that is based on the things He's already promised in His Word, He *will* answer you.

WEEK 35

"Blessed are those who hunger and thirst for righteousness, for they shall be satisfied."

MATTHEW 5:6, NASB

DAY 1

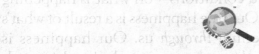

"Blessed are those who hunger and thirst for righteousness, for they shall be satisfied."

MATTHEW 5:6, NASB

This verse lands right in the middle of one of Jesus' best-known teachings: the Beatitudes, part of the famous Sermon on the Mount. People had come from towns covering more than a 100-mile radius to listen to Jesus teach (Matthew 4:25). They walked literally hundreds of miles to see Jesus that day.

Jesus began each statement of the Beatitudes with the word "*blessed*" or "*happy*" (you can read all of the Beatitudes in Matthew 5:3-11). He points out the attitudes that will successfully lead our pursuit to true happiness, which is something Americans can really get behind; one of the distinctive statements of our Constitution is that Americans have the right to the pursuit of happiness.

God wants you to be completely happy—inside and out! You may be going through some difficult times in your life right now and you're thinking to yourself, "How can I be happy when such horrible things are happening to me?" The truth is that maybe you can't; it depends on how you define happiness.

To the world, happiness is an emotional feeling based on circumstances. But if you dig a little deeper into the word "blessed," you find that it doesn't just mean "happy." The more complete definition of that word in the Beatitudes is something like "*to be envied and spiritually prosperous with life-joy and satisfaction in God's favor and salvation, regardless of the outward conditions*" (AMP).

Did you catch that last part? Our true happiness is not a variable that depends on your outward conditions—on what is happening *to* us. Our true happiness is a result of what's happening *through* us. Our happiness is dependent upon our relationship with God, and He never changes.

Our true happiness is not a variable that depends on your outward conditions. Our true happiness is a result of what's happening through us.

In his most famous psalm, David said, *"Even though I walk in the valley of deep shadow, I fear nothing, for you are with me"* (Psalm 23:4, NWT). Scientifically speaking, we know that whenever there is a shadow, then there is also a source of light. Awhile back the band *Switchfoot* recorded a song about this truth entitled "The Shadow Proves the Sunshine." David chose to focus on God's presence with him (one of God's names is Jehovah Ori: God is Light) rather than the shadow being cast over him.

David said he was just passing through the valley. He knew that the valley time was temporary and would soon pass. You may have times where you feel like things are falling apart and you may feel like doing something out of desperation, but don't do it! Instead, call out to God in faith: "Lord, I'm not going to panic; I'm not going to fear. Your word says that you will deliver me from this situation. This did not come to stay; it came to be passed through! I am going to be of good cheer."

Scripture says, *"Blessed are the people whose God is the Lord"* (Psalm 33:12, NIV). David wrote, *"Blessed (or happy) is the man whose sins are forgiven"* (Psalm 32:1, NIV). You cannot find sad, long-faced, depressed Christianity in the stories of New Testament believers, even in really terrible situations like starvation, imprisonment, torture, and horrible sickness. God's people should be the most genuinely happy people on earth.

Make the choice to live blessed today by living in the knowledge that God is with you.

In the John 16:33 Jesus says, *"In this world you will have trouble: but be of good cheer, I have overcome the world."* Joy isn't supposed to just stay down in your heart so that you are joyful on the inside but miserable on the outside. It's time for your heart to remind your face of who is in control!

Where is your focus?

Are you seeing the dark cloud or are you seeing the silver lining?

DAY 2

"Blessed are those who hunger and thirst for
righteousness, for they shall be satisfied."
MATTHEW 5:6, NASB

Craving. You know how it works. You get fixated on something specific—a food or drink gets stuck in your mind—and you want it so badly that you make a pit stop during a road trip at the first exit with that sign, or you make a 2:00am run for "4th Meal" at Taco Bell.

For me it's Mountain Dew. I *love* to drink Mountain Dew. I crave it so much sometimes that I'll choose a restaurant not by its food but by whether or not their drink menu includes it. I love to take my family to Disneyland, but you can't get Mountain Dew there. I have to choke down Coke products all week. Every time I return from a vacation to Disneyland, one of the first things I do is go to a convenience store and help myself to a 32-ounce Mountain Dew. Nothing satisfies my thirst quite like it; it's sad, I know, but it's true.

Hunger and thirst is the perfect illustration for this truth. We can all completely relate to what Jesus is saying; every day we get hungry and every day we get thirsty. We can never be completely satisfied.

Of course, Jesus isn't just talking about a good sit-down dinner after a long, hard day of work or about an electrolyte-enhanced sports drink after an exhausting workout. There is a different kind of hunger and thirst that all we all have—a need for spiritual satisfaction, for being right with God. Jesus knew it, and we all feel it.

The concept is almost cliché now but it was Blaise Pascal, a brilliant mathematician and philosopher in the 17th century, who first said, "There is a God-shaped vacuum in the heart of every man which cannot be filled by any created thing, but only by God the Creator." The common system of thought is that if we just had a bigger car, a newer house, a new boyfriend or girl-friend, a different husband or wife, a better fix or drug or drink, more than minimum wage, a trophy, a better prom picture on the wall...*then* we would be satisfied. But all of these inevitably lead to a deeper feeling of dissatisfaction and a continual search for answers. Why? Because they cannot fill that God-shaped vacuum (absence of matter; completely empty area or space).

Do you want your entire life—your family, your relationships, and your work—to be blessed? Have you been feeling spiritually empty lately? Make a new commitment today to hunger and thirst for what God offers instead of what the world offers. Start filling the void inside with more of His words, more of His truth, and more of His promises on a daily basis, even if you can't honestly say that you hunger and thirst for righteousness.

If you'll do it, you'll find your hunger and thirst for righteousness begin to increase as well. Jesus promises happiness and satisfaction to those whose deepest cravings are for spiritual blessings.

Day 3

"Blessed are those who hunger and thirst for
righteousness, for they shall be satisfied."
Matthew 5:6, NASB

Most of us know what it's like to be hungry. Some of us know what it's like to be extremely hungry. But very few of us know what it's like to be starving.

A lot of people will go hungry today, and I am in no way making light of the serious issue of hunger. I've fed hungry people under bridges in Portland and Los Angeles, and I've also helped feed starving people in those places. How can I tell the difference? Because I've seen the difference between hunger and starvation firsthand. The hungry will line up for the food, but if they don't care for or need what's being handed out that day, they will reject it. The starving will also line up for food, but they wind up at the front of the line because they show up early to be sure to get some food that day. Starving people never reject the food being offered; without it, they might not survive until food comes again. I even tell my own kids, "If you're not hungry enough to eat what's on your plate, you're not hungry enough."

The word "*hunger*" in Matthew 5:6 means to crave or to suffer want. "*Thirst*" means to painfully feel the want of those things by which the soul is refreshed. You see, Jesus is not just talking about an "I've missed a couple of meals today, so I think I'll get a snack" hunger or an "I've got a little tickle in my throat, so I think I'll take a sip" thirst. He's talking about a full-blown need to feast on and gulp down God's presence in order to not die. He's talking about the kind of desire that desperately cries out, "God, I cannot survive a day without You!"

Luke 10 tells the story of a prodigal son who takes his inheritance, leaves his father, and wanders far away. The son wastes everything he has on friends, parties, and pursuits that did not satisfy him. When his money was all gone, so were his friends. Before coming to his senses and returning home, he finds himself living with pigs and eating the slop they ate. J.N. Darby said, "To be hungry is not enough; I must be really starving to know what is in God's heart towards me. When the prodigal son was hungry he went to feed upon husks, but when he was starving, he turned to his father."

To be hungry is not enough; I must be really starving to know what is in God's heart towards me.

David said in Psalm 42:1 AMP, "*As the deer pants [cries or longs] for streams of water, so my soul pants for you, O God.*" How do your desires compare? Does your soul cry out or long for God's presence, power, provision, and protection?

Those words—hunger and thirst—are strong words. If you develop them seriously in your life towards God, these words will literally change the way you live.

Tell God that you desire more of Him in your life today.

Ask God to fill you up on a daily basis.

DAY 4

"Blessed are those who hunger and thirst for
righteousness, for they shall be satisfied."
MATTHEW 5:6, NASB

Today you are invited to read some different translations of Matthew 5:6 and write down your thoughts. Use an extra piece of paper, or your own personal journal.

"Blessed are those who hunger and thirst for righteousness, for they shall be filled." NKJV

"God blesses those who hunger and thirst for justice, for they will be satisfied." NLT

"God blesses those people who want to obey him more than to eat or drink. They will be given what they want!" CEV

"God makes happy those who are hungry and thirsty for what is right and good. They will be filled." Worldwide English Translation

"You're blessed when you've worked up a good appetite for God. *He's food and drink in the best meal you'll ever eat."* MSG

"Blessed and fortunate and happy and spiritually prosperous (in that state in which the born-again child of God enjoys His favor and salvation) are those who hunger and thirst for righteousness (uprightness and right standing with God), for they shall be completely satisfied!" AMP

Suggestions:

- Prayerfully reflect on these verses and record the thoughts that God, through the Holy Spirit, is dropping into your heart. Ask a question such as, "God, what truth are you trying to communicate to me?"
- Write a letter to God.
- Make notes about what you're learning.
- Compose a prayer.
- Draw a picture of your praise.

Day 5

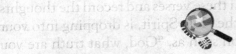

"Blessed are those who hunger and thirst for righteousness, for they shall be satisfied."

Matthew 5:6, NASB

Our culture is fixated on the pursuit of happiness. But what is it that makes happiness always seem just beyond our grasp, always pursued but never reached? I believe the answer is right here in Jesus' teaching from Matthew 5:6.

Read what Chuck Smith said in his Bible commentary: "Jesus did not say blessed (happy) is the man that pursues happiness. Happiness is found in righteousness. It is the direct by-product of righteousness."

Did you catch that? Your happiness is directly proportional to your righteousness.

Take a closer look at what righteousness means. Righteousness is "the condition of being acceptable to God; integrity; rightness; correctness of thinking, feeling, and acting." That means being a good person and living clean, right? No! What many people don't realize is that being acceptable to God has very little to do with your outside actions and everything to do with your inside conditions. Being acceptable to God is an issue of the heart. Just look at the Pharisees in the Bible. They were outwardly righteous: holy, obeying the law, and doing the right things, but inwardly hypocritical, corrupt, and missing the point.

The Scriptures say that not one of us is righteous on our own. You can't read your Bible, pray, go to church, sponsor orphans, tithe, or filter web pages and satellite TV channels enough to be acceptable to God. Why? Because we owe a debt we cannot pay with moral observances: *"Everyone sins; we all fall short of God's glorious standard"* (Romans 3:23, NLT). The good news is that righteousness is actually much easier than obeying a bunch of rules. Jesus, by the cross, already paid off our debt. It was a debt He did not owe, because *"Christ never sinned"* (2 Corinthians 5:21, CEV).

Sometimes it's easiest to wrap our heads around this in financial terms. Our debt (sin) was transferred to Jesus' account while He was on the cross, and His righteousness gets transferred to our account when we accept and choose to follow Him. From the moment of belief on, God treats us just as if we had never owed Him a dime. God's favor is the product of Christ's righteousness, period! We are legally declared "not guilty" by our association with Jesus.

> YOU CAN'T READ YOUR BIBLE, PRAY, GO TO CHURCH, SPONSOR ORPHANS, TITHE, OR FILTER WEB PAGES AND SATELLITE TV CHANNELS ENOUGH TO BE ACCEPTABLE TO GOD.

Here are some thoughts about what hungering and thirsting after righteousness looks like:

1. Desiring to love God more than you love your sin; not just to be forgiven of sin, but to be free from the desire to sin.
2. Desiring to live in constant fellowship with the Father.
3. Desiring to be like Jesus—to follow His example, to be holy and pure, and do only the things that please the Father.
4. Desiring to be in the Word and in contact with other believers on a regular basis.

Matthew 6:33 NLT tells us to, *"Seek the Kingdom of God above all else, and live righteously, and he will give you everything you need."*

I guarantee that your happiness and satisfaction are included in the "everything" else.

Years ago, I went to a Christian youth camp and the speaker said, "If God seems far away tonight, go back to the place where you left Him." He told us to picture a circle on the floor, to step inside that circle, then kneel down and "do not leave until God does what He needs to do in your heart."

If God seems far away to you, I invite you to do the same.

The opposite of hunger and thirst for God is a casual attitude towards Him.

Does full-blown hunger and thirst characterize your pursuit of God today or does "casual" better describe you?

Is your relationship with Christ a duty or a desire?

DAY 6

"Blessed are those who hunger and thirst for righteousness, for they shall be satisfied."

MATTHEW 5:6, NASB

Are you feeling full?

Satisfied means "to gorge, supply food in abundance, to fill, or fulfill the desires." The song "Satisfaction" was as controversial as it was popular when first released by the *Rolling Stones* back in June of 1965.

> 'cause I try,
> and I try,
> and I try,
> and I try.
> I can't get no...no satisfaction.

Mick Jagger wrote these lyrics as an expression of how he couldn't find satisfaction in anything. He was dissatisfied with the things he usually enjoyed: celebrity, sexuality, money, and commercialism. And Mick Jagger was absolutely right; you cannot satisfy the God-shaped hole yourself.

Ever heard of the law of diminishing returns? It says that today's input will yield less output tomorrow. In other words, not enough is being deposited to keep up with what's being withdrawn. It is the way the world's empty system operates. Today's drug won't produce the same high or help you cope tomorrow. The current relationship won't produce the same feelings as when you first hooked up. Two drinks today won't give you the same buzz or numb the pain like it did last night. The newer and better toy will make you dissatisfied with yours. The law of diminishing returns is the slippery slope that thrusts individuals down the path of a diction, divorce, pornography, abuse, alcholism, and debt. The world brings momentary happiness, but will always leave a greater thirst than ever.

> The world brings momentary happiness, but will always leave a greater thirst than ever.

Righteousness is the only pursuit that completely satisfies (or fills) the void inside. God wants to fill your life with good things (Psalm 103:5). But before you find yourself hungry for the good stuff, you have to be emptied of all the junk. If I stop at a convenience store for junk food on my way home from work, there is no way that I will be hungry for the fantastic, healthy, and well-balanced meal waiting at home. I won't have an appetite for my wife's cooking if I'm full of Mountain Dew and Funyuns.

The *Jon Courson New Testament Commentary* explains it this way:

> "Some people have lost their appetite for the Word of God. They no longer desire to worship; they no longer crave righteousness, because they are full of self-importance. When you empty yourself of self, happy you are because you're going to hunger once more for righteousness."

Begin to empty yourself of the pride of self-reliance today. Spend a little more time than usual in God's Word and in prayer. Steep yourself in the reality that God knows what you need before you even ask. You don't have to worry about missing out on anything. You will find a renewed hunger and thirst for righteousness and a deeper sense of satisfaction.

Don't hesitate. He's waiting to fill you today!

DAY 7

"Blessed are those who hunger and thirst for righteousness, for they shall be satisfied."
MATTHEW 5:6, NASB

John 4 introduces us to a Samaritan woman who has gone to the local well to draw water for the day. Jesus is there by the well and begins to dialogue with her about *"living water"* that He can give her; the kind of water that will keep a person from thirsting ever again. The woman responds by saying, *"Sir, give me this water, so I will never have to come back to the well again!"* (John 4:15, MSG)

HE KNEW SHE WASN'T JUST THIRSTY; SHE HAD A NEED.

The woman was thinking of the physical, but Jesus was talking about the spiritual and eternal. He knew she wasn't just thirsty; she had a need.

A few years ago, I had pneumonia. Before I was hospitalized and literally closer to death than life, I remember trying to get rid of my horrible cough by drinking water. I felt lousy. I couldn't figure out why I couldn't stop coughing, so I just kept drinking water. But I wasn't just thirsty or dehydrated; I needed healing.

Jesus leads the Samaritan woman to discover His identity by referring to her personal life. The woman's spiritual lights came on and she finally recognizes who Jesus is: the Messiah.

Excited, the woman runs back to her village and proclaims, *"Come see a man who knew all about the things I did, who knows me inside and out. Do you think this could be the Messiah? And they went out to see for themselves*" (John 4:29, 30 MSG). The result of her finding satisfaction in the Messiah led to a whole village coming back to meet Jesus. That group of people had to include the majority of the most important people in her life.

Do you have family, friends, teammates, coworkers, or other people around you who need hope today? When you really get thirsty for Jesus, like the woman at the well, people will naturally come to see Him—out of curiosity, if nothing else. John 7:37 NIV says, "*On the last and greatest day of the Feast, Jesus stood and said in a loud voice, "If anyone is thirsty let him come to me and drink.*""

This world is more than just thirsty; it needs a Savior.

Week 36

Her sister, Mary, sat at the Lord's feet, listening to what
he taught. But Martha was distracted by the big
dinner she was preparing. She came to Jesus and said,
"Lord, doesn't it seem unfair to you that my
sister just sits here while I do all the work?
Tell her to come and help me."
But the Lord said to her, "My dear Martha,
you are worried and upset over all these details!
There is only one thing worth being
concerned about. Mary has discovered it, and it
will not be taken away from her."

Luke 10:39-42, NLT

DAY 1

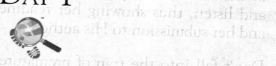

Her sister, Mary, sat at the Lord's feet, listening to what
he taught. But Martha was distracted by the big
dinner she was preparing. She came to Jesus and said,
"Lord, doesn't it seem unfair to you that my
sister just sits here while I do all the work?
Tell her to come and help me."
But the Lord said to her, "My dear Martha,
you are worried and upset over all these details!
There is only one thing worth being
concerned about. Mary has discovered it, and it
will not be taken away from her."

LUKE 10:39-42, NLT

Jesus traveled from place to place with His disciples, often meeting in private homes where He depended upon the hospitality of others. He also traveled with a lot of people, sometimes sending them out "*two by two*" into the villages ahead of Him. Some commentaries say that at least seventy traveled with Him all the time.

On the day of our verse, Jesus chose to meet at the house of Mary and Martha, who lived in Bethany with their brother Lazarus. You can picture the crowd that had just descended on their house that day!

Mary and Martha chose two different ways of responding to Jesus when He came to their house. Martha served and entertained Christ and the people with him. She welcomed them into her home with great hospitality. Interestingly, the name Martha means lady or mistress; Martha was the older of the two sisters and culturally that meant she had the role of mistress (or lady of the house). Mary, however, chose to sit at the feet of Jesus and listen, thus showing her readiness to receive His teaching and her submission to His authority.

Don't fall into the trap of prematurely judging one action over the other. Although Martha receives a reprimand about letting her well-intentioned busyness distract her from the main thing (Jesus), it is important to learn that there is a time to "sit and listen" as well as a time to "go and do." The *Luke: Interpretation Commentary* says, "If we censure Martha too harshly, she may abandon serving altogether, and if we commend Mary too profusely, she may sit there forever. There is a time to go and do; there is a time to listen and reflect. Knowing which and when are matters of spiritual discernment."

> It is important to learn that there is a time to "sit and listen" as well as a time to "go and do."

If you were to ask Jesus which example would be better for us to follow, Martha's or Mary's, His answer would most likely be "Yes." The *Jamieson Fausset Brown* commentary puts it this way: "A Church full of Mary's would perhaps be as great an evil as a Church full of Martha's. Both are needed, each to be the complement of the other." If you want to effectively serve Jesus, you must spend time listening to what He teaches. If you want to sit at His feet, He's soon going to ask you to get up and help somebody in need.

The book My Heart, Christ's Home invites readers to imagine Jesus coming into the "home" of their heart and exploring what He desires for each room. Does your "home" value hearing as well as doing God's Word (James 1:22)?

Ask God for discernment to help you balance going to church and spending time in the Word and prayer with participating on ministry teams and in active service.

Effectiveness only follows time spent at the feet of Jesus.

DAY 2

Her sister, Mary, sat at the Lord's feet, listening to what he taught. But Martha was distracted by the big dinner she was preparing. She came to Jesus and said, "Lord, doesn't it seem unfair to you that my sister just sits here while I do all the work? Tell her to come and help me."
But the Lord said to her, "My dear Martha, you are worried and upset over all these details! There is only one thing worth being concerned about. Mary has discovered it, and it will not be taken away from her."
LUKE 10:39-42, NLT

The guests have arrived, Jesus is teaching, and Martha is serving. She is busy providing the food and entertainment. She no doubt wants everything to be exactly right for her guests. My wife, Kaci, has the gift of hospitality. I've watched her make our friends and families feel welcome in our home for more than 15 years. Largely because of my wife, I can have a deep appreciation for Martha's heart. I have also traveled on mission trips with outreach teams where we relied heavily on the hospitality of strangers to help with our room and board needs.

Martha's work was absolutely worthy of praise. But her obsessiveness about it was not. Despite her good intentions, there was something to be corrected. Martha was "*distracted*" by many things. The Greek word for distracted means: "to be pulled in all directions or to be driven about mentally."

What opposing forces were pulling at Martha's life? What is pulling at our lives? Verse 38 of Luke 10 says, "*Martha welcomed him into her home*." Martha loved Jesus, but she was distracted by serving too much. She had too many tasks. She was doing so many good things, that she neglected the main thing: Jesus—the reason everyone came to her house in the first place. Being busy is a snare when it pulls us everywhere except towards sitting and learning at the feet of Jesus. Martha was busy, but she was not being blessed.

Psalm 103:5 says that God will fill your life with good things. Recreation, family, entertainment, athletics, hobbies, and religious work (like ministry and service) can bring you a certain degree of enjoyment and satisfaction. But every time you say "yes" to one of these things, you are saying "no" to something else. Do not neglect the needed things: the salvation of Christ, the favor of God, or the time spent in His presence on a daily basis!

God help us to not let our lives get so full of good things that we are pulled in all directions, or driven about mentally, to the point that we don't have time to sit and worship at the feet of Jesus.

DAY 3

Her sister, Mary, sat at the Lord's feet, listening to what
he taught. But Martha was distracted by the big
dinner she was preparing. She came to Jesus and said,
"Lord, doesn't it seem unfair to you that my
sister just sits here while I do all the work?
Tell her to come and help me."
But the Lord said to her, "My dear Martha,
you are worried and upset over all these details!
There is only one thing worth being
concerned about. Mary has discovered it, and it
will not be taken away from her."
LUKE 10:39-42, NLT

The guests have arrived, Jesus is teaching, and Mary is sitting at the feet of Jesus. The custom of sitting beneath an instructor—"sitting at one's feet"—was an action of a disciple. Mary appears three different times in the Gospels (Matthew 26, Luke 10, and John 11) and each time we see her sitting at the feet of Jesus.

In that day, a typical rabbi did not even talk to women in public, let alone allow them to sit at their feet and be disciples. But Jesus had a way of breaking all of the religious stereotypes. Jesus not only teaches the Word to Mary, but also says it is the best thing for her to concern herself with.

Riveted by both teacher and teaching, Mary does not notice the distraction of Martha's appeal for help with the work. The word used for the way Mary was listening means that she kept listening.

I've been privileged to coach many good high school basketball players, but two of them I would consider to have been outstanding. They both went on to play basketball at very high levels—one even reaching the NBA. Both players were as different from each other as two people could get, except for two characteristics. First, when I talked, their eyes were fixed on me and they listened to every word I said. Second, they refused to cut corners or give less than 100% effort in anything. While other players would be distracted, watching the clock, or not giving their best, these two guys kept listening and giving their all. This is a picture of Mary. No matter what distractions are trying to pull her away, she just keeps listening and giving her best at the feet of Jesus.

When we see Mary in the Gospels, she is not only sitting at the feet of Jesus, but she is also being misunderstood. In this passage, instead of Martha approving of her sister's devotion to Jesus, she condemned her lack of care for the household duties. The two basketball players I mentioned before also took a lot of flack from their teammates and friends for always choosing to do the right things instead of following the path of the ordinary.

> If you choose to honor God above what may be popular, you will be misunderstood. Listen and do what the Word and the Spirit say anyway.

When you choose to sit at the feet of Jesus, expect your actions to be misunderstood. When you keep listening to Christ, you will receive hostility from enemies and judgment from your friends. "Why don't you do what I am doing? Do you think you are better than me?" they will say. An interesting verse found in 1 Corinthians 2:14 NLT says, "*But people who aren't spiritual can't receive these truths from God's Spirit. It all sounds foolish to them and they can't understand it, for only those who are spiritual can understand what the Spirit means.*" If you choose to honor God above what may be popular, you will be misunderstood. Listen and do what the Word and the Spirit say anyway.

In tough economic times or when life gets difficult, many people seek God and spend time at His feet. But when life gets back to normal, they soon disappear (The *Jon Courson New Testament Commentary*). Be like Mary. In hard times or happy imes, concern yourself only with Christ. Spend time at His feet. You will experience intimacy with the Lord and He will cause everything in your life to work for your good.

He will take you to higher levels than you could ever ask or imagine.

DAY 4

Her sister, Mary, sat at the Lord's feet, listening to what
he taught. But Martha was distracted by the big
dinner she was preparing. She came to Jesus and said,
"Lord, doesn't it seem unfair to you that my
sister just sits here while I do all the work?
Tell her to come and help me."
But the Lord said to her, "My dear Martha,
you are worried and upset over all these details!
There is only one thing worth being
concerned about. Mary has discovered it, and it
will not be taken away from her."

LUKE 10:39-42, NLT

Today you have an opportunity to relate to this passage using the Ignatian Meditation method. This idea is adapted from Ignatius of Loyola, a spiritual leader in the sixteenth century who invited people to use their imaginations to recreate a story in the Scripture. This exercise can help you get face-to-face with the Scriptures and with Jesus.

Step 1 - Read the entire Bible passage: Luke 10:38-42.

Step 2 - Read the entire Bible passage again. This time, choose a new viewpoint in which to engage the story. Four viewpoint suggestions:

- **Go there!** Position yourself somewhere in the story. Where do you see yourself? Who are you standing or sitting next to? What would you have seen if you had been in the house? What do you hear? Who is there with you? Are you one of the bystanders in the crowd watching? What are people saying? What do you think? Do you meet Jesus? Do you speak to him? What does he say to you? Imagine yourself observing the story as it unfolds.

- **Be there!** Use the rest of your senses to experience the scene—touch, smell, listen, and feel.
- **Become a character in the story!** What do they see? How does the character feel?
- **Be you!** Enter the story as yourself. How would you feel if you were there?

Step 3 - Record the thoughts that God, through the Holy Spirit, drops into your heart as you reread the passage from one of the four suggested perspectives.

Suggestions:

- Prayerfully reflect on these verses and record the thoughts that God, through the Holy Spirit, is dropping into your heart. Ask a question such as, "God, what truth are you trying to communicate to me?"
- Write a letter to God.
- Make notes about what you're learning.
- Compose a prayer.
- Draw a picture of your praise.

Day 5

> Her sister, Mary, sat at the Lord's feet, listening to what he taught. But Martha was distracted by the big dinner she was preparing. She came to Jesus and said, "Lord, doesn't it seem unfair to you that my sister just sits here while I do all the work? Tell her to come and help me."
> But the Lord said to her, "My dear Martha, you are worried and upset over all these details! There is only one thing worth being concerned about. Mary has discovered it, and it will not be taken away from her."
>
> Luke 10:39-42, NLT

A seminary professor had fifteen students who were preparing for Christian ministry. As he was teaching on the story of the Good Samaritan, he passed out envelopes to the students with sealed instructions. Five students received these instructions: "Go across the campus without delay. You have 15 minutes to get to your destination. There is no time to spare. Don't loiter or do anything else, or your grade will be docked." The next five got these instructions: "Go across the campus. You have 45 minutes to do so. You have plenty of time, but don't be slow." The last five's instructions said, "Get to the other side of campus anytime before five o'clock," giving this group about five hours to complete the assignment.

What the students didn't know was that the professor had arranged for several drama majors from a nearby university to position themselves along the path that led across campus. The drama students were instructed to act as though they were suffering and in great need. One pretended to be homeless. Another sat with his head in his hands, crying as if he had just experienced a terrible tragedy. Another acted as if he were in desperate need of medical care.

What happened when the Christian ministry students tried to complete their assignments? None of the students in the first group stopped to offer any help to the "needy" people. Only two students in the second group did. But all five students in the third group took time to stop and help. In today's hectic world, it's no wonder that many people find it hard to make room to both "go and do" and "sit and listen" (adapted from *Tales of the Tardy Oxcart*, Chuck Swindoll).

If you take our passage in its full context, the verses preceding Mary sitting at Jesus' feet and Martha being busy serving Jesus tell an expert in Jewish law the story of the Good Samaritan. The lawyer says to Jesus, "I know and observe everything the Law teaches." Jesus recommends to him the illustration of servant and says, "Go and do the same yourself." Martha says, "Can't you see how hard I am working to serve you?" Jesus recommends the illustration of Mary and says, "Sit and listen for awhile; it's the best part."

> NO WONDER THAT MANY PEOPLE FIND IT HARD TO MAKE ROOM TO BOTH "GO AND DO" AND "SIT AND LISTEN."

How can you know when you should "go and do" and when you should "sit and listen"? The answer is simple: spend time at His feet. At Jesus' feet you will gain wisdom and help to have the right balance in your life.

What you do *with* Him out of love, is way more important than anything you will do *for* Him out of duty.

Day 6

Her sister, Mary, sat at the Lord's feet, listening to what
he taught. But Martha was distracted by the big
dinner she was preparing. She came to Jesus and said,
"Lord, doesn't it seem unfair to you that my
sister just sits here while I do all the work?
Tell her to come and help me."
But the Lord said to her, "My dear Martha,
you are worried and upset over all these details!
There is only one thing worth being
concerned about. Mary has discovered it, and it
will not be taken away from her."
Luke 10:39-42, NLT

Mary can teach us a lot about what it means to worship God. Each of the three times she is mentioned in Scripture we find her worshiping at the feet of Christ.

We find Mary finding her worth at Jesus' feet in Luke 10:42 NLT: *"There is only one thing worth being concerned about. Mary has discovered it, and it will not be taken away from her."* Worship can be translated as "worth-ship." When you worship God, you communicate His worth to you.

We find Mary bringing her worry to Jesus' feet in John 11:32 NLT: *"When Mary arrived and saw Jesus, she fell at his feet and said, "Lord, if only you had been here, my brother would not have died."* Worship and prayer get God's attention. Worship and prayer put us in a position to receive. Prayer is asking for God's power and intervention. Worship is saying, "God, I have faith that you just heard me; now I want to rest in you and let you know how wonderful I think you are!"

We find Mary giving her all at Jesus' feet in John 12:3 NLT: "*Then Mary took a twelve-ounce jar of expensive perfume made from essence of nard, and she anointed Jesus' feet with it, wiping his feet with her hair. The house was filled with the fragrance.*" John 12:5 says that the perfume she used was worth one year's wages. Doing what you were created to do and doing it with all of your heart, soul, mind, and strength (Mark 12:30) brings pleasure to God and glory (praise and worship) to His name.

The band *Third Day* recorded a worship song entitled, "Show Me Your Glory." The lyrics of the chorus of that song go like this:

> Show me Your glory
> Send down Your presence
> I want to see Your face
> Show me Your glory
> Majesty shines about You
> I can't go on without You, Lord

Worship is finding your worth, bringing your worry, and giving your all at Jesus' feet.

If you want to see the face of Jesus, you must kneel at His feet.

Day 7

Her sister, Mary, sat at the Lord's feet, listening to what he taught. But Martha was distracted by the big dinner she was preparing. She came to Jesus and said, "Lord, doesn't it seem unfair to you that my sister just sits here while I do all the work? Tell her to come and help me."
But the Lord said to her, "My dear Martha, you are worried and upset over all these details! There is only one thing worth being concerned about. Mary has discovered it, and it will not be taken away from her."

Luke 10:39-42, NLT

There is beauty in simplicity.

I remember my pastor telling a funny story about how his wife handed him a note right before walking up to the pulpit to preach one Sunday morning. He opened the note to find that all it said was "KISS." After the service, he went to his wife and thanked her for the encouragement of sending him a kiss right before preaching. To which his wife said, "Encouragement? That note stood for Keep It Simple, Stupid."

"There is only one thing to be concerned about, Mary has discovered it, and it will not be taken away from her" (Luke 10:42, NLT). Jesus says to Martha, "You are making things too complex–too many tasks, you're doing too much food preparation, too much of everything! All I need is one simple thing, and Mary has discovered it."

Proverbs 29:18 (KJV) tells us, *"Where there is no vision, the people perish."* In the Bible, vision usually refers to God-given revelation.

The word for "*perish*" used here is a picture of someone running around like a madman. Simply put, if a person has no God-given revelation, they will run around aimlessly. Jesus wants to give Martha, and us, vision. He says, "Keep the main thing the main thing. All you need to do is focus on me and then I will reveal your direction."

My wife, kids, and I are currently attending a large, dynamic fellowship in the Portland, Oregon area. The church currently has around 3,000 people who attend every week. The very first sentence of the first paragraph of their church vision statement reads: "A Ministry of Simplicity: The very heart of what we strive after is keeping Jesus the focal point of everything!" My daughter has attended a few of the Junior High activities at the church. The first thing listed to bring on every one of their special event flyers is a Bible. The church is in the middle of a building program, but the only time it has been mentioned in the three months that I have attended was when the Pastor made the point that they would not be talking about it. I had to Google the project and could only find information about it on the builder's own website. He didn't want to cause a new building to be a distraction from the main thing—Jesus. When they say Jesus is the focus of everything, they mean it! And people are flocking to this church (and churches like it) by the thousands.

KEEP THE MAIN THING THE MAIN THING.

Church-goers are picking up every Christian self-help book except God's Word. Many churches are scrambling to buy the newest audio-visual technology and traveling the country to find and bring back the latest church growth strategy. It's so refreshing to take my family and invite friends to a church that purposely keeps things simple. Here are the next sentences of the church vision statement: "There are many good things we could be doing in the way of programs or presentation; however, we have made the decision to keep it simple. We feel called to preserve our fellowship as a place patterned after the early church of the New Testament. Our model for this is found in Acts 2:42 NKJV: "*And they continued steadfastly in the apostles' doctrine and fellowship, in the breaking of bread, and in prayers*."

Jesus said there is only one thing needed. Mary found it at the feet of Jesus. This church is discovering it every week.

I pray that you find the beauty of simplicity as well.

Week 37

"Yes, LORD, walking in the way of your laws, we wait for you; your name and renown are the desire of our hearts. My soul yearns for you in the night; in the morning my spirit longs for you. When your judgments come upon the earth, the people of the world learn righteousness."

Isaiah 26:8-9, NIV

DAY 1

"Yes, LORD, walking in the way of your laws, we wait
for you; your name and renown are the desire
of our hearts. My soul yearns for you in the night;
in the morning my spirit longs for you.
When your judgments come upon the earth, the
people of the world learn righteousness."
ISAIAH 26:8-9, NIV

"Yes, Lord!"—the first two words of this week's Scripture—remind me of parenting. My wife and I are teaching our children to say, "Yes, sir" and "Yes, ma'am" when we speak to them about a matter. I am pretty convinced that they don't always feel like giving us that response, especially when we correct an attitude or behavior or give them difficult instructions. But we are more concerned with their immediate response and obedience than with anything else. As long as any rules or instructions we give them are for their benefit and blessing, they will eventually understand and appreciate what we've told them to do. By responding with a "Yes, ma'am!" right away, our children are immediately on the path to blessing.

SOMETIMES FEELINGS HAVE TO FOLLOW COMMITMENT.

Saying, *"Yes, Lord!"* communicates a willingness to do what God asks. It shows an attitude of readiness to take action whenever corrected or given a new or difficult direction. Saying, *"Yes, Lord!"* does not always mean that you will immediately feel like doing what the Lord has asked, but such a frame of mind is set to respond quickly to His will. Sometimes feelings have to follow commitment.

God's Word recorded in Jeremiah 29:11 declares that His plans are to prosper us and not to harm; to give us hope and a future. God spoke these words to the nation of Judah while they were in Babylonian captivity. He wanted them to know that, although things were hard, He had good things in store for their future if they would just stay faithful.

I believe these words of encouragement communicate God's heart not only for the people of Judah, but for all of His children. God is constantly at work behind the scenes for the benefit of those who obey His will. By training yourself to say, "*Yes, Lord*" immediately, you place your life on the path to receive His blessings.

DAY 2

"Yes, LORD, walking in the way of your laws, we wait
for you; your name and renown are the desire
of our hearts. My soul yearns for you in the night;
in the morning my spirit longs for you.
When your judgments come upon the earth, the
people of the world learn righteousness."
ISAIAH 26:8-9, NIV

"Yes, Lord!" indicates sensitivity to the direction of the Holy Spirit. We are taught in Romans 8:14 NLT, *"For all who are led by the Spirit of God are children of God."* The Holy Spirit will not only help you win the battle over your natural inclinations, but will also guide your steps if you will tune in to what the Spirit is saying.

Recently, after losing my job of 11 years due to cutbacks, I have been seeking the Lord's direction regarding what He wants me to do next for ministry and employment. I spend a lot of time at the local Starbucks to study, write, and pray. A couple of weeks ago, a woman—whom I do not know, have never seen before, and have not seen since—walked up and handed me a folded piece of paper, saying, "I don't know if this is going to make any sense, but I feel like I am supposed to give this to you." I unfolded the paper. Psalm 121 NLT was printed on it:

> *"I look up to the mountains—does my help come from there? My help comes from the Lord, who made heaven and earth. He will not let you stumble; the one who watches over you will not slumber. Indeed, he who watches over Israel never slumbers or sleeps. The Lord himself watches over you! The Lord stands beside you as your protective shade. The sun will not*

> *harm you by day, nor the moon at night. The Lord keeps you from all harm and watches over your life. The Lord keeps watch over you as you come and go, both now and forever."*

Below the Psalm was a handwritten note:

> "Strategy. This is the word I keep seeing for you. This is a time where God is actively and strategically aligning things for His purpose in you and your life. Be blessed. He watches over you and your loved ones with great care. Be at peace knowing this."

That note still means so much to me. I carry it everywhere I go. God reached out to me through someone led by the Spirit of God. The Spirit of God said to that woman, "I want you to go to your computer and print out Psalm 121. Take the paper down to Starbucks. No, not that Starbucks; this one! Look, over there is someone who needs a word from me. Don't worry, I will tell you what to say. Write this down and give it to him." Her response? "Yes, Lord!"

People often struggle to know God's will. But Saint Augustine said, "Love God and do whatever you want." He knew that if a person really loved God, then the Holy Spirit would change the desires of their heart to match up with His will for them (Psalm 37:4).

> SAINT AUGUSTINE SAID, "LOVE GOD AND DO WHATEVER YOU WANT."

Be led by His Spirit today. Love God, and do what you want. Say, "*Yes, Lord,*" even when the instruction doesn't make sense to you. But if you do obey, you will be doing His will. Remember, nothing we do for the King is ever in vain.

DAY 3

"Yes, LORD, walking in the way of your laws, we wait
for you; your name and renown are the desire
of our hearts. My soul yearns for you in the night;
in the morning my spirit longs for you.
When your judgments come upon the earth, the
people of the world learn righteousness."

ISAIAH 26:8-9, NIV

"*Your name and your renown are the desire of our hearts,*" declares this week's Scripture. The word "name" Isaiah uses in this passage is translated from a Hebrew word that means "reputation, fame, or glory." The people are telling God that they desire to bring glory to the name of God.

What does it mean to do everything for the glory of God? Scripture instructs us, "*So whether you eat or drink, or whatever you do, do it all for the glory of God*" (1 Corinthians 10:31, NLT). According to 1 Corinthians, the heart of a God-glorifying life is this: if you can do something in a way that gives God the glory, then that's the way to do it; if you cannot do it in a way that God would get the glory, then don't do it.

A God-glorifying life is one that does everything—relationships, finances, sports, work, school—in ways that honor God's name and reflect His character. When you glorify something, you are making it bigger. God must become the big deal in your life. God must become the bigger deal in your life. God must become the biggest deal in your life.

The *Geneva Study Bible* comments, "We must order ourselves in such a way that we seek not ourselves, but God's glory, and so the salvation of as many as we may." Never underestimate the power of example. In a God-glorifying life, the message of the Gospel is constantly present and at work.

Day 4

"Yes, LORD, walking in the way of your laws, we wait
for you; your name and renown are the desire
of our hearts. My soul yearns for you in the night;
in the morning my spirit longs for you.
When your judgments come upon the earth, the
people of the world learn righteousness."

Isaiah 26:8-9, NIV

Today you are invited to read some different translations of Isaiah 26:8-9 to gain a better understanding of the passage; then journal your thoughts.

"Lord, we show our trust in you by obeying your laws; our heart's desire is to glorify your name. All night long I search for you; in the morning I earnestly seek for God. For only when you come to judge the earth will people learn what is right." NLT

"Indeed, while following the way of Your judgments, O LORD, We have waited for You eagerly; Your name, even Your memory, is the desire of our souls. At night my soul longs for You, Indeed, my spirit within me seeks You diligently; For when the earth experiences Your judgments, the inhabitants of the world learn righteousness." NASB

"Yes, in the path of Your judgments, O Lord, we wait [expectantly] for You; our heartfelt desire is for Your name and for the remembrance of You. My soul yearns for You [O Lord] in the night, yes, my spirit within me seeks You earnestly; for [only] when Your judgments are in the earth will the inhabitants of the world learn righteousness (uprightness and right standing with God)." AMP

"Yes, in the way of Your judgments, O LORD, we have waited for You; The desire of our soul is for Your name and for the remembrance of You. With my soul I have desired You in the night, Yes, by my spirit

within me I will seek You early; For when Your judgments are in the earth, The inhabitants of the world will learn righteousness." NKJV

"You are the one we trust to bring about justice; above all else we want your name to be honored. Throughout the night, my heart searches for you, because your decisions show everyone on this earth how to live right." CEV

Suggestions:

- Prayerfully reflect on these verses and record the thoughts that God, through the Holy Spirit, is dropping into your heart.
- Ask a question such as, "God, what truth are you trying to communicate to me?"
- Write a letter to God.
- Make notes about what you're learning.
- Compose a prayer or draw a picture of your praise.

Day 5

"Yes, LORD, walking in the way of your laws, we wait
for you; your name and renown are the desire
of our hearts. My soul yearns for you in the night;
in the morning my spirit longs for you.
When your judgments come upon the earth, the
people of the world learn righteousness."

Isaiah 26:8-9, NIV

What does a God-glorifying life look like? Today's Scripture gives us a clue: "*Yes, LORD, walking in the way of your laws.*" A God-glorifying life will be obedient to His Words. Ideally, a believer's life is one big "*Yes, Lord!*" Disobedience to God dishonors Him in the eyes of those in the world looking on. Ungodly behavior may prompt observers to ask, "Aren't you supposed to be one of those Christians?" Jesus must be Lord of all or He's not Lord at all. Ask yourself: "Is my life playing the same song that my mouth is singing?" A person with a God-glorifying lifestyle is above reproach (1Timothy 3:2, NIV). "*Above reproach*" means "so good as to preclude any possibility of criticism, rebuke, blame, disgrace, or shame."

> What if the world loved God and loved others as Jesus commanded? A story is told about a man who changed the world:
>
> Once upon a time a man set out to change the world. Before long he discovered that the world was far too big for one person to change. So he decided to change his country.
>
> Unfortunately, crooked politicians and special interest groups thwarted his efforts, so he decided to change his neighborhood.

But, his neighbors simply closed theirdoors and shut their windows, so he decided to change his family.

Instead of changing, his children rebelled and his wife threatened a divorce, and things only got worse.

Finally, the man decided to change himself. And when he did that, he changed the world.

WE CANNOT EXPECT THE WORLD TO BE AFFECTED BY THE GOSPEL IF WE ARE NOT AFFECTED BY IT.

We cannot expect the world to be affected by the gospel if we are not affected by it. "The great effort of the Christian should be to act in all things as to honor his religion, as not to lead others into sin" (from *Barnes' Notes*). Take in the Word of God deep inside your heart daily. Agree with His will more and more each day. You will never be sinless, but you will sin less and less overtime (Titus 2:11).

Change starts with *you*.

DAY 6

"Yes, LORD, walking in the way of your laws, we wait for you; your name and renown are the desire of our hearts. My soul yearns for you in the night; in the morning my spirit longs for you. When your judgments come upon the earth, the people of the world learn righteousness."

ISAIAH 26:8-9, NIV

"We wait for you…My soul yearns for you in the night; in the morning my spirit longs for you." Over one billion dollars is spent every year on sleep aids. Yet the late evening through early morning hours can be some of the most amazing times of uninterrupted worship and prayer. Just ask my wife; she is often awakened in the night by God asking her to pray. Once she prays, she falls right back to sleep. Though she does not want to lose sleep, those times with God are very rewarding for her.

Isaiah uses the word yearn to describe a need for God's presence. *Yearn*, as it is used here, means "to desire, to incline, to covet, to wait longingly, to wish, to sigh, to want, to be greedy, to prefer, to long for, to lust after (used of bodily appetites)." A God-glorifying life hungers to be in His presence and only finds its satisfaction there.

What do you want more than anything else in your life right now? The thing you long for more than anything else is being glorified by you. Psalm 107:9 NLT says, *"For he satisfies the thirsty and fills the hungry with good things."* Pastor and author Chuck Smith writes in his *Text Commentary* that: "Somehow there is a consciousness in every man that life must be something more than what I have yet experienced. Somehow I feel there is more to life. The longing soul of man He satisfies."

DAY 7

"Yes, LORD, walking in the way of your laws, we wait
for you; your name and renown are the desire
of our hearts. My soul yearns for you in the night;
in the morning my spirit longs for you.
When your judgments come upon the earth, the
people of the world learn righteousness."
ISAIAH 26:8-9, NIV

Nike, Starbucks, and Apple could teach us a lot about being a believer. Everywhere we look we see their logos on walls, signs, or t-shirts. These companies are very intentional about getting your attention. In marketing, their intentionality is called "branding." Branding is not only about getting your target market to choose you over the competition. The purpose of branding is also to influence people to view your company as the only one that can provide a solution to their problem.

What can a believer learn from this? Isaiah 26:8 says, "*Your name and your renown are the desire of our hearts.*" That verse translates literally, "Your name and your brand are the desire of our hearts." It is saying, "Lord, we want to make Your name so big that it brands itself into the hearts and minds of all mankind. We will write Your name on our hearts, we will hang Your truths around our necks, and we will wear Your logo on our chests, so that people will view You as the only one that can provide a solution to their problems."

God is looking for people to carry His name and His message of hope and reconciliation to the world. In 2 Corinthians 5:20 NLT, Paul teaches that: "*We are Christ's ambassadors; God is making His appeal through us. We speak for Christ when we plead, 'Come back to God!'*" An ambassador is a person who represents all of the ideals of a country. As a follower of Christ, heaven is your home country and you are visiting here on a mission. God's reputation is going to depend on the way you represent His brand.

GOD'S REPUTATION IS GOING TO DEPEND ON THE WAY YOU REPRESENT HIS BRAND.

We get to participate in God's ministry of reconciliation by bringing the gospel—the good news—to the world. As ambassadors, we need to ask ourselves: How would God treat the waitress serving me? What would He say to my neighbor? How would God respond to the man on the off-ramp holding the sign up to my window?

Discover how God would think, feel, behave, and act in your circumstances. The world will know who God is by the way you wear His brand.

Week 38

"The thief comes only in order to steal and kill and destroy. I came that they may have and enjoy life, and have it in abundance (to the full, till it overflows)."

John 10:10, AMP

DAY 1

"The thief comes only in order to steal and kill and destroy. I came that they may have and enjoy life, and have it in abundance (to the full, till it overflows)."

JOHN 10:10, AMP

John was the author of this week's verse. He was often called "the disciple whom Jesus loved." John's message was love and his life backed up what his words preached. Henry Ward Beecher called the Gospel of John "God's love letter to the world." Many commentaries say that wherever John went he would simply deliver a one sentence sermon: "Children, love one another."

John's gospel begins with one of the most philosophically beautiful chapters in the entire Bible. *"In the beginning was the Word, and the Word was with God, and the Word was God. He was with God in the beginning. Through him all things were made; without him nothing was made that has been made. In him was life, and that life was the light of men...The Word became flesh and made his dwelling among us. We have seen his glory, the glory of the One and Only, who came from the Father, full of grace and truth."* (John 1:1-3, 14, NIV)

Do you know the Word? Not a word, but *The Word*? Eusebius (a historian) wrote that when John entered early church gatherings, people broke out into spontaneous applause because they knew that he had known Jesus—The Word—personally. The Word came so that we could enjoy an abundant and full life. The Word came so that we could have the best life possible.

Knowing The Word and living every day the way He taught us to live is the key to having the life that Jesus promises in John 10:10.

Jesus said that if a person would remain faithful to His words, then they are his disciple (John 8:31-32); "disciple" means "disciplined one." Feeding continuously on the written Word—the Bible—and disciplining yourself to study, understand, and apply what it says, will open the door to a full, overflowing, and liberated life. A disciple of The Word—of Jesus—will know what's true about life and how to live it; that knowledge combined with action will set them free.

"Free" means "to liberate from bondage." We usually cheapen the concept of freedom by boiling it down to the ability to do whatever we want whenever we want. If a person wanted to go out on the Interstate and try to play basketball, they could; they are free to do so. They might even enjoy it. They may even get away with it for awhile. But if that person continues to play basketball on the Interstate, sooner or later they will experience pain—lots of pain. Interstates were not designed for basketball. A basketball court is the place designed for playing basketball. It has definite boundaries marked that let us know when we are on or off the playing surface. There's even a play book that will teach a willing person the rules of safety and how they can get the most effectiveness and enjoyment out of playing. Learning the principles of the game and playing accordingly does not take away your freedom. It frees you up to enjoy the game to its fullest extent.

We have God's Word to teach us the rules of safety and how to get the most effectiveness and enjoyment out of life. The Bible gives us road signs and warnings about the pain life will bring if we violate God's laws. We may get away with living outside of His plan for awhile, and maybe even enjoy it while we do, but sooner or later we will get run over.

God is not a cosmic kill-joy. He doesn't want to take away your fun. He wants to take away your pain. If you will discipline yourself to play within the boundaries of The Word, you will experience God's power to set you free—the freedom to live the best life possible.

Day 2

"The thief comes only in order to steal and kill and destroy. I came that they may have and enjoy life, and have it in abundance (to the full, till it overflows)."

John 10:10, AMP

In the holiday classic *It's a Wonderful Life*, an angel helps a compassionate but frustrated businessman by showing him what life would have been like if he had never existed. He gets a clear picture of a life with George Bailey and a life without George Bailey.

In our verse this week, Jesus paints a picture for us of what two different lives look like: a life with God and a life without God. He says that the life the thief wants you to have looks one way and the life He wants you to have looks another way.

Several years ago, I ran into one of my former youth ministry students. He said "Hi, Pastor Dave. It's Jerry! Do you remember me?" I did remember Jerry. He had attended our high school ministry regularly seven or eight years earlier. I remembered that I had helped him with some family issues and, at one point, helped him get accepted into Teen Challenge (a Christian-based recovery program).

"How have you been?" I asked him.

He began to describe to me the details of his life for the past several years. Details which involved a broken marriage, kids born out of wedlock, drug use, drunk driving, and time spent in jail. He described a pretty bad life. I was happy to hear him, at the end of the story, say, "...but, I'm doing really good with God now."

I used to know Jerry pretty well, so I couldn't help but ask, "Jerry, didn't you know better? You sat in my youth group for years. Didn't I teach you all about that stuff?"

Jerry replied, "I knew what was right. I just didn't choose to do it."

Isn't that statement so true? You have the freedom to choose the direction and path you take. You can choose to live your life by going it on your own and suffering the outcome. Or, you can choose to live your life in a way that God would bless.

Jesus said, "*I came so you could have real and eternal life; more and better life than you ever dreamed of*" (John 10:10, MSG). Today, if you are living a life without God, stop right now and commit your life to Christ. Ask Him to forgive you for your wrongs and deliver you from the bondage of sin. Choose to follow His ways and let Him begin to bring you into the "Wonderful Life" that He promised.

Day 3

"The thief comes only in order to steal and kill and destroy. I came that they may have and enjoy life, and have it in abundance (to the full, till it overflows)."
John 10:10, AMP

Today I want to unpack the first twelve words of John 10:10, "*The thief comes only in order to steal and kill and destroy.*"

The truth is that Satan is a thief. His sole ambition is to rip us off and to keep us from living the full life that God has in store for us by keeping us tied to an ordinary existence. Jesus wants to rescue you from him.

The devil's lures are always tantalizing. He may whisper, "It's okay for you to mess around while you are away on your business trip. No one will ever know." But what he really came to do was steal the trust in your marriage, kill future intimacy between you and your spouse, and destroy your family.

The thief may try to convince you that you've worked hard for your company for years and if they are not going to give you the raise you deserve, then you are justified to skim a little money off the top here and there to make up for it. But he's really only coming to steal your freedom, kill your reliance on God as your provider, and destroy your integrity.

Sometimes the temptation is obviously sin, but sometimes it wears a disguise—like the old "wolf in sheep's clothing." There's a good example of this in chemistry. Every good chemist has a bottle of sodium cyanide sitting on their shelves. It smells like almond jelly beans, and it's very poisonous. If someone were to remove the label from the bottle of sodium cyanide and replace it with an almond jelly beans label, someone could possibly get a whiff of the alluring, sweet smell in the bottle, ingest its contents, and die. Changing the label on the bottle doesn't change its contents or the consequences of consuming it.

The devil is working overtime to change the labels on sin, calling what's evil "good" and what's good "evil." When people buy into that deception, it catches on and spreads around until it becomes normal; what one generation permits in moderation, the next generation will enjoy in excess. People still get hurt and die every day from consuming a sinful lifestyle, but nobody seems to know why anymore. They're just doing what everyone else does.

What about you? Do you know the truth? Can you tell the difference between the death that is socially labeled "good times" and the true life Jesus offers us? Do you know the truth about who you are and what God's purposes are for your life? The Greek word used to describe the kind of life Jesus came to teach us means "a quantity so abundant as to be considerably more than what one would expect or anticipate." God promises you a life far better than you could ever envision.

If you are unsure about the truth of God for you or if you have trouble telling the difference between the thief's deception and Jesus' life, saturate yourself with what God has said about your life. Just open up your Bible and read word after word after word. You'll find that God said things like, "You are priceless. You are pure. You are lovely. You are chosen. You are acceptable in the sight of God. There's nothing you can do to change the way I feel about you. I love you as you are. Your life has a purpose that I can help you find. My ways work. I'll supply all that you need." When you saturate your mind and spirit with those words every single day, you'll begin to replace the enemy's lies with God's truth, and your life will start to change.

When you're full of the truth, it's hard to consume a lie.

Day 4

"The thief comes only in order to steal and kill and destroy. I came that they may have and enjoy life, and have it in abundance (to the full, till it overflows)."

John 10:10, AMP

Today we're going to read some additional scriptures related to the abundant life Jesus talks about in John 10:10. At the end, journal your thoughts in your personal journal or on a separate sheet of paper.

You prepare a feast for me in the presence of my enemies. You honor me by anointing my head with oil. My cup overflows with blessings. Surely your goodness and unfailing love will pursue me all the days of my life, and I will live in the house of the Lord forever. (Psalm 23:5-6, NLT)

Trust in the Lord and do good. Then you will live safely in the land and prosper. Take delight in the Lord, and he will give you your heart's desires. (Psalm 37:3-4, NLT)

For since the world began, no ear has heard, and no eye has seen a God like you, who works for those who wait for him! (Isaiah 64:4, NLT)

You haven't done this before. Ask, using my name, and you will receive, and you will have abundant joy. (John 16:24, NLT)

What shall we say about such wonderful things as these? If God is for us, who can ever be against us? Since he did not spare even his own Son but gave him up for us all, won't he also give us everything else? (Romans 8:31-32, NLT)

Now all glory to God, who is able, through his mighty power at work within us, to accomplish infinitely more than we might ask or think. (Ephesians 3:20, NLT)

Suggestions:

- Prayerfully reflect on these verses and record the thoughts that God, through the Holy Spirit, is dropping into your heart.
- Ask a question such as, "God, what truth are you trying to communicate to me?"
- Write a letter to God.
- Make notes on what you're learning.
- Compose a prayer.
- Draw a picture of your praise.

DAY 5

"The thief comes only in order to steal and kill and destroy. I came that they may have and enjoy life, and have it in abundance (to the full, till it overflows)."

JOHN 10:10, AMP

A lot of teaching on abundance and prosperity implies that when you get Jesus, God takes away all of your problems and sets you up with all of the creature comforts you ask for. At the first moment of salvation, a person absolutely receives more peace, joy, and love than they have ever known. And Deuteronomy 28 does promise that the lives of the obedient will be extremely blessed. But interpreting John 10:10 as Jesus saying, "I came to get you the new house you've always wanted," or "Come to me so I can make all of your troubles go away" will leave a person disappointed or disillusioned with God the first time that their girlfriend dumps them or the moment they lose a job due to cutbacks.

WHEN JESUS TALKS ABOUT ABUNDANT LIFE, HE MEANS THE QUALITY OF OUR LIFE WILL BE ABUNDANT, NOT MERELY THE MEANS OF OBTAINING THE NECESSITIES.

Jesus said, "*I came so that you may have life and enjoy it.*" There's an interesting truth in two different Greek words for life: *bios* and *zoe*. Bios refers to our physical life—our useful purposefulness. *Zoe* refers to our spiritual life—our ultimate purposefulness. The word "life" used in John 10:10 is *zoe*, not *bios*. When Jesus talks about abundant life, He means the quality of our life will be abundant, not merely the means of obtaining the necessities. The *Jon Courson New*

Testament Commentary says, "The essence of the Gospel is not what Jesus will do for you; it's what he *already* did for you when he died for your sins...Get saved because Jesus Christ died for your sins."

It takes money for the gospel to be advanced and Jesus understood this. His ministry was not a poor ministry by any means. He even had to put a treasurer (Judas) in charge of all the money people gave to His ministry. But Jesus did not keep the money for His own comforts. He gave it away. He used it to meet the physical (*bios*) and spiritual (*zoe*) needs of the people around Him.

Having abundance and keeping it to fill your own storehouse, build your own kingdom, and satisfy your own needs and wants is not what God intends. Such selfishness stunts the growth of God's Kingdom—and the person who is hoarding their blessings. What God has blessed you with could reach many people with the Gospel if it were reinvested. Likewise, to say, "I only want God to give me just enough resources to meet my own needs" is not being Christ-like; it's being selfish, lacking a concern for the needs of others. This attitude also stunts the growth of God's Kingdom. God wants to overflow us on both levels—*bios* and *zoe*. They are connected to each other like hand in glove.

Use your physical purposefulness for ultimate purposefulness: the reconciliation of man to God. Remember that most of God's riches do not glitter. Let your life overflow. Let it spill out and affect the lives of others. Pass on the quality of life you've received (the joy, peace, and love) as well as the quantity of what your life provides to people who are in need.

Day 6

"The thief comes only in order to steal and kill and destroy. I came that they may have and enjoy life, and have it in abundance (to the full, till it overflows)."
John 10:10, AMP

The further we go into this verse, the more it seems like Jesus wants us to, essentially, get a life. What does that mean? Aren't we all breathing? Aren't we all alive?

I read a story about two grave diggers who were watching as a lady, who requested to be buried sitting at the wheel of her pink Cadillac, was lowered into the ground. As the Cadillac disappeared into the grave, one of the workers was overheard to say, "Now *that's* what I call real living." It's fascinating to hear what people think real living is.

In Bill Hybel's book *Becoming a Contagious Christian*, a man asked the question, "What exactly is real living?" His friend replied, "A day on my powerboat with a case of beer, a carton of Camels, and my gal in a bikini—that's real living!" While some would say living for pleasure is what life is all about, 1 Thessalonians 5:7 warns us that living for pleasure makes a person dead while they are still alive. Chuck Smith's notes about this passage say, "You may be eating, drinking, sleeping and breathing, but as God looks at you, He sees you as dead."

Real living consists of more than just eating, drinking, sleeping, and breathing. Just ask the person serving a life sentence in prison if they feel like they are really living. Or the Roman soldier who approached Julius Caesar and asked for permission to commit suicide; he was a "wretched and downcast creature" with no vitality. Caesar took one look at him and said, "Man, were you *ever* really alive?" Abraham Lincoln said, "And in the end, it's not the years in your life that count. It's the life in your years."

The Gospel of John uses the word "life" 36 times. Usually John is referring to God's gift of eternal life through Jesus. But here we need to understand the word in its deepest context. Jesus said, "*I am…the Life*" (John 11:25). He didn't say He was a kind of life. He said the Life. It is only because Jesus is the Life that there is life in anything on earth at all.

Paul finishes his first letter to Timothy by saying, "*Take hold of the eternal life…*" The phrase "*take hold*" is a present-tense verb, not a futuristic command. The eternal life that Jesus describes is not just living in God's glory forever in heaven one day. Eternal life is something you experience right now!

> "It's not the years in your life that count. It's the life in your years."

Don't try to live life on your own. Do life with Jesus. He will increase your vitality and your capacity to live in ways you've never before imagined. Take hold of eternal life now. God will add life to your years. You will be amazed at the big things He has in store for you.

DAY 7

"The thief comes only in order to steal and kill and destroy. I came that they may have and enjoy life, and have it in abundance (to the full, till it overflows)."
JOHN 10:10, AMP

I heard a great illustration at a conference I attended years ago. Imagine a man who spent his entire life living inside a closet. His meals are slid under the door. He goes to the bathroom in the corner. All he knows is the carpet that he's sitting on and the coats hanging up. One day someone knocks on the door and says, "I want to give you three wishes. If you could have anything in the world, what would it be?" All Closet Man knows is the carpet, the coats, and the hangers. He says, "Well, I'd like some shaggier carpet, some air freshener to take away the bad smell, and just a little bit more light that comes under the door. That would be awesome! That's my dream."

Now, you and I are listening to this whole conversation. We're on the outside thinking, "That's what you want? You get three wishes and you choose light, softer carpet, and something to make the smell better? Come on! Ask for the door to be opened! Right down the hall is a fully stocked refrigerator. In the next room is a big-screen TV, and right down the street is a Taco Bell! There are so many better things! Closet Man, you don't even get it."

What's your dream? To be rich? To have a big house? To get married? To earn a scholarship? That's the sort of things most of us would say. But I can imagine God is saying, "You call that a dream? You don't even get it! I could do so much more if you would allow me to invade your life. I can show you lists of people who got the house, got the money, got the girl, and got the scholarship, but are miserable. I can do anything, you know—*far more than you could ever imagine or guess or request in your wildest dreams!*" (Ephesians 3:20, MSG).

If God gives you a dream that could possibly change the world one day, will you pursue it until it becomes reality? Or will you choose to be ordinary? There is a saying that goes, "When you were born, you cried and the world rejoiced. Live your life so that when you die, the world cries and you rejoice."

Attempt something so great that it is doomed to failure unless God shows up.

Attempt something so great that it is doomed to failure unless God shows up. Dare to want an extraordinary life. A divine dream is bigger than you because it is based on the promises of God's Word. Put yourself so far out there that you can't get back without God's help.

God did not create you to settle for common or ordinary. Have the kind of faith that will let your life be big.

Week 39

But Jesus spoke to them at once. "Don't be afraid," he said. "Take courage. I am here!" Then Peter called to him, "Lord, if it's really you, tell me to come to you, walking on the water." "Yes, come," Jesus said. So Peter went over the side of the boat and walked on the water toward Jesus. But when he saw the strong wind and the waves, he was terrified and began to sink. "Save me, Lord!" he shouted. Jesus immediately reached out and grabbed him. "You have so little faith," Jesus said. "Why did you doubt me?"

Matthew 14:27-31, NLT

DAY 1

But Jesus spoke to them at once. "Don't be afraid," he said. "Take courage. I am here!" Then Peter called to him, "Lord, if it's really you, tell me to come to you, walking on the water." "Yes, come," Jesus said. So Peter went over the side of the boat and walked on the water toward Jesus. But when he saw the strong wind and the waves, he was terrified and began to sink. "Save me, Lord!" he shouted. Jesus immediately reached out and grabbed him. "You have so little faith," Jesus said. "Why did you doubt me?"

MATTHEW 14:27-31, NLT

A first-time skydiver moves closer to the open door of the plane. Fear says, "Stop!" but faith in his parachute kicks in and he makes the leap.

A young girl walking home alone at night begins to walk faster and faster until she has broken out into a run. Reaching home, faith takes over. She turns to face her fear, only to realize there was no one there all along—no mugger, no ghost, just fear.

The disciples were in a boat. Jesus had told them to go to the other side of the lake and wait for Him there. In the middle of the lake, the wind began to throw their boat around. It was the darkest part of the night when they thought they saw a ghost walking on the water. But what they thought was a ghost turned out to be Jesus, walking out to them on the lake.

Fear had definitely taken over there. The most accurate translation of their state of mind is that they were scared to death. Jesus called out, "Don't be afraid. Take courage. I'm here now."

He's telling them, "I am with you. Don't allow circumstance to dictate behavior. Make an adjustment. Walk in faith and courage."

Now, Jesus had already told them, "I'll meet you on the other side of the lake." Before they even started, He said that He was going to be joining them there. They were going to make it. When the waves are nearly capsizing the only thing between us and pretty certain death by drowning, it's not logical deduction we need so much as faith. For us, just like for them, He's saying, "I am with you. Walk in faith and courage. You are going to make it."

Don't get caught being fearful of a new, difficult, or unexpected direction God sends you. You never know; God could be releasing you from that job to give you a better one. He could be saving you from a relationship that will damage you and drag you down. That family member may have to wander away before "coming to their senses" and returning home. No matter how things logically seem like they're going to turn out, we can have faith that we're going to make it to the other side because of God's promises.

If we aren't careful, fear will take over in those circumstances. When that happens, we have to jerk ourselves out of fear and into faith, telling ourselves "I don't have to be afraid; God has me on a journey and He promised to see me through."

So make the leap. Turn and face your fear with big faith. Handled properly, adversity is an opportunity in disguise.

Are you facing a storm? Don't let fear determine your decisions! Let your faith kick in.

Take action and go to Jesus. He will reveal Himself to you in the middle of your storm.

DAY 2

> But Jesus spoke to them at once. "Don't be afraid," he said. "Take courage. I am here!" Then Peter called to him, "Lord, if it's really you, tell me to come to you, walking on the water." "Yes, come," Jesus said. So Peter went over the side of the boat and walked on the water toward Jesus. But when he saw the strong wind and the waves, he was terrified and began to sink. "Save me, Lord!" he shouted. Jesus immediately reached out and grabbed him. "You have so little faith," Jesus said. "Why did you doubt me?"
>
> MATTHEW 14:27-31, NLT

Peter is over the bow, on the water, and making his way to Jesus. Peter took action and turned his fear to faith—which is more than the other disciples did. But fear challenged him once again.

When you walk by faith, fear will always challenge again. Peter saw the wind and the waves and began to sink (Matthew 14:30).

What went wrong? Jesus had told him to *"come"* and he went. He was walking on water. No one we know of except Jesus and Peter have *ever* walked on water. But then, right in the midst of his "faith walk," fear attacked again. Peter's mind must have gone crazy with thoughts like: "This looks bad. No one walks on water. Those waves are huge. I am a dead man." He took his eyes off of Jesus and begun to look at his circumstances. Granted, those were some pretty distracting circumstances, but as Peter looked around at the waves, felt the wind, saw how far away the boat was, his faith shrank and he began to sink. ***Fear always focuses on the problem.***

Jesus immediately rescued Peter from drowning. While out on the water, before heading back to the boat, Jesus told Peter that it was doubt that began to rob his ability to walk in the supernatural. Unbelief was the source of his peril. From this we learn that if we will believe more, we will suffer less.

Most people focus on Jesus rescuing Peter when he lacks faith. And what a great promise! But there is more here to notice. Now, I can't prove it (maybe we can see instant replays or reruns in heaven), but I feel confident that Jesus didn't carry Peter back to the boat in His arms or on His shoulders. That would mean that Peter walked on water a *second* time. He was able put his eyes and his confidence back on Jesus, to put the fear in its place and resume the supernatural journey. ***Faith always focuses on the solution.***

Scripture tells us that the storm did not cease until they were both back in the boat. Do you see what that means? While Peter was still out on the water, while the circumstances that caused him to sink the first time remained unchanged, he walked successfully in the supernatural through the wind and the waves once again. Remember that even on life's stormiest days, God is present in the storm and will help you through it (Psalm 46:1-3).

> FEAR ALWAYS FOCUSES ON THE PROBLEM. FAITH ALWAYS FOCUSES ON THE SOLUTION

So put your courage in Christ! You can never find the solution when you're looking at the problem. If you begin to doubt and feel yourself sinking in the storm far away from a boat or safety net, remember that God is near. Fix your gaze on Jesus through prayer. With renewed faith, begin to walk in His supernatural power again.

Be encouraged, because even when fear challenges, faith still wins.

DAY 3

But Jesus spoke to them at once. "Don't be afraid," he said. "Take courage. I am here!" Then Peter called to him, "Lord, if it's really you, tell me to come to you, walking on the water." "Yes, come," Jesus said. So Peter went over the side of the boat and walked on the water toward Jesus. But when he saw the strong wind and the waves, he was terrified and began to sink. "Save me, Lord!" he shouted. Jesus immediately reached out and grabbed him. "You have so little faith," Jesus said. "Why did you doubt me?"

MATTHEW 14:27-31, NLT

"No, thanks. We'll wait here!"

As Peter stepped out of the boat in faith, the other eleven disciples are frozen to their seats in fear. ***Fear will stop you from doing something and make you do nothing.***

Scripture teaches that Jesus disarmed the devil at the cross. "Disarmed" means that the devil has no more weapons. His only power over you is to try to convince you that you can't do it, you can't help, you're unable, and you're useless. He will lie to you and tell you that things are worse than they really are. He wants to stop you from doing something and make you do nothing. And the moment you swallow that lie, he's got you where he wants you.

Years ago a railroad worker got himself trapped in a refrigerator freezer car. He knew he was trapped and had no way out. He knew that the trip was long and he would freeze to death before the train arrived at its destination. When they found him, he had scribbled on paper the various stages he went through before finally succumbing to death by freezing. The strange thing about the story was that the refrigeration unit on that car was not working properly and the temperature had not dropped below 50 degrees—a temperature that he could have easily survived.

I found this quote recently in some old sermon notes: "Fear and faith are two forces that have the ability and power to create something out of nothing, bringing into being that which does not exist."

Franklin Roosevelt gets quoted a lot for saying, "We have nothing to fear but fear itself," but have you ever read the rest of the quote from the fifth sentence of his 1933 inaugural address? Here it is: "So, first of all, let me assert my firm belief that the only thing we have to fear is fear itself—nameless, unreasoning, unjustified terror which paralyzes needed efforts to convert retreat into advance." ***Fear retreats, but faith advances!***

Fear will rule you, control you, and eat away at you if you allow it to.

But fear will melt away when you put your hope and trust in God.

Mark 11:23-24 tells us that our faith can move mountains!

If you don't know the truth, you may believe a lie and act accordingly. But when you know the truth of what God says about you and the things you are going through, it will set you free to move forward.

Renew your heart and mind by feeding on God's Word.

Feed your heart, mind, and spirit with words of life that will squelch the lies of fear.

DAY 4

But Jesus spoke to them at once. "Don't be afraid," he said. "Take courage. I am here!" Then Peter called to him, "Lord, if it's really you, tell me to come to you, walking on the water." "Yes, come," Jesus said. So Peter went over the side of the boat and walked on the water toward Jesus. But when he saw the strong wind and the waves, he was terrified and began to sink. "Save me, Lord!" he shouted. Jesus immediately reached out and grabbed him. "You have so little faith," Jesus said. "Why did you doubt me?"

MATTHEW 14:27-31, NLT

Today we are going to relate to this passage in a new way: Ignatian Meditation. This idea is adapted from Ignatius of Loyola, a church father who would invite people to use their imaginations to recreate a story in the Scripture. This exercise can help us get face-to-face with the Scriptures and with Jesus.

Step 1: Read the entire Bible passage so you have the context and the setting: Matthew 14.

Step 2: Read the entire Bible passage again (or maybe start with verse 22), but this time choose a new viewpoint with which to engage the story before you read it. Here are four different ways to engage with a passage. Decide on one before reading the Scripture the second time through:

- **Go there!** Position yourself somewhere in the story. Where do you see yourself? Who are you standing or sitting next to? What would you have seen if you had been in that boat? What do you hear? Who is there with you? Are you one of the bystanders in the crowd watching? What are people saying? What do you think? Do you meet Jesus? Do you speak to Him? What does He say to you? Imagine yourself observing the story as it unfolds.

- **Be there!** Use the rest of your senses to experience the scene: touch, smell, listen, and feel.

- **Become a character in the story!** What do they see? How does the character feel?

- **Be you!** Enter the story as yourself. How would you feel if you were there?

Step 3: Record the thoughts that God, through the Holy Spirit, is dropping into your heart regarding the passage you reread from one of the four perspectives listed above. Here are some ideas:

- Ask yourself a question such as, "God, what truth are you trying to communicate to me?"
- Write a letter to God.
- Make notes about what you're learning.
- Compose a prayer.
- Draw a picture of your praise.

DAY 5

But Jesus spoke to them at once. "Don't be afraid," he said. "Take courage. I am here!" Then Peter called to him, "Lord, if it's really you, tell me to come to you, walking on the water." "Yes, come," Jesus said. So Peter went over the side of the boat and walked on the water toward Jesus. But when he saw the strong wind and the waves, he was terrified and began to sink. "Save me, Lord!" he shouted. Jesus immediately reached out and grabbed him. "You have so little faith," Jesus said. "Why did you doubt me?"

MATTHEW 14:27-31, NLT

"I'm going in!"

One of the twelve is making the leap. One is turning to face the fear. Everyone else is frozen to their seats. Peter could have chosen to play it safe and be an "everyone," but his faith told him, "Take a risk!"

God wants you to be a "one," not an "everyone."

There's a story told about a man who observed that loving others required sacrifice, striving for goals might lead to disappointment, and serving people never seemed to meet all of their needs. So he decided not to soil his life with risking to love, or to strive, or to serve. When the man died, he approached God, unmarred by the filth of the world. The man stated proudly, "Here is my life!" And God said, "Life? What life?"

Sitting on the sidelines may seem safe and clean, but it insulates you from living life where we are created to live it: in a world that needs who God created you to be. When you love others, serve others, and strive to be everything God wants you to be, you will get messy. But get off of the bench anyway. Get in the game and get your uniform dirty; that's what it's designed for! After all, isn't that what Jesus did for us? 1 Peter 2:21 MSG says, "*This is the kind of life you've been invited into, the kind of life Christ lived. He suffered everything that came his way so you would know that it could be done, and also know how to do it, step-by-step.*"

FAITH ALWAYS TAKES ACTION AND FAITH ALWAYS INVOLVES A RISK.

Jesus says, "*Take courage. I am here!*"

Peter says, "Really? Then I want to get out of this boat and walk to You on the water." Peter was a fisherman; he has been in boats before and he always stays in the boat. What makes this time any different? Jesus says, "*Yes.*"

And Peter's all in.

I don't picture Peter putting one leg over the edge at a time to test the water to see if it's safe. I envision Peter jumping over the side of the boat much like a young boy puts his hands on a fence and launches both feet into the air as his body crosses over to the other side. ***Faith always takes action and faith always involves a risk.***

Scripture tells us that we are God's workmanship—a masterpiece. Everyone is born an original, but most die a copycat. Our world is made up of very few leaders and a bunch of followers. If you just do what everyone always does, you'll just get what everyone always gets. When you risk nothing, you accomplish nothing, you receive nothing, and you're left with nothing.

Answer this equation: God x 0 = what? The answer is Zero! Anything times zero is equal to zero. If you don't get out of the boat and become part of His equation, it doesn't matter what God pre-planned to accomplish in and through your life.

But watch what happens when you add a one to the same equation: God x 1 = 1,000,000,000,000,000... infinity. The "one" is *you*! When you combine your will to His power, the possibilities are infinite! ***Action is where fear ends and faith begins.***

This world needs the "one" that God created you to be.

DAY 6

But Jesus spoke to them at once. "Don't be afraid," he said. "Take courage. I am here!" Then Peter called to him, "Lord, if it's really you, tell me to come to you, walking on the water." "Yes, come," Jesus said. So Peter went over the side of the boat and walked on the water toward Jesus. But when he saw the strong wind and the waves, he was terrified and began to sink. "Save me, Lord!" he shouted. Jesus immediately reached out and grabbed him. "You have so little faith," Jesus said. "Why did you doubt me?"

MATTHEW 14:27-31, NLT

No time for prayer today? Who said prayer has to take a lot of time? Our shortest prayers can be the most effective prayers we pray.

A few prayers in the Scriptures take maybe five or six minutes, but most of the prayers we read in the Bible are very brief:

- A father (Mark 9) who prays, "*Lord, I believe; help my unbelief!*"
- A poor mother's "*Lord, help me!*" (Matthew 15)
- A woman pushes through a crowd to get to Jesus (Matthew 9). She doesn't even speak her prayer; it's just a thought: "*She said within herself, 'if I can just touch…*'"
- In this week's Scripture, Peter cries out, "*Save me, Lord!*"
- There's an evangelist who comes to my old church on a regular basis. At the beginning of his message he always prays, "*Lord, help! In Jesus name, Amen!*" I don't even close my eyes for that one.

No time for prayer? I doubt that as Peter was sinking, he thought to himself, "You know, it would be great if I could pray right now but I just don't have time." God hears and answers the cries of the desperate, the oppressed, and the people in need.

Need is a great catalyst, but need should not be the only motivation for us to pray. We should develop a habit of praying brief prayers throughout the day. A great way to start that habit is with daily detail prayers like, "Lord, thank you for that parking spot," "God, provide for that man on the corner," "Show me what to do today," or "Give me Your favor as I go into this meeting."

FAITH WILL ALWAYS TAKE ACTION.

I recently heard a story about a Puritan who was writing notes during a debate. After the debate was over, they took a look at his notes and there was nothing written but the words, "More light, Lord! More light, Lord! More light, Lord!" He simply wanted light on what they were discussing, so he asked God for it. This is the way we should pray. How else could a person ever "*pray without ceasing*" (1 Thessalonians 5:17)?

Jesus answered Peter's brief prayer. Take notice of the fact that Jesus did not save Peter until he asked to be saved even though Jesus clearly saw that Peter was going under and knew that he was going to drown. In the same way, God sees us. God knows our needs before we ask. Scripture says that we don't "*have*" because we don't ask for it. Peter had to put his faith to work and ask first. In the middle of his fear, Peter's faith took action. ***Faith will always take action.*** This time, action was in the form of prayer. He reached for Jesus' help and Jesus reached back with an answer.

God will always draw near to those who draw near to Him (James 4:8). Initiate faith by drawing near to God for whatever you need today. Call on Him and He *will* answer.

Day 7

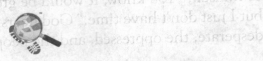

But Jesus spoke to them at once. "Don't be afraid," he said. "Take courage. I am here!" Then Peter called to him, "Lord, if it's really you, tell me to come to you, walking on the water." "Yes, come," Jesus said. So Peter went over the side of the boat and walked on the water toward Jesus. But when he saw the strong wind and the waves, he was terrified and began to sink. "Save me, Lord!" he shouted. Jesus immediately reached out and grabbed him. "You have so little faith," Jesus said. "Why did you doubt me?"

Matthew 14:27-31, NLT

Jesus told his disciples to get in the boat even though he knew the storm was coming. That brings up an excellent question: why *does* God allow storms in our lives?

The story of Jonah and the whale got started when Jonah had a problem with what God told him to do and instead got on a boat headed in the exact opposite direction from where God had asked him to go. God used a storm to get Jonah's attention and get him back on course. From that story, we know that God might use a storm to bring us back into dependence on Him and to get us back into the center of His will. Jonah's storm came to realign him.

The twelve disciples did not need correction. After all, they were doing the will of the Master; Jesus had told them to go to the other side and they were on their way. So what about their storm?

The disciple's storm was sent to refine them. "This was not a storm to correct them, but to perfect them" (*Jon Courson's New*

Testament Commentary). Like the disciples, in those situations our faith will be strengthened by the trials we overcome.

"Now faith is…being certain of things we do not see" (Hebrews 11:1, NIV). It's hard to see the comeback in the middle of a setback. Faith says, "Lord, the odds may looked stacked against me now, but I am remaining certain of Your deliverance. I may not see it, but breakthrough is coming. You are going to see me through my storm."

The same story in Mark 6:48 says that Jesus went out to the disciples on the water because He wanted to *"pass by them"*—the same language used when God's presence *"passed by"* Moses at Mt. Sinai. One of the sacred names of God is Jehovah-Shammah. It means "The Lord is There." Jesus came to the disciples during the storm to assure them of His presence in the storm.

The music group *Casting Crowns* recorded a song about God's presence through difficult times entitled "Praise You in the Storm." Here are the lyrics to the chorus of that song:

> And I'll praise you in this storm
> and I will lift my hands
> for You are who You are
> no matter where I am
> and every tear I've cried
> You hold in your hand
> You never left my side
> and though my heart is torn
> I will praise You in this storm.

If adversity comes at a time where you are running from God's direction, adjust your course. Realign yourself to His will—The Lord is There!

If challenges overtake you when you are doing God's will, continue to walk in faith and obedience. Use the storm to your advantage. See it as an opportunity for the Lord to refine and strengthen you—The Lord is There!

WEEK 40

"All Scripture is God-breathed and is useful for teaching, rebuking, correcting and training in righteousness, so that the man of God may be thoroughly equipped for every good work."

2 TIMOTHY 3:16-17, NIV

DAY 1

"All Scripture is God-breathed and is useful for teaching, rebuking, correcting and training in righteousness, so that the man of God may be thoroughly equipped for every good work."
2 TIMOTHY 3:16-17, NIV

When God breathes into something, it becomes alive. Genesis 2:7 NIV says, *"Then the LORD God formed a man from the dust of the ground and breathed into his nostrils the breath of life, and the man became a living being."*

Hebrews 4:12 tells us that God's Word is alive and active. That means His Word isn't just for those who came before us; it is alive and active for us today. God breathed life into us and breathed life into our "life manual" so that we would have clear direction and guidance. This guidance leads us into righteousness.

Righteousness is the thing we are told to aspire to (Proverbs 21:21). Righteousness is living in a complete state of correctness. For us, righteous living would be following the commands of Christ in all of their fullness—loving God with our whole hearts and loving our neighbor as ourselves, the greatest commandments of all (Luke 10:27). When we follow these commands, Jesus says we receive eternal life.

GOD'S WORD IS FULL OF ALL YOU NEED FOR LEARNING TO LIVE A RIGHTEOUS LIFE.

In order to be equipped to live righteously, we must be taught, corrected, and trained. People spend thousands of dollars sending their kids to the best schools, athletic facilities, dance studios, and music teachers so their children will be trained the correct way; dog owners spend that much getting their pets trained properly! We do this because we know the value of having correct training from the start if we want to do something a certain way. How much more important to have the training for how to rightly live our lives!

God's Word is full of all you need for learning to live a righteous life. A righteous life here on earth leads to eternal life (Matthew 25:46). God's Word is alive and active, full of His breath and life. Don't miss out on meeting with Him face-to-face each day.

Day 2

"All Scripture is God-breathed and is useful for teaching, rebuking, correcting and training in righteousness, so that the man of God may be thoroughly equipped for every good work."
2 Timothy 3:16-17, NIV

In 1 Kings 19:5-8 we read the following story of Elijah in the desert:

> *Then he lay down under the tree and fell asleep. All at once an angel touched him and said, 'Get up and eat.' He looked around, and there by his head was a cake of bread baked over hot coals, and a jar of water. He ate and drank and then lay down again. The angel of the LORD came back a second time and touched him and said, 'Get up and eat, for the journey is too much for you.' So he got up and ate and drank. Strengthened by that food, he traveled forty days and forty nights..."* NIV

Elijah was running from Jezebel, a queen who had vowed to destroy him. Elijah was afraid of this woman, so he ran into the wilderness, sat under a tree and asked the Lord to take his life (1 Kings 19:4). But the Lord did not grant Elijah's request Instead, He sent an angel to take care of Elijah's needs and give him what he needed to make the next journey. The story points out that Elijah only intended to eat once, but the angel woke him twice to eat, saying, "*Get up and eat, for the journey is too much for you.*"

There will be seasons of life that require more time in the Word than others.

There will be seasons of life that require more time in the Word than others. There will be moments that you will clearly know God is telling you to get into His Word more than you have before, because there is a journey ahead. Just like Elijah, you will need the strength to accomplish it. The more "food" you get (Hebrews 5:14), the more ready you will be to accomplish the task.

DAY 3

"All Scripture is God-breathed and is useful for teaching, rebuking, correcting and training in righteousness, so that the man of God may be thoroughly equipped for every good work."
2 TIMOTHY 3:16-17, NIV

When Jesus spoke these words, *"You are in error because you do not know the Scriptures or the power of God"* (Matthew 22:29, NIV), He was responding to the Sadducees. The Sadducees were an aristocratic, priestly group associated with the leadership of the Temple of Jerusalem. (Side note: in the gospels they are often talked about in the same sentence with the Pharisees, but they aren't the same thing; the Pharisees were a separatist Jewish religious group that considered themselves in theological opposition to the Sadducees.)

The Sadducees didn't believe in resurrection (Matthew 22:23), but they had asked a question about heaven. Their question was meant to prove how ridiculous the idea of a resurrection was. The Sadducees were the logical, rationalistic materialists of their day. Jesus let them know that although they believed they were wise, the truth was they didn't know the whole Scripture or have an understanding about eternity and God's power. Therefore, they were incorrect in their belief.

The church we attend goes through the Bible in depth each week. There is no room for misinterpretation or misunderstanding that way because we are not learning someone's opinion or thoughts. We are learning God's living, breathing Word. Years ago, before I really studied the Bible, many things I believed to be true came from sermons I heard or from people I respected. As I began to study, I discovered that many of those beliefs were correct, but some were not. When I was lacking in study, I was a judgmental, self-righteous, and ignorant person. Reading and knowing God's Word brought love, compassion, and insight into my life.

We all need to be reading the Scripture for ourselves. Relying on someone else's interpretation isn't good enough. I have yet to meet an insecure person who really studies God's Word. When you have studied and are full of Him, there is no room for shame and fear, which are the roots of insecurity. Knowing you are God's chosen one and understanding His plan of redemption will combat any attack of the enemy on your emotions or your heart.

> *"Study to show yourself approved to God, a workman that needs not to be ashamed, rightly dividing the word of truth."*
> 2 Timothy 2:15, AKJV

Day 4

"All Scripture is God-breathed and is useful for teaching, rebuking, correcting and training in righteousness, so that the man of God may be thoroughly equipped for every good work."

2 Timothy 3:16-17, NIV

I love the word "useful" in this verse. God's Word is nothing, if not useful!

When I moved into a new home a few years ago, I received the greatest house-warming gift. My friend made me a notebook to hold all of the owner's manuals for the equipment in my home. Anytime I had a question about an appliance, proper care of my countertops, or how to winterize my sprinklers, I knew right where to go. I never made a mistake, or messed up a valuable piece of equipment, because I knew how to care for them properly.

So often we grope around, asking people for advice and looking for answers to our questions from those around us. Psalm 119:105 NIV says, *"Your word is a lamp to my feet and a light for my path."* A lamp and a light can make a world of difference when you are wandering in darkness. They will illuminate the path and keep you from tripping or falling. That is what God's Word does; it lights the path of life and directs your next steps.

A lamp and a light can make a world of difference when you are wandering in darkness.

I'm going to be honest and tell you that we will often find things in the Bible that we don't understand. But don't worry about it. God will bring the understanding to you when you need it.

Let's act on the things we do understand and more will be revealed to us, as we continue to faithfully study!

> *"The unfolding of your words gives light; it gives understanding to the simple."* Psalm 119:130, NIV

DAY 5

"All Scripture is God-breathed and is useful for teaching, rebuking, correcting and training in righteousness, so that the man of God may be thoroughly equipped for every good work."
2 TIMOTHY 3:16-17, NIV

"Your word I have hidden in my heart, That I might not sin against You." (Psalm 119:11, NKJV)

"Your words were found, and I ate them, And Your word was to me the joy and rejoicing of my heart; For I am called by Your name, O LORD God of hosts." (Jeremiah 15:16, NKJV)

"Jesus answered, 'It is written: Man does not live on bread alone, but on every word that comes from the mouth of God.'" (Matthew 4:4, NIV)

"Let the word of Christ dwell in you richly in all wisdom, teaching and admonishing one another in psalms and hymns and spiritual songs, singing with grace in your hearts to the Lord." (Colossians 3:16, NKJV)

If you allow the Word of Christ to dwell in you, it will change your life. People can write books, preach great sermons, and encourage you in your faith, but the Bible is the ONLY way that you can grow to the full level that God has intended for you. It is the way that you can truly understand Him and devote your life to His purpose and plan.

Hide His Word in your heart and your heart will become reflective of His!

Day 6

"All Scripture is God-breathed and is useful for teaching, rebuking, correcting and training in righteousness, so that the man of God may be thoroughly equipped for every good work."

2 Timothy 3:16-17, NIV

In 1 Peter 1:25 NIV we read "…*'but the word of the Lord stands forever.' And this is the word that was preached to you.*"

Jesus, the Living Word, is the same yesterday, today, and forever (Hebrews 13:8). In an ever-changing world, you can trust that the truth in the Bible won't change. God has asked that we do good things in His name. This requires teaching and training from His Word—the only way we can be equipped to do every good work for God.

The Word of the Lord stands forever, and it was given to us. We have the knowledge of the Almighty God, literally, at our fingertips!

DAY 7

"All Scripture is God-breathed and is useful for teaching, rebuking, correcting and training in righteousness, so that the man of God may be thoroughly equipped for every good work."
2 TIMOTHY 3:16-17, NIV

In 1 Timothy 4:16 NLT Paul writes: "*Keep a close watch on how you live and on your teaching. Stay true to what is right for the sake of your own salvation and the salvation of those who hear you.*" Let's encourage each other to get in the Word. Let's direct others to the Bible and the truth they can find in the Word, not to our own knowledge or wisdom. If you have a friend asking you for advice, know Scripture well enough to know where to direct them.

President Ronald Reagan was quoted as saying, "Within the covers of one single book, the Bible, are all the answers to all the problems that face us today—if only we would read and believe."

Gipsy Smith told of a man who said he had received no inspiration from the Bible, although he had "gone through it several times." "Let *it* go through *you* once," Smith replied, "then you will tell a different story!"

> "LET *IT* GO THROUGH YOU ONCE, THEN YOU WILL TELL A DIFFERENT STORY!"

The Bible is a love letter, instruction manual, and adventure novel, sent to us from our Father with love and compassion. Read it, recommend it, and reap the benefits!

Week 41

He answered: "'Love the Lord your God with all your heart and with all your soul and with all your strength and with all your mind;' and, 'Love your neighbor as yourself.'"
"You have answered correctly," Jesus replied.
"Do this and you will live."

Luke 10:27-28, NIV

DAY 1

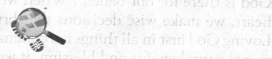

He answered: "'Love the Lord your God with all your heart and with all your soul and with all your strength and with all your mind;' and, 'Love your neighbor as yourself.'"
"You have answered correctly," Jesus replied.
"Do this and you will live."
LUKE 10:27-28, NIV

These are the two greatest commandments in the Bible (Matthew 22:37-39). Loving the Lord is the most important thing we have been instructed to do, and a close second is to love others.

Jesus gave this answer in response to a question from a lawyer who had a firm grasp of the Jewish Law, a written document that included more than 600 individual commands. The lawyer had asked Jesus what he must do to inherit eternal life. Whether the man was a sincere seeker or simply baiting Jesus, we do not know. But without hesitation Jesus handled the question by asking two more: *"What is written in the law? How do you read it?"* (Luke 10:26, NIV). The lawyer gave the correct answer.

LOVING GOD MUST BE THE FOUNDATION UPON WHICH WE LIVE OUR LIVES.

Loving God must be the foundation upon which we live our lives. Notice the Scripture does not tell us to respect God with everything, or give Him everything. The commandment is clear: *love* the Lord your God with every part of you. It may be possible to respect or sacrifice for someone without loving them. But it is impossible to truly love someone and want to withhold any good thing from them.

As with every instruction in the Bible, the command to love God is there for our benefit. When we love God with our whole heart, we make wise decisions that bring blessing into our lives. Loving God first in all things is a commandment and all commandments carry benefits and blessing. If we love Him first, respecting Him and giving everything we have to Him will easily follow, and our lives will be blessed.

DAY 2

He answered: "'Love the Lord your God with all your
heart and with all your soul and with all
your strength and with all your mind;' and,
'Love your neighbor as yourself.'"
"You have answered correctly," Jesus replied.
"Do this and you will live."
LUKE 10:27-28, NIV

Your heart, soul, strength, and mind are specific aspects of you. Your heart is the very essence of your life; it is a vital organ. But loving God with your heart also refers to your will, conscience, and emotions—your inner self. Your strength is your physical body and power. Loving God with your inner body and your outer body is necessary. Your soul is the eternal part of you that will live on forever. To love God with your mind means to direct your intellect and knowledge to love Him.

The way to love God with all of these parts is by allowing Him to have control of them. You can't give Him control of your heart, but keep your body and mind from Him. Conflict and confusion result.

Give all of yourself to God and love Him completely. You cannot conceive what He has planned for you!

"However, as it is written: 'No eye has seen, no ear has heard, no mind has conceived what God has prepared for those who love him.'" 1 Corinthians 2:9, NIV

"But the man who loves God is known by God." 1 Corinthians 8:3, NIV

Day 3

He answered: "'Love the Lord your God with all your
heart and with all your soul and with all
your strength and with all your mind;' and,
'Love your neighbor as yourself.'"
"You have answered correctly," Jesus replied.
"Do this and you will live."
Luke 10:27-28, NIV

The Bible is clear on how important the instruction to love God is, and refers to this subject many times. The love of God is perfect love (1 John 4:18), and perfect love drives out the thing that affects us the most negatively: fear.

Relying on God's love is important. We don't have enough to get by on our own, especially when it comes to loving others as ourselves. When we truly love Him, we have nothing to fear in the present or for eternity. Since perfect love casts out fear, those who really love God do not need to struggle with that emotion.

A fear-free zone sounds really great! Living in one is the result of loving God with our whole beings!

"And so we know and rely on the love God has for us. God is love. Whoever lives in love lives in God, and God in him. In this way, love is made complete among us so that we will have confidence on the day of judgment, because in this world we are like him. There is no fear in love. But perfect love drives out fear, because fear has to

do with punishment. The one who fears is not made perfect in love." 1 John 4:16-18, NIV

"Teacher, which is the greatest commandment in the Law?" Jesus replied: "'Love the Lord your God with all your heart and with all your soul and with all your mind.' This is the first and greatest commandment. And the second is like it: 'Love your neighbor as yourself.' All the Law and the Prophets hang on these two commandments." Matthew 22:36-40, NIV

Day 4

He answered: "'Love the Lord your God with all your heart and with all your soul and with all your strength and with all your mind;' and, 'Love your neighbor as yourself.'"
"You have answered correctly," Jesus replied. "Do this and you will live."
Luke 10:27-28, NIV

"*Love your neighbor as yourself*" is the second most important thing we can do in our entire lives. It's no wonder that the enemy attacks our relationships and our ability to love.

The temptation to fear and dislike others is overwhelming at times. Loving others goes hand-in-hand with loving God. We can't love God while we hate someone else.

As a speaker and writer, I have faced criticism about how I speak and what I teach. I had to learn a long time ago to only try and please one person: my Father in heaven. This stance makes criticism of me roll off my back.

> We can't love God while we hate someone else.

However, if I hear anyone say something even slightly negative about my husband or my children, or reject them in some way, I'm immediately defensive on my family's behalf! I love them fiercely and I know their hearts, minds, and motives. My love for them drives me to protect not just their physical selves but their emotions, their identity—even their reputations.

God feels the same way when someone rejects one of His children. God wants us to be loved. His design is that to be loved, you must love others first. When we love God first and others second, there is no time to be self-centered or to focus on negative things. When you walk in love and live in love, how could you stay cranky or miserable?

Everything in life is a choice. You must choose to love others, even if they don't seem particularly lovable. Loving others is beneficial to others and to you!

> *"If anyone says, 'I love God,' yet hates his brother, he is a liar. For anyone who does not love his brother, whom he has seen, cannot love God, whom he has not seen. And he has given us this command: Whoever loves God must also love his brother."* 1 John 4:20-21, NIV

> *"Now about brotherly love we do not need to write to you, for you yourselves have been taught by God to love each other."* 1 Thessalonians 4:9, NIV

DAY 5

He answered: "'Love the Lord your God with all your heart and with all your soul and with all your strength and with all your mind;' and, 'Love your neighbor as yourself.'"
"You have answered correctly," Jesus replied. "Do this and you will live."

LUKE 10:27-28, NIV

The fact that God loved us first and chose us makes it so much easier for us to love Him. John 15:16 NIV says, "*You did not choose me, but I chose you and appointed you to go and bear fruit—fruit that will last. Then the Father will give you whatever you ask in my name.*"

It feels good to be chosen. When someone loves you first, it is easy to love them back. 1 John 4:19 NIV says, "*We love because He first loved us.*" We cannot give away what we don't have. We are able to love because God has loved us with great depth and passion. We have much love to give because love has been freely given to us.

We often spend too much time trying to sell God to people and convince them to choose Him, as if He were one of several competing products. But what if we approached people in a different way and started telling them that God chose them? God isn't a big scary man in heaven waiting for us to prove ourselves. He is a perfect Father who loves us and has chosen us.

WE OFTEN SPEND TOO MUCH TIME TRYING TO SELL GOD TO PEOPLE AND CONVINCE THEM TO CHOOSE HIM, AS IF HE WERE ONE OF SEVERAL COMPETING PRODUCTS.

In elementary school, did you ever have to stand in a line-up and wait to be picked for a team? The wait could be excruciating, especially if you weren't a star athlete! Remember the relief and boost of confidence you felt when a captain finally called your name?

God has already called you out of the line and wants you on His team. It took no special skill or talent on your part. He loves you and that is all that is required!

"And so we know and rely on the love God has for us. God is love. Whoever lives in love lives in God, and God in him." 1 John 4:16, NIV

DAY 6

He answered: "'Love the Lord your God with all your heart and with all your soul and with all your strength and with all your mind;' and, 'Love your neighbor as yourself.'"
"You have answered correctly," Jesus replied.
"Do this and you will live."

LUKE 10:27-28, NIV

"*Do this and you will live*." Jesus is talking here about living well on earth and living for eternity with Him. Of course, we can't live up to these commandments all the time in our own strength. That is why we need grace.

THERE IS A DIFFERENCE BETWEEN BEING ALIVE AND REALLY LIVING.

Matthew 22:40 says all of the Jewish Law and the prophets' teachings hang on these two greatest commandments. They are the foundation from which everything flows. Practicing these commands provides a solid foundation for your life, from which blessings will flow here and for eternity.

There is a difference between being alive and really living. If you carry out these two commandments, you will experience a life worth having. You won't just survive; you will thrive and live abundantly.

When you love others, your life is full. When you reach out, you will have many arms reaching for you when you need them. If struggles come and you face challenges, you will have love returned to you in the same way you have extended it.

Make a choice to live—not just be alive. Choose to have an abundant life. Then, help someone else find theirs, too!

Day 7

He answered: "'Love the Lord your God with all your
heart and with all your soul and with all
your strength and with all your mind;' and,
'Love your neighbor as yourself.'"
"You have answered correctly," Jesus replied.
"Do this and you will live."
Luke 10:27-28, NIV

Although more than 600 specific regulations existed in the Jewish Law, these two commandments were deemed most important by Jesus. He promised that if we obeyed these important instructions, we would really live.

Love the Lord and love others—so simple in word, so challenging in action, so rewarding if completed!

Be sure to memorize this verse. Take time to know it and embed it into your heart and mind!

WEEK 42

"So encourage each other and build each other up, just as you are already doing."

1 THESSALONIANS 5:11, NLT

DAY 1

"So encourage each other and build each other up, just as you are already doing."
1 THESSALONIANS 5:11, NLT

I love spending one-on-one time with my kids. Most people call it a date, but my six year old son Jackson thinks that word is embarrassing, so we don't call it that. When it is time to hang out with him and I ask what he wants to do, the answer is always the same: "How about if you watch me play video games?" He loves nothing more than having me watch him play video games, explaining every move, level, and character in the game while I cheer him on the entire time. He loves to be told how amazing he is at something that is important to him.

DON'T LET AN OPPORTUNITY TO BUILD SOMEONE UP GO BY.

Jackson is just like all of us. We all love to be cheered on, to be encouraged. Encouragement has many forms and one of the best is noticing what is important to someone else and acknowledging their achievement.

Don't let an opportunity to build someone up go by. Too often we think great thoughts about someone, but don't let the words escape our lips. Use your voice today to be an encouragement to someone.

"Taking an interest in what others are thinking and doing is often a much more powerful form of encouragement than praise."
— Robert Martin

Day 2

"So encourage each other and build each other
up, just as you are already doing."
1 Thessalonians 5:11, NLT

The definition of "encouragement" in *Webster's Dictionary* is "to inspire with courage, spirit, or hope, and to spur on." To inspire someone with courage, spirit, and hope is an amazing human ability. Many people stand by, waiting for the chance to be negative and critical of others. Such an attitude tears people down. But building something takes time, planning, and thought. Taking the opportunity to build up a person is something that shouldn't be taken lightly or missed. The kind of encouragement that is constructive takes planning and effort at times, but the resultsare worth it!

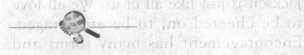

Flatter me, and I may not believe you.
Criticize me, and I may not like you.
Ignore me, and I may not forgive you.
Encourage me, and I will not forget you.
—— William Arthur Ward.

DAY 3

"So encourage each other and build each other up, just as you are already doing."

1 THESSALONIANS 5:11, NLT

Paul wrote this letter to the Thessalonican church while he was in Corinth. He had previously visited the Thessalonicans, and had received a recent report from Timothy. Paul used the opportunity of this letter to commend the church on their behavior in a time of persecution. He offered them hope by reminding them of Christ's return.

> SPIRITUAL ENCOURAGEMENT IS THE KEY TO SPURRING PEOPLE ON AND GIVING THEM THE ENDURANCE TO "FINISH THE RACE."

Paul believed enough in the concept of building others up that he wrote this letter of encouragement to the Thessalonicans. At the end of his life, Paul, in his role as Timothy's mentor, also encouraged Timothy greatly by writing: *"I have fought the good fight, I have finished the race, and I have remained faithful"* (2 Timothy 4:7, NLT).

Spiritual encouragement is the key to spurring people on and giving them the endurance to "finish the race." Today's verse refers to spiritual encouragement, which is what people need most. To have the faith, hope, and patience we need to thrive in this life, it takes spiritual encouragement from God's Word and from His people.

Day 4

"So encourage each other and build each other up, just as you are already doing."

1 Thessalonians 5:11, NLT

A few years ago I ran a marathon. It took an incredible amount of work and effort (that is my nice way of saying it was tremendously horrible!).

After training for nine months, my friend Lois and I met at the starting line and took off together. For the first thirteen miles I felt great. For the next four I began to fade. By mile 20 I wanted to lay down in the fetal position and cry for my mommy.

As we rounded a corner at mile 21, I began to hear people shouting our names. There on the side of the street stood our families, holding up signs and cheering for us with all of their might. If they had not been there, I would not have made it to the end of that race. Their encouragement gave me what I needed to make it to the finish line, and crossing that line was one of the greatest achievements of my life.

When you go to work, the store, or anywhere else, you will come across people who are at mile 21 in their life. At that moment you have the opportunity to be their cheerleader, an opportunity to change their lives.

Keep your eyes open today; you may have the opportunity to change a life. Don't miss out!

DAY 5

"So encourage each other and build each other up, just as you are already doing."

1 THESSALONIANS 5:11, NLT

My favorite verse in the Bible is at the end of this chapter: *"The one who calls you is faithful and he will do it"* (1 Thessalonians 5:24, NIV). The verses between today's verse and my favorite verse (24) are full of instructions—the kinds of things you know would make your life better if you would just do them. But they can seem overwhelming, even impossible to do, until you get to the last verse. Paul says the Faithful One will give you what you need to fulfill these directions.

The end of this week's verse shows Paul commending the Thessalonican church for already being encouraging to one another, and he tells them to continue. It is important to acknowledge others while they are going strong.

IT IS IMPORTANT TO ACKNOWLEDGE OTHERS WHILE THEY ARE GOING STRONG.

I love Victoria Osteen's take on being encouraging, which is the visual concept of filling someone's bucket with encouragement. To be a filler—not just a dipper—is an admirable goal.

Day 6

"So encourage each other and build each other up, just as you are already doing."
1 Thessalonians 5:11, NLT

In Deuteronomy 3:28 NIV God gives Moses this command: *"But commission Joshua, and encourage and strengthen him, for he will lead this people across and will cause them to inherit the land that you will see."* Moses had been told that he wouldn't enter the Promised Land himself, but that Joshua would lead in his place. The instruction to encourage and strengthen Joshua so that he would have what he needed was a serious task laid upon Moses—a man who already had a tremendous load on his shoulders!

Many people confuse flattery with encouragement, but they are very different things.

Many people confuse flattery with encouragement, but they are very different things. Encouragement often costs the giver without requiring anything from the receiver, whereas flattery often benefits the giver more than the receiver. Moses had to build Joshua up and strengthen him so that Joshua could finish the goal God had begun with Moses. Moses had to put aside his own desires to fulfill God's plan—something Moses had learned to do well over the last forty years. Moses then had to go on, to continue leading and teaching the people so they would eventually be ready to enter the Promised Land, while spendingextra time with Joshua to be sure he was prepared.

We are told in Deuteronomy 34:9 NIV: *"Now Joshua son of Nun was filled with the spirit of wisdom because Moses had laid his hands on him. So the Israelites listened to him and did what the LORD had commanded Moses.*" When Moses died in Moab, it was time for Joshua to take over. Moses had done what was required of him by teaching, encouraging, and leading. Now the ones to whom he had ministered were ready to fulfill their destinies.

Everyone has a purpose to fulfill. By living a life of encouragement, we can play a role in their destiny.

DAY 7

"So encourage each other and build each other up, just as you are already doing."

1 THESSALONIANS 5:11, NLT

In my life I can clearly identify the encouragers around me. My parents and grandparents have always told me I could do anything I put my mind to. My dad and mom are very hard working and instilled that in me. My grandparents have always been my cheerleaders and a great support. In high school my youth pastors were instrumental in encouraging me to serve the Lord and make something of my life. I know I wouldn't have survived adolescence without all of these people.

As an adult I have become a better wife and mother because of my friend Lois. I met Lois when I was a very young mom and had no idea what I was doing. The Lord brought her into my life at just the right time. Lois has always been a step ahead of me in being a wife and mother but she never made me feel less than her, she always built me up. My family is better because of her love and support. Encouragement really does build someone up, and that means the alternative is to tear them down. None of us got to where we are alone. We got there because there were others giving us advice, support, and love. Look around and acknowledge the encouragement you received and then be that for someone else!

Week 43

"Do not remember the former things, nor consider the things of old. Behold, I will do a new thing, now it shall spring forth; shall you not know it?
I will even make a road in the wilderness
and rivers in the desert."

Isaiah 43:18-19, NKJV

DAY 1

"Do not remember the former things, nor consider the things of old. Behold, I will do a new thing, now it shall spring forth; shall you not know it? I will even make a road in the wilderness and rivers in the desert."
ISAIAH 43:18-19, NKJV

It is so easy to play the "what if" game; to sit back and think about the "could haves" and "should haves" regarding past situations. But focusing on the past is a ploy of the enemy. He wants people to wallow and focus on past mistakes and missed opportunities.

THE WAY WE THINK ABOUT THE PAST CAN HOLD US BACK LIKE AN ANCHOR, MAKING IT IMPOSSIBLE TO MOVE FORWARD.

No matter how difficult any event was, it doesn't have to be a negative influence on present day life. Feeling sorry for ourselves, angry toward others, guilty, or ashamed for getting the short end of the stick in the past, will only keep us from thriving in the present and future.

Today's verse from Isaiah instructs us to neither remember *"nor consider the things of old."* Remembering them takes time and energy that can be better spent in other ways. The way we think about the past can hold us back like an anchor, making it impossible to move forward. What is past is all said and done. The present and future remain to be seen.

Your past can teach you something that spurs you on to the next level, or it can be a heavy weight that holds you back. Do not remember or consider the old stuff...God is doing a new thing!

"Therefore, if anyone is in Christ, he is a new creation; the old has gone, the new has come!" 2 Corinthians 5:17, NIV

DAY 2

"Do not remember the former things, nor consider the
things of old. Behold, I will do a new thing, now it
shall spring forth; shall you not know it?
I will even make a road in the wilderness
and rivers in the desert."
ISAIAH 43:18-19, NKJV

God makes a promise in this verse: *"Behold, I will do a new thing…."* God isn't going to concentrate on our past failures or mistakes. Instead, He is going to do a new thing in our life.

That is God's way—to look ahead. He looks ahead and wants us to fix our eyes on the future as well. Lamentations 3:22-23 NIV says, *"Because of the LORD's great love we are not consumed, for his compassions never fail. They are new every morning; great is your faithfulness."*

NEW BEGINNINGS PROVIDE A CHANCE TO START OVER AND DO THINGS DIFFERENTLY.

Recently I was with my son in a video game store. There was a certain video game he wanted, but they only had a used one. I was ready to buy it for him when we realized the last player's memory would be on the game. Jack would want to start the game fresh, not where someone else left off. So we went to another store and bought the new version of the game.

If you have ever bought a used game (I have bought many!), you know that sometimes they don't work well. Sometimes they have a scratch or defect that you can't find until you play it. They also carry someone else's history encoded into it. My kids prefer new games because they offer a fresh start right from the beginning.

New beginnings provide a chance to start over and do things differently. We can easily become complacent and ritualistic with life. Taking chances and discovering new things can seem overwhelming and cause fear within us. But the truth is: experiencing something new is exhilarating and exciting.

So today, let God do the new thing!

DAY 3

"Do not remember the former things, nor consider the things of old. Behold, I will do a new thing, now it shall spring forth; shall you not know it? I will even make a road in the wilderness and rivers in the desert."

ISAIAH 43:18-19, NKJV

"*...Now it shall spring forth,*" Isaiah writes. God is telling us that when He gives us a new thing, it will spring forth!

I remember a time in our lives when Dave was looking for a new job. Résumés were distributed and interviews attended. Two people wanted to hire him. But then, out of nowhere, someone called and offered him a completely unexpected job. That unexpected job was the one he took. Despite his best efforts and planning, the job Dave was meant to have just "sprang forth."

God is often portrayed as subtle, but I disagree. When you are walking in obedience and being faithful, you will see and hear Him loud and clear. Job 37:5 NIV says: "*God's voice thunders in marvelous ways; he does great things beyond our understanding.*" God's action may come in unexpected ways, but God's creative power and plans shouldn't be unexpected.

GOD'S ACTION MAY COME IN UNEXPECTED WAYS, BUT GOD'S CREATIVE POWER AND PLANS SHOULDN'T BE UNEXPECTED.

In the season of spring, everything is fresh and new. The stale air and dull feeling of winter melt away as everything grows and blooms. God takes us to new levels and new places in our lives so that we can grow and, for lack of a better term, blossom. But to grab hold of the new things, you must release the old—like trees do with their leaves each fall.

No matter what you have to release, let go when God asks you to and be ready to embrace the new thing. You might have a season of winter first, but it will absolutely spring forth and change your life.

"To be made new in the attitude of your minds; and to put on the new self, created to be like God in true righteousness and holiness."
Ephesians 4:23-24, NIV

DAY 4

"Do not remember the former things, nor consider the things of old. Behold, I will do a new thing, now it shall spring forth; shall you not know it? I will even make a road in the wilderness and rivers in the desert."

ISAIAH 43:18-19, NKJV

Challenges come in life.

Sometimes they are caused by an error we made along the way. We fix those situations by asking God to forgive us for our mistake and provide us with the grace we need to correct the error.

Sometimes we experience challenges because we have been wronged. These wrongs are righted by asking God to help us forgive the person and receiving His grace to carry on while He makes "*all things new*" (Revelation 21:5).

At other times, challenges are simply growing pains, helping us get to the next level. Faith and patience are usually the remedy for these challenging times of growth.

Isaiah writes: "*Shall you not know it?*" Recognizing God's voice and being immediately obedient to what He is saying and doing is the fastest way to get through a challenging time. But we have to do more than just recognize Him; we have to do what He asks of us and *not* do what He doesn't.

Sometimes God doesn't tell us how to fix it. Sometimes He asks us to hang on and wait. Do you have faith to wait during these challenging times, believing that God is going to bring out the best in every situation? Is the patience there to get you through, no matter how long it takes?

One day, Dave decided to take our son Jackson a special lunch to school as a treat. But when Jack arrived at school and realized he had no lunch box, he got very worried and had the teacher call us. When Dave arrived at school with a hot lunch from Jack's favorite fast food place, Dave reminded Jack that we have never forgotten to feed him lunch before. Jack learned that he can trust that we will never let him go hungry, that we will always get a lunch to him. For weeks after that, Jack would get to school hoping he had no lunch box, because he knew it meant a special treat!

God has always taken care of you up to this point. He has proven Himself faithful. When you remain faithful, do you recognize Him? Do you see that He is doing a new thing and trust that it will be better than the old thing?

Just because you don't see the answer to your situation, the same way Jackson didn't see his lunch box, doesn't mean God isn't bringing the answer to your door just in time. He is working on it, orchestrating a plan. And when that answer arrives, you will be so thankful that you didn't have your old lunch anymore!

> *"He was in the world, and though the world was made through him, the world did not recognize him."* John 1:10, NIV

DAY 5

"Do not remember the former things, nor consider the things of old. Behold, I will do a new thing, now it shall spring forth; shall you not know it?
I will even make a road in the wilderness
and rivers in the desert."

ISAIAH 43:18-19, NKJV

Have you ever been so deep into a forest or wilderness that all you really wanted was a road to lead you out? As long as you could see a road—even if you couldn't see where it ended—you felt confident that, eventually, you would find the way out.

I went on a long road trip through Arizona and California with my kids, mom, and step-dad this summer. I was in an air-conditioned car as we drove through the desert, but just *looking* outside made me thirsty. I imagined what it must feel like to be out in the middle of that desert with no water. It isn't something I ever want to experience. In the middle of a desert, there would be no greater relief than the sudden appearance of a river.

If you feel like you are in the middle of a desert or a wilderness right now, have faith that God will make a road, and a river! A road gives you direction and hope for getting out. A river gives you what you need to survive and thrive while you are there. So keep your eyes open, get on the road, take a drink, and rinse off the dust in the river.

Day 6

"Do not remember the former things, nor consider the things of old. Behold, I will do a new thing, now it shall spring forth; shall you not know it? I will even make a road in the wilderness and rivers in the desert."

Isaiah 43:18-19, NKJV

In Proverbs 3:6 (AMP), a wise man taught: "*In all your ways know, recognize, and acknowledge Him, and He will direct and make straight and plain your paths.*" God has a plan and a purpose for our lives. When we listen to Him, His plan and purpose for us becomes straight and plain. God's direction will become as obvious as the only road in a dense wilderness, or as clear as a river in the middle of a fiery, hot desert. But we have to choose to follow the road out. We have to choose to drink from and jump into the river.

I love Don Moen's worship chorus *God Will Make A Way*, based upon Isaiah 43:19 and Proverbs 3:6:

God will make a way,

Where there seems to be no way
He works in ways we cannot see
He will make a way for me
He will be my guide
Hold me closely to His side
With love and strength for each new day
He will make a way, He will make a way.

By a roadway in the wilderness, He'll lead me
And rivers in the desert will I see
Heaven and earth will fade
But His Word will still remain
He will do something new today.

God will make a way…

Day 7

"Do not remember the former things, nor consider the things of old. Behold, I will do a new thing, now it shall spring forth; shall you not know it? I will even make a road in the wilderness and rivers in the desert."

Isaiah 43:18-19, NKJV

I heard a story about a London businessman named Lindsay Clegg regarding a property he was selling. The building had been empty for months and needed repairs. Vandals had damaged the doors, smashed the windows, and strewn trash around the interior. As he showed a prospective buyer the property, Clegg took pains to point out everything he would do to repair the warehouse: replace the broken windows, bring in a crew to correct any structural damage, and clean out the garbage. "Forget about the repairs," the buyer said. "When I buy this place, I'm going to build something completely different. I don't want the building; I want the site."

God's plans for you are so much bigger than your own. Our efforts to improve our own lives are like putting a Band-Aid on a gaping wound. When we give our lives to the Lord, He makes all things new (2 Corinthians 5:17). All He wants is the building site and the permission to create a new thing.

After Jesus was arrested and put to death, the days were dark and frightening for His followers. They didn't know that this ultimate sacrifice had to be made for the salvation of all mankind. But after Jesus was resurrected, they understood the purpose and plan.

We may not see the full picture and understand what is going on in our lives, but don't worry. The Creator of the universe sees all and sees you, too, and His plan can be trusted.

Week 44

"Don't worry about anything; instead, pray about everything. Tell God what you need, and thank him for all he has done. Then you will experience God's peace, which exceeds anything we can understand. His peace will guard your hearts and minds as you live in Christ Jesus."

Philippians 4:6-7, NLT

Day 1

"Don't worry about anything; instead, pray about everything. Tell God what you need, and thank him for all he has done. Then you will experience God's peace, which exceeds anything we can understand. His peace will guard your hearts and minds as you live in Christ Jesus."

Philippians 4:6-7, NLT

Take note of the words "anything" and "everything" in this week's verse. It's so tempting to justify at least *some* of our worry. But clearly, we are not to worry about anything.

The beginning of worry is the end of faith. The minute worry creeps in, we are supposed to pray about it, tell God what we need, and thank Him for what He has done. Dr. E. Stanley Jones, a 20th century Methodist missionary, made the following observation on this subject:

The beginning of worry is the end of faith.

> I am inwardly fashioned for faith, not for fear. Fear is not my native land; faith is. I am so made that worry and anxiety are sand in the machinery of life; faith is the oil. I live better by faith and confidence than by fear, doubt and anxiety. In anxiety and worry, my being is gasping for breath—these are not my native air. But in faith and confidence, I breathe freely—these are my native air.
>
> A John Hopkins University doctor said, 'We do not know why it is that worriers die sooner than the non-worriers, but that is a fact.' But I, who am simple of mind, think I know: We are

> inwardly constructed in nerve and tissue, brain cell and soul, for faith and not for fear. God made us that way. To live by worry is to live against reality."

Jesus spoke to the disciples on the subject of worry: "*Can all your worries add a single moment to your life? And if worry can't accomplish a little thing like that, what's the use of worrying over bigger things?*" (Luke 12:25-26, NLT) Worry is faith in the negative and belief in defeat. As the old saying goes: worry is wasting today's time to clutter up tomorrow's opportunities with yesterday's troubles.

Retrain your brain to think: Worry = need to pray, not need to fear.

DAY 2

"Don't worry about anything; instead, pray about everything. Tell God what you need, and thank him for all he has done. Then you will experience God's peace, which exceeds anything we can understand. His peace will guard your hearts and minds as you live in Christ Jesus."

PHILIPPIANS 4:6-7, NLT

Prayer has taken on a different meaning over time. Originally, prayer was meant as a dialogue. Now, it's mostly thought of (and engaged in) as a monologue. Prayer used to be a conversation, not a confrontation. Now days we are likely to get before the Lord, say our piece, and then get out.

But the real need isn't for us to speak; the real need is for us to listen. We need to hear God more than we need to be heard by God. Matthew 6:8 tells us that He knows what we need before we even ask it. If you will get before the Lord and pray a sentence or two and then be quiet, the Lord will bring specific scripture, or even give you direction on how to pray. All prayer has power and any prayer is better than none. But I submit to you that if you will just learn to listen and be patient, clear direction will come.

> *"Cease striving, and know that I am God"* (Psalm 46:10, NASB).

> *"Trust in the Lord with all your heart and lean not on your own understanding; in all your ways acknowledge Him and He will make your paths straight"* (Proverbs 3:5-6).

These things are written in the Word to remind us to not just speak our piece and move on, but to give God time to speak peace to us before we move on.

Pray about everything, and don't worry about anything.

DAY 3

"Don't worry about anything; instead, pray about everything. Tell God what you need, and thank him for all he has done. Then you will experience God's peace, which exceeds anything we can understand. His peace will guard your hearts and minds as you live in Christ Jesus."

PHILIPPIANS 4:6-7, NLT

One day I found the following statement: "Peace that Jesus gives is not the absence of trouble, but is rather the confidence that He is there with you always." I believe this is very true.

Things come up that can cause stress or trouble. But God's peace transcends all understanding. The peace that comes from God can defy logic. Having the peace of God explains why you can be in the worst time of your life, yet feel deep down that everything is going to be all right.

Jesus promised that He will always be with you (Matthew 28:20). If you develop deep confidence in that truth, peace will come over you like a crashing wave—no matter what your situation is like. Perfect peace can only come from God. He will give it to those who are doing His will and bringing glory to Him.

When you serve the Father and something comes up, tell yourself, "It is in God's hands; I have turned it over to Him. I am not struggling with it anymore. I am not wrestling with the issues anymore; I have turned them over to God, and now I am going to rest in Him." Then, the peace that passes all human understanding will come over you. Even though you can't understand how you can feel peace in the midst of turmoil, you just *do!*

Day 4

"Don't worry about anything; instead, pray about everything. Tell God what you need, and thank him for all he has done. Then you will experience God's peace, which exceeds anything we can understand. His peace will guard your hearts and minds as you live in Christ Jesus."

Philippians 4:6-7, NLT

The peace of God transcends all understanding, because understanding simply refers to our human capacity to comprehend a situation. Our mind and our knowledge do not enable us to understand how something will work out or how we can get out of trouble unscathed. But if you live in Christ Jesus, when your understanding hits a wall (which it inevitable will), *that* is the moment when peace steps in and opens a door—if you will allow it. Isaiah 26:3-4 NLT reiterates the advice of this verse, saying, *"You will keep in perfect peace all who trust in you, all whose thoughts are fixed on you! Trust in the Lord always, for the Lord God is the eternal Rock."*

Perfect peace is what we need.

Perfect peace is what we need. We can find peace or stress relief temporarily in other things, but worry eventually creeps back. Perfect peace is never-failing and requires complete trust in God. Trust is the key. God is always in control, but it is your choice to fall into His hands or to fall apart.

Isaiah instructs us to keep our thoughts fixed on God. Keeping our thoughts focused on God is extremely important. When we follow that instruction, we overflow with more than just peace. I love Isaiah's description of God as the Eternal Rock. Eternal is forever—the sort of forever that has no ending but also no beginning, which means there was never a time when it wasn't there—and rock implies a solid foundation. Together they add up to a perfect picture of strength and stability.

When things come up that try to rob your peace, stay fixed on the Lord, trust Him always, and peace *will* come!

Day 5

"Don't worry about anything; instead, pray about everything. Tell God what you need, and thank him for all he has done. Then you will experience God's peace, which exceeds anything we can understand. His peace will guard your hearts and minds as you live in Christ Jesus."

Philippians 4:6-7, NLT

On a warm summer day, I took my children with some of my girlfriends and their kids to swim at a small lake. I am not a very strong swimmer and my husband doesn't swim at all; our children aren't very proficient at it, either. In the heat and fun of the day, my daughter was having trouble getting onto an inflatable island we had put in the middle of this lake. Tessa was unable to climb up there in her lifejacket so she just took it off. But after several attempts to hoist herself up, she grew tired of trying and decided to swim for shore—without her lifejacket.

I caught her eye when she was half-way to shore and realized she was in trouble. Without hesitation I dove into the lake and swam to her. The problem was, as stated before, I am a terrible swimmer. I got to her and grabbed her just as she was going under, but quickly realized I was going under, too. I yelled for my girlfriend Lois. She swam out and grabbed Tessa as I barely saved myself and swam back to shore.

As all of this was going on, God and I were doing some close talking. Lois helped Tess get her jacket back on and they both came to shore slightly shaken, but safe—praise God! Despite a couple human errors, He protected us. We all came home that day stronger and wiser. We also quickly enrolled in swimming lessons, and always wear our lifejackets now. We had all the tools; we just hadn't used them to their fullest before. But now we do!

The year before, at the same place, my son Jackson and I had been in a car accident that should have taken our lives. Instead, we came out of it with only minor bumps and bruises. After the day at the lake, I lay in bed that night thanking God for protecting us. I realized that in both situations I hadn't panicked. Both times I knew that everything would be okay.

Those responses were more than unusual for me. I used to be scared of everything, and stressed out all of the time. I recalled many years before telling an older pastor that I just wanted peace, hoping he would tell me the "secret" for getting it. The man didn't. He just stared at me and I realized he didn't have it, either, and couldn't tell me where to get something he didn't have himself.

I purposed that day, after talking with that pastor, to specifically study the Bible on the topic of peace, and did so for many years. But I hadn't noticed how much I had changed. God had given me the thing I so desired! My life changed that night three years ago, and I have never been the same. Reading and studying about trust and faith had changed me, slowly but surely. And when the tough things came, I had the peace that surpassed all understanding!

Isn't that exciting? We can do very little in our own power. Oh, we can do some things—even great things. But they are so small in comparison to what can be accomplished when our trust and faith are grounded in Christ.

Day 6

"Don't worry about anything; instead, pray about everything. Tell God what you need, and thank him for all he has done. Then you will experience God's peace, which exceeds anything we can understand. His peace will guard your hearts and minds as you live in Christ Jesus."

Philippians 4:6-7, NLT

In a frenzied state of worry, what happens to you physically? Your heart beats fast. Your palms sweat. Your mind spins out of control with the "what ifs." Those are short-term effects, but worry can have very negative and permanent effects on your life-long health.

But peace will protect your heart and mind in Christ Jesus. It brings physical protection and spiritual protection. Jesus commands us to love God with all of our heart, soul, strength, and mind (Luke 10:27). When you love God in this way, His protection extends to you; there is no room for worry because every part of you is busy focused on God. With your focus on the right place, there is no way your mind can get off course.

> PEACE IS THE PROTECTION YOUR HEART, SOUL, STRENGTH, AND MIND NEED.

Unlike some ancient philosophers, Jesus never condemns people for recognizing their basic needs; our Father knows we need food and clothing. He simply calls us to depend on God for our daily needs instead of depending on our job, our spouse, our investments and savings, or our ability to work hard. All of those things can fail us, which is legitimate cause for worry, but those who truly trust their heavenly Father to care for them have no need to be anxious.

Worry will not add one day to your life (it can actually subtract from it), and anxiety certainly won't solve the problem. Peace is the protection your heart, soul, strength, and mind need. You can find it in Jesus, the Prince of Peace, and His Father, Jehovah Shalom, God our Peace.

DAY 7

"Don't worry about anything; instead, pray about everything. Tell God what you need, and thank him for all he has done. Then you will experience God's peace, which exceeds anything we can understand. His peace will guard your hearts and minds as you live in Christ Jesus."

PHILIPPIANS 4:6-7, NLT

Commentator Matthew Henry writes: "This peace will keep our hearts and minds through Christ Jesus; it will keep us from sinning under our troubles, and from sinking under them; keep us calm and sedate, without discomposure of passion, and with inward satisfaction."

Henry's comments, along with Paul's instructions to pray instead of worry, compel us to look again at Jesus' teaching on how to pray:

> *"In this manner, therefore, pray: Our Father in heaven, Hallowed be Your name. Your kingdom come. Your will be done on earth as it is in heaven. Give us this day our daily bread. And forgive us our debts, as we forgive our debtors. And do not lead us into temptation, but deliver us from the evil one. For Yours is the kingdom and the power and the glory forever. Amen."* (Matthew 6:9-13, NKJV)

WEEK 45

"Finally, brethren, whatever things are true, whatever things are noble, whatever things are just, whatever things are pure, whatever things are lovely, whatever things are of good report, if there is any virtue and if there is anything praiseworthy—meditate on these things. The things which you learned and received and heard and saw in me, these do, and the God of peace will be with you."

PHILIPPIANS 4:8-9, NKJV

DAY 1

"Finally, brethren, whatever things are true, whatever things are noble, whatever things are just, whatever things are pure, whatever things are lovely, whatever things are of good report, if there is any virtue and if there is anything praiseworthy—meditate on these things. The things which you learned and received and heard and saw in me, these do, and the God of peace will be with you."

PHILIPPIANS 4:8-9, NKJV

Part of my daily study time is to look up the meaning of words in the dictionary to be sure I understand what is being said. Here are *Webster's* definitions of words from this week's Scripture:

True: honest and just

Noble: possessing very high or excellent qualities or properties; very good or excellent; moral

Just: acting or being in conformity with what is morally upright or good; righteous

Pure: free from what vitiates, weakens, or pollutes; containing nothing that does not properly belong; free from moral fault or guilt

Lovely: delightful for beauty, harmony, or grace; eliciting love by moral or ideal worth

Understanding the meaning of words makes studying so much richer and easier. Hosea 4:6 says that God's people are destroyed due to lack of knowledge. Don't allow this to happen to you and your family. Grab hold of knowledge and understanding of the Word. Instead of self-destructing, you will thrive!

Day 2

"Finally, brethren, whatever things are true, whatever things are noble, whatever things are just, whatever things are pure, whatever things are lovely, whatever things are of good report, if there is any virtue and if there is anything praiseworthy—meditate on these things. The things which you learned and received and heard and saw in me, these do, and the God of peace will be with you."

Philippians 4:8-9, NKJV

One of the pieces of spiritual armor listed in Ephesians 6:14 is the *"belt of truth."* I think the idea of a belt that protects you by only allowing in truth is phenomenal. Often we are influenced by things that have no basis in reality. We might hear gossip that someone doesn't like us or a horror story of someone else's bad experience, and we become fearful, unable to live our lives freely. Sometimes an opinion or thought that belongs to someone else keeps us from doing what we are called to do. Truth allows us to see everything the way it really is, to see people for who they really are, and to see life from God's perspective. Like a belt that is wrapped around your middle from front to back, truth will protect your whole body.

Like a belt that is wrapped around your middle from front to back, truth will protect your whole body.

Have you heard the saying "garbage in, garbage out"? It's true! By focusing on what is noble, we fill our minds with what is good, excellent, and moral. By meditating upon what is just, we begin treating other people and circumstances in a Christ-like way. Meditating upon what is pure and lovely turns our thoughts and feelings away from negative or inappropriate things, such as revenge, unforgiveness, or wrongful sexual thoughts or desires. Are you holding others hostage for past hurts, or punishing them for wrongs committed against you in the past? Dwelling on these memories will not take your mind or your actions down a peaceful path.

As your mind races with thoughts and ideas, ask yourself: "Do my thoughts fit under any of the categories in this week's Scripture verses?" If the answer is "No," ask God to help you make some changes. You will love your life much more!

Day 3

"Finally, brethren, whatever things are true, whatever things are noble, whatever things are just, whatever things are pure, whatever things are lovely, whatever things are of good report, if there is any virtue and if there is anything praiseworthy—meditate on these things. The things which you learned and received and heard and saw in me, these do, and the God of peace will be with you."

Philippians 4:8-9, NKJV

Okay: when was the last time you complained about your parents? If you are over the age of 18 and you are still harboring resentment about your parents, I have a suggestion: forgive and get over it! Continuing to criticize your mother or father just doesn't fit under such categories as: *just*, *pure*, *lovely*, *true*, or *noble*.

The praiseworthy things deserve our attention, not only because focusing on them are the right thing to do, but because we reap what we sow.

Sometimes we come up with our own ungodly definition of honoring your parents (Exodus 20:12). Focusing on the efforts and sacrifices our parents made to raise us creates more peace inside us than reviewing those times we felt let down or disappointed. Did they do it perfectly? Of course not. But that does not invalidate all they did do for us.

Truth and perspective are good. I got a huge dose of them when I had my own children. I began to appreciate my parents much more after that. Raising children requires more of me than I even knew I had, and brought to life for me the phrase "Only by the grace of God!"

When I read the word "praiseworthy" in today's passage, I always think about my parents and husband. Every day I can think of some reason to praise God for these people. The praiseworthy things deserve our attention, not only because focusing on them are the right thing to do, but because we reap what we sow. I want my kids to speak well of me and forgive my mistakes.

Day 4

"Finally, brethren, whatever things are true, whatever things are noble, whatever things are just, whatever things are pure, whatever things are lovely, whatever things are of good report, if there is any virtue and if there is anything praiseworthy—meditate on these things. The things which you learned and received and heard and saw in me, these do, and the God of peace will be with you."

Philippians 4:8-9, NKJV

Philippians is classified as the fourth of Paul's prison letters. Upon learning about Paul's imprisonment in Rome, the church in Philippi sent a gift to Paul through Epaphroditus (4:18). This letter was a thank you letter combined with encouragement and exhortation to seek humility and unity.

Paul's example of encouraging others to focus on what is noble, true, pure, and lovely while he was in prison is amazing! When we go through challenging times, it is easy to sink into self-pity. But Paul even considered his imprisonment "*all joy*," because his situation inspired others to trust God even more. Paul encouraged the Philippians to show trust in God through prayer and thanksgiving, rather than live in fear and anxiety.

Focus upon whatever is virtuous or praiseworthy in any situation, no matter what the circumstances, "*and the God of peace will be with you.*"

DAY 5

"Finally, brethren, whatever things are true, whatever things are noble, whatever things are just, whatever things are pure, whatever things are lovely, whatever things are of good report, if there is any virtue and if there is anything praiseworthy—meditate on these things. The things which you learned and received and heard and saw in me, these do, and the God of peace will be with you."

PHILIPPIANS 4:8-9, NKJV

The outstanding advice in this week's Scripture encourages us to imitate what we have learned, received, heard, and seen in action from people we love and respect. Sometimes we see and hear good things, but we don't always choose to learn and receive them. Paul's instruction is clear: do what you've learned is the right thing to do in every area of your life.

Where are you spending your time and who are you spending it with? I love friends who, when I complain about something, say, "I love you, Kaci, but let it go!" When you find yourself in relationship with people who encourage you to vent or be angry, run! If you are trying to meditate on what is true and lovely, then confide in others who are working towards the same goal. My three co-authors of this book, three of the most outstanding people I know, are the first to tell me to get myself back on track. Those times I have kept close relationship with people who have a different focus have always been a negative experience for me.

WHEN YOU FIND YOURSELF IN RELATIONSHIP WITH PEOPLE WHO ENCOURAGE YOU TO VENT OR BE ANGRY, RUN!

Matthew, the tax collector, was sitting at a table surrounded by his life and the things that he valued when Jesus said, "*Follow me*" (Matthew 9:9-12). Matthew not only followed Jesus, but he also invited his peers to meet Jesus over dinner. Although making money was no longer his goal, Matthew didn't self-righteously leave his old friends; he just rearranged their position in his life.

Jesus says in verse 12 that He came to reach the sinners and the lost, which He did. He also spent His intimate moments with people who were imperfect, but served Him faithfully. If we are focusing on what is lovely, just, noble, and good, we can be in any situation and do the right thing.

DAY 6

"Finally, brethren, whatever things are true, whatever things are noble, whatever things are just, whatever things are pure, whatever things are lovely, whatever things are of good report, if there is any virtue and if there is anything praiseworthy—meditate on these things. The things which you learned and received and heard and saw in me, these do, and the God of peace will be with you."

PHILIPPIANS 4:8-9, NKJV

Today take time to meditate on these various translations of Philippians 4:8-9. Let God speak to you through His Word.

"For the rest, brethren, whatever is true, whatever is worthy of reverence and is honorable and seemly, whatever is just, whatever is pure, whatever is lovely and lovable, whatever is kind and winsome and gracious, if there is any virtue and excellence, if there is anything worthy of praise, think on and weigh and take account of these things [fix your minds on them]. Practice what you have learned and received and heard and seen in me, and model your way of living on it, and the God of peace (of untroubled, undisturbed well-being) will be with you." (Philippians 4:8-9, AMP)

"And now, dear brothers and sisters, one final thing. Fix your thoughts on what is true, and honorable, and right, and pure, and lovely, and admirable. Think about things that are excellent and worthy of praise. Keep putting into practice all you learned and received from me—everything you heard from me and saw me doing. Then the God of peace will be with you." (Philippians 4:8-9, NLT)

"Summing it all up, friends, I'd say you'll do best by filling your minds and meditating on things true, noble, reputable, authentic, compelling,

gracious—the best, not the worst; the beautiful, not the ugly; things to praise, not things to curse. Put into practice what you learned from me, what you heard and saw and realized. Do that, and God, who makes everything work together, will work you into his most excellent harmonies." (Philippians 4:8-9, MSG)

Day 7

"Finally, brethren, whatever things are true, whatever things are noble, whatever things are just, whatever things are pure, whatever things are lovely, whatever things are of good report, if there is any virtue and if there is anything praiseworthy—meditate on these things. The things which you learned and received and heard and saw in me, these do, and the God of peace will be with you."

Philippians 4:8-9, NKJV

God's peace comes when your focus is on the good news in life. Stress and anxiety come when we let negative thoughts creep in. Paul's advice to the church reminded them that in order for the church to enjoy peace, every individual member had to develop a mind that focused on praiseworthy thoughts.

Peace, like joy, is a fruit of the Spirit (Galatians 5:22). According to a commentary I read recently, peace is especially associated with God and His relationship to His people. God is the God of peace (Philippians 4:9), the God who dwells in total *shalom* (wholeness, well-being), and who gives *shalom* to His people.

> God's peace transcends human comprehension and human anxiety.

God's peace transcends human comprehension and human anxiety. Our prayer to the God who is totally trustworthy is accompanied by His peace, not because He answers according to our wishes, but because His peace totally transcends our merely human way of perceiving the world. Fortunately, God's people do not need to have life all figured out in order to trust Him. His peace guards our hearts and minds. In the Hebrew view, the heart is the center of one's being, out of which flows all of life.

I conclude this week's devotionals with a prayer for you: May the God of peace be with you!

WEEK 46

"Be still in the presence of the Lord, and wait patiently for him to act. Don't worry about evil people who prosper or fret about their wicked schemes. Stop being angry! Turn from your rage! Do not lose your temper—it only leads to harm. For the wicked will be destroyed, but those who trust in the Lord will possess the land."

PSALM 37:7-9, NLT

DAY 1

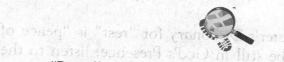

"Be still in the presence of the Lord, and wait patiently for him to act. Don't worry about evil people who prosper or fret about their wicked schemes. Stop being angry! Turn from your rage! Do not lose your temper—it only leads to harm. For the wicked will be destroyed, but those who trust in the Lord will possess the land."

PSALM 37:7-9, NLT

"Be still" is a command we hear from God, most notably in Psalm 46:10 NIV, which says, *"Be still and know that I am God."* The King James Version uses the word "rest" in place of "be still."

God has to remind us to be still and let Him take care of things for a reason. Our society really admires the "movers and shakers," the people who get things done. But when we are moving and shaking, sometimes we are also manipulating and conniving. Instead of allowing God to act, we interfere with His plan—not to mention that we wear ourselves out!

OUR SOCIETY REALLY ADMIRES THE "MOVERS AND SHAKERS," BUT WHEN WE ARE MOVING ANDSHAKING, SOMETIMES WE ARE ALSO MANIPULATING AND CONNIVING.

Psalm 55:22 reminds us to cast our burdens on the Lord. When things are overwhelming or burdensome to you, your natural reaction may be to take control and try to fix it. But if you will just wait, be still, and rest in the Lord, you can be assured that He will guide and direct your path. He will make clear to you what action, if any, you need to take. Waiting or being still does not mean being passive or lazy. It requires seeking the Lord and then responding in obedience.

One definition in *Webster's Dictionary* for "rest" is "peace of mind or spirit." Today, be still in God's Presence, listen to the Holy Spirit, and rest—knowing God is in control and will act on your behalf.

God desires for our minds and spirits to be at peace. Resting in Him is the way to get there.

DAY 2

"Be still in the presence of the Lord, and wait patiently for him to act. Don't worry about evil people who prosper or fret about their wicked schemes. Stop being angry! Turn from your rage! Do not lose your temper— it only leads to harm. For the wicked will be destroyed, but those who trust in the Lord will possess the land."
PSALM 37:7-9, NLT

I often hear questions about why dishonest people can prosper or become wealthy. But I notice time and again, in the Bible and in our society today, that their prosperity usually lasts only a short time before the truth is revealed. Even dishonest people reap what they have sown. Galatians 6:7 states that what a man sows is the ONLY thing he reaps. People can prosper for a time in the world, but this supernatural law is always eventually proven true (God even built this principle into physical reality: the law of cause and effect).

GOD TELLS US TO TURN FROM OUR RAGE. STOPPING IS ONLY THE FIRST STEP.

Failure on our part appears when we begin to obsess about the evil person and plot our revenge. If a person has gained wealth dishonestly, they are usually paying for it in ways we can't see. Today's Scripture reminds us to stop being angry.

Often we stop being angry for a time, but then it creeps back in. That is why God tells us to *turn* from our rage. Stopping is only the first step. Turning away from our anger and letting it go is the only way to become really free from the overwhelming emotions of revenge and hate.

Forgiveness is the key that unlocks so many of the chains that bind us. Forgiveness benefits us even more than it benefits the person we are forgiving. Jesus teaches us: "*If you forgive those who sin against you, your heavenly Father will forgive you. But if you refuse to forgive others, your Father will not forgive your sins*" (Matthew 6:14-15, NLT). We don't like to talk about this concept, but Jesus clearly explained that if we can't forgive, we will not be forgiven. Reaping what you sow is a spiritual law that can't be denied or defied. We must stop anger and turn from it and the only way to make this effort permanent is by forgiving the offender.

Forgiveness and faith go hand in hand. By believing that God is in control and will take care of the situation, we will be able to forgive.

DAY 3

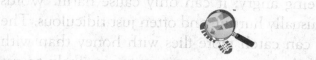

"Be still in the presence of the Lord, and wait patiently for him to act. Don't worry about evil people who prosper or fret about their wicked schemes. Stop being angry! Turn from your rage! Do not lose your temper—it only leads to harm. For the wicked will be destroyed, but those who trust in the Lord will possess the land."

PSALM 37:7-9, NLT

When my son was in the tantrum-throwing age, I waited with expectation for his first attempt at a temper tantrum. My pattern is to discipline quickly and sternly the first time, hoping to nip any future misbehavior in the bud.

One day we were watching a TV show where a child around his age kept throwing tantrums. My son stared wide-eyed at the television and I feared he was getting ideas. I was so relieved to hear him say, "That a no-no." That was four years ago; I am happy to report that Jackson has never thrown a tantrum. Apparently, Jack saw how ugly it looked and decided to not even give it a try.

NOTHING GOOD COMES FROM BEING ANGRY; IT CAN ONLY CAUSE HARM.

When you are about to lose your temper, as verse eight warns against, think about the last time you saw someone else doing it, and how unattractive and ineffective it was. Then make the choice not to go there.

Sometimes we feel losing our temper or being angry is the only way to get what we want from someone. I guess our plan is to terrify them into submission. This verse informs us that nothing good comes from being angry; it can only cause harm. Words spoken in anger are usually hurtful, and often just ridiculous. The old saying that you can catch more flies with honey than with vinegar is very true! An angry person is no more likely to get what they want than a wicked person, so don't allow your anger to take you to their level.

The next time you're about to lose it, remember you are about to take yourself farther from your goal, not closer.

Day 4

"Be still in the presence of the Lord, and wait patiently for him to act. Don't worry about evil people who prosper or fret about their wicked schemes. Stop being angry! Turn from your rage! Do not lose your temper—it only leads to harm. For the wicked will be destroyed, but those who trust in the Lord will possess the land."

Psalm 37:7-9, NLT

David wrote this chapter towards the end of his life (Psalm 37:25). David had seen and experienced many things by this point. He had observed that the wicked would eventually be destroyed and that those who trust in the Lord would possess the land. David had experienced his mentor, friends, and even his own son betraying him. But he had seen that, in the end, righteousness always prevailed. David wrote about this truth often in the Psalms, as did his son Solomon in Proverbs. Life experience teaches us that there is nothing new under the sun; all has been seen before.

Proverbs11:5 NIV says, "*The righteousness of the blameless makes a straight way for them, but the wicked are brought down by their own wickedness*." There is no reason for you to ever take revenge. The wicked person has set in motion a punishment for themselves that is stronger than anything you could do to them. Your focus is to keep trusting the Lord so that you can possess the land.

DAY 5

"Be still in the presence of the Lord, and wait patiently for him to act. Don't worry about evil people who prosper or fret about their wicked schemes. Stop being angry! Turn from your rage! Do not lose your temper—it only leads to harm. For the wicked will be destroyed, but those who trust in the Lord will possess the land."

PSALM 37:7-9, NLT

I am not proud to admit that worry is a familiar emotion for me. Worry begins as a rumble in the pit of my stomach and can quickly go straight to my neck and make me feel hot and miserable all over. One thing I have realized over the years is that worrying about things has never—not one time—solved the problem. All worry has really done is give me a few more wrinkles than I wish I had!

Worry is an emotion that can overwhelm us. If you don't resist it, worry can take over your entire life. The core of worry is fear, and fear is the opposite of faith. If we have faith that God is in control and is going to take care of things, there is no reason to worry. That is why He reminds us in this Scripture that we need to wait on Him to act. When we take control away from God, we become fearful and angry because we are trying to carry something we aren't really equipped to handle.

When you are on the edge of the cliff of worry, don't jump off. Instead, recall all the times that your worry got you nowhere—except stressed out! God is in control. If you trust in Him, you will come out safe and sound.

Day 6

"Be still in the presence of the Lord, and wait patiently for him to act. Don't worry about evil people who prosper or fret about their wicked schemes. Stop being angry! Turn from your rage! Do not lose your temper—it only leads to harm. For the wicked will be destroyed, but those who trust in the Lord will possess the land."

Psalm 37:7-9, NLT

The significance of the phrase "*possessing the land*" can be lost in our culture. At the time this Scripture was written, the amount of land you owned was a sign of wealth, importance, influence, health, and spiritual well-being. A person's ultimate goal was to gain land to pass on as an inheritance. The land held all you owned (cattle, sheep, buildings) and all that you loved (family). Acquiring the land was really only the beginning. As farmers and shepherds, these people would cultivate the land and try to improve and develop it. They also had to occupy it in order to keep it; otherwise, someone else could move in on it and claim it as their own. Back in those days there were no county clerk's offices or property titles with clearly defined boundaries to prove their claim!

In the same way, as the Lord begins to bless our trust in Him, we need to faithfully honor and care for the gifts He gives us. Your spouse, job, friends, children, material possessions, and family are all blessings from God. But as you know, once you get them, the story isn't over. Time and energy must be spent to cultivate and grow them. If they are neglected, they will be ruined or lost.

As we trust God, we will possess the land and reap blessings. But it is important to remember that once we gain these things, continued trust and faithfulness is necessary to care for these blessings the right way.

Day 7

"Be still in the presence of the Lord, and wait patiently for him to act. Don't worry about evil people who prosper or fret about their wicked schemes. Stop being angry! Turn from your rage! Do not lose your temper—it only leads to harm. For the wicked will be destroyed, but those who trust in the Lord will possess the land."

Psalm 37:7-9, NLT

In verse seven, we are told to wait patiently for God to act.

God *is* going to act! His action may not be in our timing or in the way we would do it. But isn't that a relief? Most of the time we end up messing things up with our reactions! This verse reminds us that the Lord is going to act. It tells us straight out that patience will be required on our part.

GOD IS GOING TO ACT!

My hope is that this week's devotionals have led you to be secure in the knowledge that God is in control. We can be still and not worry. What a relief!

"Who of you by worrying can add a single hour to his life?" Luke 12:25, NIV

"Those who know your name will trust in you, for you, LORD, have never forsaken those who seek you." Psalm 9:10, NIV

Week 47

"Let all that I am praise the Lord; with my whole
heart, I will praise his holy name. Let all that
I am praise the Lord; may I never forget
the good things he does for me."

Psalm 103:1-2, NLT

DAY 1

"Let all that I am praise the Lord; with my whole heart, I will praise his holy name. Let all that I am praise the Lord; may I never forget the good things he does for me."

PSALM 103:1-2, NLT

In Psalm 42, David talks to himself—to his soul, mind, and emotions. In Psalm 103, David talks to himself again and tells himself to bless the Lord. Some days we have to remind ourselves to be joyful and praise the Lord.

The other night we were at a basketball game; our six-year-old Jackson was *very* into it. He was wearing a team jersey and waving a foam finger. I had never seen him get so into a game. Every time our team made a shot, he celebrated. Every missed shot really disappointed him. Jackson was very happy as he waved his giant red finger and sucked down his lemonade. But his happiness abruptly came to an end when a close-up of his big sister, Tessa, was displayed on the JumboTron screen. Jackson sat back and pouted a little, expressing to us his disappointment that he didn't get a shirt thrown to him or have his face shown on the big screen. The next day Jackson told me he wasn't ever going to be sad like that again, because being happy and cheering for the team was way more fun than pouting.

Just like Jackson, we have the choice to rejoice or to be dissatisfied. Joy doesn't always happen automatically. Some of the time you will have to choose to be joyful. But, if you are in communion with God, you will be aware of His provision, faithfulness, and love in your life, and that will cause praise to well up in you!

DAY 2

"Let all that I am praise the Lord; with my whole heart, I will praise his holy name. Let all that I am praise the Lord; may I never forget the good things he does for me."

PSALM 103:1-2, NLT

"Let the godly sing for joy to the Lord; it is fitting for the pure to praise him." (Psalm 33:1, NIV)

"I will give thanks to the LORD because of his righteousness and will sing praise to the name of the LORD Most High." (Psalm 7:17, NIV)

"I will proclaim the name of the LORD. Oh, praise the greatness of our God!" (Deuteronomy 32:3, NIV)

"The LORD lives! Praise be to my Rock! Exalted be God, the Rock, my Savior!" (2 Samuel 22:47, NIV)

"Praise the LORD. Give thanks to the LORD, for he is good; his love endures forever." (Psalm 106:1, NIV)

"Rejoice in the Lord always. I will say it again: Rejoice!" (Philippians 4:4, NIV)

Our God is great and worthy to be praised. If we can't praise the Creator of the universe for His constant love and care, how do we expect to praise or encourage others? Living your life with an attitude of praise is life-altering and is the ultimate attitude adjustment!

DAY 3

"Let all that I am praise the Lord; with my whole heart, I will praise his holy name. Let all that I am praise the Lord; may I never forget the good things he does for me."

PSALM 103:1-2, NLT

"With my whole heart I will praise His name."

Don't keep any part of yourself back from praising the Lord. Withhold nothing from Him. Allow your mind to dwell on His goodness, your mouth to praise Him, your heart to be filled with Him, your eyes to read His Word and look for signs of His presence in your life, and your hands and feet to do His work.

EVERY PART OF US HAS TO BE INVOLVED IN PRAISING HIM.

Every part of us has to be involved in praising Him. Nothing can be held back. Like salt water and fresh water can't come from the same place, we can't be divided in our praise. We can become too good at praising God with our mouths, but feeling doubt and fear in our minds and hearts. Or we may proclaim He is great, but aren't willing to use our physical bodies to reach others in His name.

In heaven we will be praising God all of the time, but don't wait until then. Praise Him with your whole being now. He deserves it!

DAY 4

"Let all that I am praise the Lord; with my whole heart, I will praise his holy name. Let all that I am praise the Lord; may I never forget the good things he does for me."

PSALM 103:1-2, NLT

"Praise the LORD. Sing to the LORD a new song, His praise in the assembly of the saints." (Psalm 149:1, NIV)

Religious people often use the same words, songs, and prayers over and over again to praise God for His past provisions. Repeating these traditional expressions of praise for past blessings is not wrong. God did those things long ago and continues to do them today.

But God does *new* things in your life all of the time. Each day there is fresh knowledge, health, and provision that come from Him. Our praises to God each day must not become stale. Take note each day of the blessings and good things He has done for you and thank Him for them.

Take time today to write down some "good things" your Father has done. Enjoy being reminded of His great love for you.

Day 5

"Let all that I am praise the Lord; with my whole heart, I will praise his holy name. Let all that I am praise the Lord; may I never forget the good things he does for me."

Psalm 103:1-2, NLT

Most of the 150 Psalms (73 of them) were written by David. He praised God even in his darkest times—and David had some *really* dark times.

My husband Dave is just like that. No matter what is going on in life, he will not let the small stuff (or the big stuff) make him sweat. Dave hasn't spent any time in a cave with people trying to kill him, but I have seen him go through some challenging times and I always admire his faith and trust in God. Maybe it's something in the name . . .

Why was David the king able to praise so freely? David was a worshiper, a musician at heart. He had a genuine interest in establishing worship in people for the glory of God. David was a man after God's own heart (1 Samuel 13:13), and he made it his goal to praise God continually.

In Psalm 3, David talks about how many people are rising up against him. He states that many say there is no help for him in God. But David declares that God is a shield and lifter of his head (verse 3). Again and again the Psalms reveal David praising in difficult times, and his faith was not misplaced. God rescued him time and again!

Day 6

"Let all that I am praise the Lord; with my whole
heart, I will praise his holy name. Let all that
I am praise the Lord; may I never forget
the good things he does for me."

Psalm 103:1-2, NLT

Too often we forget all that God has done. Just breathing air and walking are reasons to rejoice! Each part of our lives is a testimony to God's blessing and goodness. We can so quickly forget the benefits of serving the Lord. David goes on to list the benefits in verses 3-8 NLT so we won't forget them!

He forgives all my sins
and heals all my diseases.
He redeems me from death
and crowns me with love and tender mercies.
He fills my life with good things.
My youth is renewed like the eagle's!
The Lord gives righteousness
and justice to all who are treated unfairly.
He revealed his character to Moses
and his deeds to the people of Israel.
The Lord is compassionate and merciful,
slow to get angry and filled with unfailing love.

God has forgiven our sins; salvation is always the most important reason to be thankful and to praise God! He has healed us, granted us eternal life, shown us mercy, prolonged our lives, and has given us unfailing love!

Remembering these things each day will cause us to praise Him with our whole heart.

DAY 7

"Let all that I am praise the Lord; with my whole heart, I will praise his holy name. Let all that I am praise the Lord; may I never forget the good things he does for me."

PSALM 103:1-2, NLT

Praising the Lord isn't a once-a-year, month, week, or even a once-a-day thing. Philippians 4:4 NIV says, "*Rejoice in the Lord always. I will say it again: Rejoice!*"

There is no end to God's goodness. Therefore, let there be no end to our praise of Him! C.S. Lewis, author of *The Chronicles of Narnia*, *Mere Christianity*, and several other classics, wrote this about the importance of praising God:

> I think we delight to praise what we enjoy because the praise not merely expresses but completes the enjoyment; it is its appointed consummation. If it were possible for a created soul fully to 'appreciate,' that is, to love and delight in, the worthiest object of all, and simultaneously at every moment to give this delight perfect expression, then that soul would be in supreme blessedness. To praise God fully we must suppose ourselves to be in perfect love with God, drowned in, dissolved by that delight which, far from remaining pent up within ourselves as incommunicable bliss, flows out from us incessantly again in effortless and perfect expression. Our joy is no more separable from the praise in which it liberates and utters itself than the brightness a mirror receives is separable from the brightness it sheds.

WEEK 48

"Blessed is she who has believed that what the Lord has said to her will be accomplished!"

LUKE 1:45, NIV

Day 1

"Blessed is she who has believed that what the Lord has said to her will be accomplished!"
Luke 1:45, NIV

In today's Scripture, Elizabeth is speaking to Mary and realizing Mary is pregnant with Jesus. The angel Gabriel had appeared at different times to both of these women, announcing their pregnancies.

Mary's response to Gabriel, questioning how it could be possible, was not from a lack of faith but a lack of understanding (verse 34). Elizabeth responded to Gabriel's news with great joy and she gave God the glory (verse 25). Elizabeth's husband, Zechariah, was also visited by Gabriel with the announcement and he offered the most distressing response (verse 18). Zechariah was a man of logic, and although he was a man of God, his mind couldn't understand how something like this could take place.

In life we meet many Marys, Elizabeths, and Zechariahs. Depending on the situation life brings you, your response may resemble any one of these three people. Early in our faith, we may respond like Mary. But as we grow and see God's faithfulness for ourselves, we notice God's goodness in everything, big and small, like Elizabeth. We must make a decision to stay faithful and aware of God's blessings, or we will become like Zechariah. What he and his wife Elizabeth wanted most couldn't happen naturally; he was a priest and a man of God, yet he didn't have enough faith to believe God would miraculously give them the deepest desire of their hearts. This priest had knowledge of God's law, but didn't have enough understanding of God's heart.

Elizabeth knew firsthand the consequence of lack of faith. Her husband had lost the ability to speak because of it. So when she saw Mary, she commended Mary for having enough faith to trust God when the angel appeared to her.

Elizabeth's response is our goal. She was neither surprised nor amazed at the event. She had known all along that her God was good and that all good things come from Him!

DAY 2

"Blessed is she who has believed that what the Lord has said to her will be accomplished!"
LUKE 1:45, NIV

"Blessed" is a word that is often overlooked. The meaning of "blessed" in *Webster's 1828 Dictionary* is "happy; prosperous in worldly affairs; enjoying spiritual happiness and the favor of God; enjoying heavenly felicity." Due to Mary's belief and faith, she experienced happiness in the natural world and in the spiritual realm. The blessings of obedience are abundant! (See Deuteronomy 28 for a list of them.)

Mary offers such a wonderful example of belief and trust in God. She was about 15 years old when Gabriel came to her. Mary trusted God more than the laws of the natural world she knew so well. After the angel finished speaking, verse 38 NIV shows Mary's response: *"I am the Lord's servant," Mary answered. "May it be to me as you have said."* Mary basically said, "Okay, bring it on! I want all You have planned for me!" That is why she is blessed among women (not above other women; among them). Mary was ready to play her part in God's plan, and jumped in with both feet!

"Whoever gives heed to instruction prospers, and blessed is he who trusts in the LORD." Proverbs 16:20, NIV

"But blessed is the man who trusts in the LORD, whose confidence is in him." Jeremiah 17:7, NIV

Day 3

"Blessed is she who has believed that what the Lord has said to her will be accomplished!"
Luke 1:45, NIV

Imagine how it was for Mary, a young girl, knowing deep in her heart that she had been chosen for something special, yet what she sees going on around her is common and ordinary. The mental jump in that moment, from common to extraordinary, took a special person.

> Doing big things should be ordinary for us, not extraordinary.

To see God's plan instead of ours can be a challenge to wrap our minds around. God's plans for us are no less extraordinary. But too often we talk ourselves out of them, giving into the commonness we see. Everyone, at some point, feels they are called to a certain purpose or destiny. Christians know that God has called them, promised certain things, and has a plan. Sometimes when we feel God has called us to something, we talk ourselves out of believing it and never see it come to fruition.

The truth is this: doing big things should be ordinary for us, not extraordinary. The big question is how to accomplish these things for which God has purposed us. The way Mary did it is described in Luke 1:35 NIV: *"The angel answered, 'The Holy Spirit will come upon you, and the power of the Most High will overshadow you. So the holy one to be born will be called the Son of God.'"*

The power of the Holy Spirit came over Mary and caused her to be pregnant. The Holy Spirit works in the same way with us, and what is produced is holy and from God. A human being cannot bring fruitfulness into your life—only the Holy Spirit can!

"For nothing is impossible with God." Luke 1:37, NIV

Day 4

"Blessed is she who has believed that what the Lord has said to her will be accomplished!"

Luke 1:45, NIV

Elizabeth spoke these words to Mary as the women saw each other for the first time after becoming pregnant. When an angel of God speaks to you, it is wise to pay attention, and Mary did. Gabriel did not speak Elizabeth's name to Mary by coincidence. Those two women had a divine appointment, and special bond, as did their sons later on. Elizabeth was someone who could encourage Mary. She understood the divine nature of Mary's pregnancy.

When Mary came to her older cousin, Elizabeth was instantly filled with the Holy Spirit. God had shut off Zechariah's voice and Elizabeth had removed herself from other people for five months. While it might have been lonely at times, no one could speak negative words of discouragement to her or ask questions that would cause her to doubt. Elizabeth had been spending time with God, which quickly became evident upon Mary's arrival. Elizabeth was instantly filled with the Holy Spirit in the presence of Mary, who was pregnant with Jesus.

Many people encountered Mary during her pregnancy, but only one was instantly filled with the Spirit. This speaks to Elizabeth's faith and relationship with God. Elizabeth was carrying a remarkable child—the man who would pave the way for Christ's ministry. This child knew Christ before either of them were born (Luke 1:41). Mary and Elizabeth were committed to fulfilling their destiny, and the Lord wanted them to encourage each other along the way. Elizabeth's reaction to Mary made joy well up in Mary, and caused her to rejoice through song (Luke 1:46-55). And Mary's presence brought the Holy Spirit upon Elizabeth.

Look for the people in your life who have been divinely placed there for your benefit as well as theirs!

Day 5

"Blessed is she who has believed that what the Lord has said to her will be accomplished!"

Luke 1:45, NIV

"*And happy [is] she who did believe, for there shall be a completion to the things spoken to her from the Lord.*" (Luke 1:45, YLT)

"*And blessed (happy, to be envied) is she who believed that there would be a fulfillment of the things that were spoken to her from the Lord.*" (Luke 1:45, AMP)

"*Blessed is she who believed, for there will be a fulfillment of those things which were told her from the Lord.*" (Luke 1:45, NKJV)

"*You are a woman God has blessed. You have believed that what the Lord has said to you will be done!*" (Luke 1:45, NIRV)

"*You are blessed because you believed that the Lord would do what he said.*" (Luke 1:45, NLT)

DAY 6

"Blessed is she who has believed that what the Lord has said to her will be accomplished!"

LUKE 1:45, NIV

Elizabeth was six months ahead of Mary in the process of this miraculous event. I can always find people who are six months ahead of me. When I see what God has done in their lives, how He has used, blessed, and touched them, their lives encourage me! If you are struggling to believe that you have what it takes to give birth to the dream God has put in your heart, look at the success of others and be encouraged by it!

YOU CAN BE ENCOURAGED BY THOSE AHEAD OF YOU.

My youth pastors in high school were such an encouragement to me. At a time in life when I knew I wanted to be in ministry, but had no idea how or where to go, Kevin and Teresa showed me how to minister in everyday life. They inspired me to love others, have a great family, and serve God with my whole heart. As my husband and I have gone on to live our lives together, I have often thought about those youth pastors. I appreciate all I learned by listening and watching their lives.

Elizabeth was a wonderful woman who loved Mary and invested in her. In the same way, you can be encouraged by those ahead of you. Looking around to see who you can encourage is just as important. Acknowledge those God has put in your life; they are there for a reason.

Day 7

"Blessed is she who has believed that what the Lord has said to her will be accomplished!"
Luke 1:45, NIV

Do you really believe that God will do what He has said? If you know you heard Him and you felt compelled to do something in His name, why aren't you pursuing it right now? God asking you is only half of the plan. Living the plan is in *your* hands. Do you believe that He is who He says He is and that He can do what He says He will do?

God asking you is only half of the plan. Living the plan is in your hands.

Mary was blessed because she believed. Powerful action always takes strong faith behind it. Be strong and courageous and believe that God will accomplish what He has set out to do, and be ready to be blessed in every way.

"*I can do all things through Christ who strengthens me.*" Philippians 4:13, NKJV

Week 49

"May the Lord, the God of Israel, under whose wings
you have come to take refuge, reward you
fully for what you have done."

Ruth 2:12, NLT

DAY 1

"May the Lord, the God of Israel, under whose wings
you have come to take refuge, reward you
fully for what you have done."
RUTH 2:12, NLT

The main character in this book of the Bible is a woman named Ruth. It's not just a good Bible story, but it's one of the most beautiful and romantic stories ever written.

When Benjamin Franklin was United States Ambassador to France, he would occasionally attend the Infidels Club—a group of men who spent most of their time searching for and reading literary masterpieces. On one occasion, Franklin read the book of Ruth to the club during a meeting. But he changed the names in the story so it would not be recognized as a book from the Bible. When he finished reading it, the club members were unanimous in their praise. They said it was one of the most beautiful short stories that they had ever heard. They demanded that he tell them where he had run across such a remarkable literary masterpiece. Franklin delighted in telling them that it was from the Bible, which they professed to regard with great scorn.

RUTH BRINGS A MESSAGE OF HOPE TO ANYONE WHO FEELS HURT, HELPLESS, OR WORN-OUT.

The story of Ruth brings a message of hope to anyone who feels hurt, helpless, or worn-out. Ruth represents us as the Bride of Christ. A key concept in this book is "kinsman-redeemer," or family redeemer. That phrase describes a near relative who takes responsibility for a family in difficulty. Ruth and Naomi were widows. Boaz, their close relative, stepped in to provide for them. Through him they had protection, provision, and inheritance.

This term kinsman-redeemer can easily be ascribed to Jesus. He is our Redeemer who came to earth to save us. By His death on the cross we have protection, provision, and an eternal inheritance. We also have restoration in our relationship with God; through Jesus we have access to God not just as His Father but as *our* Father.

This week's verse was actually spoken to Ruth regarding her care for her mother-in-law. But it applies to all of the players in this story, as all were selfless and loving to each other. God *does* reward faithfulness today, just as He did long ago in this remarkable story.

Day 2

"May the Lord, the God of Israel, under whose wings
you have come to take refuge, reward you
fully for what you have done."

Ruth 2:12, NLT

Today is dedicated to reflecting upon several versions of this week's Scripture. Read through them several times and pause to think about the words more deeply than you normally do. Make a note of anything that comes to mind or stands out to you. This is one of the ways God speaks to us, but we can miss it if we aren't paying attention.

> *"May the LORD repay you for what you have done. May you be richly rewarded by the LORD, the God of Israel, under whose wings you have come to take refuge."* (Ruth 1:12 NIV)

> *"May the LORD reward your work, and your wages be full from the LORD, the God of Israel, under whose wings you have come to seek refuge."* (Ruth 2:12, NASB)

> *"I pray that the LORD God of Israel will reward you for what you have done. And now that you have come to him for protection, I pray that he will bless you."* (Ruth 2:12, CEV)

> *"The LORD recompense thy work, and a full reward be given thee from the LORD God of Israel, under whose wings thou hast come to trust."* (Ruth 2:12, KJ21)

DAY 3

"May the Lord, the God of Israel, under whose wings you have come to take refuge, reward you fully for what you have done."

RUTH 2:12, NLT

God is strong and powerful, but He is also gentle and understanding. Wings are soft, yet protective and are a refuge for those who come under them. Getting under His wing requires ultimate trust in God, and that trust will be rewarded.

The following story is an example of the power and safety in wings. It was written after a fire in Yellowstone National Park.

> Following a forest fire in Yellowstone National Park, some forest rangers reportedly began their trek up a mountain to assess the inferno's damage.
>
> One ranger found a small bird literally petrified in ashes, perched statuesquely on the ground at the base of a tree. Sickened by the eerie sight, he used a stick and turned the bird over. To his amazement, three tiny chicks scurried from under their dead mother's wings.
>
> The mother bird, keenly aware of impending disaster, had carried her little ones to the base of the tree and gathered them under her wings. She instinctively knew that the toxic smoke would rise. Although she could have flown to safety, she had refused to abandon her babies.
>
> When the blaze had arrived and as the heat scorched her small body, the mother had remained steadfast.

> Because of her unselfishness and her willingness to sacrifice her own life, those under the cover of her wings lived as a testimony to her undying love.

Wings are soft enough to be comfortable underneath. But they also provide intense protection, even in the most dangerous times. Today I pray that you will find yourself under God's wing, where the protection is strong, but comfortable.

> *"He will cover you with his feathers, and under his wings you will find refuge; his faithfulness will be your shield and rampart."* Psalm 91:4, NIV

Day 4

"May the Lord, the God of Israel, under whose wings you have come to take refuge, reward you fully for what you have done."

Ruth 2:12, NLT

In the story of Ruth, Ruth follows Naomi from Moab to Bethlehem. She chooses to serve the same God as Naomi and declares Naomi as her family, leaving behind all she has known. Ruth did this out of love for Naomi and obedience to God (Ruth 1:16).

At the point of this verse, Boaz takes a moment to acknowledge Ruth's sacrifice and encourage her. Working in the field every day took great courage and stamina, and Boaz knew this. Ruth was more lowly than a servant (Ruth 2:13), so Boaz's kindness to her was gracious indeed—and greatly appreciated. Ruth had taken refuge in God. Even though she had become a follower of God later in life, her devotion and trust ran deep, as did the blessings of her obedience.

Boaz didn't just acknowledge Ruth's good deeds and faithfulness; he took active involvement in her situation. He gave her a great place to glean (Ruth 2:15-16), fed her (Ruth 2:14), and loved her. Boaz, whose name means "standing in strength," was an important person in his community. Ruth had nothing. She literally was surviving by a compassionate code of the Jewish Law (Deuteronomy 24:18-22) that God had included for the poorest of the poor.

Boaz redeemed Ruth and brought her under his covering in the same way that Jesus Christ has redeemed us, the church, and brought us under His covering. Though we are just ordinary on our own, He has redeemed us and made us a part of the family of the Most High!

You have been redeemed and you are a child of God. What better reason to rejoice all day long!

DAY 5

"May the Lord, the God of Israel, under whose wings you have come to take refuge, reward you fully for what you have done."

RUTH 2:12, NLT

The greatest part of the story of Ruth is the ending. If you cast Tom Hanks and Meg Ryan in the lead roles and put this story on the big screen, you would have a blockbuster! Boaz and Ruth get married and have a family, but the story doesn't end there.

They had a son named Obed, who was the father of Jesse; Jesse was the father of David, who became the greatest king in Israel's history. Generations later, Jesus came from the line of David. Ruth was not only rewarded for her faithfulness and obedience by having a wonderful life, but she became part of the most important family line in the history of the world!

When you take refuge in the Lord, you become freed to be fully obedient. You don't have to worry or be afraid of the outcome of the circumstances in your life. Boaz told Ruth he admired her courage, because he realized one could only have the strength to do what she was doing when they were taking refuge in God.

WHEN YOU TAKE REFUGE IN THE LORD, YOU BECOME FREED TO BE FULLY OBEDIENT.

A person who displays courage and strength may seem independent. But real courage is the ultimate dependence—dependence on God. Take refuge in Him today, and you will find the strength to be bold and courageous!

DAY 6

"May the Lord, the God of Israel, under whose wings
you have come to take refuge, reward you
fully for what you have done."

RUTH 2:12, NLT

Ruth's story is an example of God's plan to redeem and restore. Ruth's obedience and faithfulness not only gave her a better life, but also restored Naomi's life. Restoration was part of Ruth's reward for obedience.

> *So Boaz took Ruth and she became his wife. Then he went to her, and the LORD enabled her to conceive, and she gave birth to a son. The women said to Naomi: "Praise be to the LORD, who this day has not left you without a kinsman-redeemer. May he become famous throughout Israel! He will renew your life and sustain you in your old age. For your daughter-in-law, who loves you and who is better to you than seven sons, has given him birth."* (Ruth 4:13-15, NIV)

In the early part of the story, Naomi described herself as a bitter woman (Ruth 1:20-21), because things hadn't turned out the way she planned. I often wonder if, in her bitterness, Naomi may not have been the most pleasant woman to live with. Naomi had lost much. How could she know that she would end up with more than she lost? But Ruth loved her and remained faithful to her, and her faith-fulness brought restoration to them both.

If you are in a tough season of life or suffering from loss, remember that God is the Redeemer and has plans to prosper and bless you, not to harm you. If you remain faithful, you will come out better than you went in. Continue to walk in obedience and trust.

Day 7

"May the Lord, the God of Israel, under whose wings you have come to take refuge, reward you fully for what you have done."

Ruth 2:12, NLT

The book of Ruth is a beautiful story of love, compassion, faith, and redemption. The wonderful thing is that it really isn't that different from our lives.

We recall glimpses of the past and imagine hopes for the future. But we cannot see the big picture of our life—where we've been, where we're headed, and how it will all end. So we must trust that God sees the big picture of our life and has a plan. We believe that He has a better view and design than the one we have in mind.

As we take refuge under His wing and walk in obedience, we ready ourselves for the full reward for what we have done. Our lives are as full of purpose as Ruth's, and no less significant. We just have to keep being faithful.

Our lives are as full of purpose as Ruth's, and no less significant.

"One thing God has spoken, two things have I heard: that you, O God, are strong, and that you, O Lord, are loving. Surely you will reward each person according to what he has done." Psalm 62:11-12, NIV

Week 50

"So let us come boldly to the throne of our gracious God. There we will receive his mercy, and we will find grace to help us when we need it most."

Hebrews 4:16, NLT

Day 1

"So let us come boldly to the throne of our gracious God. There we will receive his mercy, and we will find grace to help us when we need it most."

Hebrews 4:16, NLT

I love the instruction to come boldly to God's throne. In clear and simple terms, this verse says to come boldly, ask for the mercy and grace you need, and you will find it. There is no need to approach God's throne with your head hanging low, begging and pleading for what you need. Just come to Him in confidence and He will meet you right there.

That God is our Provider is a fact. That God is our Father is also a fact. When you approach God to ask for what you need, He isn't surprised or disappointed. He knows who He is, and who you are, and that you have need of Him. Your Father *expects* you to come to Him and He's ready for it.

Your Father expects you to come to Him and He's ready for it.

As I began to write my portion of this devotional, I felt so overwhelmed. I am certainly not qualified to write a book and I didn't know how or where to begin, but God called me to do it. This verse was the first one that came to mind, and I quickly went to my Father's throne. I needed help, grace, and mercy in great quantity; this verse reminded me of where to get it!

I am so thankful that God is there during the overwhelming times of life. He is just waiting for us, wanting us to come with expectation that He has the answer to our question, the faith for our doubt, and the strength for our weakness.

Day 2

"So let us come boldly to the throne of our gracious God. There we will receive his mercy, and we will find grace to help us when we need it most."

Hebrews 4:16, NLT

Grace and mercy are two things I often find myself in need of, either for myself or to extend to someone else. These two things are the fuel we need to accomplish what is required of us in this life.

They are often spoken of in the same breath, used almost as synonyms, but grace and mercy are two different things. There's a good distinction made between them in the *Newsboys* song "Real Good Thing." When we don't get what we deserve, that's mercy. When we get what we don't deserve, that's grace.

The Wikipedia entry on mercy says it's "a word used to describe compassion shown by one person to another or a request from one person to another to be shown such leniency or unwarranted compassion for a crime or wrongdoing." That's an almost literal translation of the Greek word (eleos) used in this verse. But the definition of mercy in Webster's Dictionary is kind of a blending of what grace and mercy mean: "a blessing that is an act of divine favor or compassion."

Whether what we need is grace or mercy or both, God will give us what we need when we need it because He favors us and feels compassion towards us. Many times we think we know what we need, but the truth is that only God really knows what we need. So often we ask for money, time, possessions, or people when what we *really* need is the ability to emotionally or mentally handle the situation we are in.

Grace and mercy are two things that seem to be in short supply in this world and in us. The best part of mercy and grace is that they aren't earned or bought; they are freely given. Thankfully, we have been instructed on where to find them and how to ask for them—boldly at God's throne.

DAY 3

"So let us come boldly to the throne of our gracious God. There we will receive his mercy, and we will find grace to help us when we need it most."
HEBREWS 4:16, NLT

A throne speaks of authority, awe, and reverence. The throne of our "gracious God" should be a great encouragement to all of us. At God's throne, mercy and grace rule, bringing freedom, power, and prosperity. To be found at this throne, waiting on the Lord, is honorable. Our purpose at God's throne should be to obtain mercy and grace—mercy for forgiveness of all our sins and grace to fill us with what we need.

When we go to the throne of God, we should ask in faith. As children to our God and Father, we can come in a spirit of adoption. We approach with reverence and godly fear, not with terror but knowing we are kindly invited to the throne of our Father—where mercy and grace rule.

"*In him and through faith in him we may approach God with freedom and confidence*." Ephesians 3:12, NIV

"*And so, dear brothers and sisters, we can boldly enter heaven's Most Holy Place because of the blood of Jesus*." Hebrews 10:19, NLT

DAY 4

"So let us come boldly to the throne of our gracious God. There we will receive his mercy, and we will find grace to help us when we need it most."

HEBREWS 4:16, NLT

Years after the death of President Calvin Coolidge, this story came to light.

> In the early days of his presidency, Coolidge awoke one morning in his hotel room to find a cat burglar going through his pockets. Coolidge spoke up, asking the burglar not to take his watch chain because it contained an engraved charm he wanted to keep. Coolidge then engaged the thief in quiet conversation and discovered he was a college student who had no money to pay his hotel bill or buy a ticket back to campus. Coolidge counted $32 out of his wallet, which he had also persuaded the dazed young man to give back, declared it to be a loan, and advised the young man to leave the way he had come so as to avoid the Secret Service. And yes, the loan was paid back.

President Coolidge was a very merciful man in this situation. The thing about mercy is that it's a gift. This young man didn't deserve mercy, but it was given. President Coolidge had been extended mercy by God and was, therefore, able to extend it to others.

I have a great friend; every time she finds something good, she lets you know so you can get it, too. My friend doesn't want anyone to miss out on the good things she experiences. Our attitude about mercy should be like hers. Since mercy has been freely given to us, we should extend it to others.

"But because of his great love for us, God, who is rich in mercy, made us alive with Christ even when we were dead in transgressions—it is by grace you have been saved." Ephesians 2: 4-5, NIV

DAY 5

"So let us come boldly to the throne of our gracious God. There we will receive his mercy, and we will find grace to help us when we need it most."

HEBREWS 4:16, NLT

Today's verse tells us that grace is going to be given to us when we approach the throne! When we come boldly, we will get the help we need when we need it. All we have to do is ask. Grace is often spoken of in the Bible. Grace is the only word that can clearly explain why God would send His only Son to die on the cross for us. Grace is foundational for our entire belief system. Grace is extended to us daily, and we have the privilege of extending grace to others.

"*Moreover the law entered that the offense might abound. But where sin abounded, grace abounded much more.*" Romans 5:20, NKJV

"*Grace, therefore, costs us nothing, but it cost another much to get it for us. Grace was purchased with an incalculable, infinite treasure, the Son of God Himself.*" Martin Luther

"*In him we have redemption through his blood, the forgiveness of sins, in accordance with the riches of God's grace.*" Ephesians 1:7, NIV

"*Your worst days are never so bad that you are beyond the reach of God's grace. And your best days are never so good that you're beyond the need of God's grace.*" Unknown author

"*For it is by grace you have been saved, through faith—and this not from yourselves, it is the gift of God.*" Ephesians 2:8, NIV

DAY 6

"So let us come boldly to the throne of our gracious God. There we will receive his mercy, and we will find grace to help us when we need it most."

HEBREWS 4:16, NLT

My daughter Tessa is one of the most outstanding people I have ever known. One of her many gifts is reading people very well.

Early in her life she realized that if she asked her dad for something, she would most likely get it. If we were driving around, she would roll down her window and say, "Fries, nuggets, toy, diet coke, thank you." That was our signal that Tessa wanted McDonald's, and she usually got it. If Dave took Tessa on an errand with him, without fail she returned with a small treat or toy. She knew that her dad loved her and would give her what she needed and even what she wanted at times—as long as it was within reason, of course!

> OUR HEAVENLY FATHER WANTS TO GIVE US WHAT WE NEED. HE IS JUST WAITING FOR US TO APPROACH HIM AND ASK.

Just like Tessa's dad, our heavenly Father wants to give us what we need. He is just waiting for us to approach Him and ask.

In the movie Prince Caspian, Aslan the Lion shows up and wins the war after Lucy finds him and asks for his help. The people of Narnia had needed help for hundreds of years, but no one had asked Aslan for help until Lucy came along to do it.

God is gracious and wants to help us when we need it. We just need to ask!

Day 7

"So let us come boldly to the throne of our gracious God. There we will receive his mercy, and we will find grace to help us when we need it most."

Hebrews 4:16, NLT

Come to the throne boldly, not reluctantly or with hesitation.

Come boldly, because Christ has already paid the price for you to freely come. You will find grace and mercy.

When will you find grace and mercy? This is the best part: whenever you need it!

Psalm 5:3 NIV says, "*In the morning, O LORD, you hear my voice; in the morning I lay my requests before you and wait in expectation.*" You are a child of God and He feels love, compassion, patience, and mercy towards you. Approach Him with expectation, full of faith that God will answer, and be ready to receive.

Come boldly and be ready to receive the mercy and grace.

He is waiting for you.

Week 51

The LORD said to him, "What is that in your hand?"
And he said, "A staff." Then He said, "Throw it
on the ground." So he threw it on the ground, and it
became a serpent; and Moses fled from it.
But the LORD said to Moses, "Stretch out your hand
and grasp it by its tail"—so he stretched out his
hand and caught it, and it became a staff in his hand—
"that they may believe that the LORD, the God of
their fathers, the God of Abraham, the God of Isaac,
and the God of Jacob, has appeared to you."

Exodus 4:2-5, NASB

DAY 1

The LORD said to him, "What is that in your hand?" And he said, "A staff." Then He said, "Throw it on the ground." So he threw it on the ground, and it became a serpent; and Moses fled from it. But the LORD said to Moses, "Stretch out your hand and grasp it by its tail"—so he stretched out his hand and caught it, and it became a staff in his hand—"that they may believe that the LORD, the God of their fathers, the God of Abraham, the God of Isaac, and the God of Jacob, has appeared to you."

EXODUS 4:2-5, NASB

God was speaking to Moses in response to Moses' insecurity and doubt. Insecurity and fear are two things most people know all too well. People spend thousands of dollars on therapy and books (and hours watching talk shows) to conquer these overwhelming emotions. Psalm 139:13 says God formed our inmost parts and knit us together. As our Creator, God knows our makeup and our imperfections; therefore, He knows how to overcome them. His Word is full of answers to questions and problems we face each day (Psalm 119:105).

Moses felt like he wasn't good enough to do what God was requiring of him. He felt ill-equipped, and didn't think anyone would listen to him. The truth is, Moses felt ordinary, and the task God was calling him to undertake was extraordinary.

I think we can all understand Moses feeling overwhelmed; most of us have experienced that emotion. The exciting thing about God is that God will use any willing person; the only special skill required is faith. Each of us has a job to do, whether it is fulfilling a marriage commitment, raising children, doing the job we are paid to do, or accomplishing some special project. A combination of any or all of these roles can be overwhelming. God has equipped you with all you need to accomplish the task and do it successfully, just as He diiefor Moses!

What is in your hand? Therein lies the clue to beginning to actively serve Him.

Moses had a staff in his hand, David had a sling, Paul had a pen, and Peter had a net. They were used to free people, slay giants, write a large portion of God's Word, and bring people to Christ. What is in your hand? Therein lies the clue to beginning to actively serve Him.

God gave you gifts when you were born. Now that you are born again, they need to be activated for His purposes. Your abilities will be used for His glory if you are willing.

Day 2

The LORD said to him, "What is that in your hand?" And he said, "A staff." Then He said, "Throw it on the ground." So he threw it on the ground, and it became a serpent; and Moses fled from it. But the LORD said to Moses, "Stretch out your hand and grasp it by its tail"—so he stretched out his hand and caught it, and it became a staff in his hand—"that they may believe that the LORD, the God of their fathers, the God of Abraham, the God of Isaac, and the God of Jacob, has appeared to you."

Exodus 4:2-5, NASB

A staff was the most common thing about a shepherd. It was essentially an extension of his right arm and it stood as a symbol of his strength, his power, and his authority in any serious situation. Shepherds used the staff as a weapon for protection, a means of giving direction to the sheep, and a stabilizing force as they walked each day through different kinds of terrain. This common shepherd's tool was what God told Moses to use as His representative before Pharaoh.

Something that seems common to you may be what God wants to use to reach others.

In the same way, something that seems common to you may be what God wants to use to reach others. Moses' staff had been at his right hand for almost 40 years. God used such average items as David's sling and Moses' staff to do amazing things. You may find yourself average and ordinary. The good news is, that's all God needs to change the world. God can turn your staff into something much more powerful, just like God changed Moses' most familiar possession into a snake—something that was physically impossible without the power of God.

God can make you powerful and strong in ways you don't even realize. Will you let Him use you to reach others?

DAY 3

The LORD said to him, "What is that in your hand?" And he said, "A staff." Then He said, "Throw it on the ground." So he threw it on the ground, and it became a serpent; and Moses fled from it. But the LORD said to Moses, "Stretch out your hand and grasp it by its tail"—so he stretched out his hand and caught it, and it became a staff in his hand—"that they may believe that the LORD, the God of their fathers, the God of Abraham, the God of Isaac, and the God of Jacob, has appeared to you."

EXODUS 4:2-5, NASB

During this period in history, credibility was based on the ability to perform supernatural acts. Authority was shown through miracles (Exodus 7:9). A miracle would leave Pharaoh in no doubt that Moses was an important man.

In Exodus 4:10 Moses expresses his concern that he isn't eloquent or persuasive enough in speech to make Pharaoh listen to him. But God knew it didn't matter how well Moses spoke; something else would be more convincing to this leader.

GOD COMMUNICATES WITH ALL OF US IN THE WAYS WE UNDERSTAND.

God communicates with all of us in the ways we understand. He knows what we value and fully understands what makes us "tick." The staff turning into a snake was just enough to get Pharaoh's attention and allow Moses the chance to speak to him (and since Pharaoh wouldn't listen the first time, God continued to provide Moses with the miracles necessary to change his mind). Just like He did with Moses, God will equip you with what you need to communicate clearly with the people in your life. He will use supernatural means to give you favor with others, so that you can accomplish the tasks He has assigned to you.

God also knew that Moses needed a little courage and convincing. Moses' faith was built up through this private showing of God's power. Later, the supernatural sign would take place in front of Pharaoh.

When we are faithful and obedient to God, God reveals Himself to others, and our faith is built up as well.

DAY 4

The LORD said to him, "What is that in your hand?" And he said, "A staff." Then He said, "Throw it on the ground." So he threw it on the ground, and it became a serpent; and Moses fled from it. But the LORD said to Moses, "Stretch out your hand and grasp it by its tail"—so he stretched out his hand and caught it, and it became a staff in his hand—"that they may believe that the LORD, the God of their fathers, the God of Abraham, the God of Isaac, and the God of Jacob, has appeared to you."
EXODUS 4:2-5, NASB

If you have ever been close to a snake out in the woods or in the desert, you know that reaching out to grab it is not the average response. On the contrary, turning and running is a very natural reaction!

Moses reached down and picked up a snake because God told him to. To me, that took serious faith and obedience. Moses didn't know what we know about this story: that the minute he picked it up, the snake would change from being a life-threatening attacker to the trusted device of his shepherd's trade.

COURAGE IS NEEDED TO FULFILL GOD'S PLAN AND PURPOSE FOR YOUR LIFE.

God challenged Moses in the area of courage over and over again during this encounter. First, Moses was instructed to confront the Pharaoh; he responded with much hesitation. Next, God told Moses to pick up a dangerous snake with bare hands. He showed courage and bravery—two things sometimes lacking in the hearts of God's people.

Courage is needed to fulfill God's plan and purpose for your life. Boldness and bravery are the only things that will get you through when others question your call or motivation. There will be scary, snaky situations in life, where God will tell you to grab them by the tail—even though doing so defies all natural logic. His request may not make sense to you, but once that God-appointed situation is in your hand, that snake will become something that makes you stronger, better, and more capable of facing the next battle. The challenge will become a tool on your spiritual tool belt.

I am sure that there were days while the Israelites were in the wilderness that Moses thought about that staff in his hand turning into a snake. That memory must have reminded him of who was in control of all things. If you are facing a tough situation, just remember the last one you experienced and the God who pulled you through!

Day 5

The LORD said to him, "What is that in your hand?"
And he said, "A staff." Then He said, "Throw it
on the ground." So he threw it on the ground, and it
became a serpent; and Moses fled from it.
But the LORD said to Moses, "Stretch out your hand
and grasp it by its tail"—so he stretched out his
hand and caught it, and it became a staff in his hand—
"that they may believe that the LORD, the God of
their fathers, the God of Abraham, the God of Isaac,
and the God of Jacob, has appeared to you."

Exodus 4:2-5, NASB

Moses is standing in front of a burning bush as this conversation is taking place (it starts in Exodus chapter 3). As he arrives in front of the bush, God tells him to remove his shoes. I know that this was a sign of respect, but I also think it must have been astounding to have your skin exposed to Holy Ground—nothing between you and the presence of God. Imagine the sensation in Moses' feet during this time. To feel God's presence in such an intimate way would have to be life-changing.

GOD WAITS FOR US TO NOTICE THE BURNING BUSHES AND THE STAFFS IN OUR LIVES.

On this day, God was building Moses' faith; the miracles he got to experience were just the ticket. Moses' skin physically touched Holy Ground, his ears heard the voice of God, his eyes saw a burning bush, and his trusted staff transformed into a snake and then back again. Every part of Moses had to confess that he had experienced God. There was no room for argument or doubt—he had been with the God of Abraham, Isaac and Jacob.

God waits for us to notice the burning bushes and the staffs in our lives. He sends us signs of His power and love daily, but we don't always notice them. Moses saw the bush on fire and went to it (Exodus 3:3). God loves you enough to communicate with you in a way you will understand and that will be personal to you, so don't miss out; when you see a bush on fire but not burning up, head for it! Keep your heart, mind, ears, and eyes open and you will find Him.

DAY 6

The LORD said to him, "What is that in your hand?"
And he said, "A staff." Then He said, "Throw it
on the ground." So he threw it on the ground, and it
became a serpent; and Moses fled from it.
But the LORD said to Moses, "Stretch out your hand
and grasp it by its tail"—so he stretched out his
hand and caught it, and it became a staff in his hand—
"that they may believe that the LORD, the God of
their fathers, the God of Abraham, the God of Isaac,
and the God of Jacob, has appeared to you."
EXODUS 4:2-5, NASB

Moses had been a shepherd for forty years, and as far as we know, that is who he wanted to be. It might not have been his first choice (he was, after all, raised in the royal palace in a culture that found sheep and shepherds disgusting), but he found success and validity in this role.

Very often we live for our jobs, even if there's nothing dream-like about them. We are caught up in them, dependent on them, and we find our identity through them. Our job may require all of our God-given talent and skill. But remember when God told Moses to cast his staff on the ground (verse 3)? God may ask you to throw down your occupation, your job, and take a good look at its true purpose. If you are all wrapped up in it, you will get bitten.

In full-time ministry, one of the truths you learn early is that ministry is no exception to this rule. Sometimes ministers become focused on their abilities and talents and all the work *they* have to get done. Their passion stops being focused on building God's Kingdom and becomes all about building their own. No gift or talent is as valuable to God as someone who is open-handed and willing to be used.

Once you stop looking for ways to use your abilities to further yourself and you begin to look for more intimacy with God, you will understand why your job had to be pried out of your hands. No matter what it looked like, it was really a snake—something powerful and alive that was given to you for a purpose. But, when used the wrong way, that snake can hurt you and others. Once you understand this, God will allow you to pick it up once again because He knows you will use it as intended.

NO GIFT OR TALENT IS AS VALUABLE TO GOD AS SOMEONE WHO IS OPEN-HANDED AND WILLING TO BE USED.

God tells Moses to pick up the snake by the tail. Now, I've learned that to avoid a snake bite, you should pick it up behind the neck. Otherwise it will whip itself around and bite you. But this snake had no power over Moses. At this point it was just a tool to be used to complete God's plan. When you are God's child, the places where you work, live, and play are not coincidences. They are part of the big picture.

Empty your hands, and open your heart, then pick the staff back up and get moving towards Egypt!

DAY 7

The LORD said to him, "What is that in your hand?"
And he said, "A staff." Then He said, "Throw it
on the ground." So he threw it on the ground, and it
became a serpent; and Moses fled from it.
But the LORD said to Moses, "Stretch out your hand
and grasp it by its tail"—so he stretched out his
hand and caught it, and it became a staff in his hand—
"that they may believe that the LORD, the God of
their fathers, the God of Abraham, the God of Isaac,
and the God of Jacob, has appeared to you."

EXODUS 4:2-5, NASB

This is the beginning of the story for Moses. Look at how things play out when Moses and Aaron go before Pharaoh:

> *The LORD said to Moses and Aaron, "When Pharaoh says to you, Perform a miracle,' then say to Aaron, 'Take your staff and throw it down before Pharaoh,' and it will become a snake."*
>
> *So Moses and Aaron went to Pharaoh and did just as the LORD commanded. Aaron threw his staff down in front of Pharaoh and his officials, and it became a snake.*
>
> *Pharaoh then summoned wise men and sorcerers, and the Egyptian magicians also did the same things by their secret arts: Each one threw down his staff and it became a snake.*
>
> *But Aaron's staff swallowed up their staffs.* (Exodus 7:8-12, NIV)

These sorcerers are identified as Jannes and Jambres, "*men of corrupt minds, reprobate concerning the faith*" (2 Timothy 3:8, KJV). They tapped into darkness and copied the miracle. These men faced a challenge, but when Aaron's staff swallowed their staffs, there was no debate about who was in control.

As believers, we aren't immune to attack. Just as the sorcerers tried to discredit Aaron and Moses, we will be discredited and attacked. We may not be immune to attack, but we will be immune to the effects of it! Don't back away from obstacles or challenges. They are opportunities for God to show His power and for us to grow spiritually stronger.

Week 52

"I tell you the truth, anyone who has faith in me will do what I have been doing. He will do even greater things than these, because I am going to the Father. And I will do whatever you ask in my name, so that the Son may bring glory to the Father. You may ask me for anything in my name, and I will do it."

John 14:12-14, NIV

DAY 1

"I tell you the truth, anyone who has faith in me will do what I have been doing. He will do even greater things than these, because I am going to the Father. And I will do whatever you ask in my name, so that the Son may bring glory to the Father. You may ask me for anything in my name, and I will do it."
JOHN 14:12-14, NIV

Jesus is speaking to the disciples in the upper room during Passover. Jesus explains that those who believe in Him will continue to do all that He had been doing. Jesus has healed the blind, raised the dead, and spoken on a regular basis to thousands of people. The disciples had seen Jesus do so many things that no one had ever done before. Now He tells them that they will do all of those things, too. The only stipulation Jesus gives for His disciples—and anyone—being able to imitate His actions is that they have faith; we cannot do these things unless our belief is firmly planted in Christ.

IT IS EASY TO BE THE GUY BEHIND THE MAN. BUT IT IS CHALLENGING TO STEP UP AND BE THE MAN YOURSELF.

Imagine the disciples' reaction to hearing that they would do what Jesus did—feed thousands, heal the sick, confront Pharisees, and teach the truth of God's heart. I'm sure such thoughts brought excitement, but it must have felt overwhelming at the same time.

It is easy to be the guy behind the man. But it is challenging to step up and be the man yourself. Only someone of great faith can do these things.

A person with the capacity for faith who fully believes in God can accomplish much.

"And without faith it is impossible to please God, because anyone who comes to him must believe that he exists and that he rewards those who earnestly seek him." Hebrews 11:6, NIV

"This righteousness from God comes through faith in Jesus Christ to all who believe." Romans 3:22, NIV

DAY 2

"I tell you the truth, anyone who has faith in me will do what I have been doing. He will do even greater things than these, because I am going to the Father. And I will do whatever you ask in my name, so that the Son may bring glory to the Father. You may ask me for anything in my name, and I will do it."

JOHN 14:12-14, NIV

The person who has faith will not only do what Jesus did, but even greater things? WOW! The things that Jesus did were amazing! But these verses tell us that we will do *even greater* things.

Look at your résumé. Have you healed anyone lately? Walked on water? Been followed by large crowds who are waiting to hear what you have to say?

The things Jesus did best were love others and serve God with His whole heart. Jesus is telling us that we will have the ability, not just to do these things and more, but also to love others and God unconditionally. My mind cannot even wrap itself around what "*greater things*" might be done beyond what Jesus did while here on earth!

Many people feel compelled to do more, achieve more, and be more. That drive is natural, I think, but has been misdirected in most people. No amount of success at work, financially, or in status will satisfy that inner ambition. It can only be filled by doing the greater things He has planned for you.

DAY 3

"I tell you the truth, anyone who has faith in me will do what I have been doing. He will do even greater things than these, because I am going to the Father. And I will do whatever you ask in my name, so that the Son may bring glory to the Father. You may ask me for anything in my name, and I will do it."

JOHN 14:12-14, NIV

In addition to eternal life and a relationship with the Father, we have been given the privilege of prayer. This verse tells us that anything we ask for in Jesus' name will be done for us. Does this mean you can tack "in Jesus' name" onto the end of any prayer and you will receive it? Of course not!

Could you imagine a world where God was a giant Santa Claus who gave everyone what they wanted, whether it was for the best or not, whether it harmed someone else or not? That would be terrible! And yet that is often what people expect from God.

When you ask for something in someone's name, you are a representative of that person. To pray in Jesus' name means to be in line with His heart, His personality, and His desires, not just say three words. When you ask for something in Jesus' name, request for what agrees with His heart, His character, and His will. 1 John 3:22 says that we receive whatever we ask for because we obey Him and do what pleases Him.

If your heart is in line with Jesus' heart and if you are trying to obey and please Him, you will see amazing things happen. The important point about prayer is not whose name you tack onto the end, but whose name it represents!

DAY 4

"I tell you the truth, anyone who has faith in me will do what I have been doing. He will do even greater things than these, because I am going to the Father. And I will do whatever you ask in my name, so that the Son may bring glory to the Father. You may ask me for anything in my name, and I will do it."

JOHN 14:12-14, NIV

The following Scripture found in John 17:20-26 (NLT) is a beautiful prayer that Jesus prayed for all believers. The focus is on Jesus having unity with God and Christians having unity with Him. So much can be done when there is unity. When we are in this kind of unified state, we will do even greater things and see our prayers come to fruition.

"WE ARE MADE IN HIS IMAGE AND CARRY HIS GLORY."

"I am praying not only for these disciples but also for all who will ever believe in me through their message. I pray that they will all be one, just as you and I are one—as you are in me, Father, and I am in you. And may they be in us so that the world will believe you sent me. I have given them the glory you gave me, so they may be one as we are one. I am in them and you are in me. May they experience such perfect unity that the world will know that you sent me and that you love them as much as you love me. Father, I want these whom you have given me to be with me where I am. Then they can see all the glory you gave me because you loved me even before the world began! O righteous Father, the world doesn't know you, but I do; and these disciples know you sent me. I have revealed you to them, and I will continue to do so. Then your love for me will be in them, and I will be in them."

I love knowing we were created in God's image (Genesis 1:27), and we have been given His glory (Romans 8:30). "Glory" in this Scripture refers to *chabod*, the Hebrew word for the substance and reality of holiness. We are made in His image and carry His glory. When God looks at us, He does not see our failures and shortcomings, but He sees us in a glorious state in His son. He sees us with eyes full of love.

Day 5

"I tell you the truth, anyone who has faith in me will do what I have been doing. He will do even greater things than these, because I am going to the Father. And I will do whatever you ask in my name, so that the Son may bring glory to the Father. You may ask me for anything in my name, and I will do it."

John 14:12-14, NIV

Whenever I go out of town, I feel very comfortable leaving Dave and the kids on their own. Dave is a fun, responsible, and loving dad. I know that everything that needs doing will be accomplished and everyone will have fun in the process.

I believe Dave feels the same way about me, because we are in unity where our family is concerned. We are working toward the same goal, so even when one of us can't be there, we know that the important things will still be carried out.

Jesus was preparing to fulfill His destiny, and He trusted us enough to believe we would fulfill ours.

The reason why we would be given the power to do what Jesus did and more is clear. Jesus was on His way to the Father. His purpose for coming to earth was nearly completed, but there was still work to be done and His disciples are the ones to do it. Jesus was preparing to fulfill His destiny, and He trusted us enough to believe we would fulfill ours.

When we are in unity with our Father, we will continue to fulfill His plan. God has blessed us with the ability and power to accomplish great things in His name and for His glory.

DAY 6

"I tell you the truth, anyone who has faith in me will do what I have been doing. He will do even greater things than these, because I am going to the Father. And I will do whatever you ask in my name, so that the Son may bring glory to the Father. You may ask me for anything in my name, and I will do it."

JOHN 14:12-14, NIV

When Christian minister and inspirational writer Norman Vincent Peale was a boy, he found a big, black cigar, slipped into an alley, and lit up. It didn't taste good, but it made him feel very grown up—until he saw his father coming. He quickly put the cigar behind his back and tried to be casual. Desperate to divert his father's attention, Norman pointed to a billboard advertising the circus.

TO BE IN UNITY WITH GOD'S HEART, YOU MUST BE FREE OF GUILT AND HIDDEN SIN.

"Can I go, Dad? Please, let's go when it comes to town." His father's reply taught Norman a lesson he never forgot.

"Son," he answered quietly but firmly, "never make a petition while at the same time trying to hide a smoldering disobedience."

To be in unity with God's heart, you must be free of guilt and hidden sin. God knows anyway, so confess and ask forgiveness and He will give it to you. The view of a situation can change rapidly when hit with a dose of truth and perspective.

Once the fog of disobedience and guilt is cleared away, you are able to ask for the right thing in the right way—making a request that reflects God's own heart.

DAY 7

"I tell you the truth, anyone who has faith in me will do what I have been doing. He will do even greater things than these, because I am going to the Father. And I will do whatever you ask in my name, so that the Son may bring glory to the Father. You may ask me for anything in my name, and I will do it."

JOHN 14:12-14, NIV

The end of this passage states that God is the one who will answer our requests. The moment you think you are the one doing it, watch out. Correct your thinking. Remember that God is the one with the power and plan. You are an important part, but your purpose is to bring glory to Him! God's glory and power on display will draw more people to Him.

"All this is for your benefit, so that the grace that is reaching more and more people may cause thanksgiving to overflow to the glory of God." 2 Corinthians 4:15, NIV

"...to the only God our Savior be glory, majesty, power and authority, through Jesus Christ our Lord, before all ages, now and forevermore! Amen." Jude 1:25, NIV

"Then Jesus said, 'Did I not tell you that if you believed, you would see the glory of God?'" John 11:40, NIV

Appendix 1: Sin & Invitation

Sin: Look Again

I think it would be irresponsible of us to preach the need for a Savior and talk about His love and benefits without discussing the reason why He had to come rescue us in the first place. I have realized that if we do not understand sin and what it has done to humanity, a commitment to Christ will become the same as a diet. You know what I mean: we start out with good intentions but our cravings for our old habits lead us back to the same cycles that plagued us before we committed to change.

One of the reasons that evangelism, in particular, has not been as effective in the past few decades is because many leaders of faith refuse to talk about the sin that has trapped us all. We have gotten away from the "fire and brimstone" / "nuts and bolts" preaching that led many to salvation through the ministries of evangelists like Billy Graham and Luis Palau. We have turned some of the most powerful verses in the Bible like, *"for so God love the world," "the just shall live by faith,"* and *"He himself took our infirmities and carried our diseases"* into trendy catch phrases. The result is that we have sugarcoated sin so much so that we have isolated many individuals and made them think that their struggle is worse than someone else's—or maybe that they really aren't that bad. For example, our culture (sometimes even within the church) has taught that gossip, white lies, and greed are not as bad as sexual immorality, when the truth is that they all grieve the Holy Spirit because they are all sin. Many Christian fundamentalists bash homosexuals relentlessly but say nothing to a friend or colleague who watches perversion on television and brags about it. We live in a culture that sings, "Amazing grace how sweet the sound that saved a wretch like me" without realizing that we are that wretch without Jesus as our Redeemer. We have made sin culturally acceptable and determined its punishment based on our own set of rules.

But it doesn't work that way.

In an excerpt from an album by Shai Linne called *The Atonement*, C. J. Mahaney of Sovereign Grace Ministries says, "In His righteous judgment, God has determined that the just penalty for sin is death and without the shedding of blood, there is no remission of sins. Now, sin has been committed by man, therefore, only man can atone for that sin. But here's my dilemma: I can't atone for my sin; I can't. I cannot satisfy God's righteous requirements. My disobedience condemns me before a Righteous God. And...I'm captive to sin. It is humanly impossible for me to free myself from sin. A divine rescue… is necessary. I NEED A SAVIOR! I need a Savior." The truth is that ***we all do***.

In our society, we have written books and built campaigns on the ideas of "positive thinking," "good deeds," "personal confidence," and many other topics that try to alleviate the guilt we all feel at one point or another. The problem is that you can never do enough to totally get rid of this shame brought on by our fallen nature that originated in Genesis 3:6. The only thing that can eradicate this sin and make us "acceptable" to a Perfect and Holy God is faith in Jesus Christ. As Galatians 3:22 (NIV) states "*...the Scripture declares that the whole world is a prisoner of sin, so that what was promised, being given through faith in Jesus Christ, might be given to those who believe.*"

Regretfully, verses like Galatians 3:22 and Romans 3:23 have been read many times by yours truly without any contemplation or meditation. Thank God for men like Jon Courson and his commentaries on the topic of sin. In his New Testament commentary (page 1183), Courson tells a story that I think will bring my point home (I know this is long, but stay with me).

> You're in a 747 jumbo jet headed to Honolulu. Two hours into the flight, the pilot calls for the senior flight attendant and says, "There's a leak in our gas tank. We're not going to make it to Hawaii."

The flight attendant, wiping the sweat off her brow, dabbing the tears from her eyes, smiles as she returns to the cabin, saying, "Greetings passengers. Could I interest any of you in a parachute? It will make your flight more enjoyable, and in it, I think you'll discover a new measure of peace, joy, and love. *(NOTE: Sugarcoating the situation.)* Who would like a parachute?" Maybe three or four people raise their hands. *(NOTE: Just like being in church.)*

If you are among the three or four taking one, you see the other passengers snickering and pointing at you. *(NOTE: the world/peer pressure.)* Before long, you discover your parachute is tight and uncomfortable. You begin to think, *This isn't giving me any joy at all. This is ridiculous*. And after twenty minutes or so, you take it off and say to the stewardess, "You lied to me. You promised I would be comfortable, full of joy, and warmed by love. But all I got were snickers, jeers, and a rash..."

Another stewardess in the same situation hears the message from the captain. She enters the cabin, saying "STOP what you're doing. Put down your reading material. I want your full undivided attention. The captain has informed me that this plane is losing fuel fast. We're going down. Who wants a parachute?"

Suddenly, people are fighting for parachutes. No one cares if the flight for the remaining minutes is smooth, or if they have enough mobility to play video games. No, everyone is clinging to his parachute, making sure it's secure because everyone knows the plane is going down."

The parachute is salvation from the consequences of sin through faith in Jesus Christ and the plane is this world and the system that governs it. To use another analogy, unless you understand what has you in prison, the pardon and redemption will not have the impact that it should. And unless we preach against and expose sin for what it is without the fear of offending people, the people will stay away or walk away from that which can only bring them eternal life with God.

If we are not in a true state of humility that recognizes the truth about sin and our dependence on God to save us through His Son, we believers are relegated to an ineffective, trendy state at best. We will be exactly like the church of Laodicea in the book of Revelation, chapter three. In verse 16, God called that church "lukewarm" and in verse 17 He called them *"wretched, pitiful, poor, blind, and naked."* I wonder what He would call us.

Matthew 5:3 (NIV) says, *"Blessed are the poor in spirit, for theirs is the kingdom of heaven."* Poverty of spirit, as stated in John MacArthur's *Daily Reading from the Life of Christ*, means "recognizing how truly deficient we are apart from God." He also states in this same book that "no person can receive the kingdom of God until he or she realizes they are unworthy of that kingdom."

What makes us unworthy? Sin.

If you don't understand the effect of and damage caused by sin, you will never be able to appreciate the gift of salvation.

Do You Know Jesus?

The Bible says in Romans 3:23, *"For all have sinned and fall short of the glory of God."* This means every one of us has rebelled against the will of God; it only takes one sin to overcharge your credit. One sin equals death and eternity without divine companionship with God.

Jeremiah 31:31 NIV says, *"The time is coming, declares the Lord, when I will make a new covenant with the house of Israel."* The house of Israel is you and me, and the new covenant was sealed when Jesus was resurrected from the dead. Romans 10:9 states, *"If you confess with your mouth, 'Jesus is Lord,' and believe in your heart that God raised him from the dead, you will be saved."* We encourage you to pray the following prayer (or pray a similar prayer in your own words), believe the truth in your heart, and make a decision to follow Jesus with the rest of your life:

> *Heavenly Father, I acknowledge that you are God, the only true God, and that you sent your Son, Jesus, to die for my sins. With that in mind, I admit that I have sinned against you and am in need of the atonement that can only come from the perfect blood that was shed by Christ so that my sin could never be counted against me. So right now, I confess with my mouth and believe in my heart that Jesus Christ is the Lord my life. I also believe that the Holy Spirit indwells my being and He is also my God. I thank you, Father, that I now have perfect relationship with You because of Your Grace and Mercy. Amen.*

My friend, you did it! That acknowledgement of truth and the decision to follow Jesus makes you part of God's Kingdom of believers. 2 Corinthians 5:17-18 says, *"If anyone is in Christ, he is a new creation; the old has gone, the new has come! All this is from God, who reconciled us to himself through Christ and gave us the ministry of reconciliation."* This means that your past no longer holds you in bondage—God has forgotten it—and you now walk in the peace, joy, favor, grace, and mercy of God....receive it.

- I pray that you find a Christian church that believes and teaches every Word of the Bible so that you can start to fulfill the destiny that God has planned for you.
- I pray that you find an older believer that can help you along the way, as you start this new journey.
- I pray that the callings of your past life would be overwhelmed by the pull of the Holy Spirit to continue on with God.

APPENDIX 2: BIBLICAL REFERENCES

ABUV: American Bible Union Version.

AKJV: American King James Version.

AMP: The Amplified Bible, Copyright © 1954, 1958, 1962, 1964, 1965, 1987 by The Lockman Foundation. Used by permission.

ASV: American Standard Version.

BBE: The Bible in Basic English.

CEV: Contemporary English Version Copyright © 1995 by American Bible Society. Used by permission.

DAR: The Holy Scriptures: A New Translation from the Original Languages by J. N. Darby.

D-R: Douay-Rheims Bible.

EBR: J.B. Rotherham Emphasized Bible.

GW: God's Word® is a copyrighted work of God's Word to the Nations. Quotations are used by permission. Copyright 1995 by God's Word to the Nations. All rights reserved.

KJ21: 21st Century King James Version®, copyright © 1994. Used by permission of Deuel Enterprises, Inc., Gary, SD 57237. All rights reserved.

KJV: King James Version.

MOF: The Bible: James Moffatt Translation, Copyright © 1922, 1924, 1925, 1926, 1935 Harper Collins San Francisco, Copyright © 1950, 1952, 1953, 1954 James A. R. Moffatt.

MSG: The Message. Copyright © 1993, 1994, 1995, 1996, 2000, 2001, 2002. Used by permission of NavPress Publishing Group.

NIV: The Holy Bible, New International Version®. Copyright © 1973, 1978, 1984 International Bible Society. Used by permission of Zondervan. All rights reserved.

NAS/NASB: The New American Standard Bible®, Copyright © 1960, 1962, 1963, 1968, 1971, 1972, 1973, 1975, 1977,1995 by The Lockman Foundation. Used by permission.

NKJV: The New King James Version®. Copyright © 1982 by Thomas Nelson, Inc. Used by permission. All rights reserved.

NLT: The Holy Bible, New Living Translation, copyright © 1996. Used by permission of Tyndale House Publishers, Inc., Wheaton, Illinois 60189. All rights reserved.

NCV: The New Century Version. Copyright © 2005 by Thomas Nelson, Inc. Used by permission. All rights reserved.

Phi: Phillips, J.B. The New Testament in Modern English, New York: Macmillian Company, 1960.

TCNT: The Twentieth Century New Testament.

TLB: The Living Bible / Kenneth N. Taylor. electronic ed. Wheaton:Tyndale House, 1997, c1971 by Tyndale House Publishers, Inc. Used by permission. All rights reserved.

WEY: Weymouth New Testament in Modern Speech. Third Edition 1913.

WMS: The New Testament in the Language of the People, Translated from the Greek by Charles B. Williams 1937. Boston: Bruce Humphries, 1937. Slightly revised in 1950 (Chicago: Moody Press).

YLT: Young's Literal Translation.